Why Do You Need This New Edition?

If you're wondering why you should buy this new edition of *Understanding English Grammar*, here are five good reasons!

Each chapter now opens with a bulleted list outlining the purposes and goals of the chapter. Taken with the chapter-ending list of key terms, the opening goal statement provides you with a comprehensive guide for study and review.

"Usage Matters" is a new feature that provides help on issues of grammar, word choice, and writing conventions that students often find frustrating.

- Chapter 2 now includes easier to understand guidance on the basics of noun phrases and verb phrases. In addition, it includes a new helpful summary section on the structure classes.

- Many Exercises and Questions for Discussion that will likely be assigned by your instructor have been updated with new topics.

- There are many new diagrams illustrating compound structures, modifiers with hyphens, and the infinitive phrase functioning as an appositive that will help you understand these topics.

PEARS

Understanding English Grammar

Understanding English Grammar

NINTH EDITION

Martha Kolln

The Pennsylvania State University

Robert Funk

Eastern Illinois University

Boston   Columbus   Indianapolis   New York   San Francisco   Upper Saddle River
Amsterdam   Cape Town   Dubai   London   Madrid   Milan   Munich   Paris
Montreal   Toronto   Delhi   Mexico City   São Paulo   Sydney   Hong Kong
Seoul   Singapore   Taipei   Tokyo

Senior Sponsoring Editor:
  Katharine Glynn
Assistant Editor: Rebecca Gilpin
Senior Marketing Manager:
  Sandra McGuire
Senior Supplements Editor:
  Donna Campion
Production Manager: Denise Phillip
Project Coordination, Text Design, and
  Electronic Page Makeup: S4Carlisle

Cover Designer/Manager:
  Wendy Ann Fredericks
Cover Photo: © iStockphoto
Senior Manufacturing Buyer:
  Roy Pickering
Printer/Binder: Courier Corporation /
  Westford
Cover Printer: Courier Corporation /
  Westford

Library of Congress Cataloging-in-Publication Data

Kolln, Martha.
  Understanding English grammar / Martha Kolln, Robert Funk.—9th ed.
    p. cm.
Includes bibliographical references and index.
Previous ed.: 2009.
ISBN-13: 978-0-205-20952-1 (alk. paper)
ISBN-10: 0-205-20952-1 (alk. paper)
1. English language—Grammar. I. Funk, Robert. II. Title.
PE1112.K64 2011
428.2—dc23

2011028417

10 9 8 7 6 5 4 3 2—V013—14 13 12

www.pearsonhighered.com

ISBN 10: 0-205-20952-1
ISBN 13: 978-0-205-20952-1

Contents

Chapter 3
Sentence Patterns   **28**

Chapter 4
Expanding the Main Verb   63

Chapter 5
Changing Sentence Focus   86

Chapter 8
The Noun Phrase Functions: Nominals   163

Chapter 9
Sentence Modifiers   189

Chapter 10
Coordination   209

PART IV
Words and Word Classes   225

Chapter 11
Morphemes   227

Chapter 14
Pronouns   289

Preface

The central purpose of this ninth edition of *Understanding English Grammar* remains the same as it has always been: to help students understand the systematic nature of language and to appreciate their own language expertise.

We recognize that most people who use this book are speakers of English who already know English grammar, intuitively and unconsciously. But we also realize that many of them don't *understand* what they know: They're unable to describe what they do when they string words together, and they don't know what has happened when they encounter or produce unclear, imprecise, or ineffective speech and writing. Their grammatical ability is extraordinary, but knowing how to control and improve it is a conscious process that requires analysis and study.

In recent years, the widespread institution of state-mandated standards, the growth of high-stakes testing, and the increased use of diagnostic writing samples make it clear that today's students—and those who are preparing to teach them—must both *know* and *understand* grammar.

Although *Understanding English Grammar* assumes no prior knowledge on the readers' part beyond, perhaps, vague recollections of long-ago grammar lessons, we do assume that, as language users, students will learn to draw on their subconscious linguistic knowledge as they learn about the structure of English in a conscious way.

We help students tap into their subconscious grammar knowledge with a chapter on words and phrases, laying the groundwork for the study of sentence patterns and their expansion. Our focus on syntax begins where the students' own language strengths lie: in their sentence-producing ability. With a few helpful guidelines, the basic sentence patterns become familiar very quickly and provide a framework for further grammatical and rhetorical investigations. English language learners (ELLs) too will appreciate the detailed step-by-step approach, along with highlighted discussions of ELL issues. The thorough study of sentence patterns in Chapter 3 builds the foundation for the rest of the chapters.

The study of grammar, of course, is not just for English majors or for future teachers: It is for people in business and industry, in science and engineering, in law and politics, in the arts and social services. Every user of the language, in fact, will benefit from the consciousness-raising that results from the study of grammar. The more that speakers and writers know consciously about their language, the more power they have over it and the better they can make it serve their needs.

Teachers familiar with the previous editions of *Understanding English Grammar* will find the same progression of topics in this new one:

Part I: The Study of Grammar: An Overview

Part II: The Grammar of Basic Sentences

Part III: Expanding the Sentence

Part IV: Words and Word Classes

Part V: Grammar for Writers

In this revision we have tried to look at every topic, every discussion through the eyes of a novice reader; we have taken to heart the ideas and opinions of our reviewers and of others, as well, who have taken the time to comment. As a result, we have made refinements, both large and small, in the discussions, exercises, and examples throughout the book. Following are the major changes you will see:

- Chapters open with a bulleted list that lays out the purposes and the goals we have set for students. Together with the chapter-ending list of key terms, this opening set of goals can provide a comprehensive guide for study and review.

- In a new feature called "Usage Matters," we explore issues of grammar, word choice, and writing conventions—and even outright myths—that can frustrate both students and teachers. You will find them listed in the "U" section of the Index.

- Chapter 2 has undergone a makeover that clarifies the basics of noun phrases and verb phrases; it also includes a new summary section on the structure classes.

- In three new topic-centered exercises, students will learn about the Oregon Trail, the development of printing, and the game of tennis and its star players. Many other Exercises and Questions for Discussion have also been updated with new items.

- New diagrams have been added, illustrating compound structures, modifiers with hyphens, and the infinitive phrase functioning as an appositive.

Ideas and suggestions from you and your students are always welcome.

Exercises throughout the chapters reinforce the principles of grammar as they are introduced. Answers to the exercises, which are provided at the end of the book, give the book a strong self-instructional quality. Other exercises, called "Investigating Language," will stimulate class discussion, calling on students to tap into their innate language ability.

Chapters 3 through 14 end with a list of key terms, a section of practice sentences (for which answers are provided only in the *Instructor's Manual*), a series of questions for discussion that go beyond the concepts covered in the text, and several classroom applications that can be used in your college classes as well as in the future classrooms of your students. The students will also find the Glossary of Grammatical Terms and the Index extremely helpful.

Supplementing the ninth edition of the text, the *Instructor's Manual* (ISBN 0-205-20958-0) includes analyses of the practice sentences, suggested answers for the discussion questions, and suggestions for using the book. The *Instructor's Manual* is available from your Pearson representative.

Another supplement to the text is the new edition of *Exercises for Understanding English Grammar* (ISBN 0-205-20960-2), with exercises that go beyond those found in the text, many of which call for the students to compose sentences. To keep the self-instructional quality that teachers appreciate, answers for all items are included, where answers are appropriate. However, there are now ten additional "Test Exercises" for which the answers are not provided; these can be used for testing and review. An *Answer Key* for these test exercises will be available online to instructors who adopt the new edition of *Exercises for Understanding English Grammar*.

ACKNOWLEDGMENTS

Understanding English Grammar has once again been revised, corrected, and shaped by the questions and comments of students and colleagues who use the book. We are particularly grateful to the following reviewers for their thoughtful assessments of the previous edition and their recommendations for revision:

William Allegrezza, Indiana University Northwest
Booker T. Anthony, Fayetteville State University
James C Burbank, University of New Mexico
Brian Jackson, Brigham Young University
Gloria G. Jones, Winthrop University
Carlana Kohn-Davis, South Carolina State University
Mimi Rosenbush, University Of Illinois at Chicago

Rachel V. Smydra, Oakland University

Gena D. Southall, Longwood University

Duangrudi Suksang, Eastern Illinois University.

Finally, our special thanks goes to our editor and friend, Ginny Blanford, and her efficient Assistant Editor Rebecca Gilpin.

Martha Kolln

Robert Funk

Introduction

The subject of English grammar differs markedly from every other subject in the curriculum—far different from history or math or biology or technical drawing. What makes it different? If your native language is English, you do. As a native speaker, you're already an expert. You bring to the study of grammar a lifetime of "knowing" it—except for your first year or two, a lifetime of producing grammatical sentences.

Modern scholars call this expertise your "language competence." Unlike the competence you may have in other subjects, your grammar competence is innate. Although you weren't born with a vocabulary (it took a year or so before you began to perform), you were born with a language potential just waiting to be triggered. By the age of two you were putting words together into sentences, following your own system of rules: "Cookie all gone"; "Go bye-bye." Before long, your sentences began to resemble those of adults. And by the time you started school, you were an expert in your native language.

Well, almost an expert. There were still a few gaps in your system. For example, you didn't start using verb phrases as direct objects (I like *reading books*) until perhaps second grade; and not until third or fourth grade did you use *although* or *even if* to introduce clauses (I'm going home *even if you're not*). But for the most part, your grammar system was in place on your first day of kindergarten.

At this point you may be wondering why you're here—in this class, reading this textbook—if you're already an expert. The answer to that question is important: You're here to learn in a conscious way the grammar that you use, expertly but subconsciously, every day. You'll learn to think about language and to talk about it, to understand and sharpen your own reading and writing skills, and, if your plans for the future include teaching, to help others understand and sharpen theirs.

For those of you whose mother tongue is a language other than English, you will have the opportunity to compare the underlying structure of your first language as you add the vocabulary and structure of English grammar to your language awareness.

This chapter of Part I begins by recognizing English as a world language. We then take up the ways in which it has been studied through the years, along with the issues of correctness and standards and language change. In all of these discussions, a key word is *awareness*. The goal of *Understanding English Grammar* is to help you become consciously aware of your innate language competence.

CHAPTER 1

The Study of Grammar: An Overview

ENGLISH: A WORLD LANGUAGE

All over the world every day, there are people, young and old, doing what you're doing now: studying English. Some are college students in China and Korea and Tunisia preparing for the proficiency test required for admission to graduate school in America. Some are businesspeople in Germany and Poland learning to communicate with their European Union colleagues. Others are adults here in the United States studying for the written test that leads to citizenship. And in the fifty or more countries where English is either the first language or an official second language, great numbers of students are in elementary and secondary classrooms like those you inhabited during your K–12 years.

As the authors of *The Story of English* make clear, English is indeed a world language:

> The figures tell their own story. According to the best estimates available, English is now the mother tongue of about 380 million people in traditionally English-speaking countries such as Britain, Australia and the United States. Add to this the 350 million "second-language" English speakers in countries like India, Nigeria and Singapore, and a staggering further 500 to 1000 million people in countries like China, Japan and Russia that acknowledge the importance of global English as an agent of global capitalism, and you arrive at a total of nearly 2000 million, or at least a third of the world's population.[1]

⟹ Nearly 2000 million people speak English.

---

[1] McCrum et al., *The Story of English*, p. xviii. [See reference list, page 14.]

For the PBS documentary series *The Story of English*, first broadcast in 1986, Robert MacNeil traveled the world to interview native speakers of English: among them, speakers of Indian English in Delhi and Calcutta, of Scots English in the Highlands of Scotland, of Pidgin in Papua New Guinea, and of Gullah in the Sea Islands of Georgia. In many of his conversations, the language he heard included vocabulary, pronunciation, and sentence structure far removed from what we think of as mainstream English.

The theme of the documentary was clear: The story of English—or Englishes—is diversity. There is no one "correct"—no one "proper"—version of the English language: There are many.

Even the version we call American English has a wide variety of **dialects**.[2] Different parts of the country, different levels of education, different ethnic backgrounds, different settlement histories—all of these factors produce differences in language communities. Modern linguists recognize that every variety of English is equally grammatical. We could cite many examples (and so could you!) of language structures that vary from one region of the country to another. There's a word for this phenomenon: We call these variations **regionalisms**. For instance, in central and western Pennsylvania you will hear "The car needs washed," whereas in eastern Pennsylvania (and most other parts of the country) dirty cars "need washing" or "need to be washed." Clearly, there is no one "exact rule" for the form that follows the verb *need* in this context.

Another example is the well-known *you all* or *y'all* of southern dialects; in both midwestern and Appalachian regions you will hear *you'uns* or *y'uns*; in parts of Philadelphia you will hear *youse*. These are all methods of pluralizing the pronoun *you*. It's probably accurate to say that the majority of speech communities in this country have no separate form for *you* when it's plural. But obviously, some do. And although they may not appear in grammar textbooks, these plurals are part of the grammar of many regions.

It will be useful, before looking further at various grammatical issues, to consider more carefully the meaning of *grammar*.

THREE DEFINITIONS OF *GRAMMAR*

Grammar is certainly a common word. You've been hearing it for most of your life, at least during most of your school life, probably from third or fourth grade on. However, there are many different meanings, or different nuances of meaning, in connection with *grammar*. The three we will discuss here are fairly broad definitions that will provide a framework for

---

[2] Words in boldface type are defined in the Glossary of Grammatical Terms, beginning on page 349.

thinking about the various language issues you will be studying in these chapters:

Grammar 1: The system of rules in our heads. As you learned in the Introduction, on page 1, you bring to the study of grammar a lifetime of "knowing" how to produce sentences. This subconscious system of rules is your "language competence." It's important to recognize that these internalized rules vary from one language community to another, as you read in connection with the plural forms of *you.*

Grammar 2: The formal description of the rules. This definition refers to the branch of linguistic science concerned with the formal description of language, the subject matter of books like this one, which identify in an objective way the form and structure, the **syntax**, of sentences. This is the definition that applies when you say, "I'm studying grammar this semester."

Grammar 3: The social implications of usage, sometimes called "linguistic etiquette." This definition could be called do's and don't's of usage, rather than grammar. For example, using certain words may be thought of as bad manners in particular contexts. This definition also applies when people use terms like "poor grammar" or "good grammar."

TRADITIONAL SCHOOL GRAMMAR

In grammar books and grammar classes, past and present, the lessons tend to focus on parts of speech, their definitions, rules for combining them into phrases and clauses, and sentence exercises demonstrating grammatical errors to avoid. This model, based on Latin's eight parts of speech, goes as far back as the Middle Ages, when Latin was the language of culture and enlightenment, of literature and religion—when Latin was considered the ideal language. English vernacular, the language that people actually spoke, was considered inferior, almost primitive by comparison. So it was only natural that when scholars began to write grammars of English in the seventeenth century, they looked to Latin for their model.

In 1693 the English philosopher John Locke declared that the purpose of teaching grammar was "to teach Men not to speak, but to speak correctly and according to the exact Rules of the Tongue." These words of Locke define the concept that today we call **prescriptive grammar.**[3] Grammar books have traditionally been guided by normative principles, that is, for the purpose of establishing norms, or standards, to prescribe "the exact rules of the tongue."

Much of what we call traditional grammar—sometimes called "school grammar"—is the direct descendant of those early Latin-based books. Its

---

[3] From *Some Thoughts Concerning Education*, quoted in Baron, *Grammar and Good Taste*, p. 121. [See reference list, page 13.]

purpose is to teach literacy, the skills of reading and writing, continuing the normative tradition. And most language arts textbooks today continue to be based on Latin's eight parts of speech.

A more modern approach to language education, however, is guided by the work of linguists, who look at the way the language is actually used. Rather than *pre*scribing how language should be used, an accurate **descriptive grammar** *de*scribes the way people speak in everyday situations. Such a description recognizes a wide variety of grammatical forms. The standard of formal written English is, of course, one of them.

MODERN LINGUISTICS

The twentieth century witnessed important new developments in linguistics, the scientific study of language. One important difference from traditional school grammar was the emphasis on objectivity in describing the language and its word classes, together with a rejection of prescriptivism.

In the 1920s a great deal of linguistic research was carried out by anthropologists studying Native American languages, many of which were in danger of being lost. It was not unusual for a few elders to be the only remaining speakers of a tribe's language. When they died, the language would die with them.

To understand the structure underlying languages unknown to them, researchers could not rely on their knowledge of Western languages: They could not assume that the language they were hearing was related either to Latin or to the Germanic roots of English. Nor could they assume that word classes like adjective and pronoun and preposition were part of the sentences they were hearing. To be objective in their description, they had to start from scratch in their thinking about word categories and sentence structure.

Structural Grammar. The same kind of objectivity needed to study the grammar of an unknown language was applied to English grammar by a group of linguists who came to be known as structuralists. Their description of grammar is called **structuralism.** Like the anthropologists studying the speech of Native Americans, the structuralists too recognized the importance of describing language on its own terms. Instead of assuming that English words could fit into the traditional eight word groups of Latin, the structuralists examined sentences objectively, paying particular attention to how words change in sound and spelling (their form) and how they are used in sentences (their function).

You will see the result of that examination in the next chapter, where a clear distinction is drawn between the large open **form classes** (nouns, verbs, adjectives, and adverbs) and the small closed **structure classes,** such as prepositions and conjunctions.

Another important feature of structuralism, which came to be called "new grammar," is its emphasis on the systematic nature of English. The description of the form classes is a good case in point. Their formal nature is systematic; for example, words that have a plural and possessive form are nouns; words that have both an *-ed* form (past tense) and an *-ing* form are verbs. For the structuralists, this systematic description of the language includes an analysis of the sound system (**phonology**), then the systematic combination of sounds into meaningful units and words (**morphology**), and, finally, the systematic combination of words into meaningful phrase structures and sentence patterns (**syntax**).

Transformational Grammar. In the late 1950s, at a time when structuralism was beginning to have an influence on textbooks, a new approach came into prominence. Called *transformational generative grammar,* this new linguistic theory, along with changes in the language arts curriculum, finally led to the diminishing influence of structuralism. Linguistic research today carries forward what can only be called a *linguistic revolution.*

The new linguistics, which began in 1957 with the publication of Noam Chomsky's *Syntactic Structures*, deserves the label "revolutionary." After 1957, the study of grammar would no longer be limited to what is said and how it is interpreted. In fact, the word *grammar* itself took on a new meaning, the definition we are calling Grammar 1: our innate, subconscious ability to generate language, an internal system of rules that constitutes our human language capacity. The goal of the new linguistics was to describe this internal grammar.

Unlike the structuralists, whose goal was to examine the sentences we actually speak and to describe their systematic nature (our Grammar 2), the transformationalists wanted to unlock the secrets of language: to build a model of our internal rules, a model that would produce all of the grammatical—and no ungrammatical—sentences. It might be useful to think of our built-in language system as a computer program. The transformationalists are trying to describe that program.

For example, transformational linguists want to know how our internal linguistic computer can interpret a sentence such as

I enjoy visiting relatives

as ambiguous—that is, as having more than one possible meaning. (To figure out the two meanings, think about who is doing the visiting.) In *Syntactic Structures*, Chomsky distinguished between "deep" and "surface" structure, a concept that may hold the key to ambiguity. This feature is also the basis for the label *transformational,* the idea that meaning, generated in the deep structure, can be *transformed* into a variety of surface structures, the sentences we actually speak. During the past four decades the theory has undergone, and continues to undergo, evolutionary changes.

Although these linguistic theories reach far beyond the scope of classroom grammar, there are several important concepts of transformational grammar that you will be studying in these chapters. One is the recognition that a basic sentence can be transformed into a variety of forms, depending on intent or emphasis, while retaining its essential meaning—for example, questions and exclamations and passive sentences. Another major adoption from transformational grammar is the description of our system for expanding the verb in Chapter 4.

THE ISSUE OF CORRECTNESS

The structural linguists, who had as their goal the objective description of language, recognized that no one variety of English can lay claim to the label "best" or "correct," that the dialects of all native speakers are equally grammatical.

You won't be surprised to learn that the structuralists, after describing the language of all native speakers as grammatical, were themselves called "permissive," charged with advocating a policy of "anything goes." After all, for three hundred years an important goal of school grammar lessons and textbooks had been to teach "proper" grammar. Proper grammar implies standards of correctness, and the structuralists appeared to be rejecting standards and ignoring rules. But what the structural linguists were actually doing was making a distinction between Grammar 2 and Grammar 3: the formal language patterns and "linguistic etiquette."

In his textbook *English Sentences* (Harcourt, 1962), Paul Roberts labeled the following sentences, which represent two dialects of English, equally grammatical:

1. Henry brought his mother some flowers.
2. Henry brung his mother some flowers.

Roberts explains that if we prefer sentence 1,

> we do so simply because in some sense we prefer the people who say sentence 1 to those who say sentence 2. We associate sentence 1 with educated people and sentence 2 with uneducated people. . . . But mark this well: educated people do not say sentence 1 . . . because it is better than 2. Educated people say it, and that makes it better. That's all there is to it. (p. 7)

The well-known issue of *ain't* provides another illustration of the difference between our internal rules of grammar and our external, social rules of usage, between our Grammar 1 and Grammar 3. You may have assumed that pronouncements about *ain't* have something to do with in-correct or ungrammatical English—but they don't. The word itself, the contraction of *am not,* is produced by an internal rule, the same rule that gives us *aren't* and *isn't.* Any negative bias you may have against *ain't* is strictly a matter of linguistic etiquette. And, as you can hear for yourself, many speakers of English harbor no such bias.

Written texts from the seventeenth and eighteenth centuries show that *ain't* was once a part of conversational English of educated people in England and America. It was sometime during the nineteenth century that the word became stigmatized for public speech and marked a speaker as uneducated or ignorant. It's still possible to hear *ain't* in public speech, but only as an attention-getter:

> If it ain't broke, don't fix it.
>
> You ain't seen nothin' yet.

And of course it occurs in written dialogue and in written and spoken humor. But despite the fact that the grammar rules of millions of people produce *ain't* as part of their native language, for many others it carries a stigma.

Investigating Language   1.1

The stigma attached to *ain't* has left a void in our language: We now have no first-person equivalent of the negative questions *Isn't it?* and *Aren't they?* You will discover how we have filled the void when you add the appropriate tag-questions to three sentences. The tag-question is a common way we have of turning a statement into a question. Two examples will illustrate the structure:

> Your mother is a nice person, *isn't she?*
>
> Your brother is still in high school, *isn't he?*

Now write the tag for these three sentences:

1. The weather is nice today, _isn't it_ ?
2. You are my friend, _aren't you_ ?
3. I am your friend, _aren't I_ ?

You'll notice that you can turn those tag-questions into statements by reversing them. Here are the examples:

She isn't.

He isn't.

Now reverse the three that you wrote:

1. *Isn't the weather nice today?*
2. *Aren't you my friend?*
3. *Aren't I your friend?*

In trying to reverse the third tag, you have probably discovered the problem that the banishment of *ain't* has produced. It has left us with something that sounds like an ungrammatical structure. Given the linguists' definition of *ungrammatical*, something that a native speaker wouldn't say, would you call *"Aren't I?"* ungrammatical? Explain.

In summary, then, our attitude toward *ain't* is an issue about status, not grammar. We don't hear *ain't*, nor do we hear regionalisms like *I might could go* and *the car needs washed*, in formal speeches or on the nightly news because they are not part of what we call "standard English."

Modern linguists may find the word *standard* objectionable when applied to a particular dialect, given that every dialect is standard within its own speech community. To label Roberts's sentence 1 as standard may seem to imply that others are somehow inferior, or substandard. Here, however, we are using *standard* as the label for the majority dialect—or, perhaps more accurately, the status dialect—the one that is used in newscasts, in formal business transactions, in courtrooms, in all sorts of public discourse. If the network newscasters and the president of the United States and your teachers began to use *ain't* or *brung* on a regular basis, its status too would soon change.

LANGUAGE VARIETY

All of us have a wide range of language choices available to us. The words we choose and the way in which we say them are determined by the occasion—by our listeners and our purpose and our topic. The way we speak with friends at the pizza parlor, where we use the current slang and jargon of the group, is not the same as our conversation at a formal banquet or a faculty reception. "Is it correct?" is probably the wrong question to ask about a particular word or phrase. A more accurate question would be "Is it correct for this situation?" or "Is it appropriate?"

In our written language, too, what is appropriate or effective in one situation may be completely out of place in another. The language of email messages and texting are obviously different from the language you use in a job-application letter. Even the writing you do in school varies from one class or one assignment to another. The personal essay you write for your composition class has a level of informality that would be inappropriate for a business report or a history research paper. As with speech, the purpose and the audience make all the difference.

Edited American English is the version of our language that has come to be the standard for written public discourse—for newspapers and books and for most of the writing you do in school and on the job. It is the version of our language that this book describes, the written version of the status dialect as it has evolved through the centuries and continues to evolve.

LANGUAGE CHANGE

Another important aspect of our language that is closely related to the issue of correctness and standards is language change. Change is inevitable in a living organism like language. The change is obvious, of course, when we compare the English of Shakespeare or the King James Bible to our modern version. But we certainly don't have to go back that far to see differences. The following passages are from two different translations of *Pinocchio*, the Italian children's book written in the 1880s by Carlo Collodi. The two versions were published almost sixty years apart. You'll have no trouble distinguishing the translation of 1925 from the one published in 1983:

1a.   Fancy the happiness of Pinocchio on finding himself free!

1b.   Imagine Pinocchio's joy when he felt himself free.

2a.   Gallop on, gallop on, my pretty steed.

2b.   Gallop, gallop, little horse.

3a.   But whom shall I ask?

3b.   But who can I possibly ask?

4a.   Woe betide the lazy fellow.

4b.   Woe to those who yield to idleness.

5a.   Hasten, Pinocchio.

5b.   Hurry, Pinocchio.

6a.   Without adding another word, the marionette bade the good Fairy good-by.

6b.   Without adding another word, the puppet said good-bye to his good fairy.

In both cases the translators are writing the English version of 1880 Italian, so the language is not necessarily conversational 1925 or 1983

English. In spite of that constraint, we can recognize—as you've probably figured out—that the first item in each pair is the 1925 translation. Those sentences include words that we simply don't have occasion to use anymore, words that would sound out of place today in a conversation, or even in a fairy tale: *betide, hasten, bade.* The language of 1925 is simply not our language. In truth, the language of 1983 is not our language either. We can see and hear change happening all around us, especially if we consider the new words required for such fields as medicine, space science, and e-commerce.

Investigating Language 1.2

The difference between the two translations in the first pair of *Pinocchio* sentences is connected to the word *fancy,* a word that is still common today. Why did the 1983 translator use *imagine* instead? What has happened to *fancy* in the intervening decades?

The third pair involves a difference in grammar rather than vocabulary, the change from *whom* to *who.* What do you suppose today's language critics would have to say about the 1983 translation?

The last pair includes a spelling change. Check the dictionary to see which is "correct"—or is *correct* the right word? The dictionary includes many words that have more than one spelling. How do you know which one to use?

Finally, provide examples to demonstrate the accuracy of the assertion that the language of 1983 is not our language.

LANGUAGE IN THE CLASSROOM

How about the classroom? Should teachers call attention to the dialect differences in their students' speech? Should teachers "correct" them? These are questions that the National Council of Teachers of English (NCTE) has addressed in a document called "Students' Right to Their Own Language." The NCTE has taken the position that teachers should respect the dialects of their students. But teachers also have an obligation to teach students to read and write standard English, the language of public discourse and of the workplace that those students are preparing to join. There are ways of doing so without making students feel that the language spoken in their home, the language produced by their own internal grammar rules, is somehow inferior. Certainly one way is to study language differences in an objective, nonjudgmental way, to discuss individual and regional and ethnic differences. Teachers who use the technique called code-switching have had notable success in helping students not only to acquire standard English as a second dialect but also to understand in a conscious way the underlying rules of their home language. (For information on code-switching, see the book by Wheeler and Swords in the list for further reading that follows this chapter.)

In 1994 the NCTE passed a resolution that encourages the integration of language awareness into classroom instruction and teacher preparation programs. Language awareness includes examining how language varies in a range of social and cultural settings; how people's attitudes towards language vary across cultures, classes, genders, and generations; how oral and written language affects listeners and readers; how "correctness" in language reflects social, political, and economic values; and how first and second languages are acquired. Language awareness also includes the teaching of grammar from a descriptive, rather than a prescriptive, perspective.

CHAPTER *1*
Key Terms

Code-switching
Correctness
Descriptive grammar
Dialect
Edited American English
Grammar rules
Grammatical
Language change
Language variety

Linguistic etiquette
Nonstandard dialect
Prescriptive grammar
Regionalisms
Structuralism
Transformational grammar
Ungrammatical
Usage rules

For Further Reading on Topics in This Chapter

Baron, Dennis E. *Grammar and Good Taste: Reforming the American Language.* New Haven, CT: Yale University Press, 1982.

Crystal, David. *The Cambridge Encyclopedia of Language.* Cambridge, England: Cambridge University Press, 1987.

Haussamen, Brock. *Revising the Rules: Traditional Grammar and Modern Linguistics.* 2nd ed. Dubuque, IA: Kendall-Hunt, 1997.

Hunter, Susan, and Ray Wallace, eds. *The Place of Grammar in Writing Instruction: Past, Present, Future.* Portsmouth, NH: Boynton/Cook, 1995.

Joos, Martin. *The Five Clocks*. New York: Harcourt Brace Jovanovich, 1967.

Kutz, Eleanor. *Language and Literacy: Studying Discourse in Communities and Classrooms*. Portsmouth, NH: Boynton/Cook, 1997.

McCrum, Robert, Robert MacNeil, and William Cran. *The Story of English*. 3rd rev. ed. New York: Penguin Books, 2003.

Pinker, Steven. *The Language Instinct*. New York: William Morrow, 1994.

Pinker, Steven. *The Stuff of Thought: Language as a Window into Human Nature*. New York: Viking, 2007.

Schuster, Edgar H. *Breaking the Rules: Liberating Writers Through Innovative Grammar Instruction*. Portsmouth, NH: Heinemann, 2003.

Wheeler, Rebecca S., and Rachel Swords. *Code-Switching: Teaching Standard English in Urban Classrooms*. Urbana, IL: National Council of Teachers of English, 2006.

Wolfram, Walt. *Dialects and American English*. Washington, DC: Center for Applied Linguistics, 1991.

The Grammar of Basic Sentences

You might have been surprised to learn, when you read the introduction to Part I, that you're already an expert in grammar—and have been since before you started school. Indeed, you're such an expert that you can generate completely original sentences with those internal grammar rules of yours, sentences that have never before been spoken or written. Here's one to get you started; you can be quite sure that it is original:

> At this very moment, I, [Insert your name], am reading page 15 of the ninth edition of *Understanding English Grammar*.

Perhaps even more surprising is the fact that the number of such sentences you can produce is infinite.

When you study the grammar of your native language, then, you are studying a subject you already "know"; so rather than learning grammar, you will be "learning about" grammar. If you're not a native speaker, you will probably be learning both grammar and "about" grammar; the mix will depend on your background and experience. It's important that you understand what you are bringing to this course—even though you may have forgotten all those "parts of speech" labels and definitions you once consciously learned. The unconscious, or subconscious, knowledge that you have can help you if you will let it.

We will begin the study of grammar by examining words and phrases in Chapter 2. Then in Chapter 3 we take up basic sentence patterns, the underlying framework of sentences. A conscious knowledge of the basic patterns provides a foundation for the expansions and variations that come later. In Chapter 4 we examine the expanded verb, the system of auxiliaries that makes our verbs so versatile. In Chapter 5 we look at ways to change sentence focus for a variety of purposes.

CHAPTER 2

Words and Phrases

CHAPTER PREVIEW

The purpose of this chapter is to review words and phrases. It will also introduce you to some of the language for discussing language—that is, the terms you will need for thinking about sentence structure. Pay attention to the items in bold face; they constitute your grammar vocabulary and are defined in the Glossary, beginning on page 349.

This review will lay the groundwork for the study of the sentence patterns and their expansions in the chapters that follow. By the end of this chapter, you will be able to

- Distinguish between the *form classes* and the *structure classes* of words.
- Identify examples of the four form classes: *nouns, verbs, adjectives,* and *adverbs.*
- Identify *determiners* and *headwords* as basic components of noun phrases.
- Recognize the *subject–predicate relationship* as the core structure in all sentences.
- Identify the structure and use of *prepositional phrases.*
- Use your subconscious knowledge of grammar to help analyze and understand words and phrases.

THE FORM CLASSES

The four word classes that we call **form classes—nouns, verbs, adjectives,** and **adverbs**—are special in many ways. If you were assigned to look around your classroom and make a list of what you see, the words in your list would undoubtedly be the names of things and people: *books, desks,* *windows, shelves, shoes, sweatshirts, Nina, Ella, Ted, Hector, Professor Watts.* Those labels—those names of things and people—are nouns. (As you may know, *noun* is the Latin word for "name.") And if you were assigned to describe what your teacher and classmates are doing at the moment— *sitting, talking, dozing, smiling, reading*—you'd have a list of verbs.

We can think of those two sets—nouns and verbs—along with adjectives and adverbs (the *big* book; sitting *quietly*) as special. They are the content words of the language. And their numbers make them special: These four groups constitute over 99 percent of our vocabulary. They are also different from other word classes in that they can be identified by their forms. Each of them has, or can have, particular endings, or **suffixes**, which identify them. And that, of course, is the reason for the label "form classes."

NOUNS AND VERBS

Here are two simple sentences to consider in terms of form, each consisting of a noun and a verb:

> Cats fight.
> Mary laughed.

You may be familiar with the traditional definition of *noun*—"a word that names a person, place, or thing [or animal]"; that definition is based on meaning. The traditional definition of *verb* as an "action word" is also based on meaning. In our two sentences those definitions certainly work. But notice also the clues based on form: in the first one, the **plural** suffix on the noun *cat;* in the second, the **past-tense** suffix on the verb *laugh.*

The plural is one of two noun endings that we call **inflections**; the other is the **possessive case** ending, the apostrophe-plus-s (*the cat's paw*)—or, in the case of most plural nouns, just the apostrophe after the plural marker (*several cats' paws*).

When the dictionary identifies a word as a verb, it lists three forms: the **present tense**, or **base form** (*laugh*); the **past tense** (*laughed*); and the **past participle** (*laughed*). These three forms are traditionally referred to as the verb's "three principal parts." The base form is also known as the infinitive; it is often written with *to (to laugh).* All verbs have these forms, along with two more—the *-s* form (*laughs*), and the *-ing* form (*laughing*). We will take these up in Chapter 4, where we study verbs in detail.

But for now, let's revise the traditional definitions by basing them not on the meaning of the words but rather on their forms:

> *A noun is a word that can be made plural and/or possessive.*
> *A verb is a word that can show tense, such as present and past.*

THE NOUN PHRASE

The term **noun phrase** may be new to you, although you're probably familiar with the word **phrase,** which traditionally refers to any group of words that functions as a unit within the sentence. But sometimes a single word will function as a unit by itself, as in our two earlier examples, where *CATS* and *Mary* function as subjects in their sentences. For this reason, we are going to alter that traditional definition of *phrase* to include single words:

> ***A phrase is a word or group of words that functions as a unit within the sentence.***

A phrase will always have a head, or **headword;** and as you might expect, the headword of the noun phrase is a noun. Most noun phrases (NPs) also include a noun signaler, or marker, called a **determiner.** Here are three NPs you have seen in this chapter, with their headwords underlined and their determiners shown in italics:

> *the* <u>headword</u>
>
> *a* single <u>word</u>
>
> *the* traditional <u>definition</u>

As two of the examples illustrate, the headword may also be preceded by a modifier. The most common modifier in preheadword position is the adjective, such as *single* and *traditional.* You will be studying about many other structures as well that function the way adjectives function, as modifiers of nouns.

As you may have noticed in the three examples, the opening determiners are the **articles** *a* and *the.* Though they are our most common determiners, other word groups also function as determiners, signaling noun phrases. For example, the function of possessive nouns and possessive pronouns is almost always that of determiner:

> *Mary's* boyfriend
>
> *his* apartment

Another common word category in the determiner slot is the **demonstrative pronoun**—*this, that, these, those:*

> *this* old house
>
> *these* expensive sneakers

Because noun phrases can be single words, as we saw in our earlier examples (*Cats fight, Mary laughed*), it follows that not all noun phrases will have determiners. **Proper nouns**, such as the names of people and places

(*Mary*) and certain plural nouns (*cats*), are among the most common that appear without a noun signaler.

In spite of these exceptions, however, it is accurate to say that most noun phrases do begin with determiners. Likewise, it's accurate to say—and important to recognize—that whenever you encounter a determiner *you can be sure you are at the beginning of a noun phrase*. In other words, articles (*a, an, the*) and certain other words, such as possessive nouns and pronouns, demonstrative pronouns, numbers, and another subclass of pronouns called **indefinite pronouns** (e.g., *some, many, both, each, every*), tell you that a noun headword is on the way.

We can now identify three defining characteristics of nouns:

A noun is a word that can be made plural and/or possessive; it occupies the headword position in the noun phrase; it is usually signaled by a determiner.

In the study of syntax, which you are now undertaking, you can't help but notice the prevalence of noun phrases and their signalers, the determiners.

Exercise 1

The following six sentences include sixteen noun phrases. Your job is to identify their determiners and headwords.

Note: Answers to the exercises are provided, beginning on page 371.

1. The students rested after their long trip.
2. Our new neighbors across the hall became our best friends.
3. Mickey's roommate studies in the library on the weekends.
4. A huge crowd lined the streets for the big parade.
5. This new lasagna recipe feeds an enormous crowd.
6. Jessica made her new boyfriend some cookies.

THE VERB PHRASE

As you would expect, the headword of a verb phrase, or VP, is the verb; the other components, if any, will depend in part on whether the verb is **transitive** (*The cat chased the mouse*) or **intransitive** (*Cats fight*). In most sentences, the verb phrase will include **adverbials** (*Mary laughed loudly*). In Chapter 3 you will be studying verb phrases in detail because it is the variations in the verb phrases, the sentence **predicates,** that differentiate the sentence patterns.

As we saw with the noun phrase, it is also possible for a verb phrase to be complete with only the headword. Our two earlier examples—*Cats fight*; *Mary laughed*—illustrate instances of single-word noun phrases, which are fairly common in most written work, as well as single-word verb phrases, which are not common at all. In fact, single-word verb phrases as predicates are very rare. So far in this chapter, none of the verb phrases we have used comes close to the brevity of those two sample sentences.

NP + VP = S

This formula—NP + VP = S—is another way of saying "Subject plus Predicate equals Sentence." Our formula with the labels NP and VP simply emphasizes the form of those two sentence parts. The following diagram includes both labels, and their form and function:

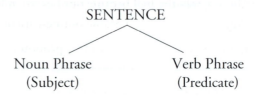

SENTENCE

Noun Phrase   Verb Phrase
(Subject)   (Predicate)

Using what you have learned so far about noun phrases and verb phrases—as well as your intuition—you should have no trouble recognizing the two parts of the following sentences. You'll notice right away that the first word of the subject noun phrase in all of the sentences is a determiner.

> Our county commissioners passed a new ordinance.
>
> The mayor's husband argued against the ordinance.
>
> The mayor was upset with her husband.
>
> Some residents of the community spoke passionately for the ordinance.
>
> The merchants in town are unhappy.
>
> This new law prohibits billboards on major highways.

As a quick review of noun phrases, identify the headwords of the subject noun phrases in the six sentences just listed:

_____   _____   _____

_____   _____   _____

Given your understanding of noun phrases, you probably had no difficulty identifying those headwords: *commissioners, husband, mayor, residents, merchants, law*. In the exercise that follows, you are instructed to identify the two parts of those six sentences to determine where the subject noun phrase ends. This time you'll be using your subconscious knowledge of pronouns.

Exercise 2

You have at your disposal a wonderful tool for figuring out the line between the subject and the predicate: Simply substitute a **personal pronoun** (*I, you, he, she, it, they*) for the subject. You saw these example sentences in Exercise 1:

Examples:

This new lasagna recipe feeds an enormous crowd.

     It   feeds an enormous crowd.

Our new neighbors across the hall became our best friends.

     They   became our best friends.

Now underline the subject; then substitute a pronoun for the subject of these sentences you read in the previous discussion:

1. Our county commissioners passed a new ordinance.

2. The mayor's husband argued against the ordinance.

3. The mayor was upset with her husband.

4. Some residents of the community spoke passionately for the ordinance.

5. The merchants in town are unhappy.

6. This new law prohibits billboards on major highways.

As your answers no doubt show, the personal pronoun stands in for the entire noun phrase, not just the noun headword. Making that substitution, which you do automatically in speech, can help you recognize not only the subject–predicate boundary but the boundaries of noun phrases throughout the sentence.

Recognition of this subject–predicate relationship, the common element in all of our sentences, is the first step in the study of sentence structure. Equally important for the classification of sentences into sentence patterns is the concept of the verb as the central, pivotal slot in the sentence. Before moving on to the sentence patterns in Chapter 3, however, we will look briefly at the other two form classes, adjectives and adverbs, which, like nouns and verbs, can often be identified by their forms. We will then describe the prepositional phrase, perhaps our most common modifier, one that adds information to both the noun phrase and the verb phrase.

ADJECTIVES AND ADVERBS

The other two form classes, **adjectives** and **adverbs**, like nouns and verbs, can usually be recognized by their form and/or by their position in the sentence.

The inflectional endings that identify adjectives and some adverbs are *-er* and *-est*, known as the **comparative** and **superlative** degrees:

Adjective	*Adverb*
big	near
bigger	nearer
biggest	nearest

When the word has two or more syllables, the comparative and superlative markers are generally *more* and *most* rather than the suffixes:

beautiful	quickly
more beautiful	more quickly
most beautiful	most quickly

Another test of whether a word is an adjective or adverb, as opposed to noun or verb, is its ability to pattern with a **qualifier,** such as *very:*

very beautiful	very quickly

You'll notice that these tests (the degree endings and *very*) can help you differentiate adjectives and adverbs from the other two form classes, nouns and verbs, but they do not help you distinguish the two word classes from each other.

There is one special clue about word form that we use to help us identify adverbs: the *-ly* ending. However, this is not an inflectional suffix like *-er* or *-est*. When we add one of these to an adjective—*happier, happiest*—the word remains an adjective (just as a noun with the plural inflection added is still a noun). In contrast, the *-ly* ending that makes adverbs so visible is actually added to adjectives to turn them into adverbs:

Adjective				*Adverb*
quick	+	ly	=	quickly
pleasant	+	ly	=	pleasantly
happy	+	ly	=	happily

Rather than inflectional, the *-ly* is a **derivational suffix**: It enables us to *derive* adverbs from adjectives. Incidentally, the *-ly* means "like": quickly = quick-like; happily = happy-like. And because we have so many adjectives that can morph into adverbs in this way—many thousands, in fact—we are not often mistaken when we assume that an *-ly* word is an adverb. (In Chapter 12 you will read about derivational suffixes for all four form classes.)

In addition to these "adverbs of manner," as the *-ly* adverbs are called, we have a selection of other adverbs that have no clue of form; among them are *then, now, soon, here, there, everywhere, afterward, often, sometimes, seldom, always*. Often the best way to identify an adverb is by the kind of information it supplies to the sentence—information of time, place, manner, frequency, and the like; in other words, an adverb answers such questions as *where, when, why, how,* and *how often*. Adverbs can also be identified on the basis of their position in the predicate and their movability.

As you read in the discussion of noun phrases, the slot between the determiner and the headword is where we find adjectives:

this <u>new</u> recipe   an <u>enormous</u> crowd

Adverbs, on the other hand, modify verbs and, as such, will be part of the predicate:

Some residents spoke <u>passionately</u> for the ordinance.
Mario <u>suddenly</u> hit the brakes.

However, unlike adjectives, one of the features of adverbs that makes them so versatile for writers and speakers is their movability: They can often be moved to a different place in the predicate—and they can even leave the predicate and open the sentence:

Mario hit the brakes <u>suddenly</u>.
<u>Suddenly</u> Mario hit the brakes.

Bear in mind, however, that some adverbs are more movable than others. We probably don't want to move *passionately* to the beginning of its sentence. And in making the decision to move the adverb, we also want to consider the context, the relation of the sentence to the others around it.

Investigating Language   2.1

Your job in this exercise is to experiment with the underlined adverbs to discover how movable they are. How many places in the sentence will they fit? Do you and your classmates agree?

1. I have <u>finally</u> finished my report.
2. Maria has <u>now</u> accumulated sixty credits towards her degree.
3. The hunters moved <u>stealthily</u> through the woods.
4. The kindergartners giggled <u>quietly</u> in the corner.
5. My parents <u>occasionally</u> surprise me with a visit.
6. Our soccer coach will <u>undoubtedly</u> expect us to practice <u>tomorrow</u>.
7. I <u>occasionally</u> jog <u>nowadays</u>.
8. The wind <u>often</u> blows <u>furiously</u> in January.

PREPOSITIONAL PHRASES

Before going on to sentence patterns, let's take a quick look at the **prepositional phrase**, a two-part structure consisting of a **preposition** followed by an object, which is usually a noun phrase. Prepositions are among the most common words in our language. In fact, the paragraph you are now reading includes nine different prepositions: *before, to, at, of* (three times), *by, among, in, throughout,* and *as* (twice). Prepositional phrases show up throughout our sentences, sometimes as part of a noun phrase and sometimes as a modifier of the verb. Because prepositional phrases are so common, you might find it helpful to review the lists of prepositions in Chapter 13 (pp. 274, 276).

As a modifier in a noun phrase, a prepositional phrase nearly always follows the noun headword. Its purpose is to make clear the identity of the noun or simply to add a descriptive detail. Several of the noun phrases you saw in Exercise 1 include a prepositional phrase:

Our new neighbors <u>across the hall</u> became our best friends.

Here the *across* phrase is part of the subject, functioning like an adjective, so we call it an **adjectival** prepositional phrase; it tells "which neighbors" we're referring to. In a different sentence, that same prepositional phrase could function adverbially:

> Our good friends live <u>across the hall</u>.

Here the purpose of the *across* phrase is to tell "where" about the verb *live*, so we refer to its function as **adverbial**. Here's another adverbial prepositional phrase from Exercise 1:

> The students rested <u>after their long trip</u>.

Here the prepositional phrase tells "when"—another purpose of adverbials. And there's one more clue that this prepositional phrase is adverbial. It could be moved to the opening of the sentence:

> <u>After their long trip</u>, the students rested.

Remember that the nouns *adjective* and *adverb* name word classes: They name forms. When we add that *-al* or *-ial* suffix—*adjectival* and *adverbial*—they become the names of functions—functions that adjectives and adverbs normally perform. In other words, the terms *adjectival* and *adverbial* can apply to structures other than adjectives and adverbs—such as prepositional phrases, as we have just seen:

> ***Modifiers of nouns are called*** adjectivals, ***no matter what their form.***
> ***Modifiers of verbs are called*** adverbials, ***no matter what their form.***

Exercise 3

In the following sentences, some of which you have seen before, identify the function of each of the underlined prepositional phrases as either adjectival or adverbial:

1. A huge crowd <u>of students</u> lined the streets <u>for the big parade</u>.
2. Mickey's roommate studies <u>in the library</u> <u>on the weekends</u>.
3. Some residents <u>of the community</u> spoke passionately <u>for the ordinance</u>.
4. The merchants <u>in town</u> were unhappy.
5. <u>In August</u> my parents moved <u>to Portland</u>.
6. <u>On sunny days</u> we lounge <u>on the lawn</u> <u>between classes</u>.

Investigating Language   2.2

A. Make each list of words into a noun phrase and then use the phrase in a sentence. Compare your answers with your classmates'—the NPs should all be the same (with one exception); the sentences will vary.

1. table, the, small, wooden
2. my, sneakers, roommate's, new
3. cotton, white, t-shirts, the, other, all
4. gentle, a, on the head, tap
5. books, those, moldy, in the basement
6. the, with green eyes, girl

Did you discover the item with two possibilities?

B. Many words in English can serve as either nouns or verbs. Here are some examples:

I made a *promise* to my boss. (noun)
I *promised* to be on time for work. (verb)

He *offered* to help us. (verb)
We accepted his *offer.* (noun)

Write a pair of short sentences for each of the following words, demonstrating that they can be either nouns or verbs:

visit   plant   point   feature   audition

THE STRUCTURE CLASSES

In addition to the form classes, so far in this chapter you have learned labels for three of our structure classes:

1. **Determiner**, a word that marks nouns. In the section headed "The Noun Phrase," you learned that the function of **articles** (*a, an, the*), **possessive nouns** and **pronouns** (*his, Mary's,* etc.), **demonstrative pronouns** (*this, that, these, those*), and **indefinite pronouns** (*some, both, each,* etc.) is to introduce noun phrases. In other words, when you see *the* or *my* or *this* or *some*, you can be very sure that a noun is coming.

2. **Qualifier**, a word that marks—qualifies or intensifies— adjectives and adverbs: *rather* slowly, *very* sure.

3. **Preposition**, a word, such as *to, of, for, by,* and so forth, that combines with a noun phrase to produce an adverbial or adjectival modifier. Prepositions are listed on pages 274, 276.

In contrast to the large, open form classes, the structure classes are small and, for the most part, closed classes. As you read in the description of the form classes, those open classes constitute 99 percent of our language—and they keep getting new members. However, although the structure classes may be small, they are by far our most frequently used words. And we couldn't get along without them.

In Chapter 3 you will be introduced to several other structure classes as you study the sentence patterns. You will find examples of all of them in Chapter 13.

CHAPTER 2
Key Terms

In this chapter you've been introduced to many basic terms that describe sentence grammar. This list may look formidable, but some of the terms were probably familiar already; those that are new will become more familiar as you continue the study of sentences.

Adjectival	Headword	Preposition
Adjective	Indefinite pronoun	Prepositional phrase
Adverb	Inflection	Pronoun
Adverbial	Noun	Qualifier
Article	Noun phrase	Structure classes
Comparative degree	Past tense	Subject
Degree	Personal pronoun	Suffix
Demonstrative pronoun	Phrase	Superlative degree
Derivational suffix	Plural	Verb
Determiner	Possessive case	Verb phrase
Form classes	Predicate	

CHAPTER
3

Sentence Patterns

CHAPTER PREVIEW

This chapter will extend your study of sentence structure, which began in the previous chapter with its focus on the noun phrase and the verb phrase. Although a speaker can potentially produce an infinite number of sentences, the systematic structure of English sentences and the limited number of elements in these structures make this study possible.

Ten sentence patterns account for the underlying skeletal structure of almost all the possible grammatical sentences. Your study of these basic patterns will give you a solid framework for understanding the expanded sentences in the chapters that follow.

By the end of this chapter, you will be able to

- Recognize four types of verbs: *be, linking, intransitive,* and *transitive.*
- Identify and diagram the ten basic sentence patterns.
- Distinguish among *subject complements, direct objects, indirect objects,* and *object complements.*
- Identify the adverbs and prepositional phrases that fill out the ten patterns.
- Understand and use *phrasal verbs* and simple *compound structures.*
- Recognize four types of sentences: *declarative, interrogative, imperative,* and *exclamatory.*

28

SUBJECTS AND PREDICATES

The first step in understanding the skeletal structure of the sentence patterns is to recognize the two parts they all have in common, the **subject** and the **predicate**:

The subject of the sentence, as its name suggests, is generally what the sentence is about—its topic. The predicate is what is said about the subject.

The terms *subject* and *predicate* refer to sentence functions, or roles. But we can also describe those sentence functions in terms of form:

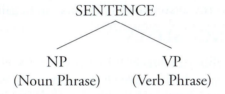

In other words, the subject slot is generally filled by a noun phrase, the predicate slot by a verb phrase. In later chapters we will see sentences in which structures other than noun phrases fill the subject slot; however, the predicate slot is *always* filled by a verb phrase.

Recognizing this subject–predicate relationship, the common element in all of our sentences, is the first step in the study of sentence structure. Equally important for the classification of sentences into sentence patterns is the concept of the verb as the central, pivotal slot in the sentence. In the following list of the ten patterns, the subjects are identical (*The students*) to emphasize that the ten categories are determined by variations in the predicates, variations in the verb headword, and in the structures following the verb. So although we call these basic forms *sentence* patterns, a more accurate label might be *predicate* patterns.

We should note that this list of patterns is not the only way to organize the verb classes: Some descriptions include fifteen or more patterns. However, rather than adding more patterns to our list, we account for the sentences that vary somewhat from the general pattern by considering them exceptions.

SENTENCE

	NP (Subject)	VP (Predicate)
I.	The students	are upstairs.
II.	The students	are diligent.
III.	The students	are scholars.
IV.	The students	seem diligent.
V.	The students	became scholars.
VI.	The students	rested.
VII.	The students	organized a dance marathon.
VIII.	The students	gave the professor their homework.
IX.	The students	consider the teacher intelligent.
X.	The students	consider the course a challenge.

THE SENTENCE SLOTS

One way to think about a sentence is to picture it as a series of positions, or slots. In the following chart, where all the slots are labeled, you'll see that the first one in every pattern is the subject, and the second—the first position in the predicate—is the **main verb**, also called the **predicating verb.**

Because the variations among the sentence patterns are in the predicates, we group the ten patterns according to their verb types: the ***be* patterns,** the **linking verb** patterns, the **intransitive verb** pattern, and the **transitive verb** patterns. You'll notice that the number of slots in the predicate varies: Six of the patterns have two, but Pattern VI has only one slot, and three of the transitive patterns, VIII to X, each have three. The label in parentheses names the function, the role, that the slot performs in the sentence.

The subscript numbers you see in some of the patterns in the chart that follows show the relationship between noun phrases: Identical numbers—such as those in Patterns III and V, where both numbers are 1—mean that the two noun phrases have the same referent; different numbers—such as those in Pattern VII, where the numbers are 1 and 2—denote different referents. **Referent** means the thing (or person, event, concept, and so on) that the noun or noun phrase stands for.

This list of patterns, with each position labeled according to its form and its role in the sentence, may look formidable at the moment. But don't worry—and don't try to memorize all this detail. It will fall into place as you come to understand the separate patterns.

are = aux verb

The Be *Patterns*

I	**NP**	**be**	**ADV/TP**
	(subject)	(predicating verb)	(adverbial of time or place)
	The students	*are*	*upstairs*
II	**NP**	**be**	**ADJ**
	(subj)	(pred vb)	(subject complement)
	The students	*are*	*diligent*
III	**NP**₁	**be**	**NP**₁
	(subj)	(pred vb)	(subj comp)
	The students	*are*	*scholars*

The Linking Verb Patterns

IV	**NP**	**linking verb**	**ADJ**
	(subj)	(pred vb)	(subj comp)
	The students	*seem*	*diligent*
V	**NP**₁	**lnk verb**	**NP**₁
	(subj)	(pred vb)	(subj comp)
	The students	*became*	*scholars*

The Intransitive Verb Pattern

VI	**NP**	**intransitive verb**
	(subj)	(pred vb)
	The students	*rested*

The Transitive Verb Patterns

VII	**NP**₁	**transitive verb**	**NP**₂	
	(subj)	(pred vb)	(direct object)	
	The students	*organized*	*a dance marathon*	
VIII	**NP**₁	**trans verb**	**NP**₂	**NP**₃
	(subj)	(pred vb)	(indirect object)	(dir obj)
	The students	*gave*	*the professor*	*their homework*
IX	**NP**₁	**trans verb**	**NP**₂	**ADJ**
	(subj)	(pred vb)	(dir obj)	(obj comp)
	The students	*consider*	*the teacher*	*intelligent*
X	**NP**₁	**trans verb**	**NP**₂	**NP**₂
	(subj)	(pred vb)	(dir obj)	(obj comp)
	The students	*consider*	*the course*	*a challenge*

THE *BE* PATTERNS

The first three formulas state that when a form of *be* serves as the main, or predicating, verb, an adverbial of time or place (Pattern I), or an adjectival (Pattern II), or a noun phrase (Pattern III) will follow it. The one exception to this rule—and, by the way, we can think of the sentence patterns as descriptions of the rules that our internal computer is programmed to follow—is a statement simply affirming existence, such as "I am." Aside from this exception, Patterns I through III describe all the sentences in which a form of *be* is the main verb. (Other one-word forms of *be* are *am, is, are, was, were;* and the expanded forms, described in Chapter 4, include *have been, was being, might be,* and *will be.*)

Pattern I: NP *be* ADV/TP

The students are upstairs.

The teacher is here.

The last performance was yesterday.

The ADV in the formula stands for adverbial, a modifier of the verb. The ADV that follows *be* is, with certain exceptions, limited to when and where information, so in the formula for Pattern I we identify the slot as ADV/TP, meaning "adverbial of time or place."[1] In the sample sentences *upstairs* and *here* designate place; *yesterday* designates time. The diagram of Pattern I shows the adverb below the verb, which is where all adverbials are diagrammed.

In the following Pattern I sentences, the adverbials of time and place are prepositional phrases in form:

The next performance is <u>on Monday</u>.

The students are <u>in the library</u>.

The diagram for the adverbial prepositional phrase is a two-part framework with a slanted line for the preposition and a horizontal line for the object:

Notice that the object of the preposition is a noun phrase, so it is diagrammed just as the subject noun phrase is—with the headword on the horizontal line and the determiner below it.

Pattern II: NP *be* ADJ

The students are diligent.

The price of gasoline is ridiculous.

The play was very dull.

In this pattern the complement that follows *be* is an adjectival. In the language of traditional grammar, this slot is the **subject complement,** which both completes the verb and modifies or describes the subject.[2] The word *complement* refers to a "completer" of the verb. On the diagram the subject complement follows a diagonal line that slants toward the subject to show their relationship.

In the three sample sentences the subject complements are adjectives in form, as they usually are, but sometimes a prepositional phrase will fill the slot. These are set phrases, or idiomatic expressions, that name an attribute of the subject:

Henry is <u>under the weather</u>.

Kim is <u>in a bad mood</u>.

Although these sentences may look like those you saw in Pattern I, you can figure out that they belong in Pattern II because you can usually think of an adjective, a single descriptive word, that could substitute for the phrase:

Henry is <u>ill</u>.

Kim is <u>cranky</u>.

You can also rule out Pattern I because "under the weather" and "in a bad mood" do not supply information of time or place.

The diagram for the prepositional phrase in a complement position has the same two-part framework that we saw before:

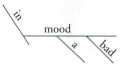

---

[2] More specifically, the traditional label for the subject complement in Pattern II (and IV) is **predicate adjective;** the traditional label for the NP in Pattern III (and V) is **predicate nominative.** We will use the more general term *subject complement* for both adjectives and noun phrases.

We attach that frame to the main line by means of a pedestal. In this way the structure is immediately identifiable in terms of both form (prepositional phrase) and function (subject complement):

Pattern III: NP$_1$ *be* NP$_1$

The students are scholars.

Professor Mendez is my math teacher.

The tournament was an exciting event.

The NP, of course, fills the subject slot in all of the patterns; in Pattern III a noun phrase following *be* fills the subject complement slot as well. The numbers that mark the NPs indicate that the two noun phrases have the same referent. For example, when we say "Professor Mendez is my math teacher," the two NPs, "Professor Mendez" and "my math teacher," refer to the same person. The subject complement renames the subject; *be*, the main verb, acts as an "equal sign," connecting the subject with its complement.

Exercise 4

Draw vertical lines to isolate the slots in the following sentences; identify each slot according to its form and function, as the example shows. Then identify the sentence pattern.

Example:

Our vacation	was	wonderful. (Pattern _____II_____)
NP	be	Adj
subject	pred vb	subj comp

1. Brian's problem is serious. (Pattern _____)
2. The workers are on the roof. (Pattern _____)
3. The excitement of the fans is really contagious. (Pattern _____)
4. Brevity is the soul of wit. [Shakespeare] (Pattern _____)
5. The final exam was at four o'clock. (Pattern _____)
6. The kids are very silly. (Pattern _____)

7. The basketball team is on a roll. (Pattern _____)
8. A foolish consistency is the hobgoblin of little minds. [Ralph Waldo Emerson] (Pattern _____)

Now do a traditional diagram of each sentence, like those you have seen next to the patterns. (See pages 56–58 for notes on the diagrams.)

THE LINKING VERB PATTERNS

The term *linking verb* applies to all verbs other than *be* completed by a subject complement—an adjectival or a noun phrase that describes, characterizes, or identifies the subject. Although many grammar books include *be* among the linking verbs, we have separated it from the linking verb category in order to emphasize its special qualities—variations of both form and function that other verbs do not have. However, it is certainly accurate to think of Patterns II and III as the "linking *be*."

Pattern IV: NP V-lnk ADJ

The students seem diligent.

I grew sleepy.

The soup tastes salty.

In these sentences an adjectival fills the subject complement slot; it describes or names an attribute of the subject, just as in Pattern II. In many cases, a form of *be* can be substituted for the Pattern IV linking verb with a minimal change in meaning: *I grew sleepy* and *I was sleepy* are certainly close in meaning. On the other hand, sentences with *be* and *seem* could have significant differences in meaning.

Pattern IV is a common category for verbs of the senses; besides *taste*, the verbs *smell*, *feel*, *sound*, and *look* often link an adjective to the subject:

The soup smells good.

The dog looks sick.

Again, as with Pattern II, an adjectival prepositional phrase sometimes fills the subject complement slot:

The piano sounds <u>out of tune</u>.

The fighter seems <u>out of shape</u>.

A complete list of all the verbs that pattern with subject complements would be fairly short. Besides *seem* and the verbs of the senses, others on the list are *appear, become, get, prove, remain,* and *turn.* But just because the list is short, don't try to memorize it. All of these verbs, with the possible exception of *seem,* hold membership in other verb classes too—transitive or intransitive or both. The way to recognize linking verbs is to understand the role of the subject complement, to recognize the form of the structure following the verb and its relationship to the subject.

Pattern V: NP₁ V-lnk NP₁

> The students became scholars.
>
> My uncle remained a bachelor.

In this pattern a noun phrase fills the subject complement slot following the linking verb. As the formula shows, the two noun phrases have the same referent, just as they do in Pattern III. We should note, too, that very few linking verbs will fit in Pattern V; most of them take only adjectivals, not noun phrases, as subject complements. The two verbs used in the examples, *become* and *remain,* are the most common. On rare occasions *seem* also takes a noun phrase rather than its usual adjective:

> That seemed a good idea.
>
> He seemed a nice person.

But in the case of these sentences, a prepositional phrase with the preposition *like* is more common:

> That seemed like a good idea.
>
> He seemed like a nice person.

The subject complement here is an adjectival prepositional phrase, so these two sentences with *like* are Pattern IV.

Again, we should remember that the most common link between two noun phrases with the same referent is *be* (Pattern III). And often the substitution of *be* for the linking verb in Pattern V makes little difference in meaning:

> The students became scholars. (Pattern V)
>
> The students are scholars. (Pattern III)

Exercise 5

Draw vertical lines to identify the sentence slots, as in Exercise 4. Then label them according to their form and function. Identify the sentence pattern. Diagram each sentence.

1. The baby looks healthy.
2. Our new neighbors became our best friends.
3. The piano sounds out of tune.
4. October turned extremely cold.
5. You look a mess!
6. That spaghetti smells wonderful.
7. Your idea seems sensible.
8. Cyberspace remains a complete mystery.

THE OPTIONAL SLOTS

Before looking at the last five patterns, we will examine an **optional slot,** the adverbial slot, which can appear in every sentence pattern. It is useful to think of the two or three or four slots in the basic patterns as sentence "requirements," the elements needed for sentence completeness. But it's obvious that most sentences include information beyond the basic requirements—words or phrases that answer such questions as *where, when, why, how,* and *how often*. Because sentences are grammatical without them, we consider the elements filling these adverbial slots as "optional." You'll recall that in the case of Pattern I, however, the ADV/TP slot is required. But a Pattern I sentence can include optional adverbials, too, along with its required time and/or place adverbial:

> The fans were in line *(where?)* for tickets to the play-offs *(why?)*.
>
> The plane was on the runway *(where?)* for an hour *(how long?)*.

All ten sentence patterns can include optional adverbials, which come at the beginning or end of the sentence or even in the middle. And a sentence can have any number of adverbials, providing information about time, place, manner, reason, and the like.

> I stopped <u>at the deli</u> *(where?)* <u>for some bagels</u> *(why?)*. (Pattern VI)
>
> <u>On Saturday night</u> *(when?)* the library was almost deserted. (Pattern II)
>
> Mario <u>suddenly</u> *(how?)* hit the brakes. (Pattern VII)

Our most common adverbials are simple adverbs (*suddenly, quickly, here, soon, always, sometimes*) and prepositional phrases (*at the deli, on Saturday night, for some bagels*). In Chapter 6 you will study other forms that add adverbial information, including noun phrases, verb phrases, and clauses.

No matter where they occur in the sentence, all adverbials are diagrammed as modifiers of the verb; the adverbs go on diagonal lines and prepositional phrases on a two-part line below the verb:

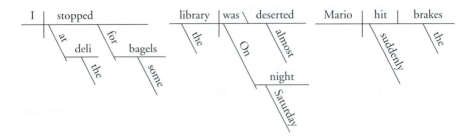

As you saw in Chapter 2, adverbs can be modified with words like *very*, known as **qualifiers**.

She walked very fast.

A qualified adverb is called an **adverb phrase**.

THE INTRANSITIVE VERB PATTERN

Pattern VI: NP V-int

> The students rested.
>
> Mary laughed.
>
> The visitors from El Paso arrived.

This formula describes the pattern of intransitive verb sentences. An **intransitive verb** has no complement—no noun phrase or adjectival—in the slot following the verb. Such skeletal sentences, however, are rare in both speech and writing; most Pattern VI sentences contain more than the simple subject and verb. You're likely to find adverbial information added:

> The students rested <u>after their long trip</u>.
>
> Mary laughed <u>loudly</u>.
>
> The visitors from El Paso <u>finally</u> arrived <u>at the airport</u>.

You may have noticed that the diagram of this pattern looks a great deal like that of Pattern I, with no complement following the verb on the main line. But there is a difference: The adverbial in Pattern I is not optional; it is required. Another important difference between Patterns I and VI is in the kind of adverbials the sentences include. Pattern I nearly always has a structure that tells where or when. The optional adverbials of Pattern VI, however, are not restricted to time and place information; they can answer other questions, such as *why* or *how* or *how long*. We can say, "John *slept* soundly" or "John *slept* for an hour" (Pattern VI), but we cannot say, "John *was* soundly" or "John *was* for an hour."

Exceptions to the Intransitive Pattern. Unlike the linking verb patterns, with their handful of verbs, the intransitive category has thousands of members. And among them are a few verbs that require an adverbial to be complete (much like the required adverbial in Pattern I). These three sentences would be ungrammatical without the adverbial:

> My best friend resides in Northridge.
>
> The boys sneaked past the watchman.
>
> She glanced at her watch.

Reside and *sneak* and *glance* are intransitive verbs that require an adverbial of place. We could provide a new sentence pattern for this subgroup of intransitive verbs, but because the number is so small, we will simply consider them exceptions to the usual Pattern VI formula.

Exercise | 6

In Chapter 2 you learned that prepositional phrases can be adverbial (modifying verbs) or adjectival (modifying nouns). In isolation, however, the two look exactly alike. You need context in order to identify the function.

Here are two sentences with identical prepositional phrases—identical in form only:

1. The puppy <u>on the porch</u> is sleeping.
2. The puppy is sleeping <u>on the porch</u>.

In sentence (1) the phrase *on the porch* tells "which puppy"; in (2) it tells where the puppy is sleeping. Of course, the position also provides a good clue. In (1) it's part of the subject. If we substituted the pronoun *she*, it would take the place of the whole NP—"the puppy on the porch"; in (2) "on the porch" fills the optional adverbial slot.

In this exercise you are to identify each prepositional phrase as either adjectival or adverbial. Underline each one, then indicate the noun or verb it modifies. Identify the sentence pattern.

Example:

The children <u>in the park</u> are playing <u>on the swing</u>. (VI)
        ADJ   ADV

1. The rug in the dining room is dirty.
2. We rarely dine in the dining room.
3. The break between classes seems very short on sunny days.
4. At the diner on Water Street, we chatted aimlessly until midnight.
5. Daylilies grow wild in our backyard.
6. In 1638 a young philanthropist of Puritan background became the founder of the oldest university in the United States.
7. The name of that young man was John Harvard.
8. My cousin from Iowa City works for a family with seven children.

Intransitive Phrasal Verbs. **Phrasal verbs** are common structures in English. They consist of a verb combined with a preposition-like word, known as a **particle;** together they form an **idiom.** The term *idiom* refers to a combination of words whose meaning cannot be predicted from the meaning of its parts; it is a set expression that acts as a unit. In the following sentence, the meaning of the underlined phrasal verb is not the meaning of *up* added to the meaning of *made:*

We <u>made up</u>.

Rather, *made up* means "reconciled our differences."
   In the following sentence, however, *up* is not part of a phrasal verb:

We jumped up.

Here *up* is simply an adverb modifying *jumped.* The meaning of *jumped up* is the meaning of the adverb *up* added to *jumped.* The two diagrams demonstrate the difference:

Another way to demonstrate the properties of verbs such as *made up* and *jumped up* is to test variations of the sentences for parallel results.

For example, adverbs can often be shifted to opening position without a change in meaning:

> Up we jumped.

But in applying this movability test to the verb *made up*, we produce an ungrammatical sentence:

> *Up we made.[3]

Here are some other Pattern VI sentences with phrasal verbs. Note that the first two include adverbial prepositional phrases. You'll discover that all five fail the movability test, just as *made up* did.

> We <u>turned in</u> at midnight.
>
> The union finally <u>gave in</u> to the company demands.
>
> Tony will <u>pull through</u>.
>
> My favorite slippers <u>wore out</u>.
>
> The party <u>broke up</u>.

Another test you can apply is that of meaning. In each case the phrasal verb has a special meaning that is different from the combined meaning of its parts: Here *gave in* means "capitulated"; *pull through* means "recover"; *broke up* means "ended." This meaning test is often the clearest indication that the word following the verb is indeed a particle producing a phrasal verb.

Exercise 7

Try both the movability test and the meaning test to help you decide whether the word following the verb is an *adverb* or a *particle* or a *preposition*. Then diagram the sentences.

1. The car turned in a complete circle.
2. The boys turned in at midnight.
3. The baby turned over by himself.
4. The students turned around in their seats.
5. A big crowd turned out for the parade.
6. The fighter passed out in the first round.
7. He came to after thirty seconds.
8. Susan came to the party late.

---

[3] An asterisk (*) marks a sentence that is ungrammatical or questionable.

THE TRANSITIVE VERB PATTERNS

Unlike intransitive verbs, all **transitive verbs** take one or more complements. The last four formulas classify transitive verbs according to the kinds and number of complements they take. All transitive verbs have one complement in common: the **direct object.** Pattern VII, which has only that one complement, can be thought of as the basic transitive verb pattern.

Pattern VII: NP₁ V-tr NP₂

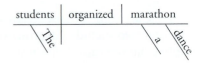

The students organized a dance marathon.

The lead-off batter hit a home run.

Amy's car needs four new tires.

In these sentences the noun phrase following the verb, the **direct object**, has a referent different from that of the subject, as indicated by the different numbers in the formula. Traditionally, we think of the transitive verb as an action word: Its subject is considered the doer and its object the receiver of the action. In many sentences this meaning-based definition applies fairly accurately. In our sample sentence, for instance, we could consider *a home run* as a receiver of the action *hit.* But sometimes the idea of *receiver of the action* doesn't apply at all:

Our team won the game.

We enjoyed the game.

It hardly seems accurate to say that *game* "receives the action." And in

Red spots covered her neck and face.

the verb indicates a condition rather than an action. So although it is true that many transitive verbs are action words and many direct objects are receivers of the action, this meaning-based way of analyzing the sentence doesn't always work.

We can also think of the direct object as the answer to a *what* or *whom* question:

The students organized (*what?*) a dance marathon.

Devon helped (*whom?*) her little brother.

However, the question will not differentiate transitive verbs from linking verbs; the subject complements in Patterns III and V also tell *what:*

Pat is a doctor. (Pat is *what?*)

Pat became a doctor. (Pat became *what?*)

The one method of distinguishing transitive verbs that works almost every time is the recognition that the two noun phrases, the subject and the direct object, have different referents. We don't have to know that *organized* and *hit* and *need* are transitive verbs in order to classify the sentences as Pattern VII; we simply recognize that the two noun phrases do not refer to the same thing. Then we know that the second one is the direct object.

An exception occurs when the direct object is either a **reflexive pronoun** (John cut *himself*) or a **reciprocal pronoun** (John and Mary love *each other*). In sentences with reflexive and reciprocal pronouns, the two NPs, the subject and the direct object, have the same referent, so the numbers 1 and 2 in the formula are inaccurate. In terms of the referents of the NPs, these sentences actually resemble Pattern V, the linking verb pattern. But clearly the purpose and sense of the verbs—*cut* and *love* in the case of these examples—are not like those of the linking verbs. We include these exceptions, where the difference is not in the verbs, in Pattern VII, simply recognizing that when the direct object is a reciprocal or reflexive pronoun the referent numbers are inaccurate.

Note: In Chapter 5 you will see another way of testing whether or not a verb is transitive. Can the sentence be turned into the passive voice? If the answer is yes, the verb is transitive.

Transitive Phrasal Verbs. Many of the idiomatic phrasal verbs belong to the transitive verb category, and like other transitive verbs they take direct objects. Compare the meaning of *came by* in the following sentences:

> He came by his fortune in an unusual way.
>
> He came by the office in a big hurry.

In the first sentence, *came by* means "acquired"; in the second, *by the office* is a prepositional phrase that modifies the intransitive verb *came*, telling where:

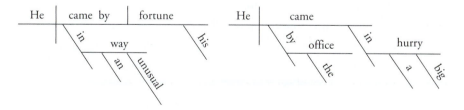

You can also demonstrate the difference between these two sentences by transforming them:

> By which office did he come?
>
> *By which fortune did he come?

It is clear that *by* functions differently in the two sentences.

The transitive phrasal verbs include both two- and three-word strings:

I don't <u>go in for</u> horse racing.   _____

I won't <u>put up with</u> your nonsense.   _____

The dog suddenly <u>turned on</u> its trainer.   _____

The principal <u>passed out</u> the new
regulations.   _____

I finally <u>found out</u> the truth.   _____

I <u>came across</u> a first edition of Hemingway
at a garage sale.   _____

You can test these as you did the intransitive phrasal verbs, by finding a single word that has the same general meaning. On the blank lines write the one-word substitutes.

Exercise 8

Identify the form and function of the sentence slots; then identify the sentence pattern. (Remember to be on the lookout for phrasal verbs.) Diagram each sentence.

1. The boys prepared a terrific spaghetti dinner.
2. An old jalopy turned into our driveway.
3. The ugly duckling turned into a beautiful swan.
4. The fog comes on little cat feet. [Carl Sandburg]
5. On Sundays the neighbor across the hall walks his dog
   at 6:00 A.M.
6. Betsy often jogs with her dog.
7. After two months the teachers called off their strike.
8. The whole gang reminisced at our class reunion about the good
   old days.

The Indirect Object Pattern. We are distinguishing among the transitive verb sentences on the basis of verb subclasses—in this case, those verbs with a second object, in addition to the direct object, called the **indirect object.**

Pattern VIII: NP₁ V-tr NP₂ NP₃

The students gave the professor their homework.

The judges awarded Mary the prize.

The clerk handed me the wrong package.

In this pattern, *two* slots follow the verb, both of which are filled by noun phrases. Note that in the formula there are three different subscript numbers on the three NPs, indicating that the three noun phrases all have different referents. (When the referents are the same, the numbers are the same, as in Patterns III and V.) The first slot following the verb is the **indirect object;** the second is the direct object. Even though both Patterns VII and VIII use transitive verbs, they are easily distinguished, because Pattern VII has only one NP following the verb and Pattern VIII has two.

We traditionally define *indirect object* as the recipient of the direct object, the beneficiary of an act. In most cases this definition applies accurately. A Pattern VIII verb—and this is a limited group—usually has a meaning like "give," and the indirect object usually names a person who is the receiver of whatever the subject gives. As with Pattern VII, however, the most accurate way to distinguish this pattern is simply to recognize that all three noun phrases have different referents: In the first sample sentence, *the students*, *the professor*, and *their homework* all refer to different people or things. Incidentally, in our third sentence, a pronoun rather than a noun phrase fills the indirect object slot.

An important characteristic of the Pattern VIII sentence is the option we have of shifting the indirect object to a position following the direct object, where it will be the object of a preposition:

The students gave their homework <u>to the professor</u>.

The judges awarded the prize <u>to Mary</u>.

The clerk handed the wrong package <u>to me</u>.

With some Pattern VIII verbs the preposition will be *for* rather than *to:*

Jim's father bought him a new car.

Jim's father bought a new car <u>for him</u>.

You'll notice that the shift will not alter the diagram—except for the added word. The indirect object is diagrammed as if it were the object in an adverbial prepositional phrase—even when there is no preposition:

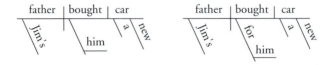

When the direct object is a pronoun rather than a noun phrase, the shift is required; without the prepositional phrase, the sentence would be ungrammatical:

> The students gave it to the professor.
>
> *The students gave the professor it.
>
> Jim's father bought it for him.
>
> *Jim's father bought him it.

Shifting of the indirect object from the slot following the verb to that of object of the preposition does not mean that the sentence pattern changes: It is still Pattern VIII. Remember that the sentence patterns represent verb categories. Pattern VIII covers the "give" group of verbs, those that include both a direct object and a "recipient" of that object. In other words, there are two possible slots for that recipient, the indirect object, in the Pattern VIII sentence.

In most Pattern VIII sentences, all three NPs have different referents, represented by the numbers 1, 2, and 3. But when the indirect object is a reflexive or reciprocal pronoun (*myself, themselves, each other*, etc.), its referent is identical to that of the subject:

> Jill gave *herself* a haircut.
>
> We gave *each other* identical Hanukkah gifts.

Exercise 9

Identify the form and function of the sentence slots. Identify the sentence patterns and diagram the sentences.

Note: Remember that Pattern VIII is the first sentence pattern you have studied in which *two* required slots follow the verb. In most cases they can be thought of as *someone* (the indirect object) and *something* (the direct object). Remember, too, that all of the sentence patterns can include optional slots— that is, adverbial information (where, when, how, why)—in addition to their required slots.

1. For lunch Manny made himself a humongous sandwich.
2. I made an A on my research paper.
3. The kids made up a story about monsters from outer space.
4. The teacher wrote a lot of comments in the margins.
5. My advisor wrote a letter of recommendation for me.
6. I wrote down the assignment very carefully.
7. I saw myself in the mirror.
8. Shirl gave herself a pat on the back.

The Object Complement Patterns. The final category of verbs, those that take an **object complement** following the direct object, is divided into two groups, depending on the form of the object complement: either an adjective or a noun phrase. This is a fairly small class, with relatively few verbs, most of which appear equally often in Pattern VII, where they take the direct object only.

Pattern IX: NP₁ V-tr NP₂ ADJ

The students consider the teacher intelligent.

The teacher made the test easy.

The boys painted their hockey sticks blue.

In this pattern the object complement is an adjective that modifies or describes the direct object. The relationship between the direct object and the object complement is the same as the relationship between the subject and the subject complement in Patterns II and IV. In Patterns II and IV the subject complement describes the subject; in Pattern IX the object complement describes the direct object. We could say, in fact,

The teacher is intelligent.

The test is easy.

The hockey sticks are blue.

The function of the object complement is twofold: (1) It completes the meaning of the verb; and (2) it describes the direct object.

When we remove the object complement from a Pattern IX sentence, we are sometimes left with a grammatical and meaningful sentence: "The boys painted their hockey sticks." (This is now Pattern VII.) However, most Pattern IX sentences require the object complement; the meaning of the first two examples under the Pattern IX formula would change without it:

> The students consider the teacher.
>
> The teacher made the test.

Other verbs commonly found in this pattern are *prefer*, *like*, and *find*. Some Pattern IX verbs, such as *consider* and *make*, also commonly appear in Pattern X.

Pattern X: NP$_1$ V-tr NP$_2$ NP$_2$

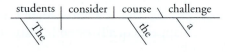

> The students consider the course a challenge.
>
> The students elected Emma chairperson.
>
> Barrie named his pug Jill.

Just as both adjectives and noun phrases can be subject complements, both forms also serve as object complements. In Pattern IX the object complement is an adjective; in Pattern X it's a noun phrase, one with the same referent as the direct object, as indicated by the numbers in the formula. Its twofold purpose is much the same as that of the adjectival object complement in Pattern IX: (1) It completes the meaning of the verb; and (2) it renames the direct object. And, again, we can compare the relationship of the two noun phrases to that of the subject and subject complement in Pattern III:

> The course is a challenge.
>
> Emma is the chairperson.

In fact, the possibility of actually inserting the words *to be* between the direct object and the following slot can serve as a test for Patterns IX and X. That is, if *to be* is possible, then what follows is an object complement. Which of the following sentences will pass the "to be" test?

> Taro finds his job easy.
>
> Taro found his job easily.
>
> Pam found her job the hard way.
>
> Pam finds her job a challenge.

If you have decided that the first and last sentences in the list could include *to be*, you have identified object complements. The other two, you'll discover, end with adverbials that tell "how" about the verb.

Sometimes the object complement is signaled by *as*, which we call an **expletive:**

> We elected Tom *as* our secretary.
>
> We refer to him *as* "Mr. Secretary."
>
> I know him *as* a good friend.
>
> The witness identified the defendant *as* the burglar.

In some cases, the *as* is optional; in other cases, it is required. With the verbs *refer to* and *know*, for example, we cannot add the object complement without *as:*

> *We refer to him "Mr. Secretary."
>
> *I know her a good friend.

The expletive is diagrammed just before the object complement but above the line:

This use of *as* is discussed further on pages 283–284.

COMPOUND STRUCTURES

Every slot in the sentence patterns can be expanded in many ways, as you'll learn in the chapters to come. We'll introduce one common expansion here—that of **coordination**, turning a single structure into a compound structure. Coordination is accomplished with another of the structure classes, the **conjunctions**, the most common of which are the **coordinating conjunctions** *and*, *or*, and *but*. The **correlative conjunctions** are two-part connectors: *both–and, not only–but also, either–or,* and *neither–nor*.

Every slot in the sentence patterns can be filled by a compound structure:

> Cats *and* dogs fight. (compound subject)
>
> They *either* drove *or* took the bus. (compound predicate)
>
> The teacher was **tough** *but* **fair**. (compound subject complement)
>
> We drove over the river *and* through the woods. (compound adverbial prepositional phrase)
>
> I finished *both* my biology project *and* my history paper. (compound direct object)

To diagram compound structures, we simply double the line and connect the two parts with a dotted line. The conjunction goes on the dotted line.

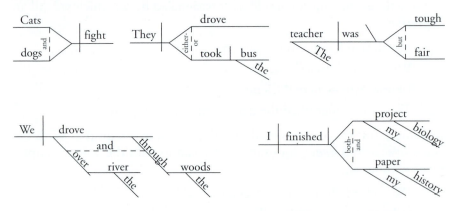

In Chapter 10 we will take up the coordination of full sentences.

Exercise 10

First identify the sentence slots according to their form and function to help you identify sentence patterns. Then diagram the sentences. (Note: The list includes sentences representing all four verb classes: *be*, linking, intransitive, and transitive.)

1. The kids on our block and their dogs drive my mother crazy.
2. She calls them a menace to the neighborhood.
3. On Friday the weather suddenly turned cold and blustery.
4. The teacher was unhappy with our test scores.
5. England's soccer fans have a reputation for wild behavior.
6. My boss at the pizza parlor promised me a raise.
7. Banquo's ghost appeared to Macbeth at the banquet.
8. The new arrivals at the animal shelter appeared undernourished.
9. Both Alaska and Hawaii attained statehood in 1959.
10. According to the latest census, Wyoming is our least populous state.
11. Some people consider Minnesota's winters excessively long.
12. Emily selected peach and lavender as the color scheme for her wedding.

EXCEPTIONS TO THE TEN SENTENCE PATTERNS

The ten sentence patterns described here represent the skeletal structure of most English sentences—at least 95 percent, if not more. However, some sentences can be thought of as exceptions to a particular pattern. For example, certain intransitive verbs, such as *reside*, *sneak*, and *glance*, would be ungrammatical without an adverbial—as we saw on page 39. Certain transitive verbs also differ from the majority because they require adverbials to be complete:

> We *placed* an ad in the paper.
>
> Joe *put* the groceries away.

To be accurate, the formulas for these sentences would have to include ADV as a requirement, not just an optional slot. However, because the number of these exceptions is small, we will simply include them as variations of Pattern VI or Pattern VII.

Another group of verbs, sometimes called "midverbs," includes characteristics of both transitive and intransitive verbs: They require a complement, as transitive verbs do, but the complement differs from mainstream direct objects. For example, rather than telling "what" or "whom," the complements following the verbs *weigh* and *cost* provide information of amount, or measure; they have almost an adverbial sense:

> The roast weighs five pounds.
>
> The roast cost twenty dollars.

Even though *weigh* and *cost* are different from the exceptional intransitive and transitive verbs cited earlier (which take straightforward adverbials of place), we will consider these uses of *weigh* and *cost* as Pattern VI, rather than add a new sentence pattern, recognizing that for them too the "optional slot" is not optional.

SENTENCE TYPES

The ten sentence pattern formulas in this chapter describe the basic structure of statements, or **declarative** sentences. The purpose of such sentences is to state, or declare, a fact or an opinion. But we don't always make straightforward statements. Sometimes we alter the formula to ask questions **(interrogative sentences)**, give commands **(imperative sentences)**, and express strong feelings **(exclamatory sentences)**:

Declarative:	He talks on his cell phone all day long.
Interrogative:	Is he talking on his cell phone now?
	Why does he talk on his cell phone so much?
	He turned off the phone, didn't he?
Imperative:	Turn that cell phone off.
Exclamatory:	What a lot of time he spends on his cell phone!

INTERROGATIVE SENTENCES (QUESTIONS)

The two most common interrogative patterns in English are the **yes/no question** and the **wh-question,** or interrogative-word question. Both kinds of questions alter the basic declarative word order by putting the verb, or part of the verb, in front of the subject:

They are going to the movies. (declarative)

Are they going to the movies? (yes/no question)

Where are they going? (*wh*-question)

In these examples, the first part of the verb *are going* is placed ahead of the subject; it is called an **auxiliary.** You'll learn a lot more about auxiliaries in the next chapter.

As their label suggests, yes/no questions permit "yes" or "no" as appropriate answers, although other responses are possible:

Q: May I go with you?   A. We'll see.

Wh-questions, also called *information questions*, use interrogative words, such as *why, where, when, who, what,* or *how,* to elicit specific details. In the question "Where are they going?" the interrogative word comes first and fills the optional adverbial slot in a Pattern VI sentence:

Where are they going?

They are going <u>where</u>.

The interrogative can also fill an NP slot:

What have you been reading?

You have been reading <u>what</u>. (Pattern VII)

Some interrogatives act as determiners:

Whose car are you taking?

You are taking <u>whose</u> car.

As the preceding examples show, the slots of the basic declarative pattern will be out of order because the interrogative word always comes first, no matter what grammatical function it has. However, when the information being elicited is a *who* or *what* that fills the subject slot, then the usual word order is maintained and the auxiliary is not shifted:

<u>Who</u> broke the window?

<u>What</u> is making that noise?

Another method of asking questions—more common in speech than in writing—is the tag-question, a repetition of the subject and auxiliary verb (or *be* as a main verb) in reverse order, which is added at the end of a declarative sentence. Its main purpose is to seek confirmation of the idea expressed in the statement. You may remember this example from Chapter 1 in the discussion of *ain't* on page 9:

Your mother is a nice person, <u>isn't she?</u>

When the sentence has neither an auxiliary verb nor *be* as a main verb, we add a form of *do* in forming the tag-question:

He turned the phone off, <u>didn't he?</u>

You'll read more about the role of *do* as a "stand-in" auxiliary in Chapter 4. See also the Classroom Application section on pages 84–85.

IMPERATIVE SENTENCES (COMMANDS)

The sentences described so far in this chapter have been two-part structures consisting of a subject and a predicate. However in the case of imperative sentences, or commands, the subject is nearly always unstated, although clearly understood; the verb is in the infinitive (base) form:

Subject	Predicate
(you)	Sit down.
(you)	Take your time.

And when Lady Macbeth says to her husband, look like the innocent flower/but be thy serpent under't, both *look* and *be* are imperative. (Note that it's the form of *be* used for the imperative that identifies the form for all commands as the infinitive form, not the present tense.)

Commands can also be negative:

Don't (you) be silly.

Don't (you) do anything I wouldn't do.

Commands are fairly common in casual speech. They are not as common in writing, although you've seem them here in the directions for the exercises:

Diagram each sentence.

Identify the form and function of the sentence slots.

EXCLAMATORY SENTENCES

We usually think of the **exclamatory sentence,** or exclamation, as any sentence spoken with heightened emotion, written with an exclamation point:

> I love your new house!
>
> Wipe that grin off your face!
>
> Are you kidding me!

But in terms of form, the first sentence immediately preceding is *declarative*, a straightforward statement; the second sentence is an *imperative;* and the third one looks like a yes/no question. By contrast, a formal exclamatory sentence involves a shift in word order that focuses special attention on a complement:

> What a lovely house you have!
>
> How proud you must be!
>
> What a piece of work is man! [Shakespeare]

The *what* or *how* that introduces the emphasized element is added to the underlying declarative sentence pattern:

> You have a lovely house. (Pattern VII)
>
> You must be proud. (Pattern II)
>
> Man is a piece of work. (Pattern III)

PUNCTUATION AND THE SENTENCE PATTERNS

There is an easy punctuation lesson to be learned from the sentence patterns with their two or three or four slots:

DO NOT PUT SINGLE COMMAS BETWEEN THE REQUIRED SLOTS.

That is, never separate

- the subject from the verb.
- the verb from the direct object.
- the direct object from the object complement.
- the indirect object from the direct object.
- the verb from the subject complement.

For example, in this sentence there is no place for commas:

> All of the discussion groups and counseling sessions I took part in during Orientation Week were extremely helpful for the incoming freshmen.

Even though the noun phrases that fill the slots may be long, the slots are never separated by commas. *A pause for breath does not signal a comma.* Sometimes punctuation is called for *within* a noun phrase slot, but even then the rule applies: no single commas between the required slots.

The one exception to this rule occurs when the direct object is a direct quotation following a verb like *say*. Here the punctuation convention calls for a comma before the quoted words:

He said, "I love you."

DIAGRAMMING THE SENTENCE PATTERNS

The **Be** *Patterns*

I. NP *be* ADV/TP

$$S \quad$$

II. NP *be* ADJ

$$S \mid \quad \backslash SC$$

III. NP₁ *be* NP₁

$$S \mid \quad \backslash SC$$

The Linking Verb Patterns

IV. NP V-lnk ADJ

$$S \mid \quad \backslash SC$$

V. NP₁ V-lnk NP₁

$$S \mid \quad \backslash SC$$

The Intransitive Verb Pattern

VI. NP V-int

$$S \mid$$

The Transitive Verb Patterns

VII. NP₁ V-tr NP₂

$$S \mid \mid DO$$

VIII. NP₁ V-tr NP₂ NP₃

$$S \mid \mid DO$$
$$\backslash IO$$

IX. NP₁ V-tr NP₂ ADJ

$$S \mid \mid DO \backslash OC$$

X. NP₁ V-tr NP₂ NP₂

$$S \mid \mid DO \backslash OC$$

The traditional sentence diagram is a visual aid to help you learn the patterns, to understand their common features, and to distinguish their differences. On page 55 you can see the relationships among them. For example, the two linking verb patterns closely resemble the two *be* patterns, II and III, above them. Likewise, the intransitive pattern, VI, placed at the left of the page, looks exactly like the main line of Pattern I. Finally, the slanted line that separates the subject complement from the verb in Patterns, II through V depicts a relationship similar to that of the object complement and object in Patterns IX and X, also separated by a slanted line. All the NP and ADJ slots are labeled according to their functions: subject (S), subject complement (SC), direct object (DO), indirect object (IO), and object complement (OC).

NOTES ON THE DIAGRAMS

The Main Line. The positions on the main horizontal line of a diagram represent the slots in the sentence pattern formulas. Only two required slots are not included on the main line: the adverbial (see Pattern I) and the indirect object (see Pattern VIII). The vertical line that bisects the main line separates the subject and the predicate, showing the binary nature of the sentence. The other vertical and diagonal lines stop at the horizontal line:

The Noun Phrase. The noun phrases we have used so far are fairly simple; in Chapter 7 we identify a wide variety of structures that can modify and expand the noun. But now we will simply recognize the feature that all noun phrases have in common—the noun head, or headword. This is the single word that fills the various NP slots of the diagrams; it always occupies a horizontal line. The modifiers slant down from the noun headword:

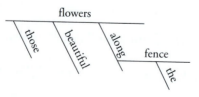

Qualifiers of adjectives are placed on diagonal lines attached to and parallel with the adjective:

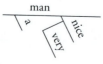

The Verb Phrase.

1. The verb and its auxiliaries go on the main line. In the case of negative verbs, the *not* is usually placed on a diagonal line below the verb. If if is contracted, it can remain attached to the verb:

2. The subject complement follows a diagonal line. The line slants toward the subject to show their relationship:

3. The direct object always follows a vertical line:

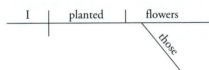

    Note that only Patterns VII through X have this vertical line following the verb: the only patterns with a direct object.

4. The object complement is set off from the direct object by a line that slants toward the object:

    I | consider | zinnias \ beautiful

5. The indirect object is placed below the verb. We can understand the logic of this treatment of the indirect object when we realize that it can be expressed by a prepositional phrase without changing the meaning or the pattern of the sentence. Both of these sentences are Pattern VIII:

    The students gave <u>the teacher</u> an apple.

    The students gave an apple <u>to the teacher</u>.

6. Adverbs are placed on slanted lines below the verb; they are modifiers of the verb:

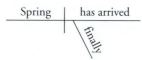

7. Like the qualifiers of adjectives, qualifiers of adverbs are placed on diagonal lines attached to the adverb:

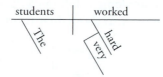

The Prepositional Phrase. The preposition is placed on a diagonal line, its object on a horizontal line attached to it. The prepositional phrase slants down from the noun or verb it modifies. When the prepositional phrase fills the subject complement slot, it is attached to the main line by means of a pedestal:

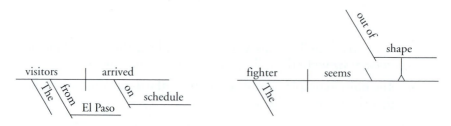

Compound Structures. The two (or more) parts of a compound structure are connected by a dotted line, which holds the conjunction. If a modifier applies to both (or all) parts of the compound structure, it is attached to a line common to them:

Punctuation. There are no punctuation marks of any kind in the diagram, other than apostrophes.

For further details of diagramming, see the Appendix, pages 366–370.

CHAPTER 3
Key Terms

In this chapter you've been introduced to the basic vocabulary of sentence grammar. Even though this list of key terms may look formidable, some of the terms are already familiar, and those that are new will become more familiar as you continue the study of sentences. You'll discover too that the patterns and their diagrams, as shown on page 55, provide a framework for helping you organize many of these concepts.

Article	Optional slot
Auxiliary	Particle
Be patterns	Phrasal verb
Command	Predicate
Complement	Predicating verb
Compound structure	Question
Coordinating conjunction	Reciprocal pronoun
Correlative conjunction	Referent
Declarative sentence	Reflexive pronoun
Direct object	Sentence pattern
Exclamatory sentence	Subject
Imperative sentence	Subject complement
Indirect object	Tag questions
Interrogative sentence	Transitive verb
Intransitive verb	Verb phrase
Linking verb	*Wh*-question
Noun phrase	Yes/no question
Object complement	

Sentences
for PRACTICE

Identify the form and function of the sentence slots; identify the sentence pattern; and diagram each sentence.

1. My boss at the pizza parlor gave everyone a raise.
2. Typhoons and hurricanes are identical storms.

3. They simply occur in different parts of the world.
4. Hank's strange behavior was out of character.
5. Some people find modern art very depressing.
6. According to the afternoon paper, the police looked into the sources of the reporter's information.
7. Is our plan workable?
8. In 2010 the Senate confirmed Elena Kagan as the third female Associate Justice of the current Supreme Court.
9. On Saturday night we left the waitress a generous tip for her splendid service.
10. At age 23, the founder and CEO of Facebook became the youngest self-made billionaire in history.
11. Yesterday my landlord was in a state of panic.
12. According to the latest UN statistics, Norway is now the world's largest exporter of seafood.

QUESTIONS ? for DISCUSSION

1. Here are some pairs of sentences that look alike. Think about their sentence patterns; label the form and function of their slots and discuss the problems you encounter; diagram the sentences to demonstrate their differences.

   The teacher made the test hard.

   The batter hit the ball hard.

   My husband made me a chocolate cake.

   My husband made me a happy woman.

   We set off through the woods at dawn.

   We set off the firecrackers at dawn.

2. The following sentences are either Pattern I or Pattern II; in other words, the prepositional phrases following *be* are either adverbial or adjectival. What test can you use to distinguish between them?

   The mechanic is under the car.

   The mechanic is under the weather.

   The teacher is in a bad mood.

   The teacher is in the cafeteria.

3. Very few verbs are restricted to a single category. Verbs like *taste* and *feel* commonly act as linking verbs, but they can fit into other classes as well. Identify the patterns of the following sentences:

    The cook tasted the soup.

    The soup tasted good.

    I felt the kitten's fur.

    The fur feels soft.

    The farmers in Iowa grow a lot of wheat.

    The wheat grows fast in July.

    We grew weary in the hot sun.

    She appeared tired.

    Black clouds appeared suddenly on the horizon.

4. Some sentences in English are not represented by one of the ten patterns described in this chapter. Among those that don't fit very well are certain sentences with *be* as the main verb:

    The book is about black holes.

    The potato salad is for the picnic.

    I am from San Francisco.

    I am in favor of the amendment.

    The misunderstanding was over a scheduling conflict.

    Pat and Jen are among the most popular students in our class.

    The prepositional phrases in these sentences are different from those we saw in Patterns I and II. How would you characterize the difference? A paraphrase of the sentence might help you to determine a possible pattern. And in the following *be* sentences, the noun phrase in subject complement position is different from those we saw in Pattern III. Do these sentences belong in Pattern III? If not, where do they belong?

    My shoes are the wrong color.

    This new wallpaper is an odd pattern.

    In what way does the following sentence change our understanding of the *be* patterns?

    The time is now.

5. People commonly say "I feel badly" when discussing their physical or mental condition. Using your understanding of sentence patterns, explain why this is sometimes considered an ungrammatical

sentence. Assuming that "I feel badly" is indeed questionable, how do you explain the acceptance of "I feel strongly about that"?

6. What is unusual about the following sentence? Think about the sentence pattern:

    The waitress served me my coffee black.

7. We have seen sentences in which prepositional phrases function as subject complements. Can they be object complements as well?

8. A sentence is **ambiguous** when it has more than one possible meaning. You can illustrate the two meanings of the following sentences by diagramming each in two different ways. Think about sentence patterns and the referents of the noun phrases.

    Herbert found his new bride a good cook.

    Rosa called her Aunt Betty.

CLASSROOM APPLICATIONS

Some of the following activities could be organized as either oral or written activities, perhaps as timed group competitions:

1. Write four sentences about summer (winter, fall, spring) in which each sentence uses a different verb category: *be*, linking, intransitive, and transitive.

2. Write ten sentences about your favorite sport or hobby, using all ten patterns.

3. Drawing on your own internal dictionary, write down as many two-word (verb + particle) idioms as you can, using the particles *up, down, in, out, on, off*, and *over*. Here are some verbs to get you started, but don't limit yourself to these: *break, take, look, run*. (Note: The resulting idioms will include both nouns and verbs—e.g., [*the*] *break-in*, [*to*] *break up*.)

4. Collect newspaper or magazine headlines that represent all ten sentence patterns. Note that in the case of the *be* patterns, the verb itself might be missing, simply understood.

CHAPTER 4

Expanding the Main Verb

CHAPTER PREVIEW

This chapter examines verbs, the most systematic of the four form classes. You will analyze the underlying rules that enable you to come up with the wide variety of verb phrases that you use every day. This analysis of your verb expertise, in fact, probably illustrates better than any other part of grammar what the word *system* means.

By the end of this chapter, you will be able to

- Identify the fives forms that all verbs have.
- Recognize auxiliary verbs and understand how they combine with main verbs.
- Understand the verb-expansion rule and use it to analyze and produce verb strings.
- Define the terms *tense, mood,* and *aspect.*
- Identify modal auxiliaries and explain their uses.
- Recognize and use the stand-in auxiliary *do.*
- Recognize the grammaticality of the African American Vernacular verb system.

THE FIVE VERB FORMS

Before analyzing the system for adding auxiliaries, we will identify the five forms that all of our verbs have so that we can conveniently discuss them, using labels that reflect our emphasis on form rather than meaning. Here again is the **regular** verb *laugh*, which we saw in Chapter 2, along with the **irregular** verb *eat:*

	Regular	*Irregular*
base form (present tense)	laugh	eat
-*s* form (present, 3rd person, singular)	laughs	eats
-*ed* form (past tense)	laughed	ate
-*ing* form (present participle)	laughing	eating
-*en* form (past participle)	laughed	eaten

Most of our verbs—all except 150 or so—are regular, as are all the new verbs that we acquire. For example, here are two recent acquisitions:

I <u>faxed</u> a letter to you yesterday.

I have <u>e-mailed</u> the invitations to our reunion.

As the verb *laugh* and these two new ones illustrate, regular verbs are those in which the past tense and the past participle are formed by adding the **suffix** -*ed* (or, in a few cases, -*t*) to the base form. Among the irregular verbs, there are many patterns of irregularity, but the deviations from regular verbs show up only in these two forms, the past and the past participle. All verbs, with minor exceptions, have regular -*s* and -*ing* forms. (The exceptions are detailed in "ELL Issues" on page 66.)

In our discussion of verbs, we will use the label -*ed* to denote the past tense form and -*en* to denote the past participle form. The past of regular verbs provides the -*ed* label; the past participle of irregular verbs like *eat* (as well as our most common verb, *be*, and about fifteen others, including *drive*, *give*, *break*, and *speak*) provides the label for the past participle, which we call the -*en* form. This means that the -*en* form of *laugh* is *laughed;* the -*ed* form of *eat* is *ate*.

Anyone familiar with a foreign language will appreciate the simplicity of our small set of only five verb forms. Instead of adding auxiliaries to express differences as we do in English, a speaker of French or Spanish must add a different suffix to the verb. French verbs, for instance, have more than seventy different forms to express variations in person, number, tense, and mood.

A speaker of English uses only two different forms (*eat, eats*) to express the present tense in first, second, and third **person**, both singular and plural; the speaker of French uses five:

	Singular	*Plural*
1st person	I eat (*je mange*)	we eat (*nous mangeons*)
2nd person	you eat (*tu manges*)	you eat (*vous mangez*)
3rd person	he eats (*il mange*)	they eat (*ils mangent*)

The speaker of English uses only one form (*ate*) to express the simple past tense in all three persons, both singular and plural. Again, the French speaker uses five, all different from the first set. In fact, for the various tenses and moods, the speaker of French uses fourteen such sets, or conjugations, all with different verb endings.

The Irregular *Be.* The only English verb with more than five forms is *be*, the most irregular of our irregular verbs. It is also the only verb with a separate form for the **infinitive**, or base (*be*); it is the only one with three forms for present tense (*am, is, are*) and two for past tense (*was, were*); and of course it has an *-en* form (*been*) and an *-ing* (*being*) form—eight forms in all. In addition to its status as a main verb, *be* also serves as an auxiliary in our verb-expansion rule and as the auxiliary that turns the active voice to passive, as you will learn in Chapter 5.

Exercise 11

Fill the blanks with the four additional forms of the verbs listed on the left. If you have a problem figuring out the *-ed* form, simply use it in a sentence with *yesterday*: "Yesterday I _____." If you have trouble figuring out the *-en* form, use it in a sentence with *have*: "I have _____."

BASE	-*s* FORM	-*ed* FORM	-*ing* FORM	-*en* FORM
1. have	_____	_____	_____	_____
2. do	_____	_____	_____	_____
3. say	_____	_____	_____	_____
4. make	_____	_____	_____	_____
5. go	_____	_____	_____	_____
6. take	_____	_____	_____	_____
7. come	_____	_____	_____	_____
8. see	_____	_____	_____	_____
9. get	_____	_____	_____	_____
10. move	_____	_____	_____	_____
11. prove	_____	_____	_____	_____
12. put	_____	_____	_____	_____
13. think	_____	_____	_____	_____
14. beat	_____	_____	_____	_____
15. meet	_____	_____	_____	_____

The first nine verbs in this exercise, along with *be*, make up a list of the ten most frequently used verbs in English.

> Q. What do these ten have in common?
>
> A. They are all irregular!

ELL Issues   **The Systematic Verb Forms**

Only two verbs have an irregular *-s* form: *be* (*is*) and *have* (*has*). In two others, the vowel sound changes for the *-s* form: *do* (*does*), *say* (*says*). So with only these minor deviations, we can certainly say that from the standpoint of form, notably the *-s* and the *-ing* forms, English verbs are highly systematic. It would be hard to find a rule in all of our grammar with fewer exceptions.

AUXILIARY–VERB COMBINATIONS

You learned in Chapter 3 that the predicating verb is the central, or pivotal, slot in the sentence. It is the verb that determines the slots that follow. The predicating verbs we have used in sentence examples so far have been one-word forms, the simple present or past tense, such as *are*, *were*, *studied*, *became*, *consider*. In our everyday speech and writing, of course, we are just as likely to use expanded forms that include one or more **auxiliaries**, also called **helping verbs**:

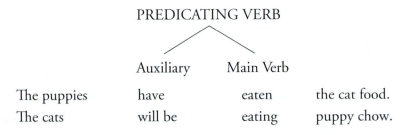

	PREDICATING VERB		
	Auxiliary	Main Verb	
The puppies	have	eaten	the cat food.
The cats	will be	eating	puppy chow.

As this branching diagram shows, we are using the term *predicating verb* as a label for the entire string that fills the verb slot in the sentence patterns, including auxiliaries and the main verb.

To discover how our auxiliary system works, we will examine a dozen sentences, all of which have a form of *eat* as the main verb, beginning with the two we have just seen:

1. The puppies <u>have eaten</u> the cat food.
2. The cats <u>will be eating</u> puppy chow today.

3. I <u>eat</u> an apple every day.

4. I <u>ate</u> one this morning.

5. My sister <u>eats</u> a banana every day.

6. I <u>should eat</u> bananas for their potassium.

7. I <u>am eating</u> healthy these days.

8. We <u>were eating</u> popcorn throughout the movie.

9. We <u>may eat</u> out on Saturday night.

10. I <u>had eaten</u> all the chips by the time the guests arrived.

11. I <u>could have eaten</u> even more.

12. We <u>have been eating</u> junk food all evening.

What is the system underlying these one- and two- and three-word verb strings? How many more variations are there? If we were going to write a computer program to generate all the possible variations, what rules and restrictions would have to be included?

To answer these questions, we will make some observations about the verb strings in our twelve sentences:

1. The base form, *eat*, is used both by itself [3] and with *should* [6] and *may* [9].

2. The *-ed* and *-s* forms of *eat* [4 and 5] are used only by themselves, never with an auxiliary word.

3. An *-en* form, *eaten* or *been*, is used after a form of *have: have* [1, 11, and 12] and *had* [10].

4. The *-ing* form, *eating*, is used after a form of *be: be* [2], *am* [7], *were* [8], and *been* [12].

5. A form of *eat*, the main verb (MV), is always the last word in the string.

We will represent these last three observations by means of a formula:

$$\textbf{(have + -en) (be + -ing) MV}$$

The parentheses in the formula mean "optional." Both *have* and *be* are optional auxiliaries: A grammatical verb string does not require either or both of them. As the formula indicates, however, when we do choose *have* as an auxiliary, we are also choosing *-en*; that is, the *-en* suffix will attach itself to the following word. And when we choose *be*, the *-ing* suffix will attach itself to the following word. In the formula the main verb is shown without parentheses because it is not optional; it is always a component of the predicating verb.

We can derive two further observations from the twelve sentences:

6. Besides *have* and *be*, the sentences illustrate another kind of auxiliary—*will* [2], *should* [6], *may* [9], and *could* [11], called **modal auxiliaries (M)**.

7. When a modal is selected, it is always first in line.

Now we can add another element, (M), to the formula:

$$\textbf{(M) (have + -en) (be + -ing) MV}$$

The formula reads as follows:

- In generating a verb string, we can use a modal auxiliary if we choose; when we do, it comes first.
- We can also choose the auxiliary *have;* when we do, an *-en* form follows it.
- We can also choose the auxiliary *be;* when we do, an *-ing* form follows.
- When we use more than one auxiliary, they appear in the order given: modal, *have*, *be*.
- The last word in the string is the main verb.

To demonstrate how the formula works, let's look at the verbs in three of our twelve *eat* sentences:

Sentence 1: **The puppies <u>have eaten</u> the cat food.**

Here we passed up (M) and chose *have* + *-en* as the auxiliary. The *-en* will be attached to the following word:

$$\text{have} + \text{-en} + \text{eat} \quad = \quad \textit{have eaten}$$

Sentence 2: **The cats <u>will be eating</u> puppy chow.**

Here we chose (M), the modal auxiliary *will;* we skipped (*have* + *-en*) and chose *be* + *-ing:*

$$\text{will} + \text{be} + \text{-ing} + \text{eat} \quad = \quad \textit{will be eating}$$

Sentence 12: **We <u>have been eating</u> junk food all evening.**

In this sentence we skipped (M) and chose both *have + -en* and *be + -ing:*

$$\text{have} + \text{-en} + \text{be} + \text{-ing} + \text{eat} \ = \ \textit{have been eating}$$

So far we have a simple but powerful formula, capable of generating a great many variations of the verb. But something is missing. How did we generate *were eating* in sentence 8 and *had eaten* in sentence 10? What is different about them? The difference is **tense**, which refers to time: *had* and *were* are **past tense**, the *-ed* forms of *have* and *be*. This means we have to add one more component to the formula: **T**, for tense. Among the five forms of the verb, you will recall, the present and past forms are the only tenses, so in the formula, **T** will represent either present or past tense.

Here, then, is the complete formula for what is known as the **verb-expansion rule**:

T (M) (have + -en) (be + -ing) MV

Notice in the following strings how the tense, either present or past, applies to the first word in the string. That verb, the one carrying the tense–whether as auxiliary or the main verb–is called the **finite** verb. Note in the third example that the first word is sometimes the main verb.

I **should have taken** the bus to class this morning.

$$\text{past} + \text{shall} + \text{have} + \text{-en} + \text{take}$$

The autumn leaves **are making** the sidewalk slippery.

$$\text{pres} + \text{be} + \text{ing} + \text{make}$$

My roommate **worked** on her project until 4:00 A.M.

$$\text{past} + \text{work}$$

You might find the branching diagram helpful for visualizing the rule:

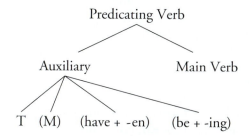

Investigating Language   **4.1**

The branching diagram illustrates the predicating verb as a two-part structure: an auxiliary and a main verb. Those two parts are obvious in a sentence such as

> We *had eaten* by the time you arrived.

> *or*

> I *was eating* when you arrived.

Sometimes the two parts of the predicating verbs are not as obvious:

> He *eats* too fast.

> Beth already *ate*.

Look again at the formula, and remember that parentheses mean "optional." The components of the verb that are shown without parentheses are required.

In sentences with *eats* and *ate*, then, what does the auxiliary consist of?

Look again at the second observation we made on page 67 about our list of twelve sentences: "The *-ed* and *-s* forms of *eat* are used only by themselves, never with an auxiliary word." It's clear then that the auxiliary component of the verbs in sentences with *ate* or *eats* is simply T.

THE MODAL AUXILIARIES

We have six major modals in English, four of which have different forms for present and past:

Present	*Past*
will	would
shall	should
can	could
may	might

Two modals have no past form:

must

ought to

Although we call these forms present and past, that meaning is not really accurate in present-day English. For example, in "I may eat" (present), the act of eating is not going on; in "I might eat" (past) the act of eating is not over; in fact, in both cases it may never happen.

Only in a few instances do the modals indicate actual time. In the company of a time adverbial, *can* and *could* will designate present or past:

This morning the groundhog <u>can</u> see his shadow.

Yesterday the groundhog <u>could</u> see his shadow.

The modals differ from the auxiliaries *have* and *be*, both of which can fill the role of main verb in addition to their auxiliary role. The modals never fill the main verb slot, nor do they have all five forms that verbs have.[1] They are so named because they affect what is called the mood of the verb. **Mood** refers to the manner in which a verb is expressed, such as a fact, a desire, a possibility, or a command. **Indicative mood** refers to a sentence dealing with a fact or a question about a fact. The modals convey conditions of probability, possibility, obligation, or necessity: *I may eat; I could eat; I should eat; I must eat.* These are known as the **conditional mood**. We should note also that the modals *will* and *shall* produce what we call the future tense: *will eat* and *shall eat,* discussed further in the next section. Modals and modal-like verbs are discussed further in "Auxiliaries" on pages 270–272.

Exercise 12

A. What is the expanded verb that each of the following strings will produce? (Assume in each case that the subject is Fred.)

Example:

past + have + -en + help = *had helped*

1. pres + have + -en + work
2. pres + will + be + -ing + play
3. past + be + -ing + be
4. pres + be + -ing + have
5. past + shall + have + -en + have
6. past + have + -en + have
7. past + can + have + -en + be
8. pres + may + have + -en + be + -ing + try

[1.] Sometimes modals appear without verbs in **elliptical clauses**, where the main verb is understood but not expressed:

Who'll cook the spaghetti? I *will*.

May I join you? Yes, you *may*.

B. Identify the components of the predicating verb in each of the following sentences. Your answers will look like the strings given in Part A.

Example:

Mike was having a bad day = *past* + *be* + *-ing* + *have*

1. The students were studying in the library.
2. I have finally found my lost scarf. [Note: Adverbs, such as *finally*, should not appear in your verb string.]
3. I lost it on the first day of classes.
4. Mickey has been skipping classes lately.
5. He could be in big trouble.
6. Joanie certainly seems happy in her new apartment.
7. She will probably be having a party this weekend.
8. I should have studied harder for this test.

THE "FUTURE TENSE"

As we saw in our discussion of the verb-expansion rule, our five verb forms include only two tenses: present and past. We're quite capable of discussing future time, of course, but we do so using means other than a special verb form. In the traditional description of verb tenses, the addition of the modal auxiliary *will* to denote a future action is called the "future tense":

I will finish my project later.

When *have* + *-en* is added, the result is called "future perfect," denoting a future action before another future action:

I will have finished it by Friday.

However, one of our most common ways of expressing future is with the semi-auxiliary *be* + *going to,* which, in speech, is pronounced "gonna":

I'm going to finish my project this afternoon.

And both the simple present and the present progressive can express future time with the addition of an appropriate adverbial:

The bus leaves at 7:00.
We're having pizza tonight.

We should also note that the modal *will* is not used exclusively for future time. In his "Language Log" posted on the Internet in March 2008, British linguist Geoffrey K. Pullum estimates that perhaps 20 percent of the occurrences of *will* do not express the future. Here are a few of his many examples:

> Step this way, if you will, sir. (Means "if you wish to". . . .)
>
> That will be Mike. (Uttered when the doorbell rings. . . .)
>
> Metallic potassium will explode on contact with water. (Means potassium already does explode on contact with water. . . .)
>
> The reason that Warren Buffet has made so much money in his life is that he will not invest in fly-by-night operations. (Means that he has a firm policy of not investing, exemplified by his past practice. . . .)

So even though we use the term *future tense*, we recognize that it does not designate a particular verb form, one with a special ending, as *past tense* does. It can refer to any of our various ways of discussing future time.

THE SUBJUNCTIVE MOOD

Unlike the conditional mood, the **subjunctive mood** does not involve modal auxiliaries. Rather, it is simply a variation of the verb that we use in special circumstances:

1. In *that* clauses after verbs conveying a strong suggestion or recommendation, we use the base form of the verb:

    > We suggested <u>that Mary go with us.</u>
    >
    > Kathy insisted <u>that Bill consult the doctor.</u>
    >
    > I move <u>that the meeting be adjourned.</u>

Even for third-person singular subjects, which would normally take the *-s* form, we use the base form in these clauses: Mary *go;* Bill *consult;* the meeting *be.* Other verbs that commonly take clauses in the subjunctive mood are *command, demand, ask, require, order, recommend,* and *propose.* A subjunctive *that* clause also follows certain nouns and adjectives related to commands and suggestions:

> The suggestion <u>that Bill see the doctor</u> was a good one.
>
> It is advisable <u>that he get a thorough checkup.</u>

2. In *if* clauses that express a wish or a condition contrary to fact, we use *were* as the standard form of *be,* no matter what the subject:

    > <u>If I were you,</u> I'd be careful.
    >
    > <u>If Joe weren't so lazy,</u> he'd probably be a millionaire.

The use of *was* is also fairly common in sentences like the second example:

> If Joe <u>was here</u>, he'd agree with me.

In writing, however, the subjunctive *were* is the standard form.

In Chapter 9 we will see *if* clauses that discuss a possible condition rather than a wish or a condition contrary to fact:

> If it <u>is cold tomorrow</u>, we'll cancel the picnic.

Here we do not use the infinitive form of *be* as we do in the subjunctive mood.

TENSE AND ASPECT

At the opening of this chapter you learned that French verbs have more than seventy different forms—in contrast to the mere five we have in English. Does that mean that our language is less expressive? Not at all. Instead of expressing concepts of time and duration and completion by adding inflectional endings to our verbs, as the French do, we use auxiliaries, either singly or in combination. The verb-expansion rule that you learned, with its tense marker and optional auxiliaries, describes our system for doing so.

The auxiliaries *be* and *have* contribute to what is called **aspect**, referring to whether an action is in progress or completed. In traditional terminology, verbs in the *-ing* form with the auxiliary *be* are called "progressive" or "continuous"; those in the *-en*, or past participle, form with the auxiliary *have* are called "perfect" tenses. The term "perfect" comes to us from Latin grammar, where it refers to "action that is completed before the present moment." However, in English our present perfect,

> Bill has lived in Florida since 1992,

while referring to past, includes a connection to the present. This sentence tells us that Bill still lives in Florida. That present connection of one kind or another is implicit in the perfect tenses with *have*. And, as the examples in the following section show, verb strings with *had* refer to a point of time in the past connected to a more recent past time.

The tense marker, T, in our verb-expansion rule, however, is limited to only two tenses: present and past. These are the only two tenses represented by the form of the verb itself. Following are illustrations of our common tenses and auxiliary–verb combinations.

USING THE VERB FORMS

The traditional labels of these common verb forms are shown in parentheses.[2]

Base form and -s form (SIMPLE PRESENT)

I <u>live</u> in Omaha.

The news <u>comes on</u> at six.

Milton's poetry <u>speaks</u> to everyone.

Spiders <u>spin</u> webs.

Historical, habitual, propensity, or timeless present

I <u>understand</u> your position.

Present point in time

Pres + be + -ing + MV (PRESENT PROGRESSIVE)

I <u>am working</u> at Wal-Mart.

John <u>is taking</u> philosophy this term.

Present action of limited duration

Past + MV (SIMPLE PAST)

I <u>moved</u> to Omaha last March.

A virus <u>erased</u> all of my data.

Specific point in time

Note that with an appropriate adverbial, this form can indicate an extended period of time in the past, not a specific point:

I <u>studied</u> Spanish *for three years in high school.*

Past + be + -ing + MV (PAST PROGRESSIVE)

A baby <u>was crying</u> during the entire ceremony this morning.

I <u>was trying</u> to sleep last night during the party, but it was no use.

Past action of limited duration (often to show one particular action during a larger span of time)

[2.] These traditional labels are called *tenses*. However, given our use of *tense* in the verb-expansion rule—that is, our restriction of T to present and past—we will adopt the linguist's term *aspect* in reference to the verb strings that are expanded with the perfect (*have* + *-en*) and progressive (*be* + *-ing*) auxiliaries.

Pres + have + -en + MV (PRESENT PERFECT)

The leaves <u>have turned</u> yellow already.

I <u>have finished</u> my work.

I <u>have memorized</u> several of Frost's poems.

A completed action extending from a point in the past to either the present or the near present—an action with relevance to the present—or occurring at an unspecified past time

Past + have + -en + MV (PAST PERFECT)

The hikers <u>had used up</u> all their water, when finally they found a hidden spring.

The students <u>had finished</u> only the first page of the test by the time the bell rang.

Past action completed before another action in the past

Pres + have + -en + be + -ing + MV (PRESENT PERFECT PROGRESSIVE)

The authorities <u>have been looking</u> for the arson suspect since last Sunday.

Past action continuing into the present

Past + have + -en + be + -ing + MV (PAST PERFECT PROGRESSIVE)

The authorities <u>had been looking</u> for the suspect even before the fire broke out.

Continuing past action completed before another action in the past

EXCEPTIONS TO THE VERB-EXPANSION RULE

The verb-expansion rule is simple, but it is powerful. With it we can expand the verb slot in all the sentence patterns to express a great many variations in meaning. Given the variety of modals we have, which we can use with or without *have + -en* and *be + -ing*, the number of possible variations adds up to fifty or more for most verbs. However, we rarely use all the possibilities for any given verb. Our system restricts the use of some, and others we simply have no occasion to use.

Although we may say,

He seems grumpy.

and

They have remained friends.

We would probably never say,

> *He is seeming grumpy.

or

> *They have been remaining friends.

Most of the exceptions involve the restriction of *be* + *-ing* with certain linking verbs, with *be* as main verb, and with a small number of transitive verbs that refer to mental processes, such as *prefer, know,* and *like,* or states, such as *own, resemble,* and *weigh.*

ELL Issues   Special Rules for *-ing* Verbs

The restriction that applies to the auxiliary *be* + *-ing* is rooted in the "continuous" or "progressive" meaning that *-ing* gives the verb; that "movement through time" is not logical with verbs like *prefer* and *know.* The restriction also applies to Pattern I, where *be* is the main verb followed by a time or place adverbial. We can use *have* + *-en* or a modal auxiliary with a time adverbial in Pattern I to describe an extended time in a particular place:

> The students *have been* in the library <u>since noon</u>.

> The students *will be* in the library <u>until this afternoon</u>.

But *be* + *-ing*, with its progressive meaning, simply doesn't work:

> *The students *are being* in the library.

The Pattern I sentence "The students *are* in the library" simply identifies the present existence of the students in a particular place, not a progressive or continuous state. The same restriction on *be* + *-ing* applies to Patterns II and III when the subject complement names a permanent, unchanging trait:

> *He is being tall.

> *He is being African-American.

See also the #2 Question for Discussion, on page 83.

THE STAND-IN AUXILIARY *DO*

You may have noticed that one common auxiliary does not appear in our verb-expansion rule (even though it appears in this sentence)—the auxiliary *do*, along with its *-s* and *-ed* forms, *does* and *did*. Why have we left those forms out of the discussion of auxiliaries? Don't they belong in our list, as modals perhaps or as alternatives to *have* + *-en* and *be* + *-ing*?

No, they don't. Even though most grammar books include the forms of *do* in their auxiliary lists along with modals and *have* and *be*, they don't really belong there. The auxiliary role played by *do* and *does* and *did* in the predicating verb is very different from that of the others. They belong in a list by themselves.

Consider which of the following sentences sound grammatical to you and which do not:

1. Boris may not work today.
2. Boris worked not yesterday.
3. Amy is not living here.
4. Amy lives not here.
5. Amy is not here.

You may have noticed that all five sentences, including the two that are ungrammatical, have something in common: They are all negative. And it's that negative marker *not* that makes sentences 2 and 4 ungrammatical. Without it, there would be no problem:

> Boris worked yesterday.
>
> Amy lives here.

What do the other three have that those two don't? Sentences 1 and 3 have auxiliaries; 5 has a form of *be* as the main verb. In order to make sentences 2 and 4 grammatical, we have to add an auxiliary. Here's where *do* comes into our grammar:

> Boris didn't work yesterday.
>
> Amy doesn't live here.

Here are two more sentences about Amy that are ungrammatical:

> *Where lives Amy?
>
> *Lives Amy in Austin?

As with negative sentences, all three kinds of questions—yes/no questions, *wh*-questions, and tag questions—also require auxiliaries:

> Where does Amy live?
>
> Does Amy live in Austin?
>
> Amy lives in Austin, doesn't she?

When an auxiliary is required for a sentence variation, including negative sentences and questions, and there is no auxiliary, then *do* comes to the rescue—it stands in as a kind of dummy auxiliary. Linguists have a more formal name for this operation: They call it ***do* support**.

There is one more occasion that calls for the assistance of *do* support: the **emphatic sentence**.

> Amy does expect to graduate in four years.
> Do come in.
> We did enjoy our holiday in the mountains.

These three sentences would be grammatical without a form of *do*, but they would lose their emphatic quality. In speech we can make our sentences emphatic simply by adding volume to either an auxiliary or to the verb itself. In writing we could put the verb in capital letters,

> I LOVE holidays in the mountains

—but of course it's not standard procedure. When the sentence has an auxiliary, we can show the emphasis with italics or possibly an adverb:

> I *have* finished my homework.
> I certainly have finished my homework.

The emphatic *do* allows us to show the emphasis without any special gimmicks:

> I did finish my homework.

The purpose of this discussion of *do* is twofold: (1) to help you understand the distinction between *do* and the other auxiliaries; (2) to help you appreciate how your grammar expertise automatically calls on *do* whenever you need an auxiliary.

Usage Matters   *Lie and Lay*

One way to think about the tricky verbs *lie* and *lay* is in terms of their sentence patterns: One is intransitive (Pattern VI) and one is transitive (Pattern VII). Read the following information adapted from *Webster's Ninth New Collegiate Dictionary*, then fill in the blanks with their various forms.

lie/ (intran) **lay**/; **lain**/; **lying** 1 a. to be or to stay at rest in a horizontal position; be prostrate: REST, RECLINE (~motionless) (~asleep) b. to assume a horizontal position—often used with *down*.

lay/ (tran) **laid**/; **laid**/; **laying** 1: to beat or strike down with force 2 a: to put or set down b: to place for rest or sleep; esp: BURY 3: to bring forth and deposit (an egg).

BASE	-*S* FORM	-*ED* FORM	-*ING* FORM	-*EN* FORM
1. lie	_____	_____	_____	_____
2. lay	_____	_____	_____	_____

Now identify the verbs in the following sentences as transitive or intransitive and indicate the base form of the verb: Is it *lie* or *lay?*

1. I should lay the papers in neat piles on the table. _____

2. The cat has never lain so still before. _____

3. Yesterday he lay very still. _____

4. I laid the baby on the bed for her nap. _____

5. I lay on the beach for two hours yesterday. _____

If you are accustomed to hearing people say "I'm going to lay down for a nap" or commanding their dogs to "lay down," you may think that the last sentence in the list sounds wrong. It's not unusual to hear people say "I laid on the beach." In fact, it is so common that at the end of the definition for *lay,* just quoted, the dictionary includes *lie* as an intransitive synonym—and labels it "nonstandard." In other words, when you say "lay down," you are using *lay* as a synonym for the intransitive *lie.* (If your dog responds only to standard usage, you'll have to say "lie down.") The reason for the common nonstandard usage becomes clear when you examine the five forms of the two verbs: Both sets include *lay.*

The confusion arising with two other pairs of tricky verbs—*rise/raise* and *sit/set*—can be resolved in the same way as with *lie/lay,* that is, in terms of their sentence pattern category. The dictionary will identify them as transitive or intransitive and list their -*ed*, -*en*, and -*ing* forms.

THE VERB SYSTEM OF AFRICAN AMERICAN VERNACULAR ENGLISH

One of the most noticeable differences between Edited American English (EAE) and African American Vernacular English (AAVE), known also as Ebonics, occurs with the verb-expansion rule.[3] In this chapter we have seen how *have* and *be* function systematically as auxiliaries to designate the perfect (*Mary has worked*) and the progressive (*Mary is working*) forms

---

[3.] This description is adapted from an article by Lisa Green: "Study of Verb Classes in African American English," *Linguistics and Education* 7 (1994): 65–81.

of the verb. We have also noted that *do* kicks in for questions (*Did Mary eat?*), negative sentences (*Mary didn't eat*), and emphasis (*Mary did eat*) when no other auxiliary is available.

The AAVE system calls for these same auxiliaries, but combines them in different ways. Here is a partial list of AAVE verb strings along with the EAE equivalent for each:

1. He eat. (present) "He is eating."
2. He be eating. (habitual) "He is usually eating."
3. He been eating. (remote past) "He has been eating for a long time."
4. He been ate. (remote past) "He ate a long time ago."
5. He done ate. (completive) "He has already eaten."
6. He been done ate. (remote past completive) "He finished eating a long time ago."
7. He had done ate. (completive) "He had already eaten."

We would need more data, of course, to come up with an accurate verb-expansion rule for AAVE. However, we can recognize certain regular features of the system from this small sample:

1. The auxiliary *done* appears in all the "completive" forms. Note that the adverb *already* or the verb *finished* is required to express the EAE equivalent.
2. The auxiliary *been* (pronounced "bin" and spoken with strong stress) carries the meaning of "remote" time. The EAE equivalent requires "a long time" or "a long time ago" to make this remote past distinction.

In terms of form, the fact that the auxiliary *done* appears in the string with other auxiliaries clearly sets this system apart from EAE, where *do* is not part of the verb-expansion rule, but, as mentioned earlier, occurs only as a stand-in auxiliary. (It should be noted that in AAVE a form of *do* also kicks in for some questions and negatives, as in EAE.) Another distinguishing feature of AAVE is the "habitual" *be*, shown in the second example. It includes the meaning "usually" or "habitually," whereas in EAE the adverb must be supplied.

It should be obvious from this brief description that the verb forms of AAVE, although different from those of EAE, are generated by a highly systematized set of rules. This recognition should also illustrate an important lesson that the linguists have contributed to language education: that all dialects of English are equally grammatical.

CHAPTER 4
Key Terms

African American Vernacular English
Auxiliary
Conditional mood
Do support
Emphatic sentence
Helping verb
Indicative mood
Infinitive
Irregular verb
Main verb

Modal auxiliary
Mood
Negative sentence
Person
Regular verb
Stand-in auxiliary
Subjunctive mood
Tense
Verb-expansion rule

Sentences
for PRACTICE

Identify the components of the main verb in each of the following sentences. Your answers will be in the form of verb strings, such as those given in Exercise 12.

1. The press has recently labeled our new senator a radical on domestic issues.
2. The teacher should have given the class more information about the exam.
3. According to the students, their teacher was being downright secretive.
4. In Florida the Coast Guard is now confiscating the boats of drug runners.
5. The president may soon name three women to top posts in the Department of State.
6. Our company will try a new vacation schedule in the summer.
7. All the workers are taking their two-week vacations at the same time.
8. Pat has been jogging regularly for six years.
9. Until last week, Mario had never told me his middle name.

10. The suspect's alibi may have been a lie.
11. I should have been studying on a regular basis throughout the semester.
12. Writers have produced almost 2,500 works about the *Bounty* mutiny during the past 200 years.

QUESTIONS
?
for DISCUSSION

1. "I've already ate" is a fairly common nonstandard usage in our country. Explain how it deviates from the standard usage described by the verb-expansion rule. Compare it with "I've already tried"; can you discover a logical reason for the nonstandard usage? Does that particular nonstandard form ever occur with regular verbs?

2. The difference between two such sentences as

> He is tall.   *and*   He is silly.

is obviously in the adjective that fills the subject complement slot. We cannot say

> *He is being tall.

but we can say

> He is being silly.

so there must be a fundamental difference between the two adjectives.

The contrast is between **stative** and **dynamic** qualities—the one describing a state, usually permanent, and the other a changing quality. What is there about *be* + *-ing* that makes this restriction seem logical? Can you think of other stative adjectives (other than *tall*) that are restricted from the subject complement slot with *be* + *-ing*?

Perhaps a better way of describing the contrast between *silly* and *tall*—between silliness and height—concerns the presence or absence of volition, the power of choice. Which of the following adjectives describe characteristics that are willed: *young, tough, nice, red, absorbent, reckless, round?* Can these adjectives serve as subject complements with *be* + *-ing?*

3. Consider further restrictions on *be + -ing* :

     *Mary is resembling her mother.

     *The blue dress is fitting you.

   Can we speak of dynamic and stative or willed and nonwilled qualities of verbs as well as of adjectives? Consider the following verbs: *assume, suit, equal, enjoy, desire, agree with, mean, know, contain, lack, like*. Do any of these have restrictions? Why?

4. Do nouns carry such distinctions, too? Try the following nouns in the subject complement slot of Pattern III: *a doctor, a nuisance, a hero, a nice person, a gentleman, a hard worker, a construction worker*. Here is the slot: "He is being _____." Can all of them be used with *be + -ing*? What conclusions can you draw about NPs? Does volition, or the power of choice, make a difference?

5. You can demonstrate the ambiguity of the following negative sentences by adding two possible follow-up sentences to each:

     I'm not taking Math 10 because it's so easy.

     He did not kill his wife because he loved her.

6. The following aphorism is ambiguous too:

     No news is good news.

   Restate the sentence in two ways to demonstrate its two meanings.

7. Why do the following sentences from Shakespeare and the King James Bible sound strange to our twenty-first-century ears? What particular change that has taken place in the language do these sentences illustrate?

     Let not your heart be troubled.

     Know you where you are?

     Wherefore weep you?

     Revolt our subjects?

     What means this shouting?

CLASSROOM APPLICATION

In this chapter we looked briefly at our system for turning sentences into questions, a process that sometimes requires *do*. The tag-question is another method for turning statements into questions:

John is washing his car, <u>isn't he?</u>

Perry should wash his too, <u>shouldn't he?</u>

Add the tags that turn the following statements into questions:

Harold has finally stopped smoking, _____?

The students are not studying Latin, _____?

Bev finished her book on schedule, _____?

Tim and Joe are good carpenters, _____?

Kris is a good carpenter, too, _____?

She builds beautiful cabinets, _____?

Now look at the system you followed for adding these questions. How many steps are involved? Imagine writing a computer program so that it, too, could generate tag-questions. What are the steps you would have to include?

Here are three more tags to supply:

Harold should stop smoking, _____?

Harold ought to stop smoking, _____?

Harold may stop smoking soon, _____?

Take a poll among your friends to get their responses to these three. Do all the respondents agree? Do they follow the procedure you described in the first set? What do these tags tell you about the changing nature of the language?

CHAPTER 5

Changing Sentence Focus

CHAPTER PREVIEW

The ten sentence-pattern formulas described in Chapter 3 represent the underlying framework of almost all the sentences we speak and write. In most of our sentences, the predicate slot following the main verb commands attention; it usually is the peak in the rhythm pattern, the place where we focus on the new information, the reason for the sentence.

This chapter will examine several ways of rearranging sentence patterns to emphasize information by shifting the focus. By the end of the chapter, you will be able to

- Recognize the difference between *active voice* and *passive voice* verbs.
- Transform active sentences into passive ones, and passive sentences into active ones.
- Understand when to use the passive voice effectively.
- Identify and use the *there transformation*.
- Recognize and construct two types of *cleft sentences*.

THE PASSIVE VOICE

The "voice" of a sentence concerns the relationship of the subject to the verb. You're probably familiar with the definition of verbs as "action words," a description commonly applied to both intransitive and transitive verbs:

> Mary laughed. (Pattern VI)
>
> The boys ate every piece of pizza. (Pattern VII)

In these sentences the subjects are performing the action; they are making something happen. Linguists use the term **agent** for this "doer" of the verbal action. Another term that describes this relationship of the subject to the verb is **active voice**.

What happens when we turn the Pattern VII sentence around, when we remove the agent from the subject slot and give that role to *every piece of pizza*, the original direct object?

> Every piece of pizza was eaten by the boys.

This reversal changes the sentence from active to **passive voice**. The diagrams clearly illustrate the changed roles:

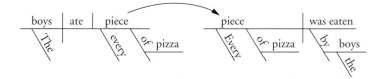

To understand the primary distinction between active and passive voice, it is important to recognize what happens to the subject–verb relationship. In our example, even though *the boys* is no longer the sentence subject, or topic, it is still the agent, or actor; and *every piece of pizza* is still the so-called "receiver of the action," still getting acted upon—still getting eaten! Only their roles in the sentence, their functions, have changed—not their relationship to each other. The passive voice simply describes the event from a different perspective.

In the active voice, while the subject is the sentence topic, the slot that follows the verb, the direct object, is the focus of the sentence—and generally the new information. In other words, what is said about the topic is generally the reason for the sentence. The passive transformation shifts the direct object from the focus position to that of sentence topic, or subject. We will see some examples of why that shift occurs in the next section. First, however, we will look at the changes to the verb string that occur in the passive voice.

The passive transformation involves three steps, all of which are fairly easy to see in the diagrams of the pizza sentences:

1. The original direct object becomes the subject.
2. A form of *be* is added as an auxiliary (in this case the past form, *was*, because *ate* is past); it teams with the past participle, the *-en* form of the verb. In other words, we add *be* + *-en* to the active verb string.
3. The original agent, if mentioned, becomes the object of the preposition *by* (or, in some cases, *for*). This third step is often missing; it is not required. Many, if not most, passive sentences do not include the active agent.

If you think about the first step in the list, you'll understand why we are not using the other example of an action verb, *Mary laughed*, to illustrate the passive voice: Intransitive verbs cannot be made passive because they have no direct object. That's why you read this statement in the discussion of Pattern VII, back in Chapter 3 (page 43):

> In Chapter 5 you will see another way of testing whether or not a verb is transitive. Can the sentence be turned into the passive voice? If the answer is yes, the verb is transitive.

As you learned in Chapter 4, the verb-expansion rule applies to all of the sentence patterns. We can think of it as the active-verb rule:

Active: T (M) (have + -en) (be + -ing) MV

As the formula shows, when we choose *be* as an auxiliary in the active voice, the main verb will be the *-ing* form. But according to Step 2 in our description of the passive transformation, the auxiliary *be* is teamed with the past participle, the *-en* form of the verb:

Every piece of pizza <u>was eaten</u> by the boys.

The passive formula shows this feature as a requirement of the passive voice; you'll note that, unlike the optional *be* + *-ing* in the active rule, the *be* + *-en* is not in parentheses:

Passive: T (M) (have + -en) (be + -ing) **be** + **-en** MV

This formula tells us that a passive verb has three requirements: (1) tense, (2) the auxiliary *be*, together with (3) the past participle form of the main verb. Here are the components of the passive verb in our pizza example:

$$\text{past} + \text{be} + \text{-en} + \text{eat} = \text{was eaten}$$

The formula also shows that a passive sentence can include optional auxiliaries, along with the required *be* + *-en*:

> The work <u>will be finished</u> soon.
> The work <u>should have been finished</u> yesterday.

We know these sentences are passive because the auxiliary *be* is not followed by the *-ing* form of the verb.

Exercise 13

Transform the active sentences into the passive by following these steps:

1. Identify the components of the verb string.
2. Add *be* + *-en*.
3. Shift the direct object to subject position.
4. Include the active subject in a *by* phrase. (Note: This step is optional.)

Example:

The Red Cross is sending aid to the earthquake victims in Haiti.

> Active verb: pres + be + -ing + send
> Passive: pres + be + -ing + be + -en + send = is being sent
> *Aid is being sent to the earthquake victims in Haiti by the Red Cross.*

1. President Lincoln signed the Emancipation Proclamation in 1862.
2. The campus paper has published several sensational news stories this semester.
3. The student government will hold a run-off election in two weeks.
4. The police are keeping the suspect in solitary confinement.
5. Your positive attitude pleases me.
6. Bill's fraternity brothers were teasing him about his new mustache.
7. You should back up your computer files on a regular schedule.
8. Heavy thunderstorms have knocked down power lines in three counties.

The Passive *Get*. It's certainly accurate to recognize *be* as the auxiliary that signals the passive voice—but *be* is not the only one. On some occasions we call on the verb *get* to team up with the *-en* form of the verb to form the passive. Such occasions are informal ones; rarely do we see sentences like these in formal writing:

> My sister gets teased about her freckles.
> Dave got fired yesterday.
> Our basement got flooded during yesterday's storm.

And here's a sentence you may recognize from the earlier passive discussion:

> The pizza is still getting eaten!

Formality—or its lack—is not the only reason that *get* falls short as an auxiliary, whether active or passive. Unlike other auxiliaries, *get* requires *do* support for negatives and questions:

> My sister doesn't get teased about her freckles.
>
> Did Dave get fired yesterday?

Some of our *get* sentences that look like passives are more accurately identified as linking verb patterns:

> I got tired of waiting.
>
> Hansel and Gretel got lost in the woods.

In these sentences, *tired* and *lost* are filling the subject complement slot. And in contrast to the first group of sentences, these two do not have an understood agent; there's no "by" phrase that's been deleted. So, in contrast to the passive sentences, here *get* is the main verb, not an auxiliary.

The Transitive-Passive Relationship. The ties between the transitive verb and the passive voice are so strong—there are so few exceptions—that we can almost define "transitive verb" in terms of this relationship. In other words, a transitive verb is a verb that can undergo the passive transformation. There are a few exceptions, including *have*, one of our most common verbs. In only a few colloquial expressions does *have* appear in the passive voice: "A good time was had by all," "I've been had." But in most cases *have* sentences cannot be transformed:

> I had a cold.
>
> *A cold was had by me.
>
> Juan has a new car.
>
> *A new car is had by Juan.

Other verbs that fit Pattern VII but are rarely transformed into passive are *lack* ("He lacks skill in debate") and *resemble* ("Mary resembles her mother"). Linguists sometimes classify these as "midverbs" and assign them to a separate sentence pattern. But on the basis of form (NP_1 V NP_2), we will classify these sentences as Pattern VII and simply look on them as exceptions to the passive rule.

Patterns VIII to X in Passive Voice. The passive examples we have seen so far are all Pattern VII. But of course, all of our transitive patterns can be transformed into the passive voice. In the case of Pattern VIII, which has an indirect object in addition to the direct object, we have two options: Either of the two objects can serve as the subject of the passive:

> *Active:* The judge awarded Prudence first prize.
>
> *Passive:* Prudence was awarded first prize.
>
> or
>
> *Passive:* First prize was awarded to Prudence.

When we diagram the version with *Prudence* as subject, the result looks exactly like an active Pattern VII:

Here, where we have two objects, we have retained the direct object in the passive; in traditional grammar this slot is called the **retained object**.

In order to identify the sentence pattern, to distinguish it from Pattern VII, we have to recognize the sentence as passive, and we do that by noting that the verb *was awarded* cannot be active (otherwise, the auxiliary *be* would be followed by *-ing*).

The diagram of the other version of Pattern VIII, with *First prize* as subject, looks exactly like Pattern VI:

Again, the only way to identify it as a transitive verb is to recognize that the verb is passive: The auxiliary *be* <u>without</u> *-ing* following is the clue.

When we transform Patterns IX and X, which also have two slots following the verb, we have only one choice for the passive: Only the direct object can serve as the subject in the passive voice:

> *Active:* The teacher considers Elizabeth bright. (Pattern IX)
>
> They named their dog Sandy. (Pattern X)

In the passive voice, the active object complement becomes a subject complement. This transformation occurs because the original object becomes the subject:

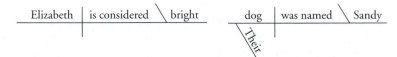

Note that we have not included a *by* phrase—that is, the active subjects—in these passive versions. They could, of course, be added.

Again, in order to identify these last two sentences as Patterns IX and X, it is important to recognize the verbs as passive. Otherwise, they will be mistaken for linking verbs. The simple fact that the verbs are passive, however, immediately sends the message that they are transitive patterns—only the transitive patterns can be transformed into the passive voice.

Exercise 14

Transform the following active sentences into the passive voice, retaining the same verb tense and aspect.

1. Many movie critics gave *Avatar* rave reviews.
2. The teacher is giving the third graders too much homework.
3. The judges have chosen three finalists for the science award.
4. These colorful murals have turned the staircase walls into an art museum.
5. Fans and sports writers often refer to Roger Federer as the greatest tennis player of all time.
6. Bach composed some of our most intricate fugues.

Changing Passive Voice to Active. To transform a passive sentence into active voice, you need to perform three operations that essentially undo the three steps that produce the passive voice:

1. First, identify the agent, or actor—the doer of the verbal action. If the agent is named, you'll usually find it in a *by* prepositional phrase. If it's not there, just add "someone":

    A party is being planned by the film club. [Agent: the film club]

    The work should be finished by Friday. [Agent: someone]

2. Next, delete *be* + *-en* from the verb string:

    is being planned = pres + be + ing + ~~be~~ + ~~-en~~ + plan

    should be finished = past + shall + ~~be~~ + ~~-en~~ + finish

3. Rewrite the sentence with the agent in subject position, the revised verb in place, and the passive subject shifted to the direct object slot:

> The film club is planning a party.

> Someone should finish the work by Friday.

Exercise | 15

Change these passive sentences to the active voice. Remember that in some cases the agent may be missing, so you will have to supply a subject for the active, such as "someone." Identify the sentence patterns for the active sentences you have produced.

1. The football team was led onto the field by the cheerleading squad.
2. The cheerleaders are chosen by a committee in the spring.
3. The new reporters had been warned by the managing editor about late submissions.
4. Three finalists have been chosen for the science award.
5. Dental floss was manufactured for the first time in 1882.
6. The possibility of recession is being talked about in financial circles.
7. The play was called a smashing success.
8. The poison has been rendered harmless.

THE PASSIVE VOICE IN PROSE

It's possible that everything you've heard or read about the passive voice has been negative. Sometimes English teachers even declare it out of bounds. This edict comes about because passive sentences sometimes have a stilted quality; and, yes, ineffective passives can often be improved by being changed to active voice. But often the reason for the problem is not the passive voice itself; the reason lies elsewhere. It's possible that an ineffective passive has the wrong subject, the wrong topic. In such a case, it's the focus that's the problem—not the mere fact that the sentence is passive.

It's fair to say that the main job of the passive voice is to provide cohesion. The passive enables the writer to shift emphasis in the sentence so that the reader will put the focus where it should be—on the new information. Below you will see the beginning of a paragraph from the discussion of verbs in Chapter 2. Note how the direct object slot in the first sentence, the new information (underlined), becomes the topic, the subject, of the three following sentences. It has gone from being the focus in the opening sentence to being the old, or known, information—the topic under discussion—in the others. Because that subject is not the agent, the doer of the action, we make use of the passive voice. The passive verbs are shown in bold type.

> When the dictionary identifies a word as a verb, it lists three forms: the base form (*laugh*), the past tense (*laughed*), and the past participle (*laughed*). These three forms **are** traditionally **referred to** as the verb's "three principal parts." The base form **is** also **known** as the infinitive; it **is** often **written** with *to* (*to laugh*). (p. 17)

Other Passive Purposes. The passive voice may also be appropriate if the identity of the agent is obscured in history or simply has no bearing on the discussion:

> In 1905 the streets of Patterson, California, were laid out in the shape of a wheel.
>
> Oregon's economy is closely tied to the lumber industry.

The passive voice is especially common—and deliberate—in technical and scientific writing, in legal documents, and in lab reports, where the researcher is the agent but to say so would be inappropriate:

> I increased the temperature to 450° for one hour. (*Active*)
>
> The temperature was increased to 450° for one hour. (*Passive*)

In some instances the passive voice is simply more straightforward:

> Joe was wounded in Iraq.

In some situations it appears that the purpose of the passive is to deliberately avoid mentioning the agent:

> It was reported today that the federal funds to be allocated for the power plant would not be forthcoming as early as had been anticipated. Some contracts on the preliminary work have been canceled and others renegotiated.

Such "officialese" or "bureaucratese" takes on a nonhuman quality because the agent role has completely disappeared from the sentences. In the foregoing example the reader does not know who is reporting, allocating, anticipating, canceling, or renegotiating.

This kind of agentless passive is especially common in official news conferences, where press secretaries and other government officials explain what is happening without revealing who is responsible for making it happen. The faceless passive does an efficient job of obscuring responsibility, but it is neither efficient nor graceful for the writing that most of us do in school and on the job.

Sometimes student writers resort to the passive voice in order to avoid using *I*, perhaps because the paper has too many of them already or because the teacher has ruled out the first-person point of view:

> The incessant sound of foghorns could be heard along the waterfront.

But English is a versatile language: First person ("I could hear . . .") is not the only alternative. Here's a version of the sentence using *sound* as the verb:

> The foghorns sounded along the waterfront.

Here's one that describes the movement of the sound:

> The incessant sound of foghorns floated across the water.

Many times, of course, the writer simply doesn't realize that the passive voice may be the culprit producing the vagueness or wordiness of that first draft. For example, the writer of the following sentence ended a family Christmas story with no awareness of voice at all:

> That visit from Santa was an occurrence that would never be
> forgotten by the family.

The active version produces a tight, straightforward sentence:

> The family would never forget that visit from Santa.

The writer could also have found an active sentence that retains *visit* as the subject:

> That visit from Santa became part of our family legend.

The passive voice certainly has a place in every kind of prose. To avoid it simply for the sake of avoiding it often results in a stilted, un-natural voice.

THE *THERE* TRANSFORMATION

Like the passive voice, the ***there* transformation** provides the writer a way of changing sentence focus by altering the word order—in this case, by opening the sentence with the unstressed *there*, known as an **expletive**; the subject of the sentence follows *be:*

> There's a fly in my soup.

> There is an error message on the computer screen.

To diagram a *there* transformation, we must identify the underlying pattern. As the diagram shows, *there* has no grammatical function in the basic sentence:

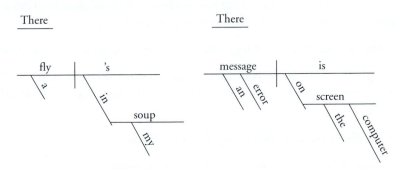

When we use the *there* transformation, we are taking advantage of the natural rhythm of language. In general, our language is a series of valleys and peaks, a fairly regular pattern of unstressed and stressed syllables:

Sentences usually begin with an unstressed valley. And more often than not, that first, unstressed slot is the subject. But the *there* transformation changes that usual word order: When the unstressed *there* fills the opening slot, it delays the subject until that first peak position of stress.

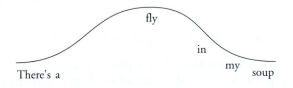

The *there* transformation applies when the subject of the sentence is indefinite: "*a* fly" or "*an* error message" rather than "*the* fly" or "*the* error message." The **indefinite article** is a signal that the subject of the *there* transformation is new information; we use the **definite article**, *the*, for old, or known, information. We might have occasion to say,

> There's the fly I told you about.

if a particular fly under discussion lands in the soup. But clearly this is a known fly, so this is not the unstressed *there*. The stress it carries marks it as an adverb providing information of place (it's called the "locative" adverb, from the word *location*). The same is true of

> There's that error message again.

In these sentences with definite subjects, we have simply shifted the order of the basic sentence pattern, as we sometimes do to emphasize adverbials:

> Here's your book.
> Right off the end of the pier plunged the getaway car.

The expletive *there* is always unstressed; the adverb *there*, when it opens a sentence, is nearly always stressed, providing an exception to the normal rhythm pattern of that opening unstressed valley we just saw. The adverb *there*, besides providing information of place, often acts as a kind of pointer. For example, read the following pair of sentences aloud and notice the difference in meaning and stress of the two *theres:*

> There's a piece of the jigsaw puzzle missing.
> There it is, on the floor.

You can almost see the finger pointing in the case of the second *there.*

In addition to the indefinite subject, the *there* transformation usually has a form of *be* either as the main verb or, in the case of the transitive and intransitive patterns, as an auxiliary. Pattern I (NP *be* ADV/ TP) is the most common pattern we transform with *there;* Patterns II and III, in which *be* acts as a linking verb, will not accept the *there* transformation.

The form of *be* will, of course, depend on the tense and on the number of the subject, whether singular or plural:

> There _were some problems_ with the heat in our new apartment.
> There _has been a problem_ with the plumbing, too.

But an exception to the general rule of **subject–verb agreement** occurs with the *there* transformation. A compound subject, which we usually treat as plural, may take the *-s* form of *be* under some circumstances:

> There _was_ some great blocking and some fine running and passing in Saturday's game.

In this sentence "there were" would be awkward, even though the subject is compound.

The *there* transformation without a form of *be* is also possible, but such sentences are not very common:

> There came from the alley a low moaning sound.
>
> There followed a series of unexplained phenomena.
>
> There remains an unanswered question.

Listen to the difference between these sentences and those with *be*. These have a tight, controlled quality about them. Notice also that when a verb other than *be* follows *there* it shares the stress with the subject.

You will read more about the rhythm of sentences and about the *there* transformation as a tool for the writer in Chapter 15. English language learners may want to review the distinction between the indefinite article "a" and the definite "the" on page 131.

Exercise 16

Identify the function of *there* in the following sentences. Is it the expletive or is it the locative adverb? Also identify the sentence patterns.

1. There's often a flock of blackbirds lining the telephone wire in our neighborhood.
2. There they are now.
3. There's nothing to do tonight.
4. There's always TV to watch.
5. There's Henry across the street.
6. There he goes.
7. Isn't there a spelling checker on your word processor?
8. There but for the grace of God go I.

CLEFT SENTENCES

Another sentence variation that provides a way to shift the focus of attention is the cleft transformation, so called because it divides a clause into two parts: It cleaves it. The **cleft sentence** allows a writer to accomplish by means of word order what a speaker can do by varying the point of main stress or loudness. The following variations show how a speaker can change the focus or meaning of a sentence simply by putting stress on different words, that is, by saying certain words louder:

> MARY wrecked her motorcycle in Phoenix during the Christmas break. (It wasn't Diane who did it.)

Mary wrecked her MOTORCYCLE in Phoenix during the Christmas break. (Not her car.)

Mary wrecked her motorcycle in PHOENIX during the Christmas break. (Not in Albuquerque.)

Mary wrecked her motorcycle in Phoenix during the CHRISTMAS break. (Not Thanksgiving.)

Because the conventions of writing do not include capital letters for words that should get main stress, as shown in the preceding sentences, the writer's intended emphasis may not always be clear. The cleft transformation solves the problem. In one kind of cleft sentence the main subject is *it* with a form of *be* as the main verb. This use of *it* is sometimes called the "anticipatory *it*." In reading the following sentences aloud, you'll notice that you automatically stress the word or phrase following *was:*

It was <u>Mary</u> who wrecked her motorcycle in Phoenix during the Christmas break.

It was <u>her motorcycle</u> that Mary wrecked in Phoenix during the Christmas break.

It was <u>in Phoenix</u> that Mary wrecked her motorcycle during the Christmas break.

It was <u>during the Christmas break</u> that Mary wrecked her motorcycle.

The cleft sentence assumes background knowledge that the writer and reader share. In other words, you would not write "It was Mary who wrecked her motorcycle" unless the accident was already known to the reader.

Another kind of cleft sentence uses a *what* clause in subject position. Note that the added *was* separates the original sentence into two parts:

Mary wrecked her motorcycle.

What Mary wrecked <u>was</u> her motorcycle.

Sometimes *what* shifts the original verb phrase into subject position. Again, a form of *be* is added as the main verb:

A branch in the road <u>caused the accident</u>.

<u>What caused the accident</u> was a branch in the road.

Thick fog <u>reduced the visibility to zero</u>.

<u>What reduced the visibility to zero</u> was the thick fog.

You'll notice in both the *it*-cleft and *what*-clefts that the sentence pattern of the main clause has changed, a change that does not occur with the other transformations. The Appendix includes a diagram of the *what*-cleft (p. 369).

The cleft transformations produce sentences that are quite complicated structurally, with clauses filling certain slots in the patterns. You'll learn about these structures in later chapters. We will not be concerned here with their diagrams.

Usage Matters   Focusing Tools

The title of this chapter, "Changing Sentence Focus," calls attention to the purpose of the structures described. All of these focusing tools—the passive voice, the *there* transformation, and the cleft variations—enable you as a writer to make sure that the reader puts the emphasis of the sentence where you intend it to be.

Unfortunately, it's fairly standard practice for handbooks and, yes, teachers to describe these structures as problems to be fixed rather than as tools to be used, warning that sentences opening with "There is" or "There are" or "It is," besides being wordy, are also "guilty" of using *be* as the verb. The passive voice receives even stronger criticism, often based on the absence of a clear agent. Sometimes, of course, the agent is irrelevant, sometimes unknown, sometimes deliberately excluded. But there are also times when the passive voice actually puts extra focus on the agent by placing it at the end of the sentence in the "by" phrase:

"That famous game-ending home run was hit by Bobby Thomson."

Writers in earlier centuries had no qualms about using the passive voice. (Before 1907 it had never been mentioned as a usage issue.) You can find many passive sentences in the words of our Founding Fathers. For example, sixteen of the nineteen main clauses in the Bill of Rights are in the passive voice: *shall not be violated, shall be examined, shall not be required, shall be held, are reserved,* and so forth.

Our purpose in this chapter is to help you recognize those occasions when these focusing tools have a job to do. In Chapter 15 you'll read more about them in connection with cohesion. (See pages 315–16, 320.)

CHAPTER 5
Key Terms

Active voice   Cleft sentence

Agent   Definite article

Case   Expletive *there*

Indefinite article

It-cleft

Objective case

Passive voice

Retained object

Subject–verb agreement

There transformation

What-cleft

Sentences

for PRACTICE

Shift the focus of the following sentences by using the structural variations you have studied in this chapter: the passive voice, the *there* transformation, and the cleft transformations. Write as many variations as you can.

1. The press has recently labeled our new senator a radical on domestic issues.

2. During the 2010 election campaign, a new conservative movement called "The Tea Party" dominated the news.

3. The transcontinental railroad brought an end to wagon trains along the Oregon Trail.

4. Many large firms are now hiring liberal arts majors for management positions.

5. Employers value liberal arts majors for their analytical ability.

6. People are constantly teasing me about my southern accent.

7. Apparently they have never heard a southern accent around here before.

8. Nutrition advocates are making positive changes to school menus.

9. Many school cafeterias are now serving more fruits and vegetables because of the alarming statistics on childhood obesity.

10. The destruction of the Amazon rain forest alarms a great many environmentalists.

11. A month of unseasonably warm weather almost ruined the ski season last winter.

12. Several gangs of kids in the neighborhood are cleaning up the empty lot on the corner.

QUESTIONS

?

for DISCUSSION

1. Do we ever need the stand-in auxiliary *do* for a passive sentence? Why or why not?

2. What do you know about a verb when it has two forms of *be* as auxiliaries?

3. In the Classroom Applications section of Chapter 4, you read about turning statements into questions using what we call tag-questions. Do the same with the following sentences—that is, add tag-questions:

> There's a good movie on television tonight, _____?
>
> There were a lot of students absent today, _____?

Now explain why some linguists prefer to call *there* the subject of the sentence rather than an expletive. Give other evidence to support or refute that position.

4. In Chapter 3 we looked briefly at sentence variations that help us distinguish verb–particle combinations (phrasal verbs) from verb–adverb combinations:

> We jumped up. → Up we jumped.
>
> We made up. → *Up we made.

The cleft and *it* transformations, introduced in this chapter, can also be useful in identifying properties of verbs:

> He came by the office in a big hurry.
>
> He came by his fortune in an unusual manner.
>
> Where he came was by the office.
>
> *Where he came was by his fortune.
>
> Joe turned on the bridge and looked around.
>
> Joe turned on the light and looked around.
>
> It was on the bridge that Joe turned and looked around.
>
> *It was on the light that Joe turned and looked around.

Here are some other pairs that look alike. Use transformations to demonstrate their differences:

> The student looked up the word.
>
> The teacher looked up the hall.

Sharon called up the stairs.

Karen called up the club members.

An old jalopy turned into the driveway.

Cinderella's coach turned into a pumpkin.

CLASSROOM APPLICATIONS

1. Examine the following newspaper headlines. You'll notice that some have incomplete verb phrases. Rewrite the headlines to complete the verbs, then identify their sentence patterns. (Note: You'll have to pay attention to voice—active or passive—in identifying the patterns.)

> Dissidents form action committee. (Pattern _____)
>
> Hurricane kills seven. (Pattern _____)
>
> Six found guilty of extortion. (Pattern _____)
>
> Team vies for championship. (Pattern _____)
>
> Battle of Verdun remembered in ceremony. (Pattern _____)
>
> Candidates ready for runoff election. (Pattern _____)
>
> Woman injured in crash. (Pattern _____)
>
> Fulbright scholarships awarded to two. (Pattern _____)

Check the headlines of your local paper. Which patterns do you find? Do you find any difference in the patterns used for sports headlines and those heading general news?

2. The following paragraph is from an article on whales by Virginia Morell in the February 2008 issue of *Smithsonian:*

The humpback's haunting songs are among the most complex animal vocalizations. They have a hierarchical syntax, one of the basic elements of language, according to recent studies. That is, they sing units of sound that together form a phrase. The phrases *are repeated* in patterns known as themes. Each song *is composed* of anywhere from two to nine themes, and the themes *are sung* in a specific order. Some phrases sound like the low moan of a cello, while others are more like the chirp of a songbird. (p. 62)

Note the three underlined clauses. In each case, the passive voice has enabled the writer to use a known element in subject position, with the new information—the reason for the sentence—in the predicate, the position of main focus.

Is there a way the author could have been just as effective without using the passive voice? Imagine that you are the author—and your teacher has asked you to revise the paragraph, declaring the passive voice out of bounds. Working in groups, see if you and your classmates can improve on the original author's version, using only the active voice.

Expanding the Sentence

I n this section we will take up three methods of expanding sentences: modification, noun phrase substitution, and coordination. You first learned about modification in Chapter 2, when you added adverbs to verb phrases and adjectives to noun phrases and prepositional phrases to both. In Chapters 6 and 7 you'll see other structures, as well as these, that function as adverbials and adjectivals. In Chapter 8 you'll see verb phrases and clauses that fill noun phrase slots; in Chapter 9, modifiers of the sentence as a whole; and in Chapter 10, the expansion of the sentence and its parts by means of coordination.

FORM AND FUNCTION

One way to organize all of these new details of sentence structure is to think in terms of form and function. The labels designating **form** that you have learned include the names of word classes such as noun, verb, adjective, adverb, preposition, and conjunction; the various phrases you have come to recognize—noun phrase, verb phrase, prepositional phrase—are also form designations. We recognize, and can label, the form of a structure like *the puppy* as a noun phrase and *on the porch* as a prepositional phrase on the basis of their forms. That is, we need not see these structures in sentences in order to recognize their forms. Until we give those structures a context, however, we have no way of discussing their **functions**. In Chapter 3, you'll recall, we saw a prepositional phrase functioning in two ways, as both an adjectival and an adverbial:

The puppy <u>on the porch</u> is sleeping.

The puppy is sleeping <u>on the porch</u>.

Only when it's in a larger structure can we discuss a word or a phrase in terms of both form and function. In the chapters that follow, the sentence expansions include verb phrases and clauses functioning as adverbials and adjectivals and nominals.

The following outline will be helpful to you in understanding the two-sided analysis of form and function and in organizing the details of sentence expansions.

FORM	FUNCTION
Word	*Adverbial*
noun	modifier of verb
verb	
adjective	*Adjectival*
adverb	subject complement
	object complement
Phrase	modifier of noun
noun phrase	
verb phrase	*Nominal*
gerund	subject
infinitive	subject complement
participle	direct object
prepositional phrase	indirect object
	object complement
Clause	object of preposition
independent clause (sentence)	appositive
dependent clause	
nominal	*Sentence Modifier*
adverbial (subordinate)	
adjectival (relative)	

You'll discover that all of the general functions listed on the right—adverbial, adjectival, nominal, and sentence modifier—can be carried out by all of the general forms listed on the left—words, phrases, and clauses. As an illustration of this principle, turn to the table of contents and read the headings for Chapter 6. You will see that the chapter title names and defines a function: "Modifiers of the Verb: Adverbials." The major subheadings name the five forms that carry out that function: Adverbs, Prepositional Phrases, Noun Phrases, Verb Phrases, and Clauses.

In this section of the book we will again use the sentence diagram to illustrate the various ways of expanding sentences, first with adverbials, then with adjectivals, nominals, and coordinated structures. The sentences are beginning to get long and complex, it's true; however, if you remember to consider the two-sided analysis of form and function, the diagrams will enhance your understanding. Each of the various forms we have discussed—noun phrase, prepositional phrase, verb phrase, clause—has a particular diagram, no matter what its function in the sentence. For example, a prepositional phrase is always diagrammed as a two-part structure, with the preposition on the diagonal line and the object of the preposition on the attached horizontal line; a noun phrase is always diagrammed with the headword on the horizontal line and its modifiers attached below it.

Always begin your analysis of a sentence by identifying the underlying pattern, one of the ten basic sentences you diagrammed in Chapter 3. Then analyze each of the slots to see how it has been expanded. If you take these expansions one step at a time, asking yourself questions about form and function, you'll come to understand the system that produces the sentences of your language.

In these five chapters on sentence expansion, you will be building on your knowledge of the basic sentence patterns. It might be a good idea at this point to revisit Chapter 3, to review the sentence patterns.

Modifiers of the Verb: Adverbials

CHAPTER 6

CHAPTER PREVIEW

When you studied the sentence patterns in Chapter 3, you learned that in addition to their various required slots all ten patterns can include "optional slots," where we add information about time, place, reason, manner, purpose, and so on. Except for Pattern I and a few other verbs where the adverbial of time or place is required, the sentence patterns are grammatical without that information; that's what we mean by "optional." But of course that doesn't mean that the adverbial information is unimportant. In fact, that information is sometimes the very reason for the sentence.

In the introduction to Part III, you learned that the term "adverbial" names a function that is defined as "modifier of the verb." By the end of this chapter, you will be able to

- Identify and use five structures that add adverbial information: *single-word adverbs, prepositional phrases, nouns and noun phrases, verb phrases,* and *clauses.*
- Identify and correct *dangling infinitives.*
- Distinguish between dependent and independent clauses.
- Define and recognize the differences among *complex sentences, compound sentences,* and *compound-complex sentences.*
- Punctuate adverbials.

THE MOVABLE ADVERBIALS

In the following sentence, each of the underlined structures—an adverb, a prepositional phrase, and a clause—adds adverbial information to the verb *gasped:*

> The audience gasped <u>nervously</u> <u>throughout the theater</u> <u>when the magician thrust his sword into the box.</u>
>
> The audience gasped (*How?*) nervously.
>
> The audience gasped (*Where?*) throughout the theater.
>
> The audience gasped (*When?*) when the magician thrust his sword into the box.

Even though all the adverbials in the preceding sentence follow the verb, there is really no fixed slot for most adverbials; in fact, movability is one of their most telling characteristics—and, for the writer, one of the most useful. In the preceding sentence, for example, there are several possibilities for ordering the three adverbials:

> When the magician thrust his sword into the box, the audience nervously gasped throughout the theater.
>
> Throughout the theater the audience gasped nervously when the magician thrust his sword into the box.

The position may depend on the writer's emphasis, on the rhythm of the sentence, on its relation to the previous sentence, or simply on the desire for sentence variety. Other structures that provide adverbial information are noun phrases and verb phrases. In this chapter we will take up each of these forms in its role as adverbial.

ADVERBS

The words we recognize as adverbs most readily are the **adverbs of manner**—the *-ly* words, such as *nervously, quietly,* and *suddenly.* These adverbs, derived from adjectives, usually tell "how" or "in what manner" about verbs:

They gasped nervously	=	in a nervous manner
They talked quietly	=	in a quiet manner
It stopped suddenly	=	in a sudden manner

The manner adverbs are probably the most movable of all the adverbials; they can appear before or after the verb, as well as at the beginning or end of the sentence:

> <u>Suddenly</u> the wind shifted.
>
> The wind <u>suddenly</u> shifted.
>
> The wind shifted <u>suddenly</u>.

Notice that all three versions of the sentence are diagrammed the same; the only clue to word order is capitalization:

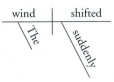

A single-word adverb can even come within the verb string, between the auxiliary word and the main verb:

The roof was <u>suddenly</u> blown off by a strong gust of wind.

Or between auxiliaries:

I have <u>actually</u> been working on my term project.

In all positions the manner adverbs can be marked by qualifiers, words such as *very, quite, so,* and *rather:*

<u>Quite suddenly</u> the crowd grew restless.
The old woman crooned <u>very softly</u>.
The airline employees handled our luggage <u>rather carelessly</u>.

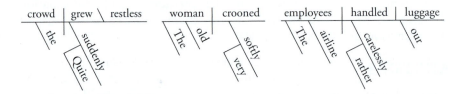

Like the adjectives they are derived from, these adverbs can be made comparative and superlative with *more* and *most:*

<u>More suddenly</u> than the police expected, the crowd grew restless.
The minister spoke <u>most eloquently</u> at the memorial service.

Besides the *-ly* adverbs, many other single-word adverbs provide information of time, place, frequency, and the like: *now, then, nowadays, today, often, always, sometimes, seldom, never, here, there, everywhere,* and many others.

I <u>still</u> jog <u>here</u> <u>sometimes</u>.
I <u>very seldom</u> eat dessert.

Some of these, like the manner adverbs, can be compared and qualified:

> I should jog <u>more often</u>.
>
> Nowadays Judd and Betty jog <u>quite often</u>.

Although movability is a characteristic of all single-word adverbs, the various subclasses are bound by certain restrictions as to order. For example, in the following sentence, the adverbials of place and time cannot be reversed:

> I am going <u>there</u> <u>now</u>.
>
> *I am going <u>now</u> <u>there</u>.
>
> <u>Now</u> I am going <u>there</u>.
>
> *<u>There</u> I am going <u>now</u>.

The rules governing the order and movement of adverbs are quite complex, but as native speakers we are unaware of that complexity; our linguistic computers are programmed to follow the rules automatically.

ELL Issues   Always

The adverb *always* isn't quite as movable as some of the other time adverbials: It doesn't fit comfortably at the beginning or the end of the sentence. It likes the preverb position, where it may be given a beat of stress and has the meaning of *habitually:*

> I always order a medium pizza.
>
> Joe always works late on Fridays.

Sometimes in that position it is given extra heavy stress—and when it is, the speaker is probably expressing annoyance rather than explaining someone's habitual behavior:

> Mac ALWAYS orders the extra-large pizza.
>
> Joe ALWAYS works late on Fridays.

Investigating Language   6.1

The adverbs of frequency, such as those in these six sentences, are among our most movable. In terms of meaning, some are positive and some negative.

1. My friends and I have pizza <u>frequently</u>.
2. <u>Occasionally</u> I order mushrooms.
3. <u>Sometimes</u> I order extra cheese.

4.   <u>Seldom</u> do I order hot sausage.

5.   <u>Never</u> will I order anchovies.

6.   I <u>rarely</u> finish the whole thing.

The movability of these adverbs enables us to change the emphasis in subtle ways. Interestingly, however, the six adverbs in this list don't always behave alike. Notice what has happened in sentences 4 and 5: How do the auxiliaries in those two differ? What rule goes into effect with these "negative" adverbs? What will happen to sentence 6 when you attempt a shift to the opening position?

PREPOSITIONAL PHRASES

The **prepositional phrase** is our most common structure of modification, appearing regularly as a modifier of both nouns and verbs, as we have seen in our sample sentences throughout the chapters.

Prepositional Phrase

Preposition	Object
throughout	the theater
during	the Christmas break
for	my sake
according to	the weather report
instead of	the elevator
over	the rainbow
because of	his stubborn streak
without	your cooperation

As you learned in Chapter 3, the diagram for the adverbial prepositional phrase is always attached to the verb:

Some prepositional phrases have modifiers that qualify or intensify them, just as adjectives and adverbs do:

He arrived <u>shortly</u> before noon.

The house was built <u>directly</u> over the water.

In the diagram the modifier will be attached to the preposition:

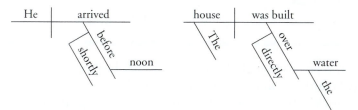

Sentences often have more than one adverbial prepositional phrase:

We hiked <u>in the woods</u> <u>for several hours</u> <u>on Saturday</u>.

And like adverbs, adverbial prepositional phrases can occupy several positions, with those referring to time often more movable than those referring to place, especially when both appear in the same sentence:

<u>For several hours</u> <u>on Saturday</u> we hiked in the woods.
<u>On Saturday</u> we hiked <u>in the woods</u> <u>for several hours</u>.

We are less likely to say:

<u>In the woods</u> we hiked <u>on Saturday</u> <u>for several hours</u>.

In general, an adverbial with a main focus will occupy a slot at or near the end of the sentence. But no matter where in the sentence they appear—whether at the beginning, the middle, or the end—in the diagram the adverbial prepositional phrases will be attached to the verb:

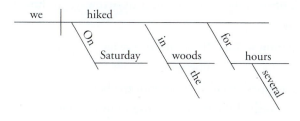

Exercise 17

Diagram the following sentences, paying particular attention to the adverbials. Your first step should be to identify the sentence pattern.

1. In winter we burn wood for our heat.
2. We can heat our house very efficiently in cold weather because of its good insulation.
3. My roommate just went to the store for a loaf of bread.
4. She'll be here in a minute.

5. Computers throughout the world are constantly being invaded by viruses.

6. Man is by nature a political animal. [Aristotle]

Because prepositional phrases can modify both verbs and nouns, ambiguity is fairly common. The prepositional phrase in the following sentence, for example, could be interpreted as meaning either "with whom" or "which problems":

They discussed their problems <u>with the teacher</u>.

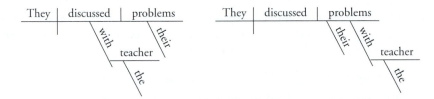

In speech, meaning is rarely a problem, and when it is, the listener can ask for clarification. But the solitary reader has no one to ask, "What do you mean?" or "How's that again?" So the writer has an obligation to make such questions unnecessary. Understanding when modifiers are ambiguous is important for writers; avoiding ambiguity is a requirement of clear writing.

Exercise 18

Rewrite each of the following sentences in two ways to show its two possible meanings:

1. I'm going to wax the car in the garage.
2. We watched the game on the porch.
3. Fred tripped his teammate with the bat.
4. Susan washed the stones she found in the river.

NOUNS AND NOUN PHRASES

Nouns and noun phrases that function adverbially form a fairly short list designating time, place, manner, and quantity. Here are some of them:

We walked <u>home</u>. _____

I'm leaving <u>Monday morning</u>. _____

I'm going <u>your way</u>. _____

<u>Every day</u> he studied <u>two hours</u>. _____

I travel <u>a great deal</u>. _____

We are flying <u>tourist class</u>. _____

I sent the package <u>airmail</u>. _____

The Boy Scouts hiked <u>single file</u> down the trail. _____

He arrived <u>this evening</u>. _____

These noun phrases may look suspiciously like direct objects or subject complements, but if you remember to think about the kind of information that adverbials contribute to the sentence, you should have no trouble in recognizing them as adverbials. In the blank following each sentence, write the adverbial question that the noun phrase answers.

These noun phrases work like prepositional phrases—like prepositional phrases with missing prepositions. The traditional grammarian labels them **adverbial objectives** and diagrams them as though they were the objects in prepositional phrases:

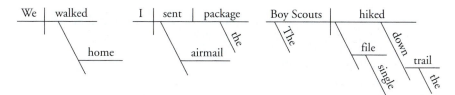

In some of these sentences the preposition is optional: (*on*) Monday morning, (*for*) two hours, (*by*) airmail, (*in*) single file. This method of diagramming the adverbial noun phrase acknowledges both its *form*—a noun headword on a horizontal line with or without modifiers—and its *function*—a modifier of the verb.

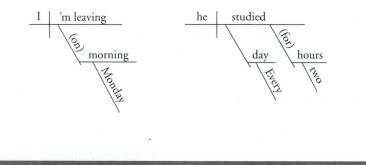

Investigating Language 6.2

In Chapter 3, when you first studied the sentence patterns, you were advised to think in terms of the referents of the NPs in determining the sentence patterns. For example, you can distinguish Pattern V,

Carmen became a doctor [NP$_1$ V NP$_1$]

from Pattern VII,

>   Carmen called a doctor [NP₁ V NP₂]

by recognizing the relationship that the two NPs have to each other. That is, when the NP that follows the verb has a referent different from that of the subject, you can assume that it's a direct object and that the verb is transitive.

In Chapter 5, you learned about another test for determining if a verb is transitive: Can you make the sentence passive? Can you say "A doctor was called (by Carmen)"? In this case, the answer is yes. This means that the verb is transitive and the sentence is Pattern VII.

Now we come to a complication of sorts—sentences that look like Pattern VII:

>   We arrived home.

>   I work Sundays.

In both cases the verb is followed by an NP with a referent different from that of the subject. What test can you apply to show that *arrived* and *work* are not transitive verbs?

Here's a pair that might fool you. How can you show that they belong to different patterns? What tests can you apply?

>   Terry is flying the plane.

>   Terry is flying first class.

You'll want to bear in mind the kind of information that adverbials and direct objects contribute, the kinds of questions that they answer. Consider also the possibility of an optional preposition.

Exercise 19

Underline the adverbials in the following sentences and identify their forms. Then identify the sentence patterns. In making your judgments, you'll want to think about the kind of information that each slot contributes to the sentence.

1. Pete is working nights this week.
2. I was awake the whole night.
3. I'll see you soon.
4. This morning Pam threw away the leftover spaghetti.
5. George will do dishes next time.
6. I love weekends.
7. Bill works weekends.
8. At the first sign of winter the birds flew south.

VERB PHRASES

The most common form of the verb in an adverbial role is the **infinitive**, the base form of the verb with *to:*

Mom cashed a check <u>to give Jody her allowance</u>.

I went home early <u>to relax before the party</u>.

Jennifer took on two paper routes <u>to earn money for camp</u>.

Remember that the infinitives—*to give, to relax,* and *to earn*—are not simply verbs with *to;* they are entire verb phrases, complete with complements and modifiers. But unlike the predicating verb strings, these infinitive phrases have no tense, so they are called non-finite—that is, infinitive.

Underlying the first infinitive phrase is a Pattern VIII sentence:

Mom gave Jody her allowance.

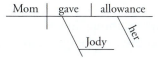

When we turn that predicate into an infinitive, the relationship of the complements and the verb stays the same, as the following diagram shows. We have a Pattern VIII infinitive, an adverbial that tells why, in a Pattern VII sentence:

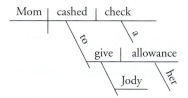

At first glance you may confuse the infinitive with a prepositional phrase, such as *to school* or *to the store; to* appears in both constructions, and the traditional diagrams are similar. But there is an important difference in form: In the prepositional phrase, a noun phrase follows *to;* in the infinitive, a verb phrase follows *to.*

Underlying the *relax* infinitive phrase in the second example is a Pattern VI sentence; underlying the *earn* phrase in the third example is a Pattern VII sentence:

I relaxed before the party.   Jennifer earned money for camp.

The Pattern VI sentence is now a Pattern VI infinitive phrase; the Pattern VII sentence is now a Pattern VII infinitive phrase. The *relax* phrase has been added to a Pattern VI sentence (*I went home early*), the *earn* phrase to a Pattern VII (*Jennifer took on two paper routes*):

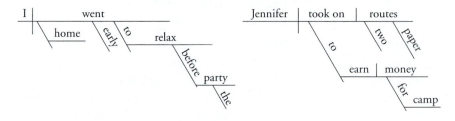

Note, too, that the subjects of the sentences are also the subjects of the infinitives.

In the first and third sentences, where the infinitive phrases follow nouns, *check* and *routes*, they may appear to modify those nouns. The clue that says otherwise is the meaning "in order to" that underlies almost all adverbial infinitives; they answer the question *why*:

> Mom cashed a check **in order to** give Jody her allowance.
>
> I went home early **in order to** relax before the party.
>
> Jennifer took on two paper routes **in order to** earn money for camp.

In fact, we often include *in order*, especially in the introductory position:

> In order to earn money for camp, Jennifer took on two paper routes.

In diagramming the expanded version, you can treat it like a phrasal preposition, with "in order to" on the diagonal line.

There are exceptions. Occasionally an infinitive functions adverbially without the meaning of "in order to," but such sentences are uncommon in speech:

> The detective glanced out the window only to see the suspect slip around the corner.
>
> I arrived at the auditorium only to find every seat taken.

These infinitives have an almost main-verb rather than adverbial quality. We could, and probably would, more often say:

> The detective glanced out the window and saw the suspect slip around the corner.
>
> I arrived at the auditorium and found every seat taken.

Other exceptions, which are fairly common idioms, occur with the verbs *come* and *live*. Here too the infinitive has main-verb status:

> I've <u>come to believe</u> in UFOs.
>
> I've <u>come to understand</u> your point of view.
>
> You'll <u>live to regret</u> that remark.

Dangling Infinitives. We noted that the subject of the sentence is also the subject of the adverbial infinitive. When this is not the case, the infinitive is said to "dangle." In the following sentences, the infinitive phrases have no stated subject:

> <u>To keep farm machinery in good repair</u>, a regular maintenance schedule is necessary.
>
> For decades the Superstition Mountains in Arizona have been explored in order <u>to find the fabled Lost Dutchman Mine</u>.

Certainly the problem with these sentences is not a problem of communication; the reader is not likely to misinterpret their meaning. But in both cases a kind of fuzziness exists that can be cleared up with the addition of a subject for the infinitive:

> <u>A farmer</u> needs a regular maintenance schedule <u>to keep the farm machinery in good repair</u>.
>
> For decades <u>people</u> [or <u>adventurers</u> or <u>prospectors</u>] have explored the Superstition Mountains in Arizona <u>to find the fabled Lost Dutchman Mine</u>.

Usage Matters **The "Split" Infinitive**

This term *split infinitive* is actually a misnomer (that's why the quotation marks are there in the heading). The infinitive is a single word, the base form of the verb; and for all verbs except *be*, the infinitive has the same form as present tense. The word *to* that usually introduces the infinitive (sometimes called "the sign of the infinitive") enables a verb phrase to function as an adverbial or adjectival or nominal. The infinitive phrase will often include modifiers and complements.

For example, note that in the following Pattern VII sentence there's an adverb in the position before the verb and a noun phrase as the direct object:

> We <u>finally</u> located <u>the road to the beach</u>.

When we turn this predicate into an infinitive phrase by adding *to* and changing the verb to its base (infinitive) form, it can become part of another sentence. Here it functions as an appositive, renaming *It*:

It took almost an hour <u>to finally locate the road to the beach</u>.

Here it's the subject:

<u>To finally locate the road to the beach</u> was a relief.

Note that *finally* precedes the verb in the infinitive phrase, just as it does in the sentence pattern that underlies it. It is that position, between *to* and the infinitive, that is called the "split" and sometimes mistakenly faulted as an error.

We know, of course, that adverbials come in many forms in addition to simple adverbs and that they are movable. In the position before the verb, however, single-word adverbs are the most common; multi-word phrases are fairly rare. And they're the ones that tend to sound awkward. So it makes sense that they would sound awkward in infinitive phrases too. We might say

Our family now and then has waffles for dinner.

But an infinitive phrase made from this sentence would be somewhat awkward; it would call attention to itself:

We like to now and then have waffles for dinner.

A reader would likely expect the adverbial *now and then* to either open or close the sentence, rather than to "split" the infinitive.

However, although the adverbial between *to* and the verb may not be the most effective placement in some cases, it is not a grammatical error. And, in the case of single-word adverbials, it is a rather common structure, as in the well-known "Star Trek" opening: "to boldly go where no man has gone before."

Exercise 20

Underline all the adverbial modifiers in the following sentences. Identify the sentence pattern of the main clause and any adverbial phrases. After doing that analysis, you should have no trouble diagramming the sentences.

1. Our cat often jumps up on the roof to reach the attic window.
2. Sometimes she even climbs the ladder to get there.
3. Last night my computer blinked ominously during an electrical storm.
4. I immediately turned it off.

5. We went to the mall last Saturday to check out the big sales.
6. Afterwards we stayed home to watch the playoff game with Uncle Dick.

Participles as Adverbials. Although we have traditionally thought of the participle as an adjectival (and that is certainly its more common role), some participles and participle phrases clearly have an adverbial function, providing information of time, place, reason, and manner, as other adverbials do:

> My uncle made a fortune <u>selling real estate</u>. (*How?*)
>
> The kids came <u>running out of the house</u>. (*How? Where?*)

The adverbial participle phrase is diagrammed below the verb, as other adverbials are:

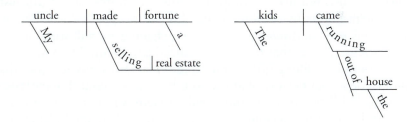

CLAUSES

What is a **clause**? When is a clause adverbial?

The label *clause* denotes a form: a group of words with a subject and a predicate. The ten sentence patterns described in Chapter 3 have this form. The branching diagram, you'll recall, illustrates the two parts:

In other words, the ten sentence patterns are essentially clause patterns.

From the standpoint of mechanical conventions, we can define **sentence** as a word or group of words that begins with a capital letter and ends with a period or other terminal punctuation. A more complete definition would read as follows:

> A *sentence* is a word or group of words based on one or more subject–predicate, or clause, patterns; the written sentence begins with a capital letter and ends with terminal punctuation.

This definition eliminates "Wow!" and "The very idea!" and "Rats!" as sentences, but it includes commands, such as "Help!" with its underlying subject–predicate "You help me." All sentences, then, are clauses, *but not all clauses are sentences.*

At the opening of this chapter we saw a *when* clause in the sentence about the magician:

> The audience gasped nervously throughout the theater <u>when the magician thrust his sword into the box.</u>

Without the word *when*, this clause would be a complete sentence. The subordinating conjunction *when*, however, turns it into a **dependent clause**—in this case, a dependent clause functioning as an adverbial.

The term *dependent clause*, in contrast to **independent clause**, refers to any clause that is not itself a complete sentence. Another set of contrasting labels traditionally given to clauses (in addition to *independent* and *dependent*) is *main* and *subordinate*. In later chapters we will see other dependent clauses, some that function as adjectivals, modifying nouns, and others as nominals, filling NP slots. In traditional terms, any sentence that includes a dependent clause of any kind is known as a **complex sentence**. A sentence with two or more independent clauses is a **compound sentence**. And one with a dependent clause and more than one independent clause is called **compound-complex**.

The most common subordinating conjuctions that introduce adverbial clauses are *if, after, because, before, since, so, until, when,* and *while*. Here in the adverbial chapter you will see examples of clauses that answer such adverbial questions as *when* and *why*, as you'll see in the following sentences:

> You should eat some breakfast <u>before you take that exam.</u>
>
> Pay close attention to your e-mail <u>because a virus could be lurking there.</u>

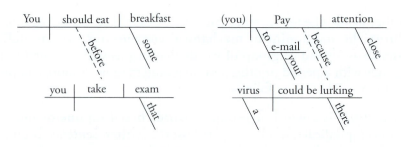

At first glance these sentence diagrams may look complicated, but as you can see, they are simply two sentence patterns connected by the subordinator that introduces the adverbial clause. Note too that the adverbial *because* clause itself includes an adverbial—the adverb *there*.

Exercise	**21**

Diagram the sentences, paying particular attention to all the sentence patterns, those of adverbial verb phrases and clauses, as well as of main clauses. Remember, too, that any adverbial that includes a verb (as clauses and verb phrases do) can also include other adverbials.

1. We will be visiting Yellowstone Park this summer, when we drive across the country in our new hybrid.
2. Last year we stayed at Silver Falls State Park for three days during our vacation in Oregon.
3. Whenever our dog sees lightning or hears thunder, he scratches frantically at the door to get our attention.
4. Is Mike really moving to Memphis to look for a job after he graduates?
5. I never take the subway home at night because my family worries about me.
6. After our building was burglarized twice in one month, we searched the ads to find a new apartment.

PUNCTUATION OF ADVERBIALS

You may have noticed in the examples that some opening adverbials are set off by commas and some are not. Their punctuation is sometimes a matter of choice, especially in the case of phrases. Generally a short prepositional phrase or noun phrase or an adverb will not be set off:

> Saturday morning we all pitched in and cleaned the garage.
> By noon we were exhausted.
> Hastily they gathered their books and left the room.

With longer prepositional phrases there is a choice:

> At the top of the hill the hikers sat down to rest.
> At the end of a long and exhausting morning, we all collapsed.

When the end of the adverbial slot is not readily apparent, the comma will be needed to prevent misreading:

> During the winter, vacation days are especially welcome.
>
> In the middle of the night, winds from the north brought subzero temperatures and the end of Indian summer.

The two opening adverbial structures that are *always* set off by commas are verb phrases and clauses—no matter what their length:

> To earn money for camp, Jennifer took on two paper routes.
>
> To succeed, you'll need self-discipline.
>
> When the speech finally ended, the audience broke into applause.

When an adverbial interrupts the verb phrase for a special effect, it will be set off by commas:

> I finally bought, on my birthday, a brand new car.
>
> The stranger asked me, quite openly, for my credit card number.

When the opening phrase is parenthetical—more clearly a comment on the whole sentence than a straightforward adverbial—then a comma is called for:

> According to all the polls, the incumbent was expected to win.
>
> On the other hand, not everyone was surprised at the outcome of the election.
>
> Luckily, no one was hurt.

The punctuation of sentence modifiers is discussed in Chapter 9.

Investigating Language   6.3

It's not at all unusual for inexperienced writers to punctuate subordinate clauses as complete sentences. It's probably the most common sentence fragment that teachers encounter:

> The children have been quite bored this summer. Because the swimming pool has been closed since July.
>
> Apparently the drought is not over yet. Although we had a lot of rain last spring.

In the second example, what's the difference between *although* and *apparently?*

If you listen carefully to the intonation of subordinate clauses and complete sentences, you will hear the difference. Read the clauses aloud:

> because you were here
>
> since Joe went away
>
> if he knows the truth

Now read them without the subordinator:

> You were here.
>
> Joe went away.
>
> He knows the truth.

You can probably hear the pitch of your voice dropping at the end of the last three. In the set with subordinators, your pitch would normally stay more level on the last word. (Even if you didn't read them with that contrast, you probably could do so to illustrate the difference.)

There's another way of reading that first group: as if they were answers to questions. In fact, such sentence fragments are common in conversation:

Q. Why did you come back?   A. Because you were here.

Q. How long have you lived alone?   A. Since Joe went away.

Q. Will Mike ever forgive you?   A. If he knows the truth.

Does this reading help explain why writers make punctuation errors? What can a writing teacher do to help students understand and correct their punctuation? (You can read about known and new information in Chapter 15 on pages 311–312.)

CHAPTER 6
Key Terms

Adverb	Independent clause
Adverbial	Infinitive
Adverbial clause	Main clause
Adverbial infinitive	Movability
Adverbial noun phrase	Prepositional phrase
Adverbial participle	Sentence
Adverbial prepositional phrase	Sentence fragment
Ambiguity	Split infinitive
Clause	Subordinate clause
Dangling infinitive	Subordinating conjunction
Dependent clause	

Sentences
for PRACTICE

Underline the adverbials in the following sentences and identify their forms. For additional practice, identify the sentence patterns and diagram the sentences. Remember also to identify the sentence patterns of the adverbial verb phrases and clauses.

1. By the end of the fifth inning, the playoff game had already become boring.

2. When the fall foliage shows its colors in New England, thousands of tourists go there to enjoy nature's astonishing display.

3. On Halloween night the neighborhood children rang every doorbell on the block to fill their bags with goodies.

4. The recent crisis in mortgage foreclosures may have occurred because most home loans these days pass through a nationwide chain of brokers, lenders, and investors.

5. According to the National Highway Traffic Safety Administration, almost 80 percent of crashes and 65 percent of near crashes involve some form of driver inattention.

6. To cut down on traffic accidents, some cities have recently declared the use of cell phones off-limits for drivers.

7. Cowards die many times before their death. [Shakespeare]

8. Be silent always when you doubt your sense. [Alexander Pope]

9. Susan plans to stay home on Friday afternoon to fix a special gourmet dinner for her roommates.

10. During the month of December there are always dozens of holiday specials on television.

11. Where were you when I needed a shove to get my car to the garage for repairs?

12. Never in the field of human conflict was so much owed by so many to so few. [Winston Churchill]

QUESTIONS
?
for DISCUSSION

1. How would you analyze the following sentences, which were spoken in a television interview by an attorney whose client had been accused of murder?

You're not talking a traffic ticket here. You're talking somebody's life.

In considering the sentence patterns and the referents of the noun
phrases, you might think that *talking* is a transitive verb. Is it?

2. How do you account for the difference in meaning of the fol-
    lowing sentences? Why is "in the mountains" so important?

    After his retirement, Professor Jones lived for six months in
    the mountains.

    After his retirement, Professor Jones lived for six months.

3. As you know, single-word adverbs are often movable, produc-
    ing a number of variations in a sentence. How many acceptable
    variations can you produce by adding the adverb *frequently* to
    the following sentence?

    I have had colds this year.

Are there any slots in the sentence where *frequently* is clearly
unacceptable?

CLASSROOM APPLICATION

Compose a cinquain (pronounced "sin-cane")—a five-line poem
in which the number of syllables increases with each line—about
an action or feeling; in other words, your topic is a verb. For
the five lines, use the five forms of adverbials you studied in this
chapter: adverb, prepositional phrase, noun phrase, verb phrase,
and clause—preferably in that order. The title of your poem will
be the verb (or, possibly, a verb + direct object or a verb +
subject complement) that you're expanding with the five
adverbials. Here is an example:

Waiting

Here

For you

One last time

To plead my case

Because you promised to listen

Here are some possible titles for you to try: Sleeping, Studying
Grammar, Worrying, Playing Soccer, Feeling Special, Making
Friends, Skiing, Thinking.

CHAPTER 7

Modifiers of the Noun: Adjectivals

CHAPTER PREVIEW

The traditional definition of *adjective* is "a word that modifies a noun." Like the word *adverb*, however, *adjective* refers to a word class with particular characteristics, not to a grammatical function. That traditional definition, then, turns out to denote an *adjectival*, the topic of this chapter. By now you've probably come to realize that the adjective is only one of many structures that modify nouns. In this chapter, you'll examine other forms and structures that function as adjectivals.

By the end of this chapter, you will be able to

- Understand the ways noun phrases can be expanded.

- Identify and punctuate preheadword modifiers: *determiners, adjectives, nouns,* and *participles*.

- Recognize and use postheadword modifiers: *prepositional phrases, relative clauses,* and *participial phrases*.

- Identify and correct *dangling participles*.

- Understand the distinction between *restrictive* and *nonrestrictive modifiers*.

- Recognize when *infinitives, noun phrases,* and *adverbs* function as postnoun modifiers.

As you know, a noun phrase occupies at least one slot in every sentence pattern—that of subject. In six of the ten patterns, noun phrases occupy one or more slots in the predicate as well: direct object, indirect object, subject complement, and object complement; the noun phrase also serves as the object of the preposition. Most of the NPs used in the sample sentences have been simple two-word phrases: determiner + headword (*the students, a scholar, an apple, their homework*). But in the sentences we actually speak and write, the noun phrases are frequently expanded with modifiers—not only with adjectives, the basic noun modifier, but with other forms as well. In preheadword position we use nouns as well as adjectives—and, as we'll see later in the chapter, single-word participles:

> We live next door to an *orange* house.
>
> My cousin lives in a *brick* house.

In postheadword position we use prepositional phrases, participial phrases, and relative clauses:

> <u>The house *on the corner*</u> is new. (prepositional phrase)
>
> <u>That house *covered with ivy*</u> looks haunted. (verb phrase)
>
> This is <u>the house *that Jack built*</u>. (clause)

We can think of the noun phrase as a series of slots (in much the same way as we looked at the expanded verb), with the determiner and noun headword as the required slots and the modifiers before and after the headword as optional:

NOUN

NP = <u>Det</u> (__) (__) <u>HEAD-</u> (__) (__) (__)

WORD

Filling the **headword** slot in the noun phrase is, of course, the noun, the word signaled by the determiner. (In the previous list of sample sentences, the word *house* fills the headword slot of the underlined noun phrases.) Traditional grammarians define noun as "the name of a person, place, or thing"—a definition based on meaning. That definition works in a limited way. But a better way to identify nouns, as you learned in Chapter 2, is to put your innate language ability to work: Is the word signaled by a determiner—or could it be? Can you make it plural? Also, an understanding of the system of pre- and postnoun modifiers in the noun phrase will make the identification of the noun headword an easy matter.

Recognition of the headword of the noun phrase can also help in preventing problems of subject–verb agreement. Such problems can arise when a postheadword modifier includes a noun itself:

> *The stack of instruction <u>forms</u> were misplaced.

> *The complicated instructions on the new income tax <u>form</u> really confuses me.

With just a few exceptions, it is the number, either singular or plural, of the headword in the subject noun phrase that dictates the form of the verb in the present tense. In the preceding sentences, the writer has used the wrong noun in making the verb selection. *Stack* and *instructions* are the headwords; *forms* and *form* are simply parts of postnoun modifiers.

The <u>stack</u> was misplaced.

The <u>stack</u> of instruction forms was misplaced.

The <u>instructions</u> really confuse me.

The <u>complicated instructions on the new income tax form</u> really confuse me.

The exceptions to this system involve noun phrases with certain **collective nouns** and pronouns in which the modifier rather than the headword determines the verb:

<u>A bunch</u> of my friends <u>are</u> coming over for dinner.
<u>Some</u> of the cookies <u>are</u> missing.
<u>Some</u> of the cake <u>is</u> missing.

This topic, along with other details of determiners, is discussed further in the "Determiner" section of Chapter 13.

THE DETERMINER

The determiner, one of the structure classes, is the word class that signals nouns. This class includes *articles, possessive nouns, possessive pronouns, demonstrative pronouns,* and *numbers,* as well as a variety of other common words. When you see one of these words, you can be fairly sure you're at the beginning of a noun phrase.

The native speaker rarely thinks about determiners; they are automatic in speech. But for the writer, the determiner's role is something to think about. For example, as the first word of the noun phrase, and thus frequently the first word of the sentence and even of the paragraph, the determiner can provide a bridge, or transition, between ideas. The selection of that bridge can make subtle but important differences in emphasis:

<u>This</u> attempt at reconciliation proved futile.
<u>The</u> attempt at reconciliation . . .

Their attempt . . .

One such attempt . . .

All their attempts . . .

Those attempts . . .

In selecting determiners, writers have the opportunity not only to make such distinctions but also to help their readers move easily from one idea to the next in a meaningful way.

Some nouns, of course, are used without determiners: proper nouns (*John, Berkeley*), noncountable nouns (*salt, water*), abstract nouns (*justice, grief*), and sometimes plural count nouns (*apples, students*). You will read more about these categories in Chapter 12.

ELL Issues | a(n)/the

The distinction between the indefinite article, *a* (or its variation *an*), and the definite *the* is a critical one, not only in the selection of the *there* transformation but in other contexts as well. We select the indefinite *a* at the first mention of a noun, when the specific referent of the noun has not yet been established; but for subsequent mentions, the definite *the* takes over:

> I read a good book last weekend. I bought the book for only a quarter at a garage sale. The sale was just down the block.

Notice that at their second mention, the referents of those nouns have become specific, particular.

ADJECTIVES AND NOUNS

These two word classes generally fill the slots between the determiner and the headword. When the noun phrase includes both an adjective and a noun as modifiers, they appear in that order; they cannot be reversed:

DETERMINER	ADJECTIVE	NOUN	HEADWORD
the	beautiful		house
the		brick	house
our	little	neighbor	boy
an	ancient	marble	bathtub
that	nervous	test	pilot
Bill's	new	kitchen	table

We do not say, "Bill's kitchen new table" or "Our neighbor little boy."

It's fairly common in traditional descriptions of grammar to see these pre-headword nouns labeled as adjectives. However, it is only their function that undergoes a change, not their form. Instead, we recognize what is called **functional shift**. This is the same phenomenon described in the previous chapter, where we saw nouns modifying verbs—in other words, functioning as adverbs do. They retain their identity as nouns while functioning adverbially.

The adjective slot frequently includes more than one adjective; all of them modify the headword:

the funny brown monkey

the little old man

You'll notice that there are no commas in the preceding noun phrases, even though there are several modifiers before the noun. But sometimes commas are called for. A good rule of thumb is to use a comma if it is possible to insert *and* between the modifiers. We would not talk about "a little and old man" or "a funny and brown monkey." However, we would say "a strange and wonderful experience," so in using these two adjectives without *and*, we would use a comma:

a strange, wonderful experience

That comma represents juncture in speech—a pause and slight upward shift in pitch. Read the following pair of sentences aloud and listen to the difference in your voice:

On the table stood a little black suitcase.

On the table stood an ugly, misshapen suitcase.

In general, the system calls for a comma between two adjectives when they are of the same class—for instance, when they are both abstract qualities such as "strange" and "wonderful" or "ugly" and "misshapen." However, in the earlier example—*funny brown monkey*—the adjectives *funny* and *brown* are not alike: "funny" is an abstract, changeable quality, a subjective quality; "brown" is a concrete, permanent quality.

The adjective can also be qualified or intensified:

the extremely bright young lady

a really important career decision

Prenoun Participles. We can also use participles to fill the adjective slot between the determiner and the headword:

> Our <u>snoring</u> visitor kept the household awake.
>
> The <u>barking</u> dog across the street drives us crazy.
>
> A <u>rolling</u> stone gathers no moss.

Because participles are verbs, they are also commonly modified by adverbs:

> Our <u>loudly snoring</u> visitor kept the household awake.
>
> The <u>peacefully sleeping</u> baby was a joy to watch.
>
> We submitted a <u>carefully conceived</u> plan to the administration.

Sometimes we have occasion to use a hyphen to make it clear that the adverbial modifies the prenoun participle, not the headword:

> a half-baked idea
>
> the Spanish-speaking community
>
> a well-developed paragraph
>
> the fast-moving train

The hyphen rule here is fairly straightforward: The *-ly* adverbs (such as *loudly, peacefully,* and *carefully*) do not take hyphens; other adverbs (such as *well* and *fast*) do take hyphens.

Other classes of words also need hyphens when the first modifier applies not to the headword but to the second modifier:

> high-technology industries
>
> two-word verbs
>
> all-around athletes
>
> free-form sculpture

Another occasion for hyphens in the preheadword position occurs when we use a complete phrase in the adjective slot:

> an off-the-wall idea   a middle-of-the-road policy
>
> the end-of-the-term party   my back-to-back exams

In a sentence diagram, these hyphenated modifiers are treated as single entities:

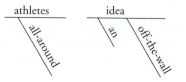

When a phrasal modifier fills the subject complement or an ending adverbial slot in the sentence pattern, however, the hyphens are generally omitted:

> Our party will be <u>at the end of the term</u>.
>
> My exams during finals week are <u>back to back</u>.

In certain idioms they would probably be retained:

> Her idea seemed off-the-wall to me.
>
> The policy he subscribes to is strictly middle-of-the-road.

The position in the sentence can also affect the earlier hyphenated examples:

> The paragraph was well developed.
>
> The industry did research in high technology.

Investigating Language 7.1

Both hyphens and commas can make an important difference in meaning.

- A. You can hyphenate the following sentence in two ways to show two different meanings:

    1. The researchers studied ten year old children.

    2. The researchers studied ten year old children.

Hyphenate sentence 1 to make it clear that the children are of school age. In sentence 2 use the hyphen to show that the children are still babies.

- B. Explain the difference the comma makes in terms of both meaning and word function:

    > Becky is a pretty, intelligent student.

Diagram the sentence in two ways, showing the meaning with and without the comma.

Exercise 22

A. Label the determiner (D) and the headword (H) to each underlined noun phrase in the following paragraph. Identify the form (adjective, noun, participle) of any modifiers that fill the slots between the determiner and headword.

Some movie reviewers say *The Social Network* is a riveting, ambitious example of modern filmmaking. The film's central premise is that a worldwide social revolution began because two middle-class college boys wanted to meet girls. Early in the film a brilliant sequence cuts back and forth between Harvard student Mark Zuckerberg and his Facebook cofounders working away while a wild party is taking place at one of the exclusive college clubs that Zuckerberg desperately wants to belong to. But instead of making a derisive contrast between the geeks with their computers and the beautiful young things at play, the sequence is really depicting a future entrepreneur and billionaire hard at work making history while the born-to-rule kids are getting drunk.

B. Underline the determiner and headword of each noun phrase in the following sentences. Identify the form of any modifiers that fill slots between them. Punctuate the noun phrases with commas and hyphens, if necessary.

1. The department's personnel committee met in the main office this morning.

2. Our whole family is impressed with the new Sunday brunch menu at the cafeteria.

3. Serena's daughter found an expensive looking copper colored bracelet in the subway station.

4. The bicycle safety commission will discuss the new regulations at their regular meeting this noon.

5. Her lovely gracious manner was apparent from the start.

6. Any mother could easily perform the job of several air traffic controllers.

7. The rising interest rates should be a serious concern for every cost conscious citizen.

The postheadword position in the noun phrase may contain modifiers of many forms; when there is more than one, they appear in this order:

Det	HEADWORD	Prepositional Phrase	Participial Phrase	Relative Clause
the	airplane	on the far runway	waiting to take off	
				which was hijacked by terrorists

In this section we will look at all of these structures that follow the headword, beginning with the most common postnoun modifier, the prepositional phrase.

PREPOSITIONAL PHRASES

The adjectival prepositional phrase, which modifies a noun, is in form identical to the adverbial prepositional phrase described in Chapter 6. In its adjectival role the prepositional phrase identifies the noun headword in relation to time, place, direction, purpose, origin, and the like:

> The *house* <u>on the corner</u> is new.
>
> The security *guard* <u>in our building</u> knows every tenant personally.
>
> I have always admired the lovely *homes* <u>along Sparks Street</u>.
>
> The *meeting* <u>during our lunch hour</u> was a waste of time.
>
> Jack is a *man* <u>of many talents</u>.

An adjectival prepositional phrase helps to identify a noun or pronoun by answering the questions "Which one?" or "What kind of?" Which house is new? The one *on the corner*. Jack is what kind of man? One *of many talents*.

Because the prepositional phrase itself includes a noun phrase, the adjectival prepositional phrase demonstrates the recursiveness of the language—the embedding of one structure in another of the same kind. Such recursiveness occurs in many parts of the sentence: a clause within a clause, a noun phrase within a noun phrase, a verb phrase within a verb phrase. In the case of the adjectival prepositional phrase, we nearly always have a noun phrase within a noun phrase. And we needn't stop with one embedding; we could continue branching that NP at the bottom of the diagram with another Det + N + PP, which would produce yet another NP:

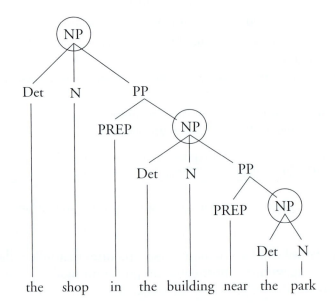

Such strings, though fairly common, especially at the end of the sentence, are sometimes open to ambiguity:

> My sister manages the flower shop in the new brick building near
> the park on Center Street.

Our linguistic computer most readily associates a modifier with the nearest possible referent:

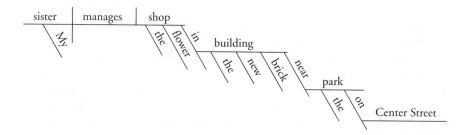

If a different meaning is intended—if, for example, it is the building rather than the park that is on Center Street—the writer must make that clear: "the flower shop in the brick building on Center Street that is near the park."

Exercise 23

Underline the adjectival prepositional phrases in the following sentences. If any of them are ambiguous, rewrite them in two ways to show their two possible meanings unambiguously.

1. A young man with a cast on his left foot hobbled down the street.
2. I will meet you in the lobby of the museum near the visitors' information booth.
3. The party after the game at Bob's house must have been a riot.
4. The threat of computer viruses is causing concern among scientists.
5. The computer world is being threatened by an enemy from within.
6. The textbook for my science course was written by a Nobel laureate from Stanford.
7. The bank will make loans to businesses of any size.
8. The candidates with the weakest qualifications usually have the most complaints about the selection process.

RELATIVE CLAUSES

Like the adverbial clause that modifies verbs, the **relative clause** (also called the **adjectival clause**) is a dependent clause. In its adjectival function, the relative clause identifies the noun or pronoun it modifies—and almost always appears immediately after that noun or pronoun:

> The arrow <u>that has left the bow</u> never returns.

> Relatives are persons <u>who live too near and visit too often</u>.

Like adjectival prepositional phrases, relative clauses answer the questions "Which one?" or "What kind of?" Which arrow? The one *that has left the bow*. What kind of persons? Those *who live too near and visit too often*.

In form, a relative clause is a sentence pattern, complete with a subject and a predicate. The only difference between a relative clause and a complete sentence is the introductory word, the relative pronoun (*who, whose, whom, which,* or *that*). Like other pronouns, the relative pronoun has an **antecedent**, the noun that it refers to and replaces. The traditional diagram clearly shows the relationship of the clause to the noun it modifies:

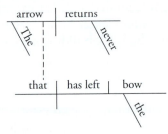

Three features of the relative pronoun will help you to recognize the relative clause: (1) The relative pronoun renames the headword of the noun phrase in which it appears; in our example, *arrow* is the antecedent of *that*. (2) The relative pronoun fills a sentence slot in its own clause; in the example, *that* is in the subject slot. And (3) the relative pronoun introduces the clause, no matter what slot it fills.

Let's look at another example of a relative clause introduced by *that*, perhaps our most common relative pronoun:

> This is the house *that Jack built.*

As the diagram shows, *that* opens its clause, even though it functions as the direct object.

In referring to people, we generally use *who* rather than *that;* and when it functions as an object in its clause, the form we use is *whom,* the **objective case**:

> A man <u>whom I knew in the army</u> phoned me this morning.
>
> The clerk at the post office, <u>to whom I complained about our mail service</u>, was very patient with me.

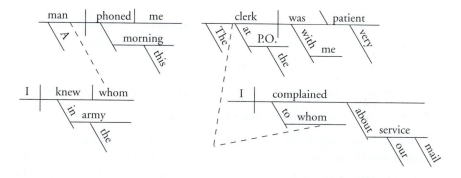

Notice in the second preceding example that *whom* is the object of a preposition. You may have noticed that the preposition, not the relative pronoun, is the first word in the relative clause. This is the only instance where the relative is not the immediate clause opener—that is, when the relative pronoun is the object of a preposition.

The following sentence illustrates the **possessive case** of *who.* Like other possessive pronouns (such as *my, his, their*), *whose* functions as a determiner in its clause:

> The student <u>whose notes I borrowed</u> was absent today.

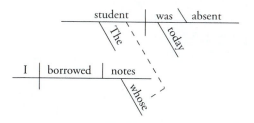

The dotted line connects the pronoun to its antecedent, *the student;* in other words, "whose notes" means "the student's notes."

Another common relative pronoun is *which:*

> *Huckleberry Finn*, <u>which we read in high school</u>, is a classic <u>that often causes controversy</u>.

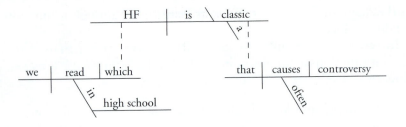

You'll read more about *which* later in the chapter, in connection with punctuation.

The following example illustrates an important feature of sentences in which the relative pronoun *that* is the direct object in its clause:

> You can choose a color <u>that you like</u>.

You will note that this sentence would be equally grammatical without *that:*

> You can choose a color you like.

The relative *that* is often deleted, but the deletion is possible only when the pronoun functions as an object in its clause, not when it acts as the subject.

The objective case relative, *whom*, like the relative *that*, can often be deleted too:

> A woman [whom] my mother knew in high school has invited me to dinner.

Even though the relative pronoun is deleted, it will have a place on the diagram; it is "understood." The deleted word can be shown in brackets, or it can be replaced by an x:

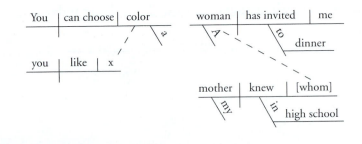

Usage Matters   *Who or Whom*

Grammarians and language experts have been discussing the question of when and whether to use *who* or *whom* for well over two hundred years, with citations that stretch from Shakespeare to the conversations of our own day:

> Who wouldst thou strike? (*The Two Gentlemen of Verona*, 1595)

Consider who the King your father sends,

To whom he sends, and what's his embassy. (*Love's Labour's Lost,* 1595)

Who shall I mail the check to?

Who did you invite for dinner?

In all four of these examples, the pronoun *who* functions as the direct object in its clause. Countless grammar books, dating as far back as 1762, maintain that *who* is incorrect in that position, that *whom* is called for. Why? Because in Latin grammar, the direct object and the object of a preposition require the objective case, not the subjective. But William Safire, in his *New York Times* column "On Language" (June 30, 1996), contends that

> at the beginning of a sentence, *whom* comes across as an affectation. In politics, formality went out with neckties, and what is comfortable to the listener's ear is to be preferred in address.

Safire agrees with many linguists who recognize that at the beginning of a sentence or clause *who* is natural in speech and that *whom* is natural only after a preposition:

To whom shall I mail the check?

If the preposition comes at the end of the sentence, however, we will probably hear *who* in speech:

Who shall I mail the check to?

The written language is a different issue. A writer can usually find a way to avoid both the affectation of *whom* and the "ungrammatical" *who* when the objective case is called for:

Where shall I mail the check?

Who should receive the check?

Another usage issue connected with substitutes for *whom* concerns the use of *that* when referring to people:

A woman that my mother knew in high school has invited me to dinner.

Most handbooks consider this use of *that* unacceptable for formal writing, prescribing the use of *who* when referring to people. In this sentence, the correct form would be the awkward *whom*. Here the obvious solution is to delete the pronoun, as the previous diagram illustrates.

However, when the relative clause is set off by commas, the pronoun cannot be deleted:

Jane Barnard, whom my mother knew in high school, has invited me to dinner.

You can probably find a way to revise this sentence in order to avoid the awkward use of *whom.*

All the relative pronouns fill slots in the clauses that nouns normally fill. However, some adjectival clauses are introduced not by relative pronouns but by the **relative adverbs** *where*, *when*, and *why*. In these clauses the relative adverb replaces an adverbial structure in its clause. The relative adverb *where* introduces clauses that modify nouns of place:

Newsworthy events rarely happen in the small *town* <u>where I was born</u>.

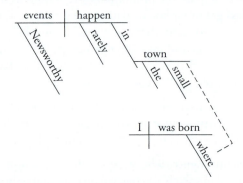

Note in the diagram that the relative adverb *where* modifies the verb *was born* in its own clause; however, the clause itself is adjectival, modifying *town*.

When clauses modify nouns of time:

I will be nervous until next *Tuesday*, <u>when results of the audition will be posted</u>.

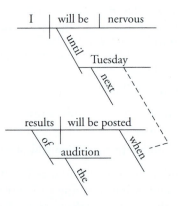

Why clauses modify the noun *reason*:

I understand the *reason* <u>why Margo got the lead in the spring play</u>.

Where, *when*, and *why* clauses are often equally acceptable, and sometimes smoother, without the relative adverb:

I understand the reason <u>Margo got the lead</u>.

I will be nervous until the day <u>the results are posted</u>.

Exercise 24

Underline the relative clauses in the following sentences. Identify (1) the noun that the clause modifies; (2) the role of the relative pronoun in its clause; and (3) the sentence pattern of the clause.

1. The story of the pioneers who traveled overland to the West in the mid-1800s has become an American epic.
2. Although the Oregon Trail is only one of three distinct emigration routes that the pioneers traveled, its name symbolizes the entire wagon emigration.
3. An important landmark for the travelers in Nebraska was Chimney Rock, which appeared on the distant horizon for many days.
4. At Interpretive Centers along the trail, today's auto travelers will learn the stories of the pioneer families who braved the hardships of the 2,000-mile journey on foot.
5. In many places from Missouri to Oregon, today's travelers can view actual ruts that those long-ago wagon wheels carved into the prairie.
6. At the Continental Divide, which was the halfway point in their journey, a large contingent of gold seekers left the main trail and headed southwest to follow the California Trail.
7. A third route was the Mormon Trail, which led to the Great Salt Lake, where the followers of Brigham Young from Nauvoo, Illinois, established their home.
8. Most of the pioneers on the main trail were farmers and their families who had been promised free land in the fertile Willamette Valley of Oregon.
9. The overland wagon trail came to an end soon after 1869, when two golden spikes were pounded into place in the transcontinental railway.
10. On today's highways, travelers can also follow the trail of the Pony Express, which became obsolete in 1861 with the click of the transcontinental telegraph.

Note: Your teacher may also want you to diagram these sentences. Having analyzed the clauses, you've done most of the work already!

PARTICIPIAL PHRASES

You'll recall that the formula describing the noun phrase includes three postheadword modifiers:

	(1)	(2)	(3)
	Prepositional	Participial	Relative
Det Adj Noun HEADWORD	Phrase	Phrase	Clause

You've been seeing the prepositional phrase as an adjectival since Chapter 2:

> the neighbors <u>from Korea</u>
>
> the president's announcement <u>about the meeting</u>

And in the previous section you studied the relative clause:

> the man <u>who lives across the street</u>

If we change the form of the verb in the relative clause by adding *be* + *-ing*,

> the man <u>who is living across the street</u>,

we can easily demonstrate that the adjectival **participial phrase** is essentially a reduced relative clause:

> the man <u>living across the street</u>

This noun phrase, with its participial phrase as a modifier, will fit in any nominal slot of the sentence:

> I know <u>the man living across the street</u>. (direct object)
>
> <u>The man living across the street</u> seems very nice. (subject)
>
> I often visit with <u>the man living across the street</u>. (object of the preposition)

Like the other adjectivals, in the diagram the participial phrase is attached below the noun. The participial phrase begins on a diagonal line, which then bends to become a horizontal line. The horizontal line will accommodate any complements and/or modifiers the participle may have. You'll notice that the diagram of the participial phrase looks exactly like the predicate of the sentence (or relative clause) that underlies it:

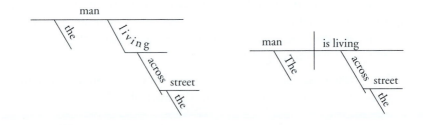

The clause—and the participial phrase—are Pattern VI.

Here are two further examples of participial phrases, the first a transitive verb, the second a linking verb:

> The students <u>taking the SAT</u> look nervous.
>
> Do you recognize those boys <u>acting so foolish</u>?

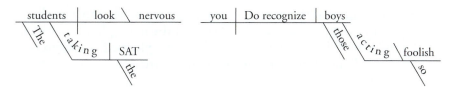

Note that the participles are diagrammed exactly like the predicates of the sentences that underlie them:

Again, you will recognize that the participial phrases are reduced versions of clauses:

> The students <u>who are taking the SAT</u> look nervous.
>
> Do you recognize the boys <u>who are acting so foolish</u>?

The only difference between the verb in the clause and the verb in the participial phrase is the presence or absence of the auxiliary *be* and tense.

As the examples illustrate, transitive participles will have direct objects (taking *the SAT*), and linking-verb participles will have subject complements (acting *so foolish*). And all participles, just like verbs in all the sentence patterns, may be modified by adverbials of various forms.

In the following sentence, we have added the adverbial noun phrase *this morning*:

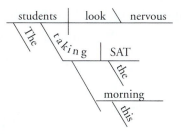

Here are three key points that will help you understand participles:

1. Verbs from all four classes—*be*, linking, intransitive, and transitive—can function as participles.
2. The noun phrases in all the NP slots can include participles (or participial phrases) as modifiers: direct objects, subject complements, object complements, indirect objects, objects of prepositions, as well as subjects.

3. The noun that the participle modifies is its subject; that is, the relationship between the headword of the noun phrase in which the participle is embedded and the participle itself is a subject-verb relationship. In the diagram, the participle is connected to its own subject.

Exercise 25

Turn each of the following sentences into a noun phrase that includes a participial phrase as a postnoun modifier. Use the noun phrase in a sentence.

Example: Two dogs are fighting over the bone.
  NP: two dogs fighting over the bone
  Sentence: I recognize those two dogs fighting over the bone.

1. An expensive sports car is standing in the driveway.
2. The baby is sleeping upstairs in the crib.
3. The fans are lining up at the ticket office.
4. The students are searching the Internet.
5. The fullback was charging through the line.
6. The teachers are walking the picket line.

Passive Participles. The participles we have seen so far are the *-ing* form of the verb (traditionally called the present participle); as you would expect, the clauses underlying them are also in the active voice. Another common form of the adjectival participle is the *-en* form. This form, which is traditionally called the past participle, might be more accurately called the "passive participle."

The houses <u>designed by Frank Lloyd Wright</u> are national treasures.

The car <u>being driven by the front-runner</u> has developed engine trouble.

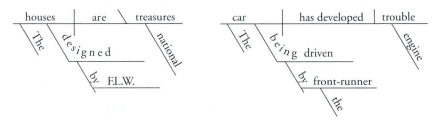

Like the *-ing* participles, the *-en* participles are also reduced clauses:

The houses <u>that were designed by Frank Lloyd Wright</u> are national treasures.

That car <u>that is being driven by the front-runner</u> has developed engine trouble.

Both of these underlying relative clauses are in the passive voice. (Note that in the last example, the active voice version of the verb includes *be* + *-ing: is driving*. When *be* + *-en* is added to make it passive, the resulting verb has two forms of *be* as auxiliaries: *is being driven*.)

Remember, we produce a passive sentence by adding *be* + *-en* to the verb, so a passive verb is always the *-en* form. When we turn such sentences into participles, they will automatically have the *-en* form.

Movable Participles. We can think of the postheadword slot in the noun phrase as the "home base" of the participle, as it is of the relative clause. But unlike the clause, the participial phrase can be shifted to the beginning of the sentence when it modifies the subject:

> Built by Frank Lloyd Wright in 1936, the Kauffman house at Falling-water is one of Western Pennsylvania's most valued architectural treasures.

> Carrying heavy packs on their backs, the hikers were exhausted when they reached the summit of Black Butte.

The participial phrase that modifies the subject can also be shifted to the end of the sentence:

> The students cheered noisily for the basketball team, standing up throughout the game.

In both of these alternative positions, at the beginning or end of the sentence, the participial phrase gets special emphasis. It is commonly known as a **free modifier**. Clearly, however, it has a connection to its subject.

No matter where it appears in the sentence, the adjectival participial phrase is attached in the diagram to its own subject, the headword of the noun phrase in which it appears:

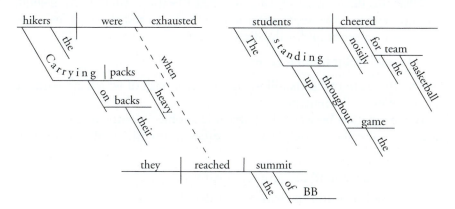

The Participle as Object Complement. You'll recall from Chapter 3 that two of the required slots in the sentence patterns, two functions, are filled by adjectivals: the subject complement slot in Patterns II and IV and the object complement slot in Pattern IX. In most cases, these slots are filled by adjectives:

> The teacher seems <u>angry</u>. (subject complement)

> We found the teacher <u>unreasonable</u>. (object complement)

We did see some examples, however, of prepositional phrases as subject complements:

> The teacher was <u>in a bad mood</u> this morning.

> The piano sounds <u>out of tune</u>.

We could easily come up with prepositional phrases as object complements as well:

> We found the teacher <u>in a bad mood</u> this morning.

> I consider your behavior <u>out of line</u>.

The object complement slot can also be filled by a participle:

> I could feel my heart <u>beating faster</u>.

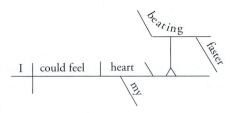

Again, we make use of the pedestal in the diagram to place the participle's characteristic bent line in the object complement slot on the main line.

What this diagram says is that "my heart beating faster" is not a single noun phrase; it is two separate structures. You can test this conclusion by substituting a pronoun for the direct object:

> I could feel <u>it</u> beating faster.

Clearly there are two slots following the verb, both of which are required for the sense of the sentence.

The distinction between the participle as object complement—a separate slot—and the participle as a modifier in the direct object slot may be subtle:

> The police found the murdered witness.

> The police found the witness murdered.

Again, you can determine the number of slots following the verb by substituting pronouns:

> The police found him.
>
> The police found him murdered.

A fairly reliable way to determine if the sentence has an object complement is to insert *to be:*

> I could feel my heart to be beating faster.
>
> The police found him to be murdered.

The resulting sentences may not be the most natural way of expressing the object complement, but they are certainly grammatical.

Exercise 26

Underline the participles and participial phrases in the following sentences; identify their sentence patterns. Diagram.

1. The award given every year to the outstanding volunteer has been announced.
2. Being a philosopher, she can propose a problem for every solution.
3. He has all the gall of a shoplifter returning an item for a refund.
4. The hostess gave the departing guests some leftover food for their pets.
5. Finding the price reasonable, they rented the apartment on the spot.
6. Congress shall make no law abridging the freedom of speech or of the press.
7. Some agencies will not fund research involving genetic manipulation.
8. The teachers' union has finally approved the last two disputed sections of the contract offered by the school district.

Usage Matters   Dangling Participles

The introductory participial phrase provides a good way to add variety to sentences, to get away from the standard subject opener. But it carries an important restriction:

> *The participle can open the sentence only when its subject is also the subject of the sentence and is located in regular subject position. Otherwise, the participle dangles.*

A dangling participle, in other words, is a verb in search of a subject:

> *Having found the rent reasonable, the apartment turned out to be perfect.

(It was not the apartment that found the rent reasonable!)

A common source of the dangling participle is the sentence with a "delayed subject." Two common delayers are the *there* transformation and the *it* cleft, which you saw in Chapter 5, in connection with sentence focus:

> *Having moved the patio furniture into the garage, there was no longer room for the car.
>
> *Knowing how much work I had to do yesterday, it was good of you to come and help.

In the previous sentence the subject of the participle, *you*, is there, but it's in the predicate rather than functioning as the sentence subject. As readers and listeners, we process sentences with certain built-in expectations. We expect the subject of an introductory verb to be the first logical noun or pronoun.

Incidentally, moving a participle to the end of the sentence will not solve the problem if the subject has been omitted. Even there, we expect the subject of the sentence to be the subject of the participle as well:

> *There was no longer room for the car, having moved the patio furniture into the garage.

Often the most efficient way to revise such sentences is to expand the participial phrase into a complete clause:

> <u>After we moved the patio furniture into the garage</u>, there was no longer room for the car.
>
> It was good of you to come and help yesterday <u>when you learned how much work I had to do.</u>

Another common source of the dangling participle is the passive sentence:

> *Having worked hard since 6:00 A.M., the project was completed before noon.

Here the problem arises because the passive transformation has deleted the agent of the verb *completed*, which is also the subject of the participle. Transforming the sentence into the active voice will solve the problem:

> Having worked hard since 6:00 A.M., <u>*we completed the project* before noon.</u>

Exercise 27

Rewrite the following sentences to eliminate the dangling participles.

1. Needing considerable repair, my parents were able to buy the house for little money.
2. Having misunderstood the assignment, my paper got a low grade.
3. Covered with the grime of centuries, the archeologists could not decipher the inscription.
4. Searching for change in her purse, the bus left without her.
5. Having spent four hours on the operating table, a double bypass was performed on the patient's severely blocked arteries.
6. Once considered only an average player, Chris's game has improved greatly in the last three months.
7. Breaking in through the window of the girls' dormitory, the dean of men surprised several members of the football team.
8. Seen from miles away, you might mistake the mountain for a cloud.

Participles as Adverbials or Adjectivals. Some participial phrases have characteristics of both adverbials and adjectivals:

Standing near a huge puddle, Jan got thoroughly splashed.

Here the opening verb phrase could be expanded into either an adjectival *who* clause (Jan, *who was standing near a huge puddle*, got thoroughly splashed) or an adverbial *while* clause (*While she was standing near a huge puddle*, Jan got thoroughly spashed). The sentence would be correctly analyzed either way.

See also the discussion of adverbial participles (page 121).

PUNCTUATION OF CLAUSES AND PARTICIPLES

The question regarding punctuation of clauses and participles is the question of **restrictive** versus **nonrestrictive modifiers**. Put simply, the question is "Should I set off the phrase or clause with commas?"

In answering this question, the writer must think about the referent of the noun being modified. Is it clear to the reader? In the case of a singular noun, is there only one possible person (or place or thing, etc.) to which the noun can refer? In the case of plurals, are the limits understood? If there is only one, the modifier cannot restrict the noun's meaning any further: The modifier is therefore nonrestrictive and will be set off by commas. It might be useful to think of these commas as parentheses and the modifier as optional; if it's optional, we can assume it's not needed to make the referent of the noun clear.

If the referent of the noun is not clear to the reader—if there is more than one possible referent or if the limits are not known—the purpose of the modifier is quite different: to restrict the meaning of the noun. Thus the modifier in this case is restrictive and is not set off by commas. You may find the terms *defining* and *commenting* easier to understand than *restrictive* and *nonrestrictive*.[1] Does the modifier define (restrict) the noun or does it merely comment on (not restrict) it?

Notice the difference in the punctuation of the following pair of sentences:

> The football players wearing shiny orange helmets stood out in the crowd.
>
> The football players, wearing shiny orange helmets, stood out in the crowd.

In the first sentence the purpose of the participial phrase is to define *which* football players stood out in the crowd. We could illustrate the situation by depicting a crowd of football players on the field, some of whom are wearing *shiny orange helmets;* they are noticeable—they *stand out in the crowd* of football players—because the others are wearing drab, dark helmets or perhaps no helmets at all. In the second sentence the modifier merely comments on the players—it does not define them. An illustration of this situation might show a group of orange-helmeted football players signing autographs in a crowd of children; those players would stand out in that crowd with or without orange helmets. The modifier does *not* tell *which* football players stood out in the crowd; they *all* did. (And, incidentally, they were all wearing orange helmets.)

Context, of course, will make a difference. What does the reader already know? For example, out of context the clause in the following sentence appears to be restrictive:

> The president <u>who was elected in 1932</u> faced problems that would have overwhelmed the average man.

Ordinarily we would say that the noun phrase *the president* has many possible referents; the *who* clause is needed to make the referent clear; it defines and restricts *the president* to a particular man, the one elected in 1932. But what if the reader already knows the referent?

---

[1] These terms are used by Francis Christensen in *Notes Toward a New Rhetoric* (New York: Harper & Row, 1967), pp. 95 ff.

> Franklin Delano Roosevelt took office at a time when the outlook for the nation was bleak indeed. The president, <u>who was elected in 1932</u>, faced decisions that would have overwhelmed the average man.

In this context the clause is simply commenting; the referent of the noun phrase *the president* is already defined by the time the reader gets to it. Many times, however, context alone is an insufficient determinant; only the writer knows if the clause defines or comments. The reader can only take the writer's word—or punctuation—at face value:

> The rain began with the first drumbeat. Only the band members <u>who were wearing rain gear</u> stayed reasonably dry. Everyone else at the parade, spectators and marchers alike, got wet.

Without commas the clause restricts the meaning of the noun phrase *the band members;* it defines those band members who stayed dry. With commas the clause suggests that all the band members were wearing rain gear.

In the case of participial phrases that modify the subject, the writer has a useful test for deciding if they are defining or commenting: Can the modifier be shifted to the beginning or end of the sentence? If that shift does not change the meaning, the modifier is nonrestrictive, simply commenting. The restrictive participial phrase will remain within the noun phrase, whereas the nonrestrictive phrase can introduce the sentence and sometimes follow it:

> <u>Wearing rain gear</u>, the band members stayed reasonably dry.

In the case of the relative clause, the relative pronoun provides some clues for punctuation:

1. The adjectival *that* clause is always restrictive; it is never set off by commas.

2. The *which* clause is generally nonrestrictive; it is set off by commas. You can test a *which* clause by substituting *that:* If it works, the clause is restrictive and should not have commas, and if not, it is nonrestrictive. NOTE: There is an exception to this general rule about *that* in restrictive and *which* in nonrestrictive clauses: Only *which* functions as the object of a preposition; *that* does not. So the relative pronoun in that position will be *which* whether the clause is restrictive or nonrestrictive:

   > I probably won't get either of the jobs for which I applied.
   > Pat got a terrific new job, for which I also applied.

3. If the relative pronoun can be deleted, the clause is restrictive:

   > The bus (that) I ride to work is always late.
   > The woman (whom) I work with is always early.

The next two rules apply to both clauses and phrases:

1. After any proper noun the modifier will be nonrestrictive.

> Herbert Hoover, elected president in 1928, was the first president born west of the Mississippi River.

2. After any common noun that has only one possible referent, the modifier will be nonrestrictive:

> My youngest sister, who lives in Oregon, is much more domestic than I.

> The highest mountain in the world, which resisted the efforts of climbers until 1953, looks truly forbidding from the air.

Exercise   28

Identify the postheadword modifiers in the following sentences as restrictive or nonrestrictive by adding commas if needed.

1. In 1440 Johannes Gutenberg who had initially trained as a goldsmith developed a technology that changed the world of printing.
2. A printing press using movable metal type was faster, cheaper, and more durable.
3. Movable type often regarded as the most important invention of the second millennium changed the way people read books.
4. Before printed texts became widely available, reading was often a communal event where one person would read to a group of people.
5. Any book printed before 1501 is called an incunabulum which literally means "swaddling clothes."
6. Today professional digital printers use an electrical charge that transfers toner or liquid ink to the material on which it is printed.
7. Inexpensive home and office printing is only possible because of digital processes that bypass the need for printing plates.
8. Text messaging which is called SMS (for short message service) in Europe and Asia has become an increasingly popular and efficient form of communication.
9. SMS is hugely popular in India where companies provide alerts, news, cricket scores, railway bookings, and banking services.
10. School authorities in New Zealand approved a policy that made text-messaging language acceptable for year-end exam papers.

MULTIPLE MODIFIERS

So far most of the sentences used to illustrate adjectivals have had a single postheadword modifier, either a clause or a phrase. But we often have more than one such modifier, and when we do, the order in which they appear is well defined: prepositional phrase, participial phrase, relative clause:

the security guard [in our building] [who checks out the visitors]

the woman [from London] [staying with the Renfords]

the DC-10 [on the far runway] [being prepared for takeoff] [which was hijacked by a group of terrorists]

In a traditional diagram, all the noun modifiers in both pre- and postposition are attached to the headword:

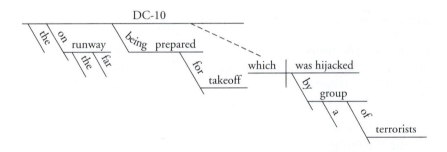

A change in the order of modifiers would change the meaning:

the DC-10 being prepared for takeoff, which was hijacked by a group of terrorists on the far runway

Here the prepositional phrase no longer specifies *which* DC-10; it has become an adverbial modifier in the relative clause, modifying *was hijacked*. In this version *DC-10* has only two postheadword modifiers, not three:

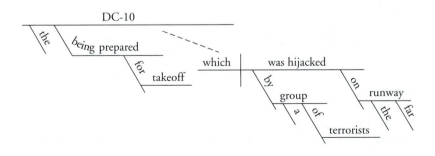

Just as ambiguity may result from a string of prepositional phrases, these multiple modifiers, too, are sometimes open to more than one interpretation:

> the driver of the bus standing on the corner
>
> a friend of my sister who lives in Tampa

In context these noun phrases may or may not be clear to the reader. In any case, the ambiguity is easily avoided:

> the driver of the bus who was standing on the corner
>
> the driver of the bus parked at the corner

> my sister's friend from Tampa
>
> my sister in Tampa's friend (or, my sister in Tampa has a friend who . . .)

OTHER POSTNOUN MODIFIERS

Infinitives. The infinitive—the base form of the verb preceded by *to*—can serve as a modifier in the postheadword position. As a verb, it will have all the attributes of verbs, including complements and modifiers, depending on its underlying sentence pattern:

> the way <u>to be helpful</u>
>
> the time <u>to start</u>
>
> the party after the play <u>to honor the director</u>
>
> the best place in San Francisco <u>to eat seafood</u>

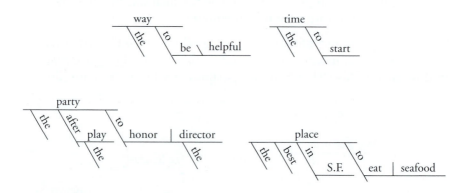

As the last two examples illustrate, the infinitive can be separated from the headword by another modifier. These examples also illustrate another common feature of the adjectival infinitive: Its subject may not be the noun it modifies; its subject is frequently just understood—the object in an understood prepositional phrase:

> That was a nice thing [for you] to do.
>
> Fisherman's Wharf is not necessarily the best place in San Francisco [for one] to eat seafood.

Noun Phrases. Nouns or noun phrases of time and place can follow the headword:

> the party <u>last night</u>
>
> the ride <u>home</u>

These adjectival noun phrases are diagrammed just as the adverbial noun phrases are—on horizontal lines:

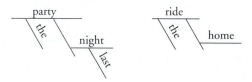

Adjectives. Qualified adjectives and compound adjectives, which usually occupy the preheadword position, can follow the headword if they are set off by commas:

> the neighbors, <u>usually quiet</u>
>
> the neighborhood, <u>quiet and peaceful</u>

Like the nonrestrictive participles, these nonrestrictive adjectives can also introduce the sentence when they modify the subject:

> <u>Usually quiet</u>, the neighbors upstairs are having a regular brawl tonight.
>
> <u>Quiet and peaceful</u>, the neighborhood slept while the cat burglars made their rounds.

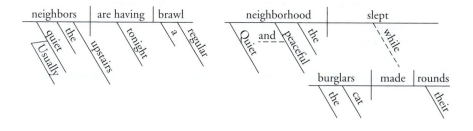

The diagram does not distinguish between pre-and postheadword modifiers—except for the capital letter. But the purpose of the diagram, after all, is to show the structural relationships, not the word order.

Adverbs. Even adverbs can occupy the postheadword position in the noun phrase:

> That was my idea <u>exactly</u>.

> The people <u>here</u> have no idea of conditions <u>there</u>.

Exercise 29

Identify all the postnoun modifiers in the following sentences and label them by form. A sentence may contain more than one postnoun modifier.

1. Curling is a game in which players slide circular, handle-topped granite stones across the ice toward a target.

2. The sport, which originated in Scotland and the Netherlands, combines the skills of bowling and shuffleboard with the strategies of billiards and chess.

3. It is played on an ice rink that is 42 yards long and 10 yards wide, in teams of four players to a side.

4. Each player propels two stones toward a target that is 38 yards away.

5. Curling stones are made from a very special granite called Blue Hone, which is known for its toughness and resiliency.

6. Players "deliver" their stones with a twist of the wrist, imparting the curling action for which the game is named.

7. The third and fourth players on a team look for ways to knock the opponents' stones out of bounds.

8. An important piece of curling equipment is the broom, used by players to melt the ice slightly in the path of a teammate's stone.

9. The winning team is the one whose stones are closest to the center of the target; for each stone that is closer, one point is scored.

10. The sport is extremely popular in Canada, where there are more than a million curlers, who play both at local clubs and on a thriving cash circuit.

CHAPTER 7
Key Terms

Adjectival	Headword
Adjectival clause	Intonation
Adjectival infinitive	Nonrestrictive modifier
Adjectival prepositional phrase	Participial phrase
Adjective	Participle
Adverbial participle	Passive participle
Antecedent	Possessive case
Case	Postheadword modifier
Dangling participle	Preheadword modifier
Demonstrative pronoun	Relative adverb
Determiner	Relative clause
Functional shift	Relative pronoun
Free modifier	Restrictive modifier

Sentences
for PRACTICE

Draw vertical lines between the slots of the sentence patterns. Mark the headword of each NP with an X, the determiner with a D; underline the pre- and postheadword modifiers; then label each according to its form. Circle any pronouns that fill NP slots.

For further practice, identify the sentence patterns and diagram the sentences. Remember that all verb phrases and clauses functioning as adverbials and adjectivals also have identifiable sentence patterns.

1. The clown, acting silly to entertain the children, was not very funny.

2. A weed is a plant whose virtues have not been discovered. [Ralph Waldo Emerson]

3. My neighbor's husband, who is a strong union man, would not cross the picket line that the clerical workers organized at the mill where he is a foreman.

4. The company's reorganization plan, voted down last week, called for the removal of all incumbent officers.

5. At midnight Cinderella's beautiful coach, in which she had been driven to the ball, suddenly became a pumpkin again.

6. According to the Sierra Club, the equivalent of eleven barrels of oil is saved for every ton of plastic bags reused or recycled.

7. Drawing on my fine command of the English language, I said nothing. [Robert Benchley]

8. The play's the thing wherein I'll catch the conscience of the king. [Shakespeare]

9. Uneasy lies the head that wears the crown. [Shakespeare]

10. Calling Pearl Harbor Day a day that would live in infamy, President Roosevelt asked Congress for a declaration of war.

11. Having been a police officer in downtown Nashville for thirty years, my neighbor grew restless after he retired from the force.

12. This is the cat that killed the rat that ate the malt that lay in the house that Jack built.

QUESTIONS
?
for DISCUSSION

1. Generate a noun phrase according to each of the following formulas:

   A. det + adj + HEADWORD + participial phrase

   B. det + adj + noun + HEADWORD + clause

   C. det + adj + HEADWORD + prep phrase + part phrase

   D. det + noun + HEADWORD + part phrase + clause

   Use your NPs in sentences as follows:

   Use A as the direct object of a Pattern VII sentence.

   Use B as the object of a preposition.

   Use C as an indirect object.

   Use D as the direct object in a relative clause.

2. In our description of the noun phrase, we saw that the headword slot is filled by a word that is a noun in form. Would you consider these underlined noun phrases as exceptions to the rule?

   The rich are different from other people.

   I was late for our meeting.

   You clean the upstairs, and I'll do the downstairs.

3. Explain the source of the ambiguity in the following sentence:

   My brother is considered the area's best foreign car mechanic.

4. In this chapter we discussed the recursive quality of the noun phrase—that is, the embedding of one noun phrase in another. Give a sentence in which a relative clause is embedded in another relative clause; give another in which a participle is embedded in another participial phrase; another with a participle in a relative clause; another with a relative clause in a participial phrase.

5. Linguist Francis Christensen, quoted in the discussion of punctuation, suggests that restrictive modifiers make one statement and imply the opposite. What opposite statements can you infer from the following?

   All the students with an average of 90 or higher will be excused from the final.

   The flight controllers who saw the strange lights in the sky became firm believers in UFOs.

   The customers who witnessed the fight were called to testify.

   How would the meaning of these sentences change if the post-noun modifiers were set off by commas?

6. What is the source of the ambiguity in the following sentences?

   Tony buried the knife he found in the cellar.

   Fred tripped his teammate with the baseball bat.

   Diagram each sentence in two ways to show its two possible meanings.

7. In what way does this famous line from Milton appear to violate the rule regarding the placement of relative clauses?

   They also serve who only stand and wait.

8. In *The Book of Lists* (Morrow, 1977), David Wallechinsky, Irving Wallace, and Amy Wallace describe a comma "that cost the government two million dollars before Congress could rectify the error." Here's the expensive sentence:

   All foreign fruit, plants are free from duty.

   The clerk who wrote the rule was supposed to use a hyphen instead of a comma. Explain the difference.

CLASSROOM APPLICATIONS

1. There are very few, if any, nouns that cannot function as modifiers of other nouns. Here's a vocabulary exercise to test this statement. Begin with a common noun, such as *light* or *tree* or *house*. Use it as a modifier; then use the noun you modified as a modifier. See how long you can keep the chain going—perhaps around the room at least once. For example,

   > *tree farm, farm building, building code, code word, word game, game player, player piano, piano bench, bench warmer, warmer oven, oven light . . .*

   If you get stuck, you can go back and change a word to start a new path.

2. The term "sentence combining" refers to a popular method of teaching sentence structure in which writers learn to combine short sentences in various ways. This method is based on the work of the transformational linguists, who hold that every modifier in the noun phrase is actually a basic sentence. For example, this sentence,

   > The silly, awkward clown is entertaining the children,

   combines three basic sentences:

   > The clown is entertaining the children.

   > The clown is silly.

   > The clown is awkward.

   There are other ways in which these same three sentences could be combined. Here are two; try for at least a dozen:

   > The silly clown entertaining the children is awkward.

   > The awkward clown who is entertaining the children is silly.

   Using your knowledge of both adverbial and adjectival modifiers, combine the following groups of sentences in as many ways as you can. (Again, try for at least a dozen!)

   > Becky stood before the magistrate.

   > Becky felt nervous.

   > The dancers kept time to the raucous music.

   > The dancers wore strange costumes.

   > The dancers acted crazy.

   > The young man waited for the train

   > The train was very late.

   > The young man looked impatient.

   > The young man paced back and forth on the station platform.

CHAPTER 8

The Noun Phrase Functions: Nominals

CHAPTER PREVIEW

In the previous two chapters you saw how the basic sentence patterns can be expanded by adding optional modifiers of various kinds—words, phrases, and clauses that function as adverbials and adjectivals. In this chapter you will learn how the NP slots can be expanded by using structures other than noun phrases. We begin this chapter by reviewing the various roles that NPs play in our basic sentence patterns, including an optional NP slot called the *appositive*. Then we examine in detail how to fill these same slots with verb phrases and dependent clauses instead of noun phrases.

By the end of this chapter, you will be able to

- Identify and use *appositives*.
- Recognize *gerunds, nominal infinitive phrases*, and *nominal clauses* and identify their functions.
- Recognize and correct *dangling gerunds*.
- Understand the *subjects* of gerunds and infinitives.
- Distinguish nominal clauses from adverbial and adjectival clauses.
- Identify and write sentences with *delayed subjects*.
- Understand these terms: *expletive, nominalizer, interrogative, subordinator*, and *anticipatory* it.

THE NOMINAL SLOTS

You have already learned that the terms *adverbial* and *adjectival* denote functions. An *adverbial* is any form—any word, phrase, or clause—that does what an adverb does—that is, modify a verb. *Adjectival* refers to any structure that does what an adjective usually does—modify a noun. But you'll notice that we have not used the parallel *-al* term for noun, **nominal**, until now. Up to this point, all of the required slots in the sentence patterns labeled NP, such as subject and direct object, have been filled with noun phrases (and sometimes with pronouns, which stand in for NPs). We did this mainly for simplicity. But now that we're going to study other forms that fill the required sentence slots, it's time to introduce the term *nominal*.

All of those NP slots you learned about in Chapter 3 are actually nominal slots. Adverbials and adjectivals have only one function each—to modify a verb or modify a noun. But nominals perform a variety of functions, most of which are required to produce a complete grammatical sentence:

> *Subject:* <u>My best buddy</u> lives in Iowa.
>
> *Direct object:* I visited <u>my best buddy</u> last Christmas.
>
> *Indirect object:* I sent <u>my best buddy</u> a card for his birthday.
>
> *Subject complement:* The town's new mayor is <u>my best buddy</u>.
>
> *Object complement:* I consider Rich <u>my best buddy</u>.
>
> *Object of a preposition:* The town has a lot of respect for <u>my best buddy</u>.

As you will see, these slots can be filled with forms other than NPs—namely, verb phrases and dependent clauses. But before we get to those other forms, let's look at one more nominal function, one that does not show up in the sentence patterns—an optional nominal slot called the **appositive**.

APPOSITIVES

An appositive is a nominal companion, a structure (usually an NP) that adds information to a sentence by renaming another nominal. It is sometimes called "a noun in apposition."

> My best buddy, <u>Rich</u>, lives in Iowa.
>
> The prosecutor cross-examined the next witness, <u>the victim's ex-husband</u>.

You can easily understand the optional nature of the appositive: These sentences would be grammatical without the added information. On the diagram the appositive occupies a place right next to the noun, or other nominal structure, that it renames, with the headword in parentheses:

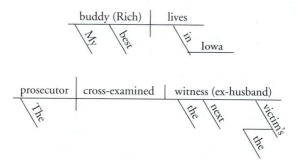

As the diagram clearly illustrates, the appositives add information to the noun phrase, as adjectivals do. But they are different from other adjectivals in that they can substitute for the nouns that they rename:

Rich lives in Iowa.

The prosecutor cross-examined the victim's ex-husband.

If the appositive renames the subject, it can be used to introduce the sentence:

<u>An ex-Marine who once played professional football</u>, the prosecutor was an intimidating presence in the courtroom.

Punctuation of Appositives. The distinction between restrictive and nonrestrictive modifiers, which you learned in connection with participial phrases and relative clauses, also applies to appositives. When the appositive defines (restricts) the meaning of the nominal it renames, no commas are needed. An altered version of the first example will illustrate the distinction:

My buddy Rich lives in Iowa.

In the earlier example, the added name simply comments:

My best buddy, Rich, lives in Iowa.

The adjective *best* makes all the difference. *My best buddy* obviously refers to one specific person, just as *my only buddy* would. *My buddy*, however, has a general reference; the added name makes the referent of the noun phrase specific, actually defining the phrase *my buddy*. You can hear the contrast when you read the two sentences aloud.

Exercise 30

Underline the noun phrases that are functioning as appositives. Remember, an appositive noun phrase has the same referent as the nominal it renames.

1. Folk songs, simple ballads sung to guitar music, became very popular in the 1960s.
2. One of the best-known folk singers of that period was Arlo Guthrie, son of the legendary songwriter Woody Guthrie.
3. An offbeat film about illegal trash dumping, *Alice's Restaurant* was inspired by Arlo's song of the same name.
4. The theme of many Arlo Guthrie songs, the search for personal freedom, is still appealing today.
5. Gillian Welch, a contemporary folk singer and songwriter, combines simple ballad-like melodies with topical lyrics in two very popular CDs, *Soul Journey* and *Time (The Revelator)*.
6. I went to the concert with my friend Casey, who is Gillian Welch's biggest fan.

In Chapter 15, we take up the use of colons and dashes in connection with appositives. And in the following sections of this chapter, we include appositives in forms other than noun phrases—verb phrases and clauses.

NOUN PHRASE SUBSTITUTES

Three other structures can perform the grammatical functions that noun phrases generally perform: the gerund phrase, the infinitive phrase, and the nominal clause. Our study of these nominal forms—these substitutes for NPs—will focus on their five primary functions: subject, direct object, subject complement, object of a preposition, and appositive.

GERUNDS

In Chapter 4 you saw the *-ing* form of the verb combined with a *be* auxiliary functioning as the predicating, or tensed, verb:

The children <u>are playing</u> in the woods.

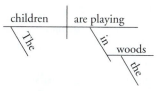

Here the diagram clearly shows the sentence as Pattern VI, with the intransitive verb *are playing* modified by an adverbial prepositional phrase.

In the previous chapter you saw the *-ing* verb functioning as a noun modifier, called the participle; and you'll recall that the noun the participle modifies is also the participle's subject:

The children <u>playing in the woods</u> look happy.

In this chapter we will use the same *-ing* verb as a nominal to fill an NP slot. In this function, it is called a **gerund**:

<u>Playing in the woods</u> is the children's favorite activity.

Here the gerund phrase is the subject of the sentence. We can think of gerunds as names. But rather than naming persons, places, things, and events, as nouns generally do, gerunds name actions or behaviors or states of mind or states of being. And because they are verbs in form, gerunds will also include all the complements and modifiers that tensed verbs include. In our gerund example, *playing* is modified by an adverbial prepositional phrase, *in the woods*, just as it was as a main verb.

Even though sentences with gerunds in the NP slots may look more complicated than those you've seen before, the system for analyzing them is the same. You do that by identifying the sentence pattern. The first step is to locate the predicating verb. No matter what structure fills the subject slot, you can determine where it ends by substituting a pronoun, such as *something* or *it*:

Playing in the woods is the children's favorite activity.

In other words,

<u>It</u> is the children's favorite activity.

Now you've identified the predicating verb, *is*, a form of *be*. Next you'll see that a noun phrase (*the children's favorite activity*) follows, so you know the sentence is Pattern III.

The next step is to identify the form of the structure filling that "it" slot. You can recognize *Playing in the woods* as a gerund because it begins with an *-ing* verb form. (You can usually identify the form of a structure by looking at the first word.)

In diagramming the gerund when it fills a slot in the main clause, we simply attach the phrase to the main line by means of a pedestal, just as we did in Chapter 3 when a prepositional phrase filled the subject complement slot. The line for the gerund itself has a small step at the left, which identifies the *-ing* verb as a gerund:

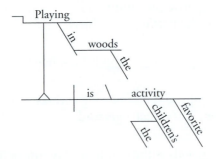

Following are examples of other NP slots occupied by gerund phrases.

> *Direct object:* Both adults and teenagers enjoy playing computer games.

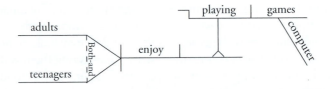

> *Subject complement:* My favorite pastime is playing computer games.

Object of a preposition: I work off a lot of tension by playing computer games.

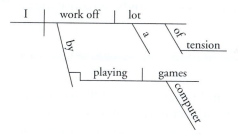

Appositive: My favorite pastime, playing computer games, is inexpensive but time-consuming.

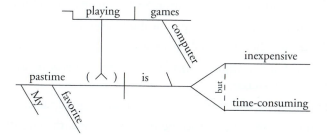

The Pattern of the Gerund. In these sentences with the gerund phrase *playing computer games*, the gerund *playing* has a direct object (*playing what?*), so we can identify the underlying sentence, with its one slot following the verb, as Pattern VII:

X is playing computer games.

The predicating verb in every pattern has the potential for becoming a gerund phrase when it is turned into the *-ing* form:

Pattern III: My little brother <u>is a pest</u>. (*being a pest*)

Pattern VIII: Tony <u>gave the landlord a bad time</u>. (*giving the landlord a bad time*)

Pattern IX: We <u>painted the bathroom orange</u>. (*painting the bathroom orange*)

In the following sentences, those *-ing* verb phrases have become gerunds filling NP slots:

My little brother enjoys <u>being a pest</u>. (direct object)

After <u>giving the landlord a bad time</u>, Tony regretted his behavior. (object of a preposition)

Our bright idea, <u>painting the bathroom orange</u>, was a decorating disaster. (appositive)

It's important to note that just because the function of the verb phrase changes—from predicating verb to nominal—its sentence pattern does not change. The three gerunds remain Patterns III, VIII, and IX, respectively.

Exercise 31

A. Identify the gerund phrases in the following sentences, and indicate the function (subject, direct object, subject complement, object of a preposition, appositive) that each one performs in its sentence. Also identify the sentence patterns of the main clause and of the gerund phrase. Diagram the sentences.

1. Flying a supersonic jet has been Sally's dream since childhood.
2. The coach enjoys playing practical jokes on his players.
3. The speaker began by telling a few jokes.
4. My hardest accomplishment last semester was staying awake in my eight o'clock class.
5. Leaving the scene of the accident was not a good idea.
6. Two witnesses reported seeing the suspect near the entrance of the bank.
7. The cost of going to college has risen dramatically in the last ten years.
8. Thinking a problem through requires time, solitude, and concentration.

B. Compose sentences that include the following verb phrases as gerunds. Try to use each gerund phrase in at least two different functions.

taking grammar tests	giving people a helping hand
being punctual	lying on the beach

Investigating Language 8.1

Compare these pairs of sentences:

Her job was selling computers in a discount store.
She was selling computers in a discount store.

My brother is getting into trouble again.
My problem is getting into law school.

How do the patterns of the two sentences in each pair differ? What are the predicating verbs? Which ones contain gerunds? How would the diagrams for each be different? Marking off the sentence slots with vertical lines will help to show the differences in the sentence patterns. You can also try substituting pronouns to help you see where the NP slots begin and end.

The Subject of the Gerund. The subject of the gerund—that is, the person or agent performing the action expressed in the gerund—is usually not part of the gerund phrase itself. However, it is often the same as the subject of the sentence, as in item 2 in Exercise 31, where "coach" is the subject of both "enjoys" (the main verb) and "playing" (the gerund). Sometimes the subject can be inferred from another word in the sentence, as in item 4, where "my" indicates who had trouble "staying awake." The subject of the gerund will usually be left unstated when it names a general, rather than a particular, action or behavior, as in items 7 and 8 in Exercise 31.

But sometimes the subject can be expressed in the gerund phrase itself. When it is, it will often be in the possessive case:

> His drinking is excessive.
>
> I objected to Jeremy's taking on another part-time job.
>
> Your complaining about the work will not make it any easier.

Although the possessive case may sometimes sound excessively formal or even incorrect, it is the form considered standard in formal writing.

In the diagram, the subject of the gerund is diagrammed like a determiner and attached to the step on the left:

Dangling Gerunds. The following sentences are likely to elicit an "awk" from your composition teacher. What is it that makes them awkward?

> Upon seeing the stop sign, the car screeched to a halt.
>
> By proofreading my papers, my grades improved greatly.
>
> The ingredients should be assembled before starting to bake a cake.

You probably recognized that these sentences aren't strictly logical: They suggest that the car saw the stop sign, the grades proofread the papers, and the ingredients baked the cake. We call that problem the "dangling gerund," a problem that occurs when the subject of the gerund is not stated or clearly implied. These sentences have the same fuzzy quality that dangling participles have.

Dangling gerunds usually turn up when the gerund serves as the object in an opening or closing prepositional phrase. To clear up a dangling gerund, you can revise the sentence in one of two ways:

1. Make sure that the subject of the main clause is also the subject of the gerund:

    Upon seeing the stop sign, I brought the car to a screeching halt.

    By proofreading my papers, I improved my grades greatly.

2. Turn the prepositional phrase with the gerund into an adverbial clause:

    Assemble the ingredients before you start to bake a cake.

Exercise 32

Improve the following sentences by providing a clear subject for the gerund.

1. After finishing the decorations, the ballroom looked beautiful.
2. Your revising time will be reduced by following a few helpful pointers.
3. In making a career decision, your counselor will be a big help.
4. By signing this waiver, no claims against the owner can be made.
5. Our backpacks got really heavy after hiking up that steep mountain trail.

ELL Issues *Go + -ing* verbs

The verb *go* is used with a great many *-ing* verbs, but, interestingly, those verbs are limited to recreational activities of various kinds:

    Let's go hunting (fishing, bowling, swimming, shopping, jogging, etc.).

We don't say "Let's go gardening," "Let's go cooking," or "Let's go doing homework."

This is one of those "why" questions that we have no answer for! Another is what to call that *-ing* verb that follows *Let's go*. Because *go* is nearly always intransitive, the *-ing* activity can probably be interpreted as an adverbial, a participle functioning adverbially. But because that *-ing* verb names an activity, we could also make a case for calling it a gerund. Perhaps the best answer is to recognize its special usage and call it an idiom.

INFINITIVES

Another form of the verb that functions as a nominal is the **infinitive phrase**—the base form of the verb with *to*. Like the gerund, the nominal infinitive names an action or behavior or state of being. In fact, the infinitive closely parallels the gerund and is often an alternative to it:

> *Gerund:* <u>Remaining neutral on this issue</u> is unconscionable.
>
> *Nominal infinitive:* <u>To remain neutral on this issue</u> is unconscionable.

You have already seen infinitives functioning as modifiers of verbs (Chapter 6, "Adverbials") and as modifiers of nouns (Chapter 7, "Adjectivals"). In this chapter you will see the nominal infinitive functioning as subject, direct object, subject complement, and appositive:

> *Subject:* <u>To be a successful farmer these days</u> requires stamina and perseverance.
>
> *Direct object:* My cousin wants <u>to be a successful farmer.</u>
>
> *Subject complement:* My cousin's ambition is <u>to be a successful farmer.</u>
>
> *Appositive:* My cousin's ambition, <u>to be a successful farmer,</u> requires stamina and perseverance.
>
> It requires stamina and perseverance <u>to be a successful farmer.</u>

As with gerunds, you can substitute a pronoun to help you decide what nominal slot the infinitive phrase fills:

> <u>Something</u> requires stamina and perseverance.
>
> My cousin wants <u>something.</u>
>
> My cousin's ambition is <u>this.</u>

Infinitives, like gerunds, are verb forms; they may include complements and/or adverbial modifiers. And like gerunds, infinitive phrases can be derived from all the sentence patterns. Our "farmer" infinitive is Pattern III. In the first example it fills the subject slot in a Pattern VII sentence:

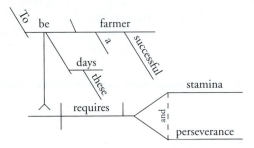

In the diagram, the infinitive phrase, like the gerund, is connected to the main line with a pedestal. The infinitive itself is on a two-part line exactly like that of a prepositional phrase. (It's easy to tell the difference, however: In the infinitive phrase, *to* is followed by a verb, not by a noun phrase.)

The second appositive example makes use of the anticipatory *it* to change sentence focus, much like the *it*-cleft that you saw in Chapter 5:

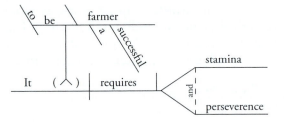

In the following sentence, a Pattern VII infinitive phrase functions as an appositive:

My job, to hand out the diplomas, was a last-minute assignment.

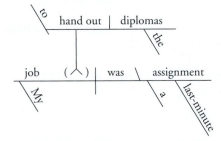

The action expressed in the infinitive phrase renames the subject, *My job;* it tells what the job is.

Exercise 33

Identify the sentence pattern of each infinitive phrase and its function in the sentence. Diagram the sentences.

1. Ruth plans to give her father a necktie for Christmas.
2. Our only hope is to beg for mercy.
3. To walk across campus alone at night could be dangerous.
4. Both candidates desperately want to become president.
5. Winston Churchill had a rule to never take strong drink before lunch.
6. A mother bird will attempt to distract predators from the nest.
7. My friend Renato likes to shock people with his outrageous political views.
8. To know him is to love him.

The Subject of the Infinitive. In most of the infinitive sentences we have seen so far, the subject of the tensed verb is also the subject of the infinitive. For example, in item 7 of the previous exercise, "My friend Renato likes to shock people with his outrageous political views," *friend* is the subject of both *likes* and *to shock*. But when an infinitive has a general meaning, the sentence may not include that infinitive's actual subject, especially if the infinitive occupies the subject slot:

To listen to Norah Jones is pure delight.

In some cases, however, the subject of the infinitive will be expressed in a prepositional phrase:

For Conchita to win this match would be a miracle.

For the district attorney to take part in this discussion is a conflict of interest.

Conchita and *district attorney* are the subjects of the infinitives *to win* and *to take part*.

Prepositional phrases with embedded infinitives also occur in the direct object position after verbs like *hope, like, want,* and *prefer*:

Conchita's fans would like for her to win this match.

We are hoping for our legislature to make a wise decision about school taxes.

In the diagram for these sentences, the vertical line between the object of the preposition and the infinitive indicates the subject–verb boundary:

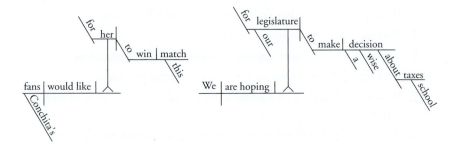

Some verbs that can appear in such sentences are also grammatical without the preposition *for:*

Conchita's fans would like her to win this match.

In these examples we have treated the infinitive and its subject as a single unit filling the direct object slot:

Conchita's fans would like <u>something</u>.

We are hoping <u>something</u>.

But in the following sentence, there are two slots:

We asked <u>the uninvited guests to leave the party</u>.

In this sentence, we have both a "someone" and a "something" following the verb; so rather than analyze the sentence as Pattern VII, we would explain it as Pattern VIII, with the "someone" as an indirect object:

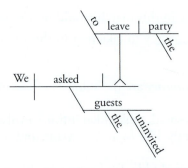

You might argue that the verb *asked* is not a "give" verb, as most Pattern VIII verbs are, and that *uninvited guests* isn't really a "recipient," as most indirect objects are. However, the two slots clearly have different referents, so the Pattern VIII formula, with its NP_2 and NP_3, seems to fit. We can also transform the sentence into passive voice to show that *to leave the party* occupies a separate slot from *the uninvited guests*:

> The uninvited guests were asked to leave the party.

Other verbs that follow this pattern include *tell, advise, invite, require, order,* and *expect.*

Exercise **34**

Underline the nominal verb phrases—both gerunds and infinitives—in the following sentences. Then identify the function of each nominal verb phrase. Finally, diagram the sentences. Be sure to think about sentence patterns.

1. The best thing would be for you to tell the truth.
2. By remaining silent, you are merely making the situation worse.
3. It would be foolhardy to ignore the judge's order.
4. Raising the company's national profile was the new owner's long-term goal.
5. Our composition teacher instructed us to write three drafts of every assignment.
6. I appreciate your proofreading this final version for me.
7. I like to watch the goldfinches at the bird feeder in the morning.
8. The baby's crying upset the rest of the passengers.

NOMINAL CLAUSES

In the preceding sections you have seen examples of verb phrases—gerunds and infinitives—filling NP slots. In this section you will see that nominal clauses can do so as well:

> I understand <u>that several students have launched a protest</u>.
>
> I wonder <u>what prompted their action</u>.

These nominal clauses (also called "noun clauses") are further examples of dependent clauses, just as adverbial and adjectival clauses are: They do not function as complete sentences, as independent clauses do.

The trick of substituting a pronoun to determine the boundaries of the NP slot is especially useful when the nominal slot it filled by a clause, as in the two previous examples:

> I understand <u>something</u>.
>
> I wonder <u>something</u>.

The pronoun substitutes for the entire nominal slot.

These two examples also illustrate the two kinds of introductory words that signal nominal clauses: the **expletive** *that* and **interrogative** words such as *what*. The diagrams will show a basic difference between them:

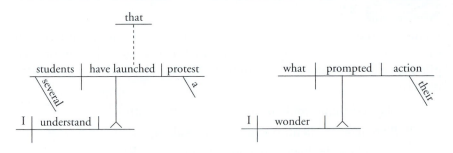

The interrogative *what* fills a grammatical role in the clause it introduces—in this case, that of subject; the expletive does not.

(*Diagramming note:* The pedestal can be attached to the nominal clause wherever it is convenient to do so. The expletive is placed above the clause it introduces and attached with a broken line, again wherever convenient.)

The Expletive *That*. The term *expletive* refers to a sentence element that plays no grammatical role itself; it's an added element that enables us to manipulate a structure for reasons of emphasis and the like. The expletive *that* makes it possible to embed one sentence as a nominal in another sentence. This use of *that* is sometimes labeled a *nominalizer*. In the previous example, the Pattern VII sentence "Several students have launched a protest" becomes the direct object in another Pattern VII sentence. The diagram illustrates the added-on quality of the expletive.

The expletive *that* can turn any declarative sentence into a nominal clause:

The guests from El Paso will arrive soon.	⟶	I hope that the guests from El Paso will arrive soon.
The common cold is caused by a virus.	⟶	That the common cold is caused by a virus has been clearly established by science.

When the *that* clause fills the direct object slot, as in the first example, the sentence may be grammatical without the expletive:

I hope the guests from El Paso will arrive soon.

When the clause is in the subject position, however, the expletive is required:

*The common cold is caused by a virus has been clearly established by science.

Nominal *that* clauses can also function as subject complements and appositives, as the following examples illustrate:

Subject complement: Your assumption is <u>that interest rates will remain relatively low</u>.

Appositive: The reviewer's criticism, <u>that the characters lack conviction</u>, is fully justified.

Exercise 35

Create a nominal *that* clause to fill the following slots. Identify the function of the clause that you've added.

1. You should know _____ .
2. _____ makes everyone angry.
3. My parents realize _____.
4. _____ has not occurred to them.
5. The truth is _____
6. The fact _____ disturbs me.

Investigating Language 8.2

Nominal clauses that begin with the expletive *that* should not be confused with adjectival clauses that begin with the relative pronoun *that*. Compare the following examples:

Nominal clause: I know <u>that I reminded you about the deadline</u>.

Adjectival clause: You ignored the reminders <u>that I gave you</u>.

Because the expletive *that* plays no grammatical role in its clause, the nominal clause will be a complete sentence without the *that: I reminded you about the deadline.* But the relative pronoun *that* does have a role to play within its clause; if you remove it, the remaining words won't be a complete sentence: **I gave you.*

You can also distinguish between *that* clauses by replacing the *that* with *which*. If the clause is adjectival, the sentence will still be grammatical:

> You ignored the reminders <u>which I gave you</u>.

But if you substitute *which* for the expletive *that* in a nominal clause, the result will be clearly ungrammatical:

> *I know which I reminded you about the deadline.

Here are some more sentences with clauses introduced by *that*. Decide which clauses are nominal (introduced by an expletive) and which are adjectival (introduced by a relative pronoun):

> The color that you chose for the walls doesn't match the rug.
> _____
>
> Milton suspects that someone has been using his computer.
> _____
>
> The books that I need for chemistry class are expensive.
> _____
>
> I suppose that the books that I need for art history will be expensive
>   too. _____, _____
> The idea that I need your help is absurd. _____
> The idea that you proposed to the committee is a brilliant one.
> _____
>
> He gave her a look that you could have poured on a waffle. [Ring
>   Lardner] _____

You can check your answers by doing a diagram to make sure that you've identified the *that* correctly.

Interrogatives. One of the sample sentences we saw earlier included a nominal clause introduced by the interrogative *what:*

> I wonder <u>what prompted their action</u>.

Other **interrogatives**, or question words, that introduce nominal clauses are *who, whose, whom, which, where, when, why,* and *how*. Unlike the expletive, the interrogative always plays a grammatical role in its own clause. In the previous example, *what* functions as the subject of *prompted*. In the following sentence, *what* is the direct object in its clause:

I wonder <u>what the students are demanding</u>.

In both of these examples, the *what* clause functions as the direct object. Another common function of nominal clauses introduced by interrogatives is that of subject, as shown in the next two examples:

Where <u>you are going</u> is no business of mine.

Where is an interrogative adverb, so it acts as an adverb in its clause. The interrogative pronoun *who* will be the subject in its own clause:

Who <u>will be at the party</u> remains a mystery.

Who can also be the subject complement in its clause. Here the clause fills the direct object slot:

I don't know *who* <u>that stranger is.</u>

In the following sentences *which* and *what* function as determiners in their clauses; both clauses fill the direct object slot:

I wonder *which* <u>brand of yogurt has the least fat.</u>
I can't decide *what* <u>brand I should buy.</u>

Nominal clauses introduced by interrogatives can also function as objects of prepositions and as appositives:

Object of a preposition: Clarice knows a lot about <u>how computers work</u>.

Appositive: The dean's question, <u>why the students didn't object sooner</u>, has not been answered.

Exercise 36

Both *when* and *where* hold membership in two word classes. As **subordinating conjunctions** they introduce adverbial clauses; as interrogatives they introduce nominal clauses. Identify the function of the *where* and *when* clauses in the following sentences. Are they adverbial or nominal? If the clause is nominal, identify the NP slot it fills. Also identify the sentence patterns of both the independent and dependent clauses.

1. Julie could not remember where she had left her keys.
2. Rob lost his keys when he misplaced his backpack.

3. When I get in late, my roommate gets upset.

4. When I get home is my own business.

5. The starship *Enterprise* ventures where explorers have never gone before.

6. When you decide where we are having dinner, give me a call.

7. When you don't know where you are going, any road will take you there.

8. They have finally decided where the wedding will be held.

9. When I am an old woman, I shall wear purple. [Jenny Joseph]

10. The police asked where we were when the accident occurred.

Yes/No Interrogatives. In Chapter 3 you read about our two kinds of questions: those that ask for specific information, the so-called *wh*-questions; and yes/no questions. Here we've seen those same interrogative words used to introduce nominal clauses, filling NP slots in sentences. We also have nominal clauses based on yes/no questions, introduced by two expletive-like elements, *if* and *whether (or not)*:

> I can't remember <u>if I turned off the television.</u>
>
> <u>Whether or not I turned it off</u> doesn't really matter.

We consider these introductory words as expletives because, like the expletive *that*, they play no part in the clause; they simply act as operators that allow us to use yes/no questions as nominal clauses:

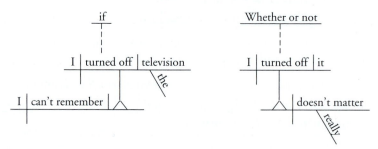

Unlike the expletive *that*, which can sometimes be omitted, these introducers of interrogative clauses will always be included.

Exercise 37

Underline the nominal clause in each of the following sentences. Then identify its function in the sentence: What NP slot does it fill? Diagram the sentences.

1. Until yesterday I never realized how awesome a redwood tree could be.

2. The main complaint about his presentation was that it was too short.

3. What Carlos said about his cousin is unfair and inaccurate.

4. Our psychology teacher is writing a book about why people fear intimacy.

5. My sister told her children that they could have a dog.

6. Who invented calculus is a matter of some dispute.

7. We could not tell which twin was Elaine.

8. Percy wondered if we could come for the weekend.

9. I wish he would explain his explanation. [Lord Byron]

10. The decision that they should replay the point upset both contestants.

Punctuation of Nominal Clauses. As many of the previous examples and exercise items illustrate, sentences with nominal clauses can get fairly long. But with one exception, the punctuation of these sentences remains exactly the same as the punctuation of the basic sentence: no single commas between the sentence pattern slots. The exception occurs when the direct object is a direct quotation. The standard convention calls for a comma between a verb like *say* or *reply* and the quotation:

He said, "I will meet you at the gym at five o'clock."

In this sentence the quoted passage is essentially a nominal clause in direct object position.

Exercise 38

Underline the nominal clauses, gerund phrases, and nominal infinitives in the following sentences, and identify the function that each performs in the sentences. Also, put parentheses around all adverbials: one-word adverbs, prepositional phrases, noun phrases, infinitive phrases, and clauses. And finally, put square brackets around all adjectival phrases (prepositional and participial phrases) and relative clauses.

1. In 1874 Major Walter Wingfield registered his patent in London for the equipment and rules of an outdoor lawn tennis game that was the first version of what we play today.

2. Some fans dislike how graphite rackets and synthetic strings have transformed the game of tennis.

3. Multiplying the advantage of a powerful serve has taken away the finesse and strategy that many spectators enjoy.

4. Introduced in 1970, the tiebreak system revolutionized the sport of tennis by making the matches shorter and more attractive.

5. In the 1980 Wimbledon final, Bjorn Borg failed to convert seven match points in a fourth-set tiebreaker, which John McEnroe won.

6. Unless Serena Williams is injured, it's nearly impossible to beat her, because she really hates losing.

7. Roger Federer's goal is to win twenty major championships before he retires.

8. Two years after getting married and having a baby, Kim Clijsters won her second U.S. Open title.

9. Instead of using a conventional shot, Maria Sharapova often prefers to hit a powerful "swinging volley" when approaching the net or attacking a lob.

10. Although their opponents claim that Bob and Mike Bryan possess "twin chemistry," the brothers, who have won more doubles titles than any men's team in professional tennis, reject the idea that common DNA has resulted in uncommon results.

NOMINALS AS DELAYED SUBJECTS

We have seen nominal clauses that fill the subject slot, some of which have a formal quality more characteristic of writing than speech; in fact, such sentences are uncommon in speech:

> That the common cold is caused by a virus has been clearly established.
>
> That Sherry left school so suddenly was a shock to us all.

In conversation we are more likely to delay the information in that opening clause, substituting for the subject what is called the **anticipatory *it***:

> It has been clearly established that the common cold is caused by a virus.
>
> It was a shock to us all that Sherry left school so suddenly.

The infinitive phrase as subject can also be delayed in this way, as you saw earlier in the discussion of infinitives:

> To play computer games is fun.   ⟶   It is fun to play computer games.
>
> To be a successful farmer requires   ⟶   It requires stamina and stamina and perseverance   perseverance to be a successful farmer.

The anticipatory *it* allows us to change the stress of the sentence, in much the same way that we saw with the cleft sentence in the discussion of sentence transformations in Chapter 5 (pages 99–100). This use of *it* as a tool for writers is discussed in Chapter 15 (pages 315–316).

CHAPTER 8
Key Terms

Anticipatory *it*

Appositive

Clause

Dangling gerund

Delayed subject

Dependent clause

Direct quotation

Expletive *that*

Gerund

Independent clause

Infinitive

Interrogative

Nominal

Nominal clause

Nominal verb phrase

Subordinating conjunction

Tensed verb

Sentences
for PRACTICE

Draw vertical lines to show the sentence slots. Label the form of the structure that occupies each slot. Identify the sentence pattern for each verb phrase and clause. Diagram the sentences.

1. I wonder what Jeff's problem is.

2. I think that I know what the solution to Jeff's problem is.

3. Chondra said that she would call me today when the audition results were posted.

4. In rejecting *Plessy vs. Ferguson* in its 1954 *Brown* decision, the Supreme Court declared that separate educational facilities are inherently unequal.

5. Where you will be in ten years is a question you probably think about sometimes.

6. The defendant's claim that he was kidnapped by aliens did not impress the jury.

7. I know how men in exile feed on dreams. [Aeschylus]

8. The hen is an egg's way of producing another egg.

9. My roommate, who will graduate this month, wonders why finding a job in his field, business management, is so difficult.

10. I haven't figured out which Shakespeare play is my favorite.

11. According to the U.S. Customs Service, smuggling birds from the Caribbean has become a big business.

12. Our biological rhythms play a crucial role in determining how alert we feel.

QUESTIONS
?
for DISCUSSION

1. Why is the appositive set off with commas in the second of these two sentences?

      Mark's brother George coaches basketball in Indiana.

      Mark's brother, George, coaches basketball in Indiana.

   Which sentence tells you that Mark has only one brother? Which sentence implies that Mark has more than one brother? Why does the following sentence need commas?

      The senator's husband, Reuben, accompanied her to Washington.

2. Consider the differences in meaning in these two pairs of sentences. How do you account for these differences? Do the differences involve different sentence patterns?

      Mel stopped to talk to Walt.

      Mel stopped talking to Walt.

      Mel started talking to Walt.

      Mel started to talk to Walt.

3. Show by a diagram how the following two sentences are different. Identify their sentence patterns.

      I went to work.

      I want to work.

4. Your understanding of participles and gerunds will help you understand and explain the ambiguity of these two sentences:

      Flying planes can be dangerous.

      I don't like burping babies.

Diagram each of them in two ways to show their two meanings.

5. What are two possible meanings of the following ambiguous sentence?

   The shooting of the hunters was a wanton act.

   In what way is the traditional diagram inadequate to account for that ambiguity?

6. In Chapter 5 we examined the passive voice of predicating verbs. Can gerunds and infinitives be passive?

7. The traditional grammarian would label the *who* clause in this famous line by Shakespeare an adjectival clause. Why? Why is it not nominal? How would you as a twenty-first-century speaker word this statement?

   Who steals my purse steals trash.

8. Perhaps the best way to explain this *that*-filled sentence is to diagram it.

   I know that that *that* that that student wrote is wrong.

CLASSROOM APPLICATIONS

The following can be organized as either oral or written activities, perhaps as timed group competitions:

1. The fact that verb phrases and clauses can fill NP slots gives the language great embedding capabilities. For example, a gerund phrase could easily fill the direct object slot in a nominal clause. Picture the diagram:

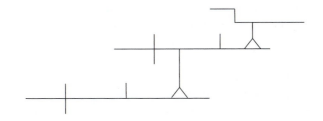

Here's a six-word sentence that would fit:

I know that Joe enjoys swimming.

Now try two other patterns:

(Hint: Bear in mind that the expletive *that* can turn almost any sentence into a nominal clause. Now write a sentence with a gerund in the position shown—as subject or direct object; then turn that sentence into a nominal clause. In the first example, the sentence "Joe enjoys swimming" has been embedded as the direct object following the verb *know*.)

2. This time your task is the opposite of #1: Write a sentence in which a nominal clause is embedded in a gerund phrase.

3. Write a sentence in which an adjectival clause is embedded in a nominal clause.

4. Write a sentence in which an adverbial infinitive phrase is embedded in a gerund phrase.

5. Write a sentence in which a gerund phrase is embedded in an adverbial clause.

Note: These exercises can be organized for group or individual competition in the class. To add to the challenge, the topic of the sentences can be specified: Write about baseball, summer, winter sports, health, rap music, competition, the election campaign, movies, and so forth. And, of course, other specific directions could be included: Use a nominal *who* clause; use the passive voice; include two prepositional phrases; include an indirect object, and so forth.

CHAPTER 9

Sentence Modifiers

CHAPTER PREVIEW

The modifiers and nominals you studied in the three preceding chapters add information that expands units within the sentence: adverbials (Chapter 6), adjectivals (Chapter 7), and noun phrase substitutes (Chapter 8). The structures you will study in this chapter, however, have no direct connection to a particular sentence slot; instead, the information they add relates to the sentence as a whole.

The fact that these structures lie outside the boundaries of the main sentence does not diminish their importance in terms of meaning. Sentences may be grammatical without the independent structures described in this chapter, but that fact does not lessen the impact they have on the meaning or intent of the discourse.

By the end of this chapter, you will be able to

- Distinguish between *adverbial adverbs* and *sentence-modifier adverbs*.
- Identify and use six structures that function as sentence modifiers: *vocatives, interjections, subordinate clauses, absolute phrases, appositives,* and *relative clauses*.
- Punctuate subordinate clauses.
- Recognize *elliptical clauses* and revise ineffective ones.
- Identify *broad reference clauses* and rewrite unclear ones.

Like the modifiers of nouns and verbs, modifiers of the sentence as a whole also come in the form of single words, phrases, and clauses. Because most of the single-word modifiers are adverbs in form, you may be tempted to label them adverbials. However, as the following pair of sentences illustrates, there is a clear contrast in meaning between (1) the adverb as adverbial and (2) the adverb as **sentence modifier**:

1. Mark did not explain the situation <u>clearly</u>.
2. <u>Clearly</u>, Mark did not explain the situation.

The adverbial says something about the verb, about the manner in which Mark did the explaining; *-ly* adverbs are called "manner adverbs." The sentence modifier, on the other hand, indicates the attitude of the writer toward the message stated in the main clause, a signal that provides a guidepost for the reader. This kind of message expressing the writer's feeling or attitude is called **metadiscourse**; in other words, discourse about the discourse. We will look more closely at the topic of metadiscourse in Chapter 15 (pages 327–329).

The diagrams make the difference in meaning clear:

There are a number of tests you can apply to verify the difference. For example, the adverb in sentence 1 can be moved to the preverb position:

Mark did not clearly explain the situation.

We probably wouldn't make the same change in 2, but if we did, we would have to include the commas, to retain the parenthetical meaning:

Mark did not, clearly, explain the situation.

The commas would also stay if we moved the sentence modifier to the end:

Mark did not explain the situation, clearly.

The substitution of close synonyms would also clarify the difference:

Obviously, Mark did not explain the situation.
*Mark did not explain the situation obviously.
Mark did not explain the situation very well.
*Very well, Mark did not explain the situation.

Not all single-word sentence modifiers are as easy to demonstrate as this one, where a clear contrast in meaning exists between *clearly* in its two roles. But many adverbs do have this same parenthetical quality, this metadiscourse function:

> <u>Invariably</u>, the dress or pair of shoes I like best is the one with the highest price tag.
>
> <u>Luckily</u>, the van didn't get a scratch when it hit the ditch.
>
> <u>Undoubtedly</u>, we will see interest rates gradually rise.
>
> The book you want is out of print, <u>unfortunately</u>.

But not all sentence modifiers are separated by commas:

> <u>Perhaps</u> the entire starting lineup ought to be replaced.

Here it is fairly clear that *perhaps* raises a question about the idea of the sentence as a whole. If it were moved to a position within the sentence, it would probably be set off by commas:

> The entire starting lineup, <u>perhaps</u>, ought to be replaced.

So the absence of a comma after an introductory modifier does not rule it out as a sentence modifier; but neither does the presence of a comma rule it in. As we saw in the earlier chapters on noun and verb modifiers, both adjectivals and adverbials can sometimes be shifted to the opening position. That shift does not in itself make them sentence modifiers. For example, in the following sentences the introductory phrases are adjectival, modifiers of the subject:

> <u>Hot and tired</u>, we loaded the camping gear into the station wagon for the long trip home.
>
> <u>Limping noticeably</u>, the runner rounded third base and managed to beat the throw at home plate.

Verb modifiers in introductory position are somewhat more open to interpretation as sentence modifiers, because adverbials do tend to add information that relates to the whole idea. In Chapter 6 we classified phrases like the following as modifiers of the verb, although admittedly the designation is somewhat arbitrary; a case could be made for such modifiers to be classified as sentence modifiers rather than adverbials:

> <u>To polish his skills for his trip to Las Vegas</u>, Tim plays poker every night.
>
> <u>Almost every Monday morning</u>, I make a vow to start counting calories.
>
> <u>On a day like today</u>, I prefer to stay in bed.

The less clearly a modifier is related to a particular part of the sentence, the more clearly we can classify it as a modifier of the sentence as a whole. English has many idiomatic expressions—unvarying formulas that have an independent or parenthetical quality—that are clearly sentence modifiers. Unlike the previous three adverbial examples, the introductory modifiers in the following sentences are not added for information such as *when* or *where* or *why:*

> <u>Frankly</u>, I didn't expect sailing to be so much work.
>
> <u>To our amazement</u>, the driver of the Corvette walked away from the accident.
>
> <u>To my regret</u>, I've never seen the Grand Canyon.
>
> <u>Speaking of the weather</u>, let's decide on the place for our picnic.
>
> <u>To tell the truth</u>, I have never read *Silas Marner*.

Besides the adverb, these examples include two prepositional phrases, a participial phrase, and an infinitive phrase.

You might think that the last two sentence modifiers in the list, which are verb phrases in form, look suspiciously like the danglers that we have seen in earlier discussions of gerunds and infinitives and participles. But it's probably accurate to say that, in contrast to those earlier examples, *speaking of the weather* and *to tell the truth* have achieved the status of independent idiomatic expressions, or set phrases.

Another set phrase that is becoming fairly common in spoken news reports—*having said that*—has that same almost-dangling effect. Speakers use this phrase as a transition device, usually to an idea in support of the topic under discussion or sometimes to a new topic:

> <u>Having said that</u>, the economic indicators tell us a different story.
>
> <u>Having said that</u>, we can't forget the long-term effects of the deficit.

These set phrases are diagrammed apart from the rest of the sentence with their usual pattern:

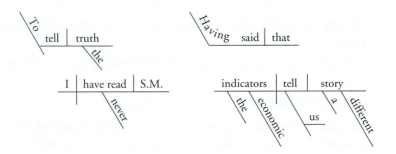

Usage Matters | "Hopefully"

Beginning in the 1960s, the adverb *hopefully* got the attention of a number of prominent language commentators, who condemned its usage as a sentence modifier in sentences like this:

Hopefully, we will get to the theater before the play starts.

Here the writer means "I hope" or "It is to be hoped." However, the critics—along with many writers of grammar and usage books—maintained that because *hopefully* is a "manner" adverb, it can mean only "in a hopeful manner." (Interestingly, the criticism did not extend to the *–ly* adverbs such as *clearly* and *obviously*, which we have included in our discussion of sentence modifiers.)

By the 1990s, however, the anti-*hopefully* vogue had faded. Several of the critics publicly admitted they had changed their minds; for others, however, the battle goes on. The 2004 edition of *The Associated Press Stylebook* still denounces the usage: "Do not use it to mean it is hoped, let us [hope] or we hope" (page 117).

In *The Oxford Dictionary of American Usage and Style* (2000), author Bryan A. Garner maintains that "the battle is now over." However, he goes on to explain that "some stalwarts continue to condemn the word, so that anyone using it in the new sense is likely to have a credibility problem with some readers" (p. 172).

In other words, don't be surprised to see your teacher's red circle around *hopefully* if you have used it as a sentence modifier. But bear in mind that current usage—along with the opinion of many language professionals—is on your side.

NOUNS OF DIRECT ADDRESS: THE VOCATIVES

Another structure set off by a comma is the noun or noun phrase of direct address, known as a **vocative**:

Ladies and gentlemen, please be seated.

Jennifer, your date is here.

Although the vocative is not a modifier in the same sense that other structures are, in that it does not modify the meaning of the sentence, it does have a relationship to the sentence as a whole. And like other modifiers, it can come at the beginning, middle, or end of the sentence:

We certainly hope, my dear friends, that you will visit again soon.

I promise you won't see me here in court again, your honor.

Tell us, Mr. President, how your new tax plan will benefit the economy.

The purpose of the vocative, as the term "direct address" implies, is to direct the writer's or speaker's message to a particular person or group. (In most cases it's the speaker's message: This structure is much more common in speech than in writing.) And, as the foregoing examples illustrate, the vocative can express the attitude of the writer or speaker and reflect the tone, whether formal or informal, serious or light, familiar or distant. In that sense, certainly, the vocative is a "sentence modifier": It can affect the meaning of the words.

The vocatives are diagrammed just as the other sentence modifiers are, on a line set apart from the main clause.

INTERJECTIONS

The **interjection**—usually a single word or short phrase—can also be considered as a modifier of the sentence as a whole:

> <u>Oh</u>, don't frighten me like that!

> <u>Wow</u>! That's not what I expected.

The traditional view of grammar treats the interjection as one of the eight parts of speech, probably because there is no other way to categorize such "nonwords" as *oh* and *ah* and *wow* and *ouch*. However, many words that we recognize as nouns and verbs are also used as exclamatory sentence modifiers of this kind:

> <u>Heavens</u>, I don't know what to say.

> <u>Good grief</u>! Don't confuse me with the facts!

> <u>My word</u>! This will never do.

Like the vocatives, interjections are much more likely to occur in speech than in writing (other than written dialogue).

It might seem logical to consider these actual words as interjections, the same as we treat *oh* and *wow;* however, we do not put all such "interjections" into a single parts-of-speech class, as the traditional grammarians do. Such a classification distorts the principle on which we make judgments about word categories. Except for *oh* and *ah* and *whew* and a few others, we recognize interjections strictly by their exclamatory, or emotional, function in the sentence. It's true, of course, that the familiar definitions given to the traditional eight parts of speech are not necessarily consistent in their criteria; for example, nouns and verbs are defined according to their meaning (as names and as actions) and adjectives and adverbs by their function (as modifiers). Nevertheless, out of all eight traditional "parts of speech," only the interjection category is denoted strictly by sentence function, rather than as a word type; that is, the other seven traditional parts of speech (noun, verb, adjective, adverb, pronoun, preposition, and conjunction) are names of word classes. It is for this reason that the interjection is not included in our inventory of structure words, described in Chapter 13, but, rather, is included here as a function, one kind of sentence modifier.

Interjections, like the other sentence modifiers, are diagrammed on a separate line.

Exercise 39

Underline any sentence modifiers in the following sentences.

1. Amazingly, the money held out until the end of the month.
2. The twins look amazingly alike.
3. Well, I plan to stay, myself.
4. Myself, I plan to stay well.
5. Strangely, he seemed to look right through me.
6. I thought he looked at me strangely.
7. Without a doubt our team will win the league championship.
8. We will no doubt win the league championship.
9. I told my friend I was not interested in her scheme.
10. I told you, my friend, that I am not interested.

SUBORDINATE CLAUSES

In Chapter 6 we looked at the adverbial clauses, recognizing that they, too, often seem to relate to the sentence as a whole rather than to the verb specifically. Those introduced by *where, when, before,* and *after* seem to be the most "adverbial" of all in that they convey information of time and place about the verb; but certainly we could make an equal case for classifying even these as sentence modifiers. **Subordinate clauses** introduced by such subordinators as *if, since, as,* and *although* seem even more clearly to modify the idea of the whole sentence, because the subordinator explains the relationship of one idea to another:

If you promise to be there, I'll go to Sue's party.

I'll go with you, *although* I would rather stay home.

The phrasal subordinators, too, may relate one complete clause to another:

Provided that the moving van arrives on schedule, we'll be ready to leave by three o'clock.

All the members of the city council, *as far as* I know, voted in favor of the new dog ordinance.

(See page 281 for a list of the simple and phrasal subordinators.)

Some of the interrogatives and **indefinite relative pronouns** introduce conditional clauses that are clearly sentence modifiers:

> *Whatever* decision you eventually make, I'll support you.
>
> *Whichever* route we take, there's no way we'll get there on time in this traffic.
>
> *No matter how much* overtime I work, my paycheck never seems to stretch far enough.

The subjunctive *if* clauses that we saw in Chapter 4 can also join this list of clauses that say something about the sentence as a whole:

> If I were you, I'd skip the party.

Punctuation of Subordinate Clauses. In opening position the subordinate clause is always set off by a comma; in closing position, punctuation is related to meaning. As a general rule, when the idea in the main clause is conditional upon or dependent upon the idea in the subordinate clause, there is no comma. For example, the idea of the main clause—the opening clause—in the following sentence will be realized only if the idea in the subordinate clause is carried out; thus here the main clause depends on the *if* clause:

> I'll go to Sue's party *if you promise to be there.*

But in the next sentence the subordinate clause does not affect the fulfillment of the main clause:

> I'm going to the party that Sue's giving on Saturday night, *even though I know I'll be bored.*

The distinction between these two functions is comparable to the restrictive/nonrestrictive distinction we examined in connection with adjectivals in Chapter 7. If the subordinate clause "defines" the situation, it will not be set off from the main clause; if it simply "comments," it will take the comma.

In general, *even though* and *although* are preceded by commas; *if* is not. The point to be made here is that the subordinator relates the idea in its clause to the idea in the main clause, so the subordinate clause clearly functions as a modifier of the sentence as a whole—even though it is not preceded by a comma. But in opening position, the clause is always followed by a comma. The use of the comma with final subordinate clauses is probably one of the least standardized of our punctuation rules. The final criteria must be readability and clarity for the reader.

Exercise 40

Add commas to the following sentences, if necessary.

1. We left the party as soon as we politely could.
2. Jim agreed to leave the party early and go bowling with us although he was having a good time.
3. When the storm is over we can head for home.
4. We might as well put on the coffee since we're going to be here for another hour.
5. I know that Jerry and I will never be able to afford that much money for rent even if it does include utilities.
6. I won't be able to stay in this apartment if the rent goes any higher.
7. I won't be able to stay in this apartment even if the rent stays the same.
8. If you can't stand the heat get out of the kitchen. [Harry Truman]

Elliptical Clauses. Many subordinate clauses are **elliptical**—that is, certain understood words are left out:

> <u>While</u> [we were] <u>waiting for the guests to arrive</u>, we ate all the good hors d'oeuvres ourselves.

> <u>When</u> [I am] <u>in doubt about the weather</u>, I always carry an umbrella.

As a reader, you have no problem understanding either of those elliptical clauses: In both cases the missing words, the subject of the elliptical clause, show up as the subject of the main clause.

What would happen if that understood subject did not show up? The result would be a fuzzy sentence, similar to those we have seen with dangling participles and gerunds and infinitives. Like the opening verb phrase, the elliptical element sets up certain expectations in the reader; it's the writer's job to fulfill those expectations. Consider what you expect in the main clause following these elliptical openers:

> *<u>When late for work</u>, the subway is better than the bus.

> *<u>If kept too long in hot weather</u>, mold will grow on the bread.

> *<u>While driving to the game on Saturday</u>, an accident tied up traffic for over an hour.

As with many of the dangling structures we have seen, the message of the sentence may be clear; but there's simply no reason for a writer to set up a situation in which the reader must make the connections—and must do so in a conscious way. Those connections are the writer's job.

In some cases only the elliptical version is grammatical:

I'm a week older <u>than Bob</u>.

My sister isn't <u>as tall as I</u>.

or

I'm a week older <u>than Bob is</u>.

My sister isn't as tall <u>as I am</u>.

We would never include the entire clause:

*I'm a week older <u>than Bob is old</u>.

*My sister isn't as tall <u>as I am tall</u>.

In both of these examples, we are comparing an attribute of the subjects of the two clauses. But the ellipses in such comparisons can produce ambiguity when the main clause has more than one possible noun phrase for the subordinate clause to be compared with:

The Packers beat the Patriots worse <u>than the Panthers</u>.

Joe likes Mary better <u>than Pat</u>.

In these sentences we don't know whether the comparison is between subjects or objects because we don't know what has been left out. We don't know whether

The Packers beat the Patriots worse <u>than</u>	}	the Packers beat the Panthers. *or* the Panthers beat the Patriots.
Joe likes Mary better <u>than</u>	}	Joe likes Pat. *or* Pat likes Mary.

See the Appendix for diagrams illustrating these clauses (page 370).

The comparison in the clauses with *as . . . as* can become a problem when an alternative comparison is added. Here is how such comparisons should read:

Our team is <u>as good as</u>, or <u>better than</u>, the Wildcats.

But sometimes the writer (or speaker) omits the second *as:*

*Our team is as good, or better than, the Wildcats.

*My sister is just as strong, or stronger than, you.

These omissions do not result in ambiguity, but the sentences clearly have a grammatical problem—an incomplete comparison.

Incidentally, these clauses of comparison are actually modifying adjectives—*older, tall, worse, better, good,* and *strong*—the qualities that are being compared, rather than modifying the sentence as a whole. We are discussing them here with the sentence modifiers because of the shared elliptical feature.

Exercise 41

A. Rewrite the three sentences on page 197 to include a subject in the elliptical clause. You may have to make changes in the main clause as well.

1. When late for work, the subway is better than the bus.
2. If kept too long in hot weather, mold will grow on the bread.
3. While driving to the game on Saturday, an accident tied up traffic for over an hour.

B. Now rewrite the following sentences, supplying the words missing in the elliptical clauses. Are the sentences clear?

1. I picked up a Midwestern accent while living in Omaha.
2. My accent is not as noticeable as Carlo's.
3. Holmes hit Ali harder than Norton.
4. If necessary, strain the juice before adding the sugar.
5. While waiting at the train station in Lewistown, there was no place to sit.
6. If handed in late, your grade will be lowered 10 percent.
7. Love goes toward love, as schoolboys from their books. But love from love, toward school with heavy looks. [Shakespeare]
8. The weather in Little Rock is not as humid as New Orleans.

ABSOLUTE PHRASES

The absolute phrase (also known as the *nominative absolute*) is a structure independent from the main sentence; in form the absolute phrase is a noun phrase that includes a postnoun modifier. The modifier is commonly an *-en* or *-ing* participle or participial phrase, but it can also be a prepositional phrase, an adjective phrase, or a noun phrase. The absolute phrase introduces an idea related to the sentence as a whole, not to any one of its parts:

> Our car having developed engine trouble, we stopped for the night at a roadside rest area.

> The weather being warm and clear, we decided to have a picnic.

> Victory assured, the fans stood and cheered during the last five minutes of the game.

Absolute phrases are of two kinds—with different purposes and different effects. (Moreover, both are structures generally used in writing, rather than in speech.) The preceding sentences illustrate the first kind: the absolute that explains a cause or condition. In the first sentence, the absolute phrase could be rewritten as a *because, when,* or *since* clause:

> When our car developed engine trouble,
> *or*
> Since our car developed engine trouble,   } we stopped for the night. . . .
> *or*
> Because our car developed engine trouble,

The absolute construction allows the writer to include the information without the explicitness that the complete clause requires. In other words, the absolute phrase can be thought of as containing all the meanings in the three versions shown here rather than any one of them.

In the following sentence the idea in the *because* clause could be interpreted as the only reason for the picnic:

> <u>Because the weather was warm and clear</u>, we decided to have
> a picnic.

The absolute construction, on the other hand, leaves open the possibility of other reasons for the picnic:

> <u>The weather being warm and clear</u>, we decided to have a picnic.

It also suggests simply an attendant condition rather than a cause.

Perhaps the most famous absolute phrase is the one found in the Second Amendment to the U.S. Constitution. And, as we know, it is open to more than one interpretation:

> <u>A well-regulated militia, being necessary to the security of a free state</u>, the right of the people to keep and bear arms, shall not be infringed.

The author might have been well advised to use a structure other than the absolute phrase: A full clause or a separate sentence could have forestalled the controversy that surrounds the amendment's meaning. We should note, too, that the convention of comma use has changed in the intervening years; two of those commas are superfluous by today's standards.

In the second kind of absolute phrase, illustrated by the sentences following, a prepositional phrase (*above his head*), adjective phrase (*alert to every passing footstep*), or noun phrase (*a dripping mess*), as well as a participle (*trembling*), may serve as the postnoun modifier. This second kind of absolute adds a detail or point of focus to the idea stated in the main clause:

> Julie tried to fit the key into the rusty lock, <u>her hands trembling</u>.
>
> The old hound stood guard faithfully, <u>his ears alert to every passing footstep</u>.
>
> <u>Hands above his head</u>, the suspect advanced cautiously toward the uniformed officers.
>
> <u>Her hair a dripping mess</u>, she dashed in out of the rain.

This technique of focusing on a detail allows the writer to move the reader in for a close-up view, just as a filmmaker uses the camera. The absolute phrase is especially effective in writing description. Notice how the authors of the following passages use the main clause of the sentence as the wide lens and the absolute phrase as the close-up:

> There was no bus in sight and Julian, <u>his hands still jammed in his pockets and his head thrust forward</u>, scowled down the empty street.
>
> Flannery O'Connor, *Everything That Rises Must Converge*

> The man stood laughing, <u>his weapons at his hips</u>.
>
> Stephen Crane, *The Bride Comes to Yellow Sky*

> To his right the valley continued in its sleepy beauty, mute and understated, <u>its wildest autumn colors blunted by the distance</u>, placid as a water color by an artist who mixed all his colors with brown.
>
> Joyce Carol Oates, *The Secret Marriage*

The traditional diagram of the absolute simply shows the noun phrase on a line separate from the main clause, with the headword on the horizontal:

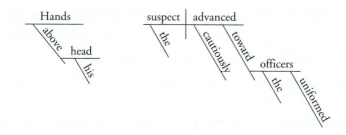

Exercise 42

Underline any absolute phrases in the following sentences. Is the modifier of the headword an adjective, a prepositional phrase, a noun phrase, or a participle?

1. The cat lay by the fire, purring contentedly, her tail moving from side to side like a metronome.

2. Chuck and Margie kicked their way through the fallen leaves, their arms draped across each other's shoulders.

3. The rain having persisted for over an hour, the game was officially stopped in the sixth inning.

4. Michelle lounged in front of the fire, her book open on the floor, her eyes intent on the flames.

5. He saw the city spread below like a glittering golden ocean, the streets tiny ribbons of light, the planet curving away at the edges, the sky a purple hollow extending into infinity. [Anne Tyler]

6. Then the boy was moving, his bunched shirt and the hard, bony hand between his shoulder-blades, his toes just touching the floor, across the room and into the other one, past the sisters sitting with spread heavy thighs in the two chairs over the cold hearth, and to where his mother and aunt sat side by side on the bed, the aunt's arms about his mother's shoulders. [William Faulkner]

APPOSITIVES

You'll recall that one of the nominals described in Chapter 8 is the appositive, a structure that in form is often a noun phrase:

> Our visitor, <u>a grey-haired lady of indeterminate age</u>, surprised us all when she joined in the volleyball game.

In this example, the appositive renames the subject of the sentence. But sometimes we use a noun phrase to rename or, more accurately, to encapsulate the idea in the sentence as a whole. We call these structures sentence appositives:

> He waved his pink right hand in circles, <u>his favorite gesture</u>.
>
> JOHN FOWLES, *The Magus*

We often use a dash to set off the sentence appositive:

> The musical opened to rave reviews and standing-room-only crowds—<u>a smashing success</u>.
>
> A pair of cardinals has set up housekeeping in our pine tree—<u>an unexpected but welcome event</u>.

Like the absolutes, which are also noun phrases in form, these sentence appositives are related to the sentence as a whole, but their purpose is quite different: They simply label, or restate, the idea of the main clause; they do not introduce a new, subordinate idea, as both kinds of absolute phrases do.

The rhetorical effects of sentence appositives are discussed further in Chapter 15, page 319.

RELATIVE CLAUSES

Most relative clauses are modifiers of nouns, and most are introduced by a relative pronoun that refers to that noun:

> Joe's car, <u>which he bought just last week</u>, looks like a gas guzzler to me.

In this sentence the antecedent of *which* is the noun *car;* the noun is modified by the clause.

But in some sentences *which* refers not to a particular noun but to a whole idea; it has what we call *broad reference.* In the following sentence, the antecedent of *which* is the idea of the entire main clause:

> Joe bought a gas guzzler, <u>which surprised me</u>.

All such broad-reference clauses are introduced by *which*, never by *who* or *that*, and all are nonrestrictive—that is, they are set off by commas:

> Tom cleaned up the garage without being asked, <u>which made me suspect that he wanted to borrow the car</u>.
>
> This summer's heat wave in the Midwest devastated the corn crop, <u>which probably means higher meat prices for next year</u>.

Many writers try to avoid the broad-reference relative clause, instead using *which* only in the adjectival clause to refer to a specific noun. In inexperienced hands the broad-reference *which* clause often has the vagueness associated with dangling modifiers:

> I broke out in a rash, <u>which really bothered me</u>.

In this sentence the referent of *which* is unclear; *which* could refer to either the *rash* or the *breaking out.* There are a number of alternatives in which the meaning is clear:

> Breaking out in a rash really bothered me.
>
> The rash I got last week really bothered me.

Even though they are not particularly vague, the earlier examples, too, can be revised in ways that avoid the broad-reference *which:*

> When Tom cleaned up the garage without being asked, I suspected that he wanted to borrow the car.
>
> Tom's cleaning up the garage without being asked made me suspect that he wanted to borrow the car.
>
> This summer's heat wave in the Midwest, which devastated the corn crop, probably means higher meat prices for next year.

Exercise 43

Rewrite the following sentences to eliminate the broad-reference *which.*

1. I had to clean the basement this morning, which wasn't very much fun.

2. Otis didn't want to stay for the second half of the game, which surprised me.

3. The president criticized the Congress rather severely in his press conference, which some observers considered quite inappropriate.

4. The first snowstorm of the season in Denver was both early and severe, which was not what the weather service had predicted.

5. We're having company for dinner three times this week, which probably means hot dogs for the rest of the month.

CHAPTER 9
Key Terms

Absolute phrase

Broad-reference clause

Direct address

Elliptical clause

Idiomatic expression

Independent modifier

Interjection

Metadiscourse

Relative clause

Sentence appositive

Sentence modifier

Subordinate clause

Vocative

Sentences
for PRACTICE

Draw vertical lines to set off sentence modifiers; identify them by form. If the sentence modifier is, or includes, a verb phrase or clause, identify its sentence pattern.

1. My brother will finish basic training next month if everything goes smoothly.

2. If you don't mind, I want to be alone.

3. Speaking of travel, would you like to go to Seattle next week to see the Seahawks play?

4. Incidentally, you forgot to pay me for your share of the expenses.

5. The weather being so beautiful last Sunday, we decided to go to Silver Creek Falls for a picnic.

6. The invitations having been sent, we started planning the menu for Maria's birthday party.

7. Jennifer stayed in bed all day, her fever getting worse instead of better.

8. The giant redwoods loomed majestically, their branches filling the sky above us.

9. Luckily, Sunday was a nice day, so we didn't miss our weekly hike.

10. Freddie suggested we take a taxi instead of the subway—a splendid idea.

11. Old Town was festive, indeed—the stores decorated with bright-colored banners, the air alive with music, the streets crowded with people.

12. If I can stop one heart from breaking, I shall not live in vain. [Emily Dickinson]

QUESTIONS
?
for DISCUSSION

1. Many of the simple and phrasal subordinators listed on page 281 introduce clauses that could be interpreted as either sentence modifiers or verb modifiers. How would you classify

the underlined clauses in the following sentences—as sentence modifiers or as verb modifiers? Why?

> I'll return your book <u>as soon as I finish it</u>.
>
> He'll lend me the money <u>provided that I use it for tuition</u>.
>
> The dog looked at me <u>as if he wanted to tell me something important</u>.
>
> Nero fiddled <u>while Rome burned</u>.

2. The following sentences are both illogical and ungrammatical. What is the source of the problem?

> The summer temperatures in the Santa Clara Valley are much higher than San Francisco.
>
> The Pirates' stolen-base record is better than the Cardinals.

3. The following sentence is less elliptical than those you just read, but it's equally fuzzy. What is the source of its problem?

> The people of Atlanta are much friendlier than they are in New York.

4. Consider the pronouns in these elliptical clauses. Are they the correct form? Is it possible that both sentences are correct?

> I think my little sister likes our cat better than me.
>
> I think my little sister likes our cat better than I.

5. How do you explain the difference in meaning between the following sentences, which appear so similar on the surface? Discuss the effect of the understood elliptical clause in the second sentence. Are both sentences negative?

> I have never been happy with our living arrangement.
>
> I have never been happier with our living arrangement.

6. The little comma can carry a great deal of meaning. Explain why it's so important in this sentence.

> You should call the boss, Herbert.

What happens to the meaning of the sentence when the comma is removed? Use your knowledge of sentence patterns in thinking about the two meanings.

7. As you consider the ambiguity of the following sentence, think about two of the topics you have studied in this chapter and in the previous one, vocatives and appositives:

> I am taking a trip with Mildred, my dear friend.

Rewrite the sentence in two ways to show its meanings unambiguously.

CLASSROOM APPLICATIONS

1. Combine the following pairs of sentences, reducing one of them to a sentence modifier. Experiment with variations.

   Example:

   I was lucky. I knew how to swim.
   <u>Luckily, I knew how to swim</u>.

   1. The door was closed. We climbed in the back window.
   2. The guests departed. We resumed our normal household routine.
   3. Consider the circumstances. He was lucky to escape alive.
   4. Felice is the best tenor in the choir. That's my opinion.
   5. I'll tell you the truth. I don't like your new haircut.
   6. She did not complete her thesis. That is unfortunate.
   7. The copy machine has been malfunctioning. That was apparent.
   8. It doesn't matter what you say. Graham is going to quit school.

2. One popular technique for teaching writing, which dates back to the schools of ancient Greece, is known as modeling. Students learn to write by copying the form of sentences, using the same blueprint while supplying new words. For this exercise, you are to model the following sentences, some of which you saw earlier as examples of absolute phrases. Remember the comparison of the absolute to the close-up view; the main clause provides the wide-angle shot.

   Example:

   The man stood laughing, his weapon at his hips. [Stephen Crane]

   Modeled version:

   The woman sat smoking, a black poodle in her lap.

   1. With a breathy shriek the train pulled away, the crowd cheering, waving at the caboose until it was out of sight. [E. Annie Proulx]
   2. There was no bus in sight and Julian, his hands still jammed in his pockets and his head thrust forward, scowled down the empty street. [Flannery O'Connor]

3. He smiled to himself as he ran, holding the ball lightly in front of him with his two hands, his knees pumping high, his hips twisting in the almost girlish run of a back in a broken field. [Irwin Shaw]

4. Soon afterwards they retired, Mama in her big oak bed on one side of the room, Emilio and Rosy in their boxes full of straw and sheepskins on the other side of the room. [John Steinbeck]

Coordination

CHAPTER PREVIEW

Throughout the previous chapters you have been seeing coordination within sentences, both in the samples for discussion and in the text itself. In fact, the sentence you just read includes one such structure, a compound prepositional phrase connected by the correlative conjunction *both–and*. We make these connections at every level—word, phrase, and clause; in speech we do so automatically.

In this chapter we will take up several features of compound structures within the sentence and then look at the coordination of whole sentences, with special emphasis on the punctuation conventions that apply to them.

By the end of this chapter you will be able to

- Punctuate coordinate structures within sentences.
- Recognize *elliptical coordinate structures* and revise unclear ones.
- Use correct *subject-verb agreement* with coordinate noun phrases in the subject slot.
- Identify and use *parallel forms* with coordinate constructions.
- Use the three methods for creating *compound sentences: coordinating conjunctions, semicolons,* and *colons.*
- Understand the difference between *coordinating conjunctions* and *conjunctive adverbs.*

COORDINATION WITHIN THE SENTENCE

Punctuation. A simple punctuation rule applies to nearly all the compound pairs of words, phrases, and clauses that occur within the sentence: *We use no comma with the conjunction.* Notice in the following examples that no comma appears even when the two parts being joined are fairly long:

> On Homecoming weekend our frat party <u>started at noon *and* lasted until dawn</u>. (compound verb phrase)
>
> I will buy <u>*either* the blue dress with the long sleeves *or* the green print with a matching jacket</u>. (compound noun phrase)
>
> He said <u>that he would get here sooner or later *and* that I shouldn't start the rehearsal without him</u>. (compound nominal clause)

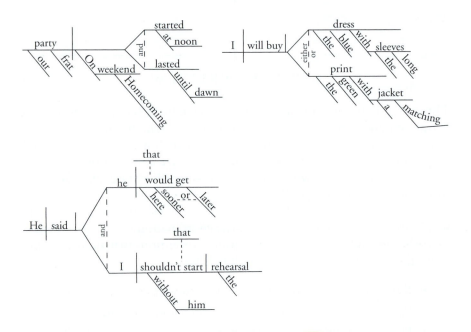

An exception to the rule against commas with compound elements occurs when the conjunction is *but:*

> I have visited a lot of big cities, <u>but</u> never Los Angeles.
>
> I worked hard all night, <u>but</u> just couldn't finish my project.
>
> My new white dress is beautiful, <u>but</u> not very practical.

There's a clear disjunction with *but*, resulting, of course, from its meaning: It introduces a contrast. Furthermore, the phrase introduced by *but* could almost be thought of as an elliptical clause, another reason that the comma seems logical:

> I worked hard all night, but [I] just couldn't finish my project.
>
> My new white dress is beautiful, but [it is] not very practical.

Another exception to the comma restriction occurs when we want to give special emphasis to the second element in a coordinated pair:

> I didn't believe him, and said so.
>
> My new white dress is beautiful, and expensive.

This emphasis will be even stronger with a dash instead of a comma:

> I didn't believe him—and said so.
>
> My new white dress is beautiful—and expensive.

We also use commas with a series of three or more elements:

> We gossiped, laughed, and sang together at the class reunion, just like old times.

These commas represent the pauses and slight changes of pitch that occur in the production of the series. You can hear the commas in your voice when you compare the two—the series and the pair. Read them aloud:

> We gossiped, laughed, and sang.
>
> We laughed and sang.

You probably noticed a leveling of the pitch in reading the pair, a certain smoothness that the series did not have. In the series with conjunctions instead of commas, you'll notice that same leveling:

> We gossiped <u>and</u> laughed <u>and</u> sang together at the class reunion, just like old times.

When conjunctions connect all the elements, we use no commas.

In the series of three, some writers—and some publications as a matter of policy—use only one comma, leaving out the **serial comma,** the one immediately before *and:*

> We gossiped, laughed <u>and</u> sang together at the class reunion, just like old times.

Perhaps they do so on the assumption that the conjunction substitutes for the comma. But it really does not. In fact, this punctuation misleads the reader in two ways: It implies a closer connection than actually exists between the last two elements of the series, and it ignores the pitch change, however slight, represented by the comma. The main purpose of punctuation, after all, is to represent graphically the meaningful speech signals—pitch, stress (loudness), and juncture (pauses)—that the written language otherwise lacks. That small pitch change represented by the comma can make a difference in emphasis and meaning.[1]

Exercise 44

Punctuate the following sentences.

1. Pete sanded the car on Friday and painted it with undercoating on Saturday.

2. Even though the car's new paint job looks terrific now I suspect it will be covered with rust and scratches and dents before next winter.

3. I spent a fortune on new tires shock absorbers and brake linings for the car last week.

4. The car that my grandfather had back in the 1960s and 1970s a 1959 Chevy required very little maintenance and no major repairs during the ten or more years he drove it.

5. I have decided to park my car until gas prices go down and to ride my bicycle instead.

6. I don't suppose I'll ever be able to afford either the down payment or the insurance on a new Corvette the car of my dreams.

Elliptical Coordinate Structures. Elliptical structures are those in which something has been left out. You'll recall from the discussion in the previous chapter that fuzziness or ambiguity sometimes results when the "understood" element is not, in fact, understood. The same kind of problem can occur with coordinate structures.

One common ellipsis is the elimination of the second determiner in a coordinate noun phrase:

The cat and dog are sleeping on the porch.

A problem can arise when the noun phrase includes modifiers:

Our new cat and dog are sleeping on the porch.

The clear implication of the noun phrase is that both the cat and the dog are new. If that's not the case, then *dog* needs its own determiner:

Our new cat and our dog are sleeping on the porch.

or

Our dog and new cat are sleeping on the porch.

---

[1] *The Chicago Manual of Style*, fifteenth edition, concurs with this view of the serial comma.

Postnoun modifiers can also be the source of ambiguity in coordinate structures:

> Visitors to this area always admire the flower gardens and stately elms on campus.

Without a determiner for *elms*, the reader is justified in inferring that both the flowers and trees are on the campus, although it's certainly possible that the writer had a different intention. The problem of ambiguity is much more blatant when both noun phrases have determiners:

> Visitors to this area always admire the flower gardens and the stately elms on campus.

Now the reader has no way to decide what *on campus* modifies. If only the elms are on campus, the writer can either reverse the two noun phrases or add another modifier so that both locations are clear:

> . . . the stately elms on campus and the flower gardens.
> . . . the flower gardens near City Hall and the stately elms on campus.

Here's a similar problem sentence, one with an ambiguous *by* phrase:

> Penn State's administration building, Old Main, is best known for its presidential portraits and [its] murals by Henry Varnum Poor.

With or without the determiner for *murals*, this sentence is ambiguous. Another problem can occur with numbers as determiners:

> There were six men and women waiting in line.
> There were six dogs and cats on the porch.
> There were six mothers and daughters at the mother-daughter reception.

We don't, of course, know whether the noun phrases include six or twelve people or animals.

There are many possibilities for structural ambiguity, where the reader simply has no way of knowing the writer's intention. Coordinate structures are especially open to misinterpretation. It's the job of the writer to make sure that the meaning is clear.

Subject–Verb Agreement. When nouns or noun phrases in the subject slot are joined by *and* or by the correlative *both–and*, the subject is plural:

> My roommate and his brother are coming to the wedding.

However, the coordinating conjunction *or* and the correlatives *either–or* and *neither–nor* do not have the additive meaning of *and;* with *or* and *nor* the relationship is called disjunctive. In compound subjects with these conjunctions, the verb will be determined by the closer member of the pair:

> Neither the speaker nor <u>the listeners were</u> intimidated by the protestors.
>
> Either the class officers or <u>the faculty advisor makes</u> the final decision.
>
> <u>Do the class officers</u> or the faculty advisor make the final decision?
>
> <u>Does the faculty advisor</u> or the class officers make the final decision?

If the correct sentence sounds incorrect or awkward because of the verb form, you can simply reverse the compound pair:

> Either the faculty advisor or <u>the class officers make</u> the final decision.

When both members of the pair are alike, of course, there is no question:

> Either <u>the president</u> or <u>the vice president is</u> going to introduce the speaker.
>
> Neither <u>the union members</u> nor <u>the management representatives were</u> willing to compromise.

For most verb forms, you'll recall, there is no decision to be made about subject–verb agreement; the issue arises only when the *-s* form of the verb or auxiliary is involved. In the following sentences, there is no *-s* form:

> Either the class officers or the faculty advisor <u>will make</u> the final decision.
>
> Either the faculty advisor or the class officers <u>will make</u> the final decision.

Another situation that sometimes causes confusion about number—that is, whether the subject is singular or plural—occurs with subjects that include a phrase introduced by *as well as* or *in addition to* or *along with:*

> *The sidewalk, in addition to the driveway, need to be repaired.
>
> *The piano player, as well as the rest of the group, usually join in the singing.
>
> *Mike, along with several friends, often help out at the bakery on weekends.

These additions to the subject are parenthetical; they are not treated as part of the subject. To make the subject compound—to include them—the writer should use a coordinating conjunction, such as *and:*

> The sidewalk <u>and</u> the driveway <u>need</u> to be repaired.
> The piano player <u>and</u> the rest of the group usually <u>join</u> in the singing.
> Mike <u>and</u> several friends often <u>help</u> out at the bakery on weekends.

Parallel Structure. An important requirement for coordinate structures is that they be **parallel**. A structure is parallel when all the coordinate parts are of the same grammatical form. The conjunctions must join comparable structures, such as pairs of noun phrases or verb phrases or adjectives:

> The <u>short blonde woman</u> *and* <u>her apricot poodle</u> seemed to belong together.
> The stew <u>smells delicious</u> *and* <u>tastes even better</u>.
> The entire cast gave <u>powerful</u> *and* <u>exciting</u> performances.

Unparallel structures occur most commonly with the correlative conjunctions: *both–and, either–or, neither–nor,* and *not only–but also*. For example, in the following sentence, the two coordinators introduce structures of different forms:

> **Either* <u>they will fly straight home</u> *or* <u>stop overnight in Dubuque</u>.

Being able to picture the diagram can be helpful in preventing such unparallel structures. With the sentence above, you'll discover that the conjunction line would connect a complete sentence (*they will fly straight home*) and a verb phrase (*stop overnight in Dubuque*). Because the two structures are not parallel, the diagram simply won't work.

A diagram of the following sentence won't work either:

> **I'll *either* <u>take a bus</u> *or* <u>a taxi</u>.

The conjunction line would have to connect a verb phrase and a noun phrase; again the two structures are not parallel.

Such problems are easy to correct. It's just a matter of shifting one part of the correlative pair so that both introduce the same kind of construction:

> They will *either* <u>fly straight home</u> *or* <u>stop overnight in Dubuque</u>.
> I'll take *either* <u>a bus</u> *or* <u>a taxi</u>.

Further examples of the correlative conjunctions are given on page 279.

Rewrite the following sentences, paying particular attention to unparallel structures and agreement errors.

1. I can't decide which activity I prefer: to swim at the shore in July, when the sand is warm, or jogging along country roads in October, when the autumn leaves are at their colorful best.

2. I almost never watch television. There is either nothing on that appeals to me or the picture disappears at a crucial moment.

3. I neither enjoy flying across the country nor particularly want to take the train.

4. Either the members of the school board or the superintendent make the final decision.

5. The recipe was either printed wrong, or I misread it.

6. I was unhappy with what he said and the way he said it.

7. The coach announced an extra hour of drill on Saturday and that the practice on Sunday would be canceled.

8. My history class, as well as both English classes, require a term paper.

9. Aunt Rosa has promised to fix her famous lasagna for my birthday dinner and will also bake my favorite cake.

10. For the picnic we brought baskets of chicken and lemonade.

COORDINATING COMPLETE SENTENCES

We have three methods of joining independent clauses to produce **compound sentences:** (1) using coordinating conjunctions; (2) using the semicolon, either with or without conjunctive adverbs; and (3), for limited situations, using the colon.

Conjunctions. The compound sentence with a coordinating conjunction such as *and* shows up at an early stage of the writer's development:

> We went to the fair, <u>and</u> we had a good time.
> Robby is mean, <u>and</u> I don't like him.

Such sentences can, of course, be effective when they are used sparingly, but they will strike the reader as immature when overused. The compound sentence is most effective when the coordinate ideas have relatively equal importance—when the two ideas contribute equal weight:

> I disapprove of her spending money on lottery tickets, <u>and</u> I told her so.
>
> The curtain rose to reveal a perfectly bare stage, <u>and</u> a stillness settled over the audience.
>
> Pete filled the bags with hot roasted peanuts, <u>and</u> I stapled them shut.

Note that the punctuation rule that applies to the compound sentence differs from the rule regarding internal coordinate constructions. Between the sentences in a compound sentence we do use a comma with the conjunction; between the parts of a coordinate structure within the sentence we do not. When the clauses of a compound sentence are quite short and closely connected, however, we sometimes omit the comma. The following sentence, for example, would probably be spoken without the pitch change we associate with commas:

> October came <u>and</u> the tourists left.

The coordinators *and* and *or* can link a series of three or more sentences:

> Pete filled the bags, <u>and</u> I stapled them shut, <u>and</u> Marty packed them in the cartons.
>
> The kids can wait for me at the pool, <u>or</u> they can go over to the shopping center and catch the bus, <u>or</u> they can even walk home.

In these two sentences, the first conjunction can be replaced by a comma:

> Pete filled the bags, I stapled them shut, <u>and</u> Marty packed them in the cartons.

But usually joins only two clauses:

> Jill wanted me to wait for her, <u>but</u> I refused.

But can introduce the final clause when *and* or *or* joins the first two:

> Pete filled the bags, <u>and</u> I stapled them, <u>but</u> Marty refused to lift a finger.
>
> The kids can wait for me at the pool, <u>or</u> they can walk to the bus stop, <u>but</u> I really think they ought to walk home.

Semicolons. When a semicolon connects two coordinate clauses, the conjunction can be omitted:

> Pete packed the hot roasted peanuts into bags; I stapled them shut.
>
> The curtain rose; a stillness settled over the audience.

The semicolon is also used when a **conjunctive adverb** introduces the second clause. Note, too, that the conjunctive adverb is set off by a comma:

> We worked hard for the Consumer Party candidates, ringing doorbells and stuffing envelopes; <u>however</u>, we knew they didn't stand a chance.
>
> We knew our candidates didn't have a hope of winning; <u>nevertheless</u>, for weeks on end we faithfully rang doorbells and stuffed envelopes.

Of all the adverbial conjunctions, only *yet* and *so* can be used with a comma instead of a semicolon between clauses:

> Several formations of birds were flying northward, <u>so</u> I knew spring was on the way.
>
> Several formations of birds were flying northward, <u>yet</u> I suspected that winter was far from over.

In both of these sentences, a semicolon could replace the comma, depending on the writer's emphasis. The semicolon would put extra emphasis on the second clause. *So* and *yet* straddle the border between the coordinating conjunctions and the conjunctive adverbs; they are often listed as both. In meaning, *so* is similar to *therefore* and *yet* to *however;* but unlike these conjunctive adverbs, *so* and *yet* always introduce the clause, so in this respect they are perhaps closer to the coordinating conjunctions. Sometimes we use both the conjunction and the adverbial: *and so; but yet.*

Because they are also adverbials, most conjunctive adverbs are movable; they can appear in the middle of the clause or at the end, as well as at the beginning:

> We worked hard for the Consumer Party candidates; we knew, <u>however</u>, they didn't stand a chance.
>
> *or*
>
> . . . we knew they didn't stand a chance, <u>however</u>.

Other common conjunctive adverbs are listed on page 280.

Colons. As a sentence connector, the colon is rather specialized. Unlike the semicolon, which connects sentences with the meaning of *and*, the colon makes an announcement of sorts: It means "namely." You're probably familiar with the colon that signals an appositive or a list:

> I'm taking three English courses this semester: advanced grammar, American lit, and Shakespeare.

Here the colon says, "Here it comes, the information I promised." When the colon signals a complete sentence, the message is similar. It promises to complete the idea set up in the first clause:

> We finally made our decision: we would sell the house and move.
>
> Easton, Pennsylvania, is a most colorful city: It's where Crayolas are made.
>
> Ideas are like children: There are none so wonderful as your own.

(Note: We have a choice of either capitalizing the word following the colon or using lower case, as the examples illustrate. A quotation following the colon calls for upper case.)

Diagramming the Compound Sentence. In the diagram a broken line connects the two verbs, with the connector on a solid line approximately halfway between the two clauses:

> Pete filled the bags, and I stapled them shut, but Marty refused to lift a finger.

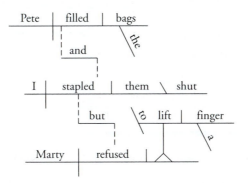

Investigating Language   10.1

Combine the following groups of sentences into compound sentences, using conjunctions of your choice, including conjunctive adverbs. In each case there are a number of possible ways to combine them, depending on the emphasis.

1. The library closes at noon on Thursdays.
   It is open until 9:00 p.m. on Fridays.

2. The food at the new French restaurant is exceptionally good.
   The prices are exceptionally high.

3. I am going to take piano lessons this fall.
   I may take guitar lessons, too.

4. My first-period students are bright.
   They are wide awake at 8:00 a.m., too.

5. Our trip across Kansas was long and straight and uneventful.
   The trip across Kansas took an entire day.

Now turn your compound sentences into **compound-complex sentences** by adding a dependent clause to each one. The dependent clause can be nominal, adverbial, or adjectival. (You may have to make other changes to accommodate the dependent clauses.)

1. _____

_____

2. _____

_____

3. _____

_____

4. _____

_____

5. _____

_____

CHAPTER 10
Key Terms

Colon

Compound sentence

Compound structure

Compound-complex sentence

Conjunction

Conjunctive adverb

Coordinating conjunction

Coordination

Correlative conjunction

Elliptical coordinate structure

Parallel structure

Semicolon

Serial comma

Subject–verb agreement

Sentences
for PRACTICE

Underline the sentence slots that have coordinate structures; circle the conjunctions. For further practice, identify the sentence patterns and diagram the sentences.

1. The housing market is caught in a cycle of falling prices and surging foreclosures.

2. I lent my son and daughter-in-law a sizable sum of money.

3. They have recently moved to Ohio and will soon be buying a new house.

4. To get your rebate, simply fill out the coupon and mail it to the company's headquarters in Michigan.

5. I have battled beetles and aphids and tent caterpillars for the entire summer.

6. During spring break many students and tourists will be going to our nation's capital to visit the historical monuments or perhaps to stroll along the streets and simply enjoy that beautiful city.

7. My friends and I, finding the movie boring, left at intermission and adjourned to our favorite hangout.

8. Thousands of Americans, united by a deep and urgent concern about the quality of life for themselves and future generations, have given both their money and their time to the environmental movement.

9. The hundreds of separate groups that make up the environmental movement are demonstrating to get the support of their fellow citizens and their legislators.

10. Having found an apartment that was inexpensive, roomy, and close to the subway, we made a split-second decision and rented it on the spot.

11. The boom in cosmetic surgery is apparently the result of new, more sophisticated procedures, safer anesthetics, and the desire for self-improvement.

12. Only two knots are required for most fly-fishing situations: a knot for tying on the fly and a knot for joining monofilament.

QUESTIONS
?
for DISCUSSION

1. In the following sentences the coordinate ideas are unparallel in form. Do some seem more acceptable than others? Rank them in order of acceptability. Rewrite those that can be improved.

    Almost every lineman on the squad was overweight and out of condition when the season started.

    She volunteered her services at the senior citizens' center frequently and with boundless enthusiasm.

    The old man, broke and having no friends to turn to, simply disappeared from the neighborhood.

    I have always loved sports of all kinds and jog regularly.

2. Consider the following compound sentences. Are they parallel? Can you find a way to improve them? What is their special problem?

    I fixed three bowls of popcorn for the party, but it was eaten up before most of the guests even got there.

    Burglars broke into the art museum last night, and three valuable paintings were stolen.

    The television lost its sound last week, but luckily it got fixed before the World Series started.

3. Explain the ambiguity of the compound structures in these two sentences.

    Six red and blue banners were hanging from the ceiling.

    My uncle sells used cars and motorcylces.

4. Explain why the verbs or auxiliaries in the following sentences would not be the *-s* form even though the subject headwords *crime* and *stamina* are singular.

> Blue-collar and white-collar crime are on the increase.
>
> Both physical and mental stamina are required for long-distance running.

5. The following passage commonly appears on labels of movie videos:

> This film has been modified from its original version. It has been formatted to fit your screen.

In what way would the meaning change if, instead of the period, a colon followed the first sentence? In what way is the passage ambiguous as written?

CLASSROOM APPLICATIONS

1. Notice how choppy and repetitious the following passage sounds:

> I know very little about laboratory science. I have the impression that conclusions are supposed to be logical. From a given set of circumstances a predictable result should follow. The trouble is that in human behavior it is impossible to isolate a given set of circumstances. It is also impossible to repeat these circumstances. That is true of history, too. Complex human acts cannot be reproduced. They cannot be deliberately initiated. They cannot be counted upon like the phenomena of nature.

Now read the original of that choppy passage (from an article by Barbara Tuchman, "Is History a Guide to the Future?"). Observe how coordination makes it smoother and more concise. (The coordinating conjunctions and transitional expressions have been italicized.)

> I know very little about laboratory science, *but* I have the impression that conclusions are supposed to be logical; *that is*, from a given set of circumstances a predictable result should follow. The trouble is that in human behavior *and* history it is impossible to isolate *or* repeat a given set of circumstances. Complex human acts cannot be *either* reproduced *or* deliberately initiated—*or* counted upon like the phenomena of nature.

Now revise the following passage (a "de-combined" section from Lewis Thomas's *Lives of a Cell*), using coordination to eliminate choppiness and unnecessary repetition:

> The Iks, a nomadic tribe in northern Uganda, have become celebrities. They have also become literary symbols for the ultimate fate of disheartened mankind. They are also symbols of heartless mankind at large. Two disastrous things happened to them. They were compelled to give up hunting. They had to become farmers on poor hillside soil. Also, an anthropologist detested them. The anthropologist wrote a book about them.

2. The following is a typical sentence-combining exercise—a list of sentences to be formed into an effective paragraph. As you can see, these sentences include a great deal of repetition, some of which you can eliminate by using coordination. Experiment with both coordination and modification in combining these ideas.

   1. The Anza-Borrego Desert State Park is California's largest state park.
   2. The Anza-Borrego encompasses 600,000 acres.
   3. The park reaches south to within three miles of the border with Mexico.
   4. The Santa Rosa Mountains form the western border of the Anza-Borrego.
   5. The Santa Rosa Mountains rise to a height of 8,700 feet.
   6. The San Ysidro Mountains form the southwestern border of the Anza-Borrego.
   7. The Anza-Borrego holds a rich archaeological heritage.
   8. Archaeologists have found evidence of early inhabitants.
   9. These early people lived in the Anza-Borrego 6,000 years ago.
   10. The technology of these people did not yet include pottery.
   11. Their technology did not include the bow and arrow.
   12. The Anza-Borrego is rich in fossil remains.
   13. The extinct North American camel has been uncovered in the Anza-Borrego.
   14. This camel is known as Camelops.
   15. The age of the camel fossils is estimated to be 800,000 years.

IV

Words and Word Classes

I f you studied traditional grammar in middle school or high school, you may remember learning about the eight "parts of speech": noun, verb, adjective, adverb, pronoun, preposition, conjunction, and interjection. As you may recall from Chapter 1, early grammarians came up with those eight categories in order to make their description of English conform to the word categories of Latin. Scholarly grammarians, however, recognize that the accurate description of a language—any language—requires a framework of its own.

When the structural linguists went about identifying the word categories of English, they did so by examining the language as it is actually used, by reading personal letters and listening to phone conversations. They looked at the words themselves, at their forms, their meanings, and their functions in the sentence, and then established two main categories: the **form classes** and the **structure classes**. We can think of the form-class words as the bricks of the language and the structure words as the mortar that holds them together.

Probably the most striking difference between the form classes and the structure classes is characterized by their numbers. Of the half million or more words in our language, the structure words—with some notable exceptions—can be counted in the hundreds. The form classes, however, are large, open classes; new nouns and verbs and adjectives and adverbs regularly enter the language as new technology and new ideas require them. They are sometimes abandoned, too, as the dictionary's "obsolete" and "archaic" labels testify. The structure classes, on the other hand, remain constant—and limited. It's true that we don't hear *whilst* and *betwixt* and *thy* anymore, nor do we see them in contemporary prose and poetry, but most of our structure words are identical to those that Shakespeare and his contemporaries used.

FORM CLASSES	STRUCTURE CLASSES	
Noun	Determiner	Pronoun
Verb	Auxiliary	Conjunction
Adjective	Qualifier	Interrogative
Adverb	Preposition	Expletive
		Particle

An important difference between the classes has to do with form. As their label suggests, the form classes are those that can undergo changes in form—that are, in fact, distinguishable by their form—whereas the structure classes are not. But, as with almost every "rule" of the language, we will encounter exceptions. For example, auxiliaries are among the structure classes, although some of them, because they are verbs, show form variations; *be, have,* and *do,* as you know, can be both auxiliaries and verbs. Some of the pronouns also have variations in form. On the other hand, there are many words in the form classes that have no distinctions in form and do not undergo change—nouns like *chaos,* adjectives like *main,* and adverbs like *there.*

Another complication in our two-part form/structure division is the inclusion of the determiner and qualifier classes, both of which are more accurately described as *functions,* rather than word classes. The determiner class, as you have seen, includes words from other classes, such as pronouns; the fact that it also includes possessive nouns actually makes it an open class. The qualifier class, too, includes words from other classes, such as adverbs, so that class, also, is open to membership.

Before looking at the classes individually, we need to examine the basic unit of word formation, the morpheme; an understanding of the morpheme is central to the conscious understanding of words. Then we will take up the form classes, the structure classes, and, in a separate chapter, pronouns.

A caveat, a word of caution, is in order here: Don't be intimidated by the amount of detail you find about the word classes in these four chapters. These are not details for you to memorize—not at all. For the most part, in fact, they are simply descriptions of details you already know, not only from your study of grammar but also from your everyday use of the language, even though you may not have thought consciously about them.

CHAPTER 11

Morphemes

CHAPTER PREVIEW

In this chapter, in preparation for the study of word classes, you will learn about morphemes, basic units of meaning that make up words. You'll find that an understanding of morphemes will help to trigger your unconscious language expertise, as you consciously study the form of words. You'll learn that nouns, verbs, adjectives, and adverbs have characteristics that enable you to identify them, not by their meanings but by their forms.

Some of the detail in this chapter may also trigger memories of vocabulary and dictionary lessons from your early grades. When you study morphemes, you are actually studying in a conscious way the lexicon in your head—your internal dictionary. In fact, for this chapter you'll need access to the other kind of dictionary too—the alphabetical kind that sits on your desk.

By the end of this chapter you will be able to

- Understand the *morpheme structure* of words.
- Distinguish between *bases* and *affixes*.
- Recognize *bound* and *free morphemes*.
- Identify the grammatical significance of *derivational* and *inflectional morphemes*.
- Tell the differences among *allomorphs, homonyms*, and *homophones*.
- Identify the characteristic stress pattern of *compound words*.

When we study sentence patterns and their expansions, we are studying **syntax**. The structural linguist, however, begins the study of grammar not with syntax, but with **phonology**, the study of individual sounds. At the next level, before syntax, comes **morphology**, the study of **morphemes**, combinations of sounds with meaning.

This definition of *morpheme* may sound to you like the definition of *word*. Many morphemes are, in fact, complete words; *head* and *act* and *kind* and *walk* (as well as *and*) are words consisting of a single morpheme, a single meaningful combination of sounds. But others, such as *heads* and *actively* and *unkindly* and *walking*, consist of two or more morphemes, each of which has meaning itself. The success you had years ago in learning to read and spell was in part dependent on your awareness of the parts of words. For instance, in spelling a word like *actively*, you probably break it into its three morphemes automatically: Its stem, or **base morpheme**, is the verb *act;* the suffix *-ive* turns it into an adjective; and the suffix *-ly* turns the adjective into an adverb. Each of these three morphemes, the base and the two suffixes, has meaning itself; and each appears in other environments (other words) with the same meaning. These are the two primary criteria that we use to identify the morphemes in a word: They have meaning; they appear with the same meaning in other words.

We should also emphasize that *morpheme* and *syllable* are not synonymous—even though the morphemes discussed so far consist of a single syllable. There are, in fact, many two-syllable words in English that are single morphemes: *carrot, college, jolly, merit, over.* Furthermore, many two-morpheme words are single syllables: *acts, walked, dog's.* So even though it may be understandable to think of syllable boundaries as boundaries for morphemes, it is inaccurate to do so.

The individual morphemes in a word are not always quite as obvious as they are in words like *actively*. In the word *reflections*, for example, we can recognize the verb *reflect*, the *-ion* ending that turns it into a noun, and the *-s* that makes it plural: *reflect + ion + s*. But how about the word *reflect?* Is that a single morpheme, or is it two? Are *re* and *flect* separate morphemes? Do they both have meaning? Do they appear in other environments with the same meaning? Certainly there are many words that begin with the prefix *re-: reverse, rebound, refer.* In all these, *re-* means "back," so *re* passes the morpheme test. How about *flect?* We have *inflect* and *deflect.* The dictionary reveals that all three words with *flect* are based on the Latin verb *flectere*, meaning "to bend." So in the word *reflections* we can identify four morphemes: *re + flect + ion + s*.

Incidentally, it's not unusual to need the dictionary to understand the morpheme structure of a word. The meanings of words often change, and their origins become obscure. Take the word *obscure*, for example. How many morphemes does it have, one or two? What does *scure* mean? Does it appear in other words with the same meaning? Is *ob* the same morpheme we find in *observe?* What does it mean? And how about *observe?* Is that the verb *serve?* Such meanderings into the dictionary in search of clues about morphemes can heighten our awareness of words and appreciation of language.

And certainly an awareness of morphemes can enhance the understanding of language essential to both reader and writer. When we study etymology and historical linguistics, we begin to understand the intricacies of morphemes, their changes, and their variations. But our interest in morphemes here is a limited one. We will look mainly at those that signal the form classes, that contribute to our understanding of the parts of speech.

BASES AND AFFIXES

All words, as we have seen, are combinations of morphemes, or, in the case of a word like *act* (as well as the eight words preceding it in this sentence), single morphemes. All morphemes are either **bases** (*act*), which we define as the morpheme that gives the word its primary lexical meaning, or **affixes** (*-ive*, *-ly*); and all affixes are either **prefixes,** those that precede the base (*re-*), or **suffixes**, those that follow it (*-ion*):

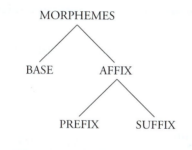

Exercise 46

The following four sets of words illustrate some of the relationships of morphemes. In each set find the common base. What does the base mean? Draw vertical lines in the words to show the separate morphemes.

nova	auditor	durable	conceive
renovation	audience	endure	capable
innovate	inaudible	duration	susceptible
novice	auditorium	during	capture
novelist	audio	endurance	intercept

BOUND AND FREE MORPHEMES

One other feature of morphemes concerns their ability to stand alone. Many cannot. For example, the affixes are **bound,** or attached, to another morpheme rather than **free** to stand alone; that's what *affix* means. In the word *actively*, only the first morpheme is free: *-ive* and *-ly* are bound. In *reflections*, even the base is bound; *flect* is not a word that can stand by itself. We call this a bound base. Other examples of words without free morphemes are *concur*, *conceive*, *depict*, *expel*, and many others with these common prefixes. There are also a few affixes that are free, such as *able*, *like*, and *less*. A free morpheme is a word; a bound morpheme is not. The solid arrows in the following diagram represent the most common circumstance, the broken ones the less common:

Exercise 47

Find a word to fit each of the following formulas. Include only the morphemes called for.

Examples:

free + bound = **birds**
bound + free = **rerun**

1. free + bound
2. bound + free
3. free + bound + bound
4. bound + free + bound
5. free + free
6. bound + free + bound + bound
7. bound + bound
8. bound + bound + bound

DERIVATIONAL AND INFLECTIONAL MORPHEMES

Another feature of affixes we want to recognize is their classification as either derivational or inflectional. Although we have several hundred suffixes, distinguishing between the derivational and inflectional ones is easy to do. Only eight are **inflectional**. You'll recognize four of them from the discussion of verbs in Chapter 4.

-*s* (plural)
-*s* (possessive) } Noun inflections

-*s* (3rd-person singular)
-*ed* (past tense)
-*en* (past participle)
-*ing* (present participle) } Verb inflections

-*er* (comparative)
-*est* (superlative) } Adjective and adverb inflections

All the other suffixes, as well as all the prefixes, are **derivational**.

As the branching diagram shows, all prefixes are derivational, whereas suffixes are either derivational or inflectional:

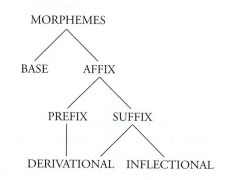

The term *derivational* refers to the change that a word undergoes when a derivational morpheme is added: Either the meaning of the word changes or the class, the part of speech, changes—or both. Take the word *inactivity*, for example. With the derivational morpheme -*ive*, the verb *act* becomes the adjective *active*—that is, we derive one class of word from another. When we add *in-*, the class remains the same—*active* and *inactive* are both adjectives—but the prefix does affect the meaning, as prefixes generally do; in other words, we derive a new meaning. Finally, with the addition of -*ity* the adjective becomes the noun *inactivity*.

The significance, then, of derivational morphemes is this ability they give us to derive new words: *Active* and *inactive* are two different words; so are *active* and *actively;* so are *act* and *action*.

The inflectional affixes also change words, of course, but the changes do not represent new words in the same sense that the changes with derivational morphemes do. It is probably accurate to consider the verb *acting* as simply a variation of *act;* likewise, the inflections we add to nouns—the plural and possessive—produce variations of the singular noun; we think of *dogs* and *dog's* simply as variations of *dog*, rather than as different words.

Two other attributes of derivational morphemes distinguish them from the inflectional morphemes:

1. **Derivational morphemes are arbitrary.** Unlike the inflectional morphemes, which apply in a systematic way to all, or at least to a significant number of, the words in a class, the derivational morphemes are quite unsystematic. For example, all verbs— with only two or three exceptions—take the inflectional *-s* and *-ing* endings; and almost all verbs have an *-ed* and *-en* inflection as well. However, there's nothing systematic about the derivational endings that we add to other word classes to form verbs: The adjective *able* becomes a verb with the addition of the prefix *en-* (*enable*); *sweet* takes the suffix *-en* (*sweeten*); *legal* takes *-ize* to become a verb (*legalize*); *active* takes *-ate* (*activate*). For many adjectives, however, we have no derivational morpheme at all for producing verbs; we have no way to turn such adjectives as *big, good, happy*, and *vicious* into verbs. On the other hand, we can derive nouns from these particular adjectives by adding *-ness*. As you might expect, however, *-ness* is not our only noun-forming suffix: Others include *-ity* (*generosity, activity, creativity*); *-acy* (*supremacy, literacy*); *-er* (*singer, helper*); *-ion, -tion* (*action, preparation*); and *-ment* (*contentment, enlargement*). We have no rules to explain what goes with what, no system to account for these differences; that lack of system is what "arbitrary" means.

2. **Derivational morphemes often change the class of the word.** Most of the time, in fact, that change in class is their very purpose; they produce new words. Inflectional morphemes, on the other hand, never change the class. And, as mentioned earlier, we generally don't even consider the inflected form of a word as a different word.

If all these derivational and inflectional morphemes seem complicated to you, it's probably because you haven't thought about them before. If you're a native speaker, they're really not complicated at all; you use them without even thinking. In fact, there is probably no feature of English that illustrates more clearly the innate ability that native speakers have than this inventory of prefixes and suffixes that gives the language such versatility.

Investigating Language **11.1**

Consider the following sets:

  A. *X* can dorf; *X* dorfs; *X* is dorfing; *X* has dorfed already.

  B. Give me that dorf. No, I mean those dorfs. Where's your dorf's snape?

  C. You're pretty dorf, but *X* is dorfer, and *Y* is the dorfest of all.

  1. In which set is *dorf* an adjective? What morphological—not syntactic—evidence tells you that?

  2. In which set is *dorf* a verb? Again, what morphological evidence tells you that?

  3. In which set is *dorf* a noun? Once more, what morphological evidence tells you that?

  4. What type of morphemes have you been dealing with in these questions: inflectional or derivational?

  5. The traditional definition of *noun* is "the name of a person, place, or thing" and that of *verb* is "a word that denotes action, being, or state of being." Instead of using those criteria of meaning, write your own definitions of *noun* and *verb* that are based on form.

ALLOMORPHS

In Exercise 46 the base morphemes *aud* and *dur* are pronounced and spelled the same in all five words in their lists. However, the morpheme *nov* in that same exercise has two pronunciations; in *nova* and *novelist* the vowel sounds are different, comparable to the difference between *node* and *nod*. In the last group in the exercise, the difference from one word to the next is greater still, with variations in spelling as well as pronunciation. In fact, without the help of a dictionary we would be tempted to label *ceive* and *cap* and *cept* as different morphemes altogether, rather than variations of the same one. Such variations of morphemes, which are extremely common in English, are known as **allomorphs**.

Sometimes the base morphemes have allomorphic variations as the result of suffixes. For example, a word ending in *f* often takes a *v* in the plural:

    leaf → leaves   wife → wives   elf → elves

We would call *leav* and *wiv* and *elv* allomorphs of *leaf* and *wife* and *elf*. Here are some other examples in which the pronunciation of the base morpheme changes with the addition of a suffix: *type/typify; please/pleasant; press/pressure; able/ability; oblige/obligation; child/children*. Because these allomorphs of the base are not used without the suffix, we would include them in the category of bound bases.

Prefixes and suffixes, too, undergo such variation; that is, they also have allomorphs. For example, notice the negative prefix we add to these adjectives: *unkind, improper, illegal, irrelevant, ineligible*. All these prefixes mean *not*, so it is probably accurate to consider *im, il, ir,* and *in* as allomorphs of the prefix *un,* the most common among them. At any rate, their sounds are determined by their environment.

Suffixes also have allomorphic variation. Consider, for example, the sound you add to make nouns plural:

cat → cats   dog → dogs   kiss → kisses

Even though the first two are spelled the same, the sounds are different: in *cats* the sound is an *s*; in *dogs*, it's a *z*. And in *kisses*, the *es* represents an unstressed vowel sound followed by *z*.

HOMONYMS

You're probably familiar with homonyms, words with different meanings that happen to have the same spelling and the same sound, such as *saw* (the tool) and *saw* (the past-tense verb). The concept refers also to morphemes, in some cases to parts of words that sound the same but have different meanings. Prefixes and suffixes, for example, can be homonyms. The *ex* in *exchange* and the *ex* in *ex-husband* have two different meanings: "from" and "former." So do the *er* in *singer* and the *er* in *brighter*: "one who" and "more." In the case of *er*, one is derivational and one is inflectional. And the *s* endings we add to verbs and nouns also have different meanings. All of these are examples of homonyms.

You might find it useful to think of homonyms as simply accidents of language, mere coincidences. It's coincidence that the word *bell* and the bound morpheme *bell* (in *rebellion*) sound and look alike. The dictionary will show they have no connection: The free morpheme *bell* has its origin in the Old English word meaning roar; *rebellion* comes from the Latin word for war. And certainly it's coincidence that the name of the carpenter's tool sounds the same and shares the same spelling as the past-tense form of *see*.

A subclass of homonyms, called **homophones**, includes those words with identical sounds in which both meaning and spelling are different: *to, two, too; sale, sail.*

COMPOUND WORDS

Merriam-Webster's Collegiate Dictionary (eleventh edition) lists three examples in the definition of **compound word:** *rowboat, high school, devil-may-care.* All three of these are combinations of free morphemes, which is the standard definition of the term. Even though the three are connected differently (or not at all, in the case of *high school*), they share one common characteristic, one that helps us to recognize their grammatical framework as compound—their common stress pattern:[1]

/ \\	/ \\	/ \\
rowboat	high school	devil-may-care

When you read the following compound words aloud, you'll hear their stress pattern in the same way, with primary stress on the first word:

newspaper	snowman	blackboard
girl crazy	blacktop	candlelight
dog house	bag lady	workweek
dog catcher	bagman	storehouse

It's the stress pattern that makes the distinction between a house that is green and a greenhouse; between a teacher from France and a teacher of French, a French teacher; between a big load that's a heavy weight and a boxer who's a heavyweight; between a room that's dark and a photographer's darkroom.

We often have to consult a recent dictionary to find out how a compound word is written: with or without hyphens, as separate words or one word. You might be reluctant to call two separate words a compound word, but in the case of *high school,* the dictionary does! By the time the twelfth edition of *Webster's* is published, *high school* may have gained a hyphen, and by the thirteenth, it may be closed up.

What we are distinguishing in the case of *dark room* versus *darkroom* or *French teacher* versus *French teacher* is the difference between a noun phrase and a compound noun. In a noun phrase with the headword

---

[1] Linguists generally recognize four degrees of stress in intonation: / (primary), ∧ (secondary), \\ (tertiary), and ∪ (weak or unstress).

preceded by an adjectival, the main stress in most cases will be on the headword. Intonation can always be altered in speech for a different emphasis, but generally the stress pattern—along with meaning, of course—provides the best clue for recognizing a compound word.

Exercise 48

Draw vertical lines in the following words to indicate their morpheme boundaries. Identify each morpheme as follows: *bound* or *free; base* or *affix*. Identify each affix as *derivational* or *inflectional*. You will probably need to consult your dictionary.

precision	unaware	illegal
candidate	money	wealthy
detoured	sidewalks	television
excessively	promotion	revises

CHAPTER 11
Key Terms

Affix
Allomorph
Base morpheme
Bound morpheme
Compound words
Derivational morpheme
Free morpheme
Homonyms

Homophones
Inflectional suffix
Morpheme
Morphology
Phonology
Prefix
Suffix

QUESTIONS
?
for DISCUSSION

...norphemes are made up of combinations of sounds. Give ...amples of morphemes that are single sounds.

2. Consider how the meaning of a word comes about. Explain the origin of the following words:

ambulance	cohort	fancy	mayhem
budget	daisy	hussy	meal
calculate	dial	infant	money
candidate	easel	lunatic	pilot
cigar	escape	magazine	vaccine

3. What do the following compound words have in common: *fingerprint, sourpuss, overland, walkway*? In what way are they different?

4. Consider the difference between derivational and inflectional suffixes. What can you say about their positions when both appear on the same word? Is the rule fairly constant? Is it possible for more than one derivational and/or inflectional suffix to appear on a single word?

5. Which of the following words appear to violate the system that you described in Question 4?

    inflectional   sportsmanship   microscopy   teaspoonsful

6. How can the awareness of morphemes be of help in spelling problem words, such as the following?

entirely	innovate	disappoint
safety	inaudible	roommate
professor	misspell	vineyard

7. Explain the difference between the words "painful" and "pained." Under what circumstances would the following sentences be accurate?

    > He had a pained expression on his face.
    >
    > He had a painful expression on his face.

    Now think about the difference between "healthy" and "healthful." Would you say that carrots are a healthy food to eat? And what's the difference between "masterly" and "masterful"?

8. Our vocabulary expands in many ways. Sometimes we give new meanings to old words or to their combinations, as in *waterbed, whistle-blower, gridlock*, and *moonshot*. And sometimes we combine two words into a completely new one: We made *brunch* from *breakfast* and *lunch*. What two words

do you suppose were combined in the formation of these: *bash, clash, flare, blog, smash,* and *motel?* What are the origins of *radar* and *scuba?*

CLASSROOM APPLICATIONS

1. Homophones are words with the same pronunciation but with different spellings and different meanings, like *pear* and *pair* or *haul* and *hall.* In his book *A Chocolate Moose for Dinner,* Fred Gwynne plays with homophones, as you can see from the title. Before eating your dessert of chocolate moose, what would you have for your main course? Stake, perhaps? Plan a complete menu for your meal using (misusing!) homophones.

2. Homophones usually occur in pairs. But sometimes there are three or even four words in English that sound alike but differ in meaning and spelling. See how many trios or quartets of homophones you can come up with. (For starters, think of another to go with *pair* and *pear.*)

3. Another tricky class of our words is that of *heteronyms*—pairs of words that are spelled alike but differ in both meaning and pronunciation: *bass/bass, sewer/sewer, row/row.* See how many others you can come up with; then try to use both in the same sentence.

4. Among the bound bases of our vocabulary, some are combined with the suffix *-logy,* meaning a science. For example, the bound base *herpeto,* which means "to creep," when combined with *-logy* means the scientific study of creatures that crawl and creep— reptiles. When we add *-ist,* we get the title of the scientist who studies reptiles: *herpetologist.*

   Use your dictionary to figure out the jobs and the job titles that can be produced from the following bound bases:

   socio-

   bio-

   anthropo-

   ethno-

   cardio-

   eco-

   patho-

   zoo-

   geol-

   entomo-

The Form Classes

As you read in the opening of Part IV, an important difference between traditional and structural grammar is in the classification of words. The structuralists' definitions of the form classes—nouns, verbs, adjectives, and adverbs—make use of the native speaker's inherent language ability. For example, does the word have both -*s* and -*ing* forms? Then it's a verb. Can it be made plural or possessive? Then it's a noun. In traditional grammar, the definitions of *noun* (the name of a person, place, or thing) and *verb* (a word showing action) are based on meaning.

In this chapter, you will study words in a "formal" way, as classes with certain characteristics of form. By the end of the chapter you will be able to

- Use derivational and inflectional suffixes to identify words in the four form classes: nouns, verbs, adjectives, and adverbs.
- Recognize the structure words that signal the four form classes.
- Write the correct *possessive forms* of nouns.
- Differentiate between *count* and *noncount* nouns.
- Distinguish between *attributive* and *predicative* adjectives.
- Identify *flat adverbs*.

NOUNS

We traditionally define *noun* on the basis of meaning, as the *name* of a person, place, thing, idea, event, or the like, and that definition works fairly well. After all, we've been learning names since we spoke our first words: *mama, daddy, cookie, baby*. The word *noun*, in fact, comes from *nomen*, the Latin word for "name."

We also get a sense of "nounness" from the words that signal nouns—the determiners. A word such as *the, my,* or *an* tells us a noun will follow, although not necessarily as the next word: *the* books, *my* sister, *an* honest opinion. Determiners are simply not used without nouns.

But certainly the most reliable clue for recognizing nouns is form. We can often differentiate the form classes from one another without reference to either meaning or context, simply on the basis of their derivational and inflectional suffixes.

Noun Derivational Suffixes. Each of the four form classes has its own inventory of derivational suffixes. The ending *-ion,* for example, converts the verb *reflect* into a noun, so we call it—or its variations, *-tion, -sion, -cion,* and *-ation*—a noun-forming suffix. A quick check of the dictionary reveals that all the *-ion* words listed on the first few pages are also nouns formed from verbs:

abbreviation	abstraction	accusation
abolition	accommodation	acquisition
abortion	accumulation	action

Some *-ion* words function as both nouns and verbs: *question, partition, mention,* and, yes, *function;* you may be able to think of others. But you will find few, if any, *-ion* words that are not nouns; *-ion* is a reliable signal. Many other derivational suffixes do the same job, that of converting verbs into nouns:

accomplish<u>ment</u>	break<u>age</u>
accept<u>ance</u>	deliver<u>y</u>
arriv<u>al</u>	depart<u>ure</u>
assist<u>ant</u>	teach<u>er</u>

This variety of noun-forming suffixes that we add to verbs—and, incidentally, there are many more than these—illustrates not only our versatility in changing one part of speech to another but also the arbitrary way in which we do so. Why, for example, do we say "delivery" and "deliverance" but not "deliverment"? Why "departure" rather than "departation"? Why "deportation" rather than "deporture"? There are no good answers to such questions.

The same arbitrariness runs through all the word classes. For example, many adjectives become nouns with the addition of *-ness:* pretti*ness,* lazi*ness,* strange*ness,* happi*ness,* helpless*ness.* But there is a long list of other suffixes that do the same job: tru*th*, wis*dom*, jus*tice*, partial*ity*. And a number of suffixes simply alter the meaning of the word without changing the class; for example, we derive the abstract noun *boyhood* from the concrete noun *boy*. Other examples of suffixes that produce new meanings include *kingdom, friendship, Spaniard, gardener,* and *terrorism*.

Finally, the nouns *partiality* and *activation* illustrate another feature of derivational suffixes, where a noun-forming suffix is added to a word that already has one or more derivational suffixes:

part + -*ial* = partial + -*ity* = partiality
(noun)   *(adj)*   *(noun)*

act + -*ive* = active + -*ate* = activate + -*ion* = activation
(verb)   *(adj)*   *(verb)*   *(noun)*

This feature also illustrates another difference between derivational and inflectional suffixes. The inflectional suffixes do not add on in this way. With the exception of the plural and possessive morphemes of nouns, which may appear in combination, the form-class words will have only one inflectional suffix, and it will always come at the end of the word, after any derivational suffixes.

Exercise 49

Transform the following verbs into nouns by adding a derivational suffix. Are there any that have more than one noun form?

1. please   + _____ = _____
2. regulate + _____ = _____
3. steal   + _____ = _____
4. seize   + _____ = _____
5. derive   + _____ = _____
6. retire   + _____ = _____
7. form   + _____ = _____
8. revive   + _____ = _____

Noun Inflectional Suffixes. The other aspect of form that differentiates the four form classes both from the structure classes and from one another is the set of inflectional morphemes that each form class has, which we saw in Chapter 2. Our nouns have only two grammatical inflections, one indicating **number (plural)** and one indicating **case (possessive)**. Most nouns will fit into the following framework:[1]

SINGULAR	PLURAL	SINGULAR POSSESSIVE	PLURAL POSSESSIVE
cat	cats	cat's	cats'
dog	dogs	dog's	dogs'
horse	horses	horse's	horses'
mouse	mice	mouse's	mice's

The nouns *cat* and *dog* and *horse* illustrate that in speech we can't always distinguish among inflected forms of nouns: *Cats, cat's,* and *cats'* are all pronounced exactly the same. Only in writing can we differentiate the plural from the possessive and from the plural possessive. In the case of *mouse,* with its irregular plural, we of course make the distinction in speech as well as in writing.

The preceding examples illustrate another point about noun inflections: Sometimes the plural inflection is not a single /s/ or /z/ sound, as in *cats* and *dogs.* It may be two sounds, an entire syllable, complete with vowel, as in *horses.* The sound we add is determined by the final sound of the noun. With words ending in what is called a sibilant sound—usually spelled with *s, z, sh, ch, dge,* or *ge*—we must add a syllable to pronounce the *-s* plural (as well as the possessive): kiss*es,* maz*es,* sash*es,* church*es,* judg*es,* pag*es.*

Exercise 50

The possessive marks are missing from the following noun phrases. Read each one aloud; then punctuate each phrase in two ways to show its two possible meanings.

all my teachers assignments   the horses sore legs

all my teachers assignments   the horses sore legs

my sisters husbands business   my sons problems

my sisters husbands business   my sons problems

---

[1] In words where the plural noun has no *-s,* as in the case of irregular plurals such as *men* and *women,* both the singular and the plural possessive forms take the apostrophe plus *-s:*

man	men	man's	men's
woman	women	woman's	women's

Recognizing whether or not the added sound is a complete syllable can be a useful clue in spelling. Spelling the plural and possessive of words that end in an /s/ or /z/ sound is sometimes confusing; they not only sound strange, they tend to look strange when they're written:

> Mr. and Mrs. Jones are the Joneses. (*Plural*)
>
> Their cat is the Joneses' cat. (*Possessive*)

To turn *Joneses*, the plural of *Jones*, into the possessive case, we add only the apostrophe, the usual procedure for possessive plurals: cats', horses', leaders'.

The policy for forming possessive names followed by *The Chicago Manual of Style*, which is generally considered the bible of publishing, is a restatement of William Strunk's "Rule No. 1" in the famous *Elements of Style*. Strunk's rule is, simply,

> Form the possessive singular of nouns by adding *'s*.

In other words, according to the *Manual* (and Strunk), there should be no question with a name like Martinez or Williams, multisyllable names ending with a sibilant (/s/ or /z/) sound. Even though you may not pronounce the extra *s* when you say "Martinez's batting average" or "Mr. Williams's Hummer," you should include the *s* with the apostrophe when you write the possessive case.

However, both Strunk and *The Chicago Manual* list exceptions for certain proper names that have multiple sibilant (/s/ or /z/) sounds, such as Moses' and Jesus'. The *Manual* also makes exceptions for words with an unaccented ending pronounced /eez/, among them Euripedes' plays, Ramses' tomb, Surtees' novels. And Strunk's exceptions include such forms as "for conscience' sake" and "for righteousness' sake." All of these are words in which an added syllable would not be pronounced, so the *s* is not added with the apostrophe. In most of these cases, the final syllable both begins and ends with a sibilant sound.

As *The Chicago Manual* makes clear, however, names ending with a single sibilant follow the basic rule:

> Maria Callas's performance.
>
> Dylan Thomas's poetry.
>
> Roy Harris's compositions.

In these cases, the possessive -*s* is an added syllable when pronounced. A word's pronunciation, whether or not you add a syllable in speech, is sometimes used as the guideline for whether to add apostrophe plus -*s* or only the apostrophe; as the *Manual* points out, this issue is a well-known matter of disagreement among editors. However, you won't go wrong if you stick to Strunk's No. 1 rule and add apostrophe plus -*s*.

The plural and possessive inflections provide a test of sorts for "noun-ness." Can the word be made plural and/or possessive? If so, it's a noun. If not? Well, the possibility for nounness is still there. In applying the inflection test to the nouns in the preceding section on derivational suffixes, we find that all the words on the *-ion* list can take the plural inflection, but most of them will not take the possessive *-s*. With many nouns the *of* prepositional phrase is more common than the possessive *-s* inflection: In general, the more specific or concrete the sense of the noun, the more likely it is that the inflections will be acceptable.

Exercise 51

Transform the *of* possessive phrase into the inflected noun.

1. The son of Mr. Price is Mr. _____ son.
2. The daughter of Ms. Hedges is Ms. _____ daughter.
3. The computer belonging to James is _____ computer.
4. The governor of Massachusetts is _____ governor.
5. The blanket belonging to Linus is _____ blanket.
6. The garden of the neighbor is the _____ garden.
7. The garden of the neighbors is the _____ garden.
8. The curls on the head and tail of Miss Piggy are _____ curls.
9. The club the women belong to is the _____ club.
10. The wisdom of Confucius is _____ wisdom.

The Meaning of the Possessive Case. In the examples we have seen so far, the relationship between the possessive noun and the headword is actually one of possession, or ownership, but such a relationship is not always the case. As the following examples show, the possessive noun can be simply a description:

> an evening's entertainment
>
> a bachelor's degree
>
> today's news

It can also be a measure of value or time:

> a day's wages
>
> a moment's notice
>
> a dollar's worth

It can denote origin:

> the teacher's suggestion
> Lincoln's Gettysburg Address

Sometimes the actual relationship is unclear, even in context:

> We admired Van Gogh's portrait.

This possessive could refer either to a portrait *of* the artist or to a portrait *by* the artist.

Irregular Plural Inflections. Before leaving the noun inflections, we should note the many instances of irregular plurals, such as *mice,* in our lexicon. Some are old forms of English that have resisted becoming regularized: *foot–feet, tooth–teeth, man–men, child–children, ox–oxen.* A number of animal and fish names are irregular in that they have no inflection for the plural: *sheep, deer, bass, salmon, trout.* A large number of borrowed words have retained their foreign plural inflections: *larva–larvae, criterion–criteria, alumnus–alumni, appendix–appendices.* Incidentally, some of these borrowings are now in the process of acquiring regular plurals. *Appendixes* appears along with *appendices; indexes* and *formulas* are even more common than *indices* and *formulae; stadiums* has all but replaced *stadia. Memorandum* is giving way to the shortened *memo,* along with its regular plural, *memos;* and the added complication of gender in *alumnus–alumni* (masculine) and *alumna–alumnae* (feminine) no doubt encourages the use of the simpler, gender-free—and informal—*alum* and *alums.* The borrowed words ending in *-s—analysis–analyses, nucleus–nuclei, hypothesis–hypotheses, stimulus–stimuli*—are less likely to lose their foreign inflections; the addition of *-es* to the singular would be cumbersome.

The irregularity of noun inflections, incidentally, applies only to the plural; the possessive follows the regular rule:

SINGULAR	SINGULAR POSSESSIVE	PLURAL	PLURAL POSSESSIVE
man	man's	men	men's
child	child's	children	children's
deer	deer's	deer	deer's
mouse	mouse's	mice	mice's
larva	larva's	larvae	larvae's

Note that these plural possessives look different from regular plural possessives *(dogs'),* only because for regular plural nouns we don't add an *-s* to make the word possessive; the regular plural already has one.

Plural-Only Forms.   Some nouns, even when singular in meaning, are plural in form. One such group refers to things that are in two parts—that are bifurcated, or branching: *scissors, shears, pliers, pants, trousers, slacks, shorts, glasses, spectacles.* As subjects of sentences, these nouns present no problems with subject–verb agreement: They take the same verb form as other plural subjects do. Interestingly, even though a pair of shorts is a single garment and a pair of pliers is a single tool, we use the plural pronoun in reference to them:

> I bought a new pair of shorts today; they're navy blue.
>
> I've lost my pliers; have you seen them?

Other plural nouns that have no singular form include *measles, mumps, means, tidings, clothes,* and *athletics.*

A different situation arises with certain plural-in-form nouns that are sometimes singular in meaning. A noun such as *physics, mathematics,* and *linguistics,* when referring to an academic discipline or course, is treated as singular:

> Physics is my favorite subject.
>
> Linguistics is the scientific study of language.

But sometimes such nouns as *mathematics* and *statistics* are used with plural meanings:

> The mathematics involved in the experiment are very theoretical.
>
> The statistics on poverty levels are quite depressing.

These uses also call for plural pronouns.

Collective Nouns.   Nouns such as *family, choir, team, majority, minority*—any noun that names a group of individual members—can be treated as either singular or plural, depending on context and meaning:

> The family have all gone their separate ways.
>
> The whole family is celebrating the holidays at home this year.
>
> The majority of our city council members are Republicans.
>
> The majority always rules.

Other singular-in-form nouns, such as *remainder, rest,* and *number,* also have a plural meaning in certain contexts; their number depends on their modifiers:

> The remainder of the job applicants are waiting outside.
>
> The rest of the books are being donated to the library.
>
> A number of customers have come early.

This system also applies to certain indefinite pronouns, such as *some, all,* and *enough:*

> <u>Some of the books</u> *were* missing.
> <u>All of the cookies</u> *were* eaten.

Notice what happens to the verb in such sentences when the modifier of the subject headword is singular:

> <u>The rest of the map</u> *was* found.
> <u>Some of the water</u> *is* polluted.
> <u>All of the cake</u> *was* eaten.
> <u>The remainder of this chapter</u> *is* especially important.

The pronoun to use in reference to these noun phrases will depend on the meaning, and it will usually be obvious:

> <u>They</u> (some of the books) *were* missing.
> It (some of the water) *is* polluted.

One special problem occurs with the word *none,* which has its origin in the phrase *not one.* Because of that original meaning, many writers insist that *none* always be singular, as *not one* clearly is. However, a more accurate way to assess its meaning is to recognize *none* as the negative, or opposite, of *all* and to treat it in the same way, with its number (whether singular or plural) determined by the number of the modifier or of the referent:

> <u>None of the guests</u> *want* to leave.
> <u>None of the cookies</u> *were* left.
> <u>None of the cake</u> *was* eaten.
> <u>All of the guests</u> *are* staying; <u>none of them</u> *are* leaving.

Semantic Features of Nouns. Nouns can be classified according to certain built-in semantic features that affect their distribution. At an early age we begin this process of classification, recognizing, for example, whether a noun can be counted. We can say "one cookie" or "two cookies"; but a noun like *milk* is not countable. This understanding is evident in our selection of determiners:

> I want milk.
> I want <u>a</u> cookie.
> I want <u>some</u> milk.

Within a few short years our linguistic computers have become programmed to make distinctions like this that we are hardly aware of. The non-native speaker, on the other hand, must work conscientiously to make such distinctions. The person who says "I need a new luggage" or "I have a lot of homeworks" or "I am looking forward to a peace and quiet this weekend" has not distinguished between **countable** and **noncountable nouns**. Linguists have described these features of our nouns in a hierarchy, each level of which has consequences for selecting determiners and other parts of the sentence:

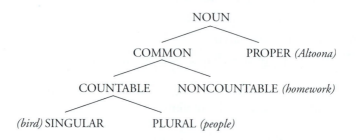

The restrictions built into the word determine its place in the hierarchy; each word carries with it only those features in the higher intersections (or *nodes*) that it is connected with: *Homework* is a noncountable, common noun; *bird* is a singular, countable common noun. Determiners have related built-in features or restrictions; the determiner *a* (or *an*) includes the features "singular" and "countable," so we are restricted from using it with *homework*. It will signal only those nouns that fit in the lowest, left-hand branch, like *bird*. Some nouns appear in both branches of a node, depending on their meaning. For example, some nouns can be both countable and noncountable:

> I had a strange experience yesterday.
>
> I've had experience working with animals.
>
> I baked a cake today.
>
> I'll have some cake.

The term **proper noun** refers to a noun (or noun phrase) with a specific referent—a single meaning: Empire State Building, Grand Canyon, William Shakespeare, London, the *CBS Evening News*, Aunt Mildred, November, Pearl Harbor Day, Thanksgiving. Proper nouns name people, geographic regions and locations, buildings, events, holidays, months, and days of the week; they are usually written with initial capital letters. Although most proper nouns are singular, exceptions occur in the case of mountain ranges and island groups—the Rockies, the Andes, the Falklands—which are plural.

Usage Matters Capitalization

You read in the previous section that proper nouns are written with initial capital letters. Because the names of days and months (Saturday, August) are included as proper nouns, you might think that the names of seasons would also be in line for capitals. But apparently they're not proper enough! The words *winter* and *spring* and *summer* and *fall*—as well as *autumn*—are all written with a lowercase opener. They will, of course, be capitalized when they're part of a title for a specific event: the Winter Olympics; our annual Spring Fling.

Another easy mistake to make is to forget the capital letter for direction words that designate an area of the country: the East; the Northwest.

And another is the rule for capitalizing the words we use for parents and grandparents. Mother and Father—also Mom and Dad and Granny and other such names—are capitalized when they are used as names—in other words, when used like proper nouns:

1. I told Mother I'd be home for dinner.

But the words take no capital when used as common nouns:

2. People tell me that I look like my mother, but my dad doesn't agree.

3. Mom thinks I look like Dad.

Note that a determiner makes a difference: It's the clue that tells you that *mother* and *dad* in (2) are common, not proper, nouns. Note also that in (1) and (3) we could substitute the parents' given names for *Mother* and *Dad*; we cannot do so when there's a determiner as part of the noun phrase.

Investigating Language 12.1

A careful writer would avoid writing sentences like these two:

*There have been less accidents in the county this year.

*I have also noticed an increase in the amount of bicycles on the roads.

But there's no problem with these:

There are fewer students enrolled in the advanced ceramics class this year.

There is an increase in the number of students enrolled in the beginning course.

Think about where in the noun hierarchy on page 248 you would find *accidents*, *bicycles*, and *students*. How would a careful writer revise those first two sentences? If you were helping a non-native speaker revise those sentences, how would you explain the changes?

Would that careful writer avoid any of the following sentences?

> There were less than a dozen accidents in the county this year.
>
> We had fewer accidents than last year.
>
> We have less dollars than we need.
>
> We have less money than we need.
>
> We have less than ten dollars to last until payday.

You probably gave that non-native speaker some advice about the use of *less/fewer* and *amount of/number of*. Should you revise your explanation? In what way?

VERBS

The traditional definition of *verb*, like that of *noun*, is based on meaning: a word denoting action, being, or state of being. When we look for the verb in a sentence, we look for the word that tells *what is happening*, and most of the time this method works. But a much more reliable criterion for defining *verb* is that of form. Some verbs have derivational endings that signal that they are verbs; and, with only two or three exceptions, all verbs fit into the verb-expansion rule, the system of adding auxiliaries and inflections described in Chapter 4.

Verb Derivational Affixes. Many of the root words, or bases, that take noun-forming suffixes are verbs to begin with; for example, most of our nouns with *-ion* are formed from verbs. The opposite operation—deriving verbs from other form classes—is less common. We are more likely to turn a noun into a verb without changing its form at all, another example of **functional shift**—in other words, shifting the function of the word. We *chair* meetings and *table* motions; the carpenter *roofs* the house; the cook *dishes* up the food; the painter *coats* the wall with paint; the gardener *seeds* the lawn and *weeds* the garden; we *butter* the bread, *bread* the chicken—and who among us hasn't *chickened out* at one time or another?

But we also have a few verb-forming affixes that combine with certain nouns and adjectives:

typ*ify*   dark*en*   activ*ate*   legal*ize*

In addition to these suffixes, the prefixes *en-* and *be-* and *de-* and *dis-* can turn nouns and adjectives into verbs and can alter the meaning of other verbs: *enable, enact, enchant, encounter, encourage, encrust, endear, enforce, enlighten, enthrone, bedevil, bewitch, besmirch, dethrone, derail, disable*. But compared with the large number of derivational morphemes that signal nouns, the inventory of verb-forming affixes is fairly small.

Verb Inflectional Suffixes. The verb-expansion rule describes the system of adding auxiliaries and inflectional suffixes to verbs. So as a clue in identifying the part of speech we call *verb*, the inflectional system is extremely reliable. All verbs, with only one or two exceptions—even those with irregular *-en* and *-ed* forms—have both *-s* and *-ing* forms. This means we can identify a word as a verb simply by noting its *-s* and *-ing* forms. Every verb has the other three forms as well—the base, the *-ed*, and the *-en*—but they may not be as recognizable: Verbs such as *hit* and *put*, for instance, show no changes in form from the base (*hit, put*) to the *-ed* form (*hit, put*) to the *-en* form (*hit, put*); others include *cast, hurt, shut, split*, and *spread*. Yet the *-s* and the *-ing* forms are exactly like those of every other verb: *hits, puts, hitting, putting*. The verb inflectional system is so regular, in fact, that we can define *verb* on that basis alone. A word that doesn't have an *-s* or an *-ing* form is simply not a verb.

Investigating Language 12.2

It is easy to demonstrate the "verbness" of *ground, water, air*, and *fire*, even though these words may, at first glance, appear to be nouns. First, add the verb inflections. Then write a sentence for each of the four verbs, using the form called for. Remember that the *-en* form will follow the auxiliary *have;* and if you begin your sentence with *yesterday,* you'll automatically use the *-ed* form.

BASE	*-s* FORM	*-ed* FORM	*-ing* FORM	*-en* FORM
1. GROUND				
(-ed)				
2. WATER				
(-s)				
3. AIR				
(-ing)				
4. FIRE				
(-en)				

Now test the "verbness" of the verbs in the following sentences (*rumor, beware*) by listing their five forms:

> It was rumored that Marcus broke his leg.
>
> You should always beware of rumors.

What have you discovered about the reliability of identifying verbs by their inflections? Would a different criterion be more accurate—perhaps one based on the possibility of auxiliaries?

The verbs *rumor* and *beware* are indeed exceptions to the inflectional-suffix rule for identifying verbs. The verb *rumor* is used exclusively in the passive voice, although the dictionary does include the *-ing* form—perhaps used at one time or place in a particular dialect. The verb *beware* is used exclusively with *you*—or, in commands, with the understood *you*. The dictionary lists only the base form for *beware*. But we shouldn't let these two exceptions—and they do appear to be the only two—discourage us from relying on the almost infallible inflection test for identifying verbs.

ADJECTIVES

In terms of form, adjectives are not as easily identifiable in isolation as are nouns and verbs. Often we need either meaning or context for clues. One reliable way to discover if a word is an adjective is this "adjective test frame":

> The _____ NOUN is very _____.

Only an adjective will fit into both slots. For example,

> The diligent student is very diligent.
>
> The ordinary house is very ordinary.

Because these sentences are grammatical (although perhaps not sentences you'd ever be likely to use), we have shown that the words *diligent* and *ordinary* are adjectives. But in some cases the form of the word also provides clues. A number of derivational suffixes signal adjectives.

Adjective Derivational Suffixes. The most reliable derivational suffix identifying a word as an adjective is *-ous;* we know that *gorgeous, famous,* *porous, courageous,* and *contagious* are adjectives simply on the basis of form. Here are some other adjective-forming suffixes:

mer<u>ry</u>, fun<u>ny</u>	child<u>ish</u>, redd<u>ish</u>
beauti<u>ful</u>, wonder<u>ful</u>	fragment<u>ary</u>, compliment<u>ary</u>
terrif<u>ic</u>, ascet<u>ic</u>	puni<u>tive</u>, act<u>ive</u>
fortun<u>ate</u>, temper<u>ate</u>	vari<u>able</u>, amen<u>able</u>

As clues to adjectives, these suffixes are not as reliable as *-ous* because they show up occasionally on other form classes too: hand *ful* (noun), pan*ic* (noun, verb), pun*ish* (verb). But it is safe to say that most words with these endings are adjectives.

Adjective Inflectional Suffixes. The inflectional suffixes that pattern with adjectives are *-er*, the sign of the **comparative degree**, and *-est*, the **superlative:**

Positive:	big	young	smart
Comparative:	bigger	younger	smarter
Superlative:	biggest	youngest	smartest

The *-er* form is used in the comparison of two nouns—that's why this form is called the comparative degree:

Pat is <u>younger</u> than Phyllis.

Phyllis is the <u>better student</u> of the two.

The comparative degree with *than* can also be followed by a clause rather than a noun phrase:

Pat is younger <u>than I suspected</u>.

The *-est* form, the superlative degree, is used when singling out one of more than two nouns:

Tom was the <u>oldest</u> person in the room.

Of the three candidates, Sarah is the <u>best campaigner</u>.

For many adjectives the comparative and superlative degrees are not formed with *-er* and *-est* but with *more* and *most*, which we can think of as alternative forms, or allomorphs, of the morphemes *-er* and *-est*. In fact, adjectives of more than one syllable generally pattern with *more* and *most*, with certain exceptions: two-syllable adjectives ending in *-y* or *-ly* (*prettiest,* *friendlier, lovelier*); some ending in *-le* (*nobler, noblest*), *-ow* (*narrower, narrowest*), and *-er* (*tenderest*).

But *more* and *most* are not exclusive to adjectives either. The *-ly* adverbs, those derived from adjectives, also have comparative and superlative versions: *more quickly, most frequently*. And there are some adjectives, such as *former, main*, and *principal*, that have no comparative and superlative forms.

A small group of words that have comparative and superlative forms can serve as either adjectives or adverbs, so the inflectional test is not completely reliable in identifying a word as an adjective:

early	fast	late	high
earlier	faster	later	higher
earliest	fastest	latest	highest
hard	long	low	deep
harder	longer	lower	deeper
hardest	longest	lowest	deepest

Another word we could add to this list is *near* (*nearer, nearest*), which can serve not only as an adjective and an adverb, but also as a preposition ("Our seats were *near* the fifty-yard line")—the only preposition that takes inflections. In short, the possibility of making a word comparative or superlative is not exclusive to adjectives.

In spite of all these limitations, we have no difficulty distinguishing adjectives in sentences. First, we know the positions they fill in the sentence patterns—as subject and object complements and in noun phrases as prenoun modifiers. And although nouns can also fill all these slots, the differences in the form of nouns and adjectives make it easy to distinguish between them.

On the subject of the comparative and superlative degrees, we should also note that adjectives can be compared in a negative sense with *as, less,* and *least:*

This picnic is not <u>as enjoyable as</u> I thought it would be.

This picnic is <u>less enjoyable than</u> I thought it would be.

This is the <u>least enjoyable</u> picnic I've ever attended.

We should also note some exceptions to the regular comparative and superlative forms:

good	bad	far	far
better	worse	farther	further
best	worst	farthest	furthest

Exercise 52

Fill in the blanks with the comparative and superlative degrees of the adjectives listed. Do any of them require *more* and *most?*

POSITIVE	COMPARATIVE	SUPERLATIVE
friendly	_____	_____
helpful	_____	_____
wise	_____	_____
awful	_____	_____
rich	_____	_____
mellow	_____	_____
expensive	_____	_____
valid	_____	_____
pure	_____	_____
able	_____	_____

Subclasses of Adjectives. The adjective test frame, The _____ NOUN is very _____, is useful in identifying adjectives. It is also useful in helping distinguish subclasses of adjectives: those that are limited to the prenoun slot and those that are limited to the complement slots.

Adjectives actually fill three slots in the sentence patterns: as subject complement and object complement (where they are called **predicative adjectives**) and as modifiers in the noun phrase (where they are called **attributive adjectives**). Most adjectives can fill all three slots; the test frame uses two of them: attributive and subject complement.

But a small number will not fill the complement slots. The following adjectives are attributive only: *main, principal, former, mere, potential, atomic, late* (meaning "dead"), and such technical adjectives as *sulfuric* and *hydrochloric*. These do not serve as either subject or object complements in the verb phrase, nor do they take qualifiers, such as *very:*

He is the former president.

*The president is former.

*My reason is main.

*My main reason is very main.

She is a mere child.

*The child is mere.

Many of the so-called A-adjectives—*ablaze, afraid, aghast, alone, awake*—are predicative only:

> The house was ablaze.
> *The ablaze house burned down in an hour.
> The children were awake.
> *The awake children were noisy.

There are a few others—*fond, ready, ill, well*—that rarely appear in attributive position in reference to animate nouns. We may refer to a "ready wit" but rarely to a "ready person." We may talk about an "ill omen" but rarely an "ill person"; we are more likely to say a "sick person."

Incidentally, not all predicative adjectives take *very*, the sample qualifier in the test frame. We usually don't say "very afraid" or "very awake"; we are more likely to say "very much afraid" or "very much awake." But these adjectives do combine with other qualifiers: *quite* afraid, *extremely* afraid, *completely* awake, *wide* awake.

A number of adjectives in predicative position appear frequently with complements in the form of phrases or clauses; some adjectives, such as *fond* and *aware*, are rarely used without them.

> The children were <u>afraid that the dog would bite</u>.
> The children were <u>aware that the dog would bite</u>.
> The dog was <u>fond of biting children</u>.
> We were <u>conscious of the problem</u>.
> Our team is <u>certain to win</u>.

We call these "complements" rather than, simply, modifiers or qualifiers because they complete the idea expressed by the adjective, in much the same way that direct objects are complements of verbs.

Another subclassification of adjectives relates to their ability to combine with qualifiers. Certain adjectives denote meanings that are considered **absolute** in nature: *unique, round, square, perfect, single, double, fatal, empty, right, wrong, impossible*. These can fill both the attributive and predicate slots, but they generally cannot be qualified or compared. We can, of course, say "almost perfect" or "nearly square," but most writers avoid "more perfect" or "very perfect." For most of these words, however, we recognize more than a single, absolute meaning. In the case of *unique*, it has come to mean "rare" or "unusual," in which case "very unique" would be comparable to "very unusual." However, given the historical meaning "one of a kind," the qualified "very unique" is generally avoided.

Investigating Language   12.3

In discussing word stems and affixes in his book *The Language Instinct* (Morrow, 1994), Steven Pinker makes the following statement:

> [The suffix] *-able* combines with any verb to create an adjective, as in *crunch–crunchable*. The suffix *-er* converts any verb to a noun, as in *crunch–cruncher*, and the suffix *-ness* converts any adjective into a noun, as in *crunchy–crunchiness*. (pp. 133–134)

Test those rules on your own vocabulary to see if you can find exceptions. Can you think of other suffixes or prefixes that have similar powers?

ADVERBS

Of all the form classes, adverbs are the hardest to pin down in terms of both form and position. Many of them have no distinguishing affixes, and except in Pattern I they fill no required slots in the sentence patterns. (We have identified certain verbs in Patterns VI and VII, however—among them, *lay*, *put*, *place*, and *set*—that do require adverbials.) The fact that adverbs are often movable is perhaps their most distinguishing characteristic.

The class we are calling "adverb" differs from the class identified as "adverb" in traditional grammar. You'll recall the traditional definition as "a word that modifies a verb, an adjective, or another adverb." This definition includes words that we call "qualifiers," words that intensify or qualify the meaning of adjectives and adverbs: *very* nice, *quite* slow, *rather* quickly. But even when we leave out adjectives and other adverbs from the traditional definition, we are left with a definition of "adverbial"—that is, the definition of a function, not a word class. (Chapter 6 describes many structures—not only adverbs—that function adverbially.) Remember, we are defining the four form classes on the basis of their inflectional and derivational affixes and of the words that signal them—not on the basis of their function in the sentence. You'll read more about the distinction between qualifiers and adverbs in the section on "Qualifiers" in Chapter 13.

Adverb Derivational Suffixes.   One common indicator of form we do have is the derivational suffix *-ly*, which we use to derive adverbs of manner from adjectives—adverbs that tell *how* or *in what way* about the verb:

He walked <u>slowly</u>.
She answered <u>correctly</u>.

But *-ly* is not completely reliable as a signaler of adverbs; it also occurs on nouns (*folly*) and on adjectives (*lovely, ugly*). But we are safe in saying that most *-ly* words are adverbs, simply because there are so many adjectives that we can turn into adverbs with this derivational morpheme.

There are some restrictions on this process, however: Not all adjectives can become manner adverbs. These restrictions are related to meaning. Some adjectives describe a state, such as *tall* and *old*, or a fixed or inherent characteristic, such as *Norwegian;* others describe characteristics that change, such as *weak, active,* and *industrious.* Another distinction can be drawn between objective characteristics, such as *tall* and *old*, and subjective ones, such as *nice* and *splendid.* The adjectives that refer to objective or stative or inherent qualities rarely become manner adverbs: *tall, old, fat, young, short, thick, large, flat, round, red.* When they do, they are likely to have a specialized, often metaphorical, meaning: *shortly, hardly, flatly, squarely, widely.*

Besides *-ly*, two other derivational suffixes produce adverbs: *-ward* and *-wise.* Words ending in *-ward* signal direction: *homeward, forward, backward, upward, downward.* Words ending in *-wise,* which indicate manner, include both old usages, such as *otherwise, lengthwise,* and *crosswise,* and new ones that are considered by some writers as unnecessary jargon, such as *budgetwise, weatherwise, moneywise,* and *profitwise.*

Investigating Language 12.4

One of our most reliable derivational suffixes is *-ly*. In most cases the message it sends is "adverb of manner": *Quickly* means "in a quick manner," and *slowly* means "in a slow manner." But, as with most rules in our language, there are exceptions to both parts of that message—both the "adverb" part and the "of manner" part.

Consider the *-ly* words in the following sentences. Are they adverbs? Are they adjectives? Could they be nouns or verbs?

1. We're leaving <u>immediately</u> and driving <u>directly</u> to Austin.
2. Bob will be leaving <u>directly</u>.
3. The natives around here are not always <u>friendly</u>.
4. One person I met tried to <u>bully</u> me.
5. He wasn't <u>particularly neighborly</u>.
6. Shedding tears is not considered <u>manly</u>.
7. That is <u>hardly</u> a universal belief, however.
8. My <u>belly</u> aches, but I <u>flatly</u> refuse to stay home.

Use your understanding of form to test these -*ly* words. Remember the inflectional paradigms for nouns and verbs; remember the adjective test frame. And is it possible that -*ly* adverbs have a meaning other than manner? Use your intuition, too!

Adverb Inflectional Suffixes. The comparative and superlative inflections, -*er* and -*est*, combine with adverbs as well as with adjectives, although in a much more limited way. The comparative form of -*ly* adverbs, usually formed by adding *more* rather than -*er*, is fairly common. The superlative degree—*most* suddenly, *most* favorably—is rare in both speech and writing; it invariably calls attention to itself and will often have the main focus of the sentence:

> The committee was most favorably impressed with the proposal.
>
> The crime was planned most ingeniously.

In the discussion of adjectives, we listed a few words that serve as both adjectives and adverbs: *early, late, hard, fast, long, high, low, deep,* and *near.* These are simply adverbs made from adjectives without the addition of -*ly;* they are referred to as **flat adverbs**. Except for a few others such as *soon* and *often,* they are the only adverbs that take -*er* and -*est;* most of the -*ly* adverbs take *more* and, occasionally, *most* in forming the comparative and superlative degrees.

A great many adverbs have neither derivational nor inflectional affixes that distinguish them as adverbs. Instead, we recognize them by the information they provide, by their position in the sentence, and often by their movability:

Time:	now, today, nowadays, yesterday
Duration:	already, always, still, yet
Frequency:	often, seldom, never, sometimes, always
Location:	there, here, everywhere, somewhere, else-where, upstairs, abroad, outside, nearby
Direction:	away, thence
Concession:	still, yet
Sequence:	afterward, next, then

There are also a number of words without form distinctions that can serve as either prepositions or adverbs: *above, around, behind, below, down, in, inside, out, outside, up.*

Exercise 53

Fill in the blanks with variations of the words shown on the chart, changing or adding derivational morphemes to change the word class.

	NOUN	VERB	ADJECTIVE	ADVERB
1.	grief	grieve	grievous	grievously
2.	varience	vary		variously
3.	ability	enable	able	ably
4.		defend		
5.	economy			
6.			pleasant	
7.	type			
8.		prohibit		
9.				critically
10.			valid	
11.		appreciate		
12.	beauty			
13.		accept		
14.			pure	
15.		continue		

CHAPTER 12
Key Terms

Absolute adjective

Adjective

Adjective complement

Adjective derivational suffix

Adjective inflectional suffix

Adverb

Adverb derivational suffix

Adverb inflectional suffix

Attributive adjective

Case

Collective noun

Common noun

Comparative degree

Countable noun

Flat adverb

Form classes

Functional shift

Indefinite pronoun

Noncountable noun	Possessive
Noun	Predicative adjective
Noun derivational suffix	Proper noun
Noun inflectional suffix	Superlative degree
Number	Verb
Plural	Verb derivational suffix
Plural-only noun	Verb inflectional suffix
Positive degree	

QUESTIONS

?

for DISCUSSION

1. A government spokesperson used the following clauses in a discussion of the economy:

    When we were approaching crunch.

    When push comes to shove.

    What part of speech are *crunch, push,* and *shove?*

2. The traditional Latin term for possessive case is *genitive.* Consider the relationship between the possessive noun and its headword in the following noun phrases:

    the teacher's explanation

    the car's overhaul

    Explain what is meant by *subjective genitive* and *objective genitive.* Now consider the following ambiguous sentence:

    I was disturbed about Tom's punishment.

    What is the source of the ambiguity?

3. We often use verbs adjectivally, as noun modifiers, as you saw in Chapter 7. But many words that look like verbs—that were, in fact, originally verbs—now have the characteristics of adjectives. We have said that we can identify a word as an adjective if it can fit into the adjective test frame (The _____ NOUN is very _____). We also have an inflectional test: Can the word be made comparative and superlative? Using these two tests, identify the underlined words in the following sentences: Are they adjectives or verbs?

    Joe took the <u>broken</u> chair to the dump.

    That <u>disgusting</u> movie wasn't worth five dollars.

I feel <u>tired</u>.

Many <u>working</u> mothers have problems with day care.

The <u>decorated</u> tree looks beautiful.

4. In 1625 Francis Bacon described the value of language in the following words:

> Reading maketh a full man, conference a ready man, and writing an exact man.

How might a twenty-first-century philosopher express these ideas?

5. Explain the ambiguity of the following sentences in terms of their possible sentence patterns and parts of speech:

> My mother is always entertaining.

> They are frightening people.

6. Shakespeare, as you know, used language in all sorts of original ways. Here are two lines from *Romeo and Juliet*. What has he done with word classes?

> Thank me no thankings nor proud me no prouds.

> O flesh, flesh, how art thou fishified!

7. When a banner was hung across a city's main street to recognize the local bus company's service to the community, some of the citizens objected to the wording. The banner was printed with the company's name, followed by the verb phrase "serving our community" and, in bold print, these three words: SAFELY ECONOMICALLY FRIENDLY. To discover the problem, check out those three *-ly* words.

8. *Bully, belly,* and *silly* all look a great deal alike. Consider what you know about *-ly* and about the inflectional endings on nouns and verbs. How can you show what word classes these three belong to? Do any of them fit in more than one class?

9. In meeting a very tall person, you might ask the question, "How tall are you?" Strangely enough, we would ask the same question of a short person: We don't usually ask, "How *short* are you?" In this pair of adjectives, *tall* is called the unmarked version. Think of other adjectives we use for quantity or size or age or speed: *old/young, big/little, heavy/ light, fast/slow.* Does our usage suggest marked and unmarked versions? Under what circumstances would we use the unmarked version?

CLASSROOM APPLICATIONS

1. Here's a sentence with a message you may not understand:

    The frabous gricks were brocking my parmy dorfer very
    botly.

    As you see, it's filled with nonsense words. But even though the
    sentence has no semantic, or dictionary, meaning, it still sounds
    like English. It has structural meaning. In fact, you can prob-
    ably figure out the classes of the separate words, as well as the
    sentence pattern. Identify the derivational and inflectional clues
    that enable you to do so.

    Noun(s):

    Verb(s):

    Adjective(s):

    Adverb(s):

    What other clues, in addition to the form of the nonsense
    words, helped you?

    The traditional definitions of *noun* ("the name of a person,
    place, or thing") and *verb* ("a word showing action") are of
    no help here. Write new definitions based on the clues you
    identified.

    Noun: _____

    Verb: _____

2. Here's another grammatical nonsense sentence for you to
   interpret:

    Stear, the frabous grick botly brocked my parmy dorfer in
    the alflit because the dorfer jilked the grick.

    First, answer the following questions:

    1. What happened to the dorfer?
    2. Why did it happen?
    3. Who or what did it?
    4. Where did it happen?
    5. Describe the grick and the dorfer.

    Now diagram the sentence. Then write a version in which the
    main clause is in the passive voice. Write a version in which the
    subordinate clause is passive.

3. Here's an altered version of the sentence in 2:

> Stear, the frabous grick, botly brocked my parmy dorfer in the alflit because the dorfer jilked the grick.

Explain how the addition of one comma changed the syntax. Note that the class of one word has changed in the new version. Which word? Diagram the new version.

4. In his book *Words and Rules: The Ingredients of Language* (Basic Books, 1999), Steven Pinker discusses our ability to form new words with prefixes and suffixes:

> The psychologists Harald Baayen and Antoinette Renouf calculated that every time you open a newspaper you will be faced with at least one word with *un-* that you have never seen before, one with *-ness,* and one with *-ly:* words like *uncorkable, uncheesey, headmistressly, breathcatchingly, pinkness,* and *outdoorsiness.* (p. 122)

Check the front page of your daily paper or a current magazine article to test this calculation. See how many such words your class can find, words that do not appear in the dictionary.

CHAPTER 13

The Structure Classes

CHAPTER PREVIEW

In contrast to the large, open form classes, the categories of words known as structure classes are small and, for the most part, closed. Although new words regularly enter the language as nouns and verbs as the need arises for new vocabulary, the structure classes remain constant from one generation to the next. As native speakers, we pay little attention to structure words. Until we notice a nonnative speaker omitting a determiner or using the wrong preposition, we probably don't appreciate the grammatical sense that structure words contribute.

Part of that grammatical sense comes from the stress–unstress pattern of speech, the rhythm of the language. Most structure words have weak stress: They have the lowest volume, providing valleys between the peaks of loudness that fall on the stressed syllables of the form-class words.

By the end of this chapter you will be able to

- Identify the signalers of form-class words: *determiners, auxiliaries,* and *qualifiers.*
- Tell the difference between *qualifiers* and adverbs.
- Recognize *prepositions, conjunctions,* and *interrogatives.*
- Understand the structural operations that *expletives* perform.
- Distinguish among *prepositions, adverbs,* and *particles.*

DETERMINERS

The **determiner** class is one of the structure classes that straddle the line between a word class and a function. On the one hand, our most common determiners, the articles, do indeed constitute a small, closed structure class. At the other end of the spectrum are the possessive nouns, which function as determiners while retaining their membership in the open class "noun." In between are the subclasses of determiners that belong to the pronouns, a closed class: Demonstrative, possessive, and indefinite pronouns all function as determiners; and, of course, as pronouns they also function as nominals (in fact, "pronominal" would be a more accurate label than "pronoun").

Determiners signal nouns in a variety of ways: They may define the relationship of the noun to the speaker or listener (or reader); they may identify the noun as *specific* or *general;* they may *quantify* it specifically or refer to quantity in general. Because determiners have an important role in the noun phrase, as signalers, we also include them under the umbrella term *adjectival,* as you learned in Chapter 7. Following are the most common classes of determiners, many of which have appeared in our sample sentences:

ARTICLES	POSSESSIVE NOUNS	DEMONSTRATIVE PRONOUNS	NUMBERS
the	John's	this/these	one
a(n)	my son's	that/those	two
	etc.		*etc.*

POSSESSIVE PRONOUNS		INDEFINITE PRONOUNS			
my	its	several	few	each	all
your	our	little	fewer	every	both
his	their	many	more	either	some
her	whose	much	most	neither	any
		no	enough	less	

We should note that possessive nouns as determiners may have their own determiners: *my daughter's* teacher; *the week's* groceries; *our cat's* fur.

Many of the features of nouns in the hierarchy shown on page 248 affect our selection of determiners. A noun appearing in the lowest, left-hand branch of the diagram, for example—a singular, countable noun—rarely appears without a determiner:

<u>This cookie</u> tastes good.
*<u>Cookie</u> tastes good.

John is <u>my friend</u>.
*John is <u>friend</u>.

There are certain exceptions to this rule. For example, the nouns *town*, *school*, and *car* are singular, countable nouns; nevertheless, in some prepositional phrases they appear without determiners:

> the other side of <u>town</u>
>
> going to <u>school</u>
>
> the best kind of <u>car</u>

These exceptions present no problems for native speakers, of course. We're used to the sometimes arbitrary nature of the determiner:

> We say, "I walked to town," but not "I walked to city."
>
> We say, "I have a cold," but not "I have a flu."
>
> We say, "I attend college," but not "I attend university."
>
> We say, "I'm going into town," but not "I'm going into hospital."

(The British and Australians, incidentally, do "go into hospital," "attend university," and "look out of window.")

The difficulty for the nonnative speaker comes with learning which nouns are countable nouns and which are not. Other complications arise because determiners have built-in restrictions. Some will signal only plural nouns *(these, those, many, few, several)*, some only singular nouns *(a, one, each, every)*, some only noncountables *(much, less)*, and others only countables *(few, many, a, one)*.

Another fairly regular rule concerns the limitation of determiners with certain noncountable nouns, sometimes called mass nouns, such as *luggage, furniture, beer, cake, sugar, rice, coal, steel, water*. When mass nouns are used as noncountable, they cannot be plural, so they do not combine with determiners that have either the "plural" or "countable" feature: *a, one, two, these, several, many*.

> *<u>These furnitures</u> are sturdy.
>
> *<u>Many furnitures</u> are expensive.
>
> *<u>Each furniture</u> has its own charm.

Some determiners have both countable and noncountable features built into them *(this, some, most, all)*, so they can combine with both kinds of nouns:

> <u>This furniture</u> is lovely.
>
> <u>This chair</u> is comfortable.
>
> <u>Some furniture</u> is expensive.
>
> <u>Some chairs</u> are expensive.
>
> <u>Most chocolate cake</u> is high in calories.

<u>Most coconut macaroons</u> are delicious.

<u>All polluted water</u> is undrinkable.

<u>Not all rules</u> are necessarily good rules.

The nonnative speaker must consciously learn these features of both nouns and determiners. But a further complication arises when these mass nouns take on countable meanings:

<u>These</u> whole-grain <u>flours</u> are popular now.

<u>The</u> light <u>beers</u> are getting better all the time.

Abstract nouns also present problems for the nonnative speaker because they may appear either with or without determiners:

I have finally regained <u>peace</u> of mind.

I have finally regained <u>my peace</u> of mind.

In some cases the determiner is tied to the presence of a modifier, such as a *that* clause:

*<u>The peace</u> of mind is hard to acquire in these insecure times.

<u>The peace of mind that comes with financial security</u> is my goal.

Even a proper noun may require a determiner when it has certain kinds of modifiers:

<u>The Altoona of my childhood</u> was a railroad town.

And for some inexplicable reason, the article *a* changes the meaning in sentences with *few* and *little:*

I have few friends.	I've had little trouble with my car.
I have a few friends.	I've had a little trouble with my car.

Finally, some determiners are extremely versatile. The **definite article**, *the*, can signal all classes of nouns that can take determiners when the definite meaning is called for—unlike the **indefinite** *a*, which is restricted to countables. The possessives, too—both nouns and pronouns—are wide-ranging, without built-in distribution restrictions.

Exercise 54

Identify the determiners in the following sentences.

1. My sister doesn't have enough money for her ticket.
2. John's roommate went home for the weekend.

3. Every course I'm taking this term has a midterm exam.

4. Bill spent more money on the week's groceries than he expected to.

5. I spend less time studying now than I did last term.

6. I haven't seen either movie, so I have no preference.

The Expanded Determiner. A determiner is not always a single word. In fact, we can think of the determiner slot itself as a series of slots with optional pre- and postdeterminers. The following formula will account for some fairly common **expanded determiners**, although a description that accounted for all the possibilities would be far more complex. This simplified scheme, however, should help you appreciate the intricacies of the grammar rules built into your linguistic computer:

(predeterminer) + DETERMINER + **(postdeterminer)**

		ORDINAL NUMBERS	CARDINAL NUMBERS
all (of)	the	first	one
both (of)	a	second	two
half (of)	my	*etc.*	*etc.*
only	these	next	
especially	*etc.*	last	
just			

The pre- and postdeterminers are, of course, optional, so they are shown in parentheses in the formula.

In the following sentences, the pre- and postdeterminers are underlined; the determiner is written with capital letters:

<u>All of</u> THE cookies disappeared.

<u>Only</u> MY pretzels disappeared.

THE <u>first ten</u> students in line were chosen.

<u>Only</u> THE <u>next two</u> students complained.

<u>Both (of)</u> THESE students wrote A papers.

<u>Half (of)</u> THE class took part in the demonstration.

I have <u>just</u> ENOUGH gas for the trip.

Another type of expanded determiner is the phrasal quantifier; it can occur with either countable or noncountable nouns:

<u>a lot of</u> classes

<u>a lot of</u> homework

<u>a great many</u> friends

<u>a large number of</u> people

In terms of **subject–verb agreement**, it is the number of the noun—whether singular or plural—that determines the verb: homework *is;* classes (friends, people) *are*. Expanded determiners present a problem for traditional diagramming. This topic is discussed on pages 368–369.

AUXILIARIES

Like the determiners and the other structure classes, the auxiliary class is limited in membership and closed to new members. Counting the forms of *have* and *be*, the modals, and the forms of *do*, the list of regular auxiliaries numbers around two dozen:

have	be	can	do
has	is	could	does
had	are	will	did
having	am	would	
	was	shall	
	were	should	
	been	may	
	being	might	
		must	
		ought to	

The following modal-like verbs also function as auxiliaries; they are sometimes referred to as semi-auxiliaries or marginal modals:

have to   be going to   used to   be to

We <u>have to leave</u> soon.

We<u>'re going to take</u> the bus to Iowa City today.

We <u>used to live</u> there.

The bus <u>is to leave</u> at noon.

(We should note that *ought to* is sometimes classified with this group as a marginal modal rather than as a major modal. But because it patterns freely with the auxiliaries *have* and *be* and can also act as an operator in forming negatives and questions without *do* support, *ought to* meets the criteria for major modals.)

The marginal modals are diagrammed just as other auxiliaries are, on the main line:

There are a number of other phrasal modals that are often listed with the marginal modals shown here. In fact, we could make the case to include them with the four listed above: *be able to, be due to, be meant to, be obliged to, be supposed to, had better.* Even though many traditional grammarians do not recognize the marginal modals as a category, it's clear that in some cases the meaning is very close to that of a major modal: *be able to = can; be obliged to = should; had better = must.*

Two other modal-like verbs, *dare* and *need*, commonly appear in negative sentences and in questions:

She <u>need not</u> go.   <u>Dare</u> we go?

I <u>don't dare</u> go.   <u>Need</u> you go?

In function, the auxiliaries are perhaps more intimately connected to verbs than are determiners to nouns, because they alter the verb's meaning in important ways and often determine the form that it takes. Another important difference between the auxiliaries and the other structure classes lies in their systematic distribution. Determiners and qualifiers are somewhat arbitrary in distribution; but with few exceptions every verb can be signaled (preceded) by every auxiliary. The modals, *have,* and *do* combine with every verb; only *be* is restricted in any way, as we saw in Chapter 4, where we noted a few verbs, such as *seem,* that rarely appear with *be + -ing.*

Exercise   55

Underline the auxiliaries in the following sentences. Circle the main verb.

1. I have been having problems with my car.
2. I should not have eaten those tomatoes.
3. Apparently some people can't even look at tomatoes.
4. Sally will be helping us with the party.

5. Margie has to leave early.

6. The kids are really frustrating me today.

7. The teens can be frustrating years for some adolescents.

8. The gymnasts should continue practicing their balance-beam routines.

ELL Issues   **Would**

There are a great many variations and subtleties in the use of modal auxiliaries, one of the most problematic areas of English grammar. Like all the modals, *would* has many uses.

To express a wish about a present condition or a future happening:

I wish it would stop raining.

I wish the teacher would speak more slowly.

To express a past or unrealized possibility:

I would help you if I could. (I'd help you . . .)

I would have helped, but I wasn't asked. (I'd have helped . . .)

(When the contracted *'d* is followed by the base form of the verb, it's short for *would*.)

For polite requests:

Would (could, will) you help me with this math problem?

(Of the three choices, *will* is somewhat less polite than *could* or *would*.)

To express exasperation or surprise:

She **would** say that, wouldn't she!

Who would have believed she was that old?

QUALIFIERS

As the following lists demonstrate, many words can act as **qualifiers** or **intensifiers** to alter the meaning of adjectives and adverbs. (In the adjective test frame the word *very* is used to represent all the possible qualifiers.) On the diagram the qualifier is attached to the adjective or adverb:

The diagrams illustrate that *very* says something about *slowly* and *nice;* it is the whole adverb phrase *very slowly* that modifies *walked* and the whole adjective phrase *very nice* that modifies *young man.*

The following list of qualifiers can be used with the positive form of most adjectives, such as *good* and *soft,* and with adverbs of manner, such as *rapidly:*

very	really	fairly
quite	pretty	mighty
rather	awfully	too

A second group of qualifiers can be used with the comparative degree of adjectives, such as *better* and *nicer,* and with comparative adverbs, such as *sooner, later, nearer,* and *farther:*

still	some	no
even	much	

A number of others have a limited distribution:

<u>right</u> now	<u>just about</u> there
<u>wide</u> awake	<u>almost</u> there
<u>just</u> so	

Many others are used in colloquial expressions:

<u>right</u> nice	<u>darn</u> right
<u>damn</u> sure	<u>real</u> pretty

Some of the adverbs of manner, the *-ly* adverbs, are themselves used as qualifiers with certain adjectives:

<u>dangerously</u> close	<u>politically</u> expedient
<u>particularly</u> harmful	<u>technically</u> possible
<u>absolutely</u> true	<u>especially</u> difficult

Because of the *-ly* adverbs in their ranks, the qualifier class, like that of the determiners, is not a closed class. In fact, the qualifier, like the determiner, can be thought of as both a word class and a sentence function. It has attributes of both.

In their relationship to the form classes, the qualifiers are different from the determiners and auxiliaries in that they are optional; all the adjectives and adverbs they modify can appear without them. This is not true of the relationship of nouns and verbs to their signal words: Many nouns cannot appear without a determiner; and two of our verb forms—the *-en* and the *-ing* forms—require auxiliaries to function as the main verb. But like the other structure words, the qualifiers signal the form classes; they provide a useful test to differentiate adjectives and adverbs from other parts of speech.

PREPOSITIONS

The **preposition** (meaning "placed before") is a structure word found in pre-position to—preceding—a noun phrase or other nominal. Prepositions are among our most common words in English; in fact, of our twenty most frequently used words, eight are prepositions: *of, to, in, for, with, on, at,* and *by.*[1] Prepositions can be classified according to form as simple (one-word) or phrasal (multiple-word).

Simple Prepositions. The following list includes the most common simple prepositions:

aboard	below	in	since
about	beneath	into	through
above	beside	like	throughout
across	between	near	till
after	beyond	of	to
against	but (except)	off	toward
along	by	on	under
amid	concerning	onto	underneath
among	despite	out	until
around	down	outside	up
as	during	over	upon
at	except	past	with
atop	for	per	within
before	from	regarding	without
behind			

[1.] This frequency count, based on a collection of 1,014,232 words, is published in Henry Kučera and W. Nelson Francis, *Computational Analysis of Present-Day English* (Providence, RI: Brown University Press, 1967).

Note that we label these words as prepositions only when they are followed by a nominal—that is, only when they are part of prepositional phrases. In the following sentence, for example, *up* functions as an adverb, not a preposition; *up* holds membership in both classes.

The price of sugar went <u>up</u> again.

Words like *up* also function as particles in two-word, or phrasal, verbs, such as *hold up:*

A masked gunman <u>held up</u> the liquor store.

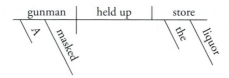

But in the following sentence, *up* is a preposition, part of a prepositional phrase:

We hiked <u>up the steep trail</u>.

Investigating Language 13.2

Speaking of *up*, a "Dear Abby" correspondent sent in the following passage, which he had clipped from the *Reader's Digest* many years ago:

It's easy to understand UP, meaning toward the sky or toward the top of a list. But when we waken, why do we wake UP? At a meeting, why does a topic come UP? And why are participants said to speak UP? Why are officers UP for election? And why is it UP to the secretary to write UP a report?

The little word is really not needed, but we use it anyway. We brighten UP a room, light UP a cigar, polish UP the silver, lock UP the house and fix UP the old car.

At other times, it has special meanings. People stir UP trouble, line UP for tickets, work UP an appetite, think UP excuses and get tied UP in traffic.

To be dressed is one thing, but to be dressed UP is special. It may be confusing, but a drain must be opened UP because it is stopped UP.

We open UP a store in the morning, and close it UP in the evening. We seem to be all mixed UP about UP.

In order to be UP on the proper use of UP, look UP the word in the dictionary. In one desk dictionary, UP takes UP half a page; and the listed definitions add UP to about 40.

If you are UP to it, you might try building UP a list of the many ways in which UP is used. It may take UP a lot of your time, but if you don't give UP, you may wind UP with a thousand.

Try your hand at writing a similar passage using DOWN or OUT or OFF.

Phrasal Prepositions. Two-word, or **phrasal, prepositions** consist of a simple preposition preceded by a word from another category, such as an adverb, adjective, or conjunction:

according to	because of	next to
ahead of	but for	out of
along with	contrary to	prior to
as for	except for	thanks to
aside from	instead of	up to

Most three-word prepositions consist of preposition + noun + preposition:

by means of	in charge of	in spite of
in accordance with	in front of	on account of
in back of	in lieu of	on behalf of
in case of	in search of	

In a traditional diagram, we usually treat these phrases as we do the simple prepositions. They can also be analyzed as one prepositional phrase embedded in another:

The foregoing lists include the most common, although certainly not all, of the prepositions. We use prepositions automatically, as we do the other structure words, in spite of the sometimes subtle differences in meaning they can express: *below* the stairs, *beneath* the stairs, *under* the stairs, *underneath* the stairs; *in* the room, *inside* the room, *within* the room. As native speakers we understand these distinctions, and, except for a few idioms that sometimes cause problems of usage, we rarely hesitate in selecting the right preposition for the occasion.

Exercise 56

Identify the prepositions in the following sentences.

1. The Renfords have lived in San Diego since 1985.
2. They like it there because of the climate.
3. I like Minnesota in spite of the cold winters.
4. Prior to 1985, the Renfords lived in Baltimore.
5. According to some economists, the financial health of the Social Security System is in jeopardy.
6. I look on such predictions with skepticism.
7. Except for eggs, which rarely go up in price, the cost of groceries is going out of sight.
8. Between you and me, my grocery money may not hold out until payday.

Usage Matters The Ending Preposition

For a long time we have heard that it's ungrammatical to end a sentence with a preposition. *Nothing could be further from the truth.* In fact, that little word we so often see at the end of a sentence may not be a preposition at all! It's much more likely to be a particle:

Did he look the word up?

That's one way to turn

He looked the word up

into a question. In this case, *up* is a particle, part of the phrasal verb *look up;* it's not a preposition. Here's another example, where the particle *down* falls at the end of a sentence:

When we sign up to be tutors in the writing center, I hope we are not turned <u>down</u>.

I, too, am planning to sign <u>up</u>.

Sometimes, of course, those little ending words really are prepositions:

Who shall we talk <u>to</u>? (i.e., To whom shall we talk?)

We would probably have a hard time finding anyone who preferred the "to whom" version in ordinary conversation—or even in writing of any but the most formal kind. As with many grammatical structures, some are more formal than others. That doesn't mean that the informal versions are ungrammatical.

The "never end a sentence with a preposition" is, in fact, a non-rule—or, as *The Chicago Manual of Style* puts it, "an ill-founded superstition."

CONJUNCTIONS

As you saw in Chapter 10 on coordination, we use **conjunctions** to connect words and phrases and clauses within the sentence and to connect the sentences themselves. Within the sentence our most common connectors are the simple *coordinating* conjunctions and the *correlative* conjunctions. For joining sentences we also use *conjunctive adverbs*. The *subordinating* conjunctions connect dependent clauses to the main clause.

Coordinating Conjunctions. We can use a coordinate structure for any slot in the sentence by using a coordinating conjunction (*and, or, but, yet, nor, for*):

Riley <u>and</u> Tim worked out on Saturday.

I'll meet you at the ticket window <u>or</u> in the grandstand.

The dessert was simple <u>yet</u> elegant.

Eager to start her new job <u>but</u> sad at the thought of leaving home, Kris packed the car <u>and</u> drove away from the familiar house on Maxwell Avenue.

The coordinating conjunctions also join complete sentences:

I disapproved of his betting on the horses, <u>and</u> I told him so.

He claims to have won fifty dollars, <u>but</u> I suspect he's exaggerating.

She won't come to the party, <u>nor</u> will she explain why.

Notice that the clause introduced by *nor* requires a subject–auxiliary shift.

The coordinating conjunction *for* joins only complete sentences, not structures within the sentence. Even though it is close in meaning to *because*, it differs from the subordinating conjunctions: The *for* clause cannot open the sentence.

We should also mention that well-respected writers use both *and* and *but* as sentence openers (in spite of what you may have read or been told to the contrary). They are even used to open paragraphs. In Chapter 15, you'll find an example of *but* as a paragraph opener on page 334, the *Time* paragraph about the Vikings. And the opening of the passage that introduces the paragraph is *and* (as is the opener of this sentence!).

Correlative Conjunctions. Like the coordinating conjunctions, the **correlative conjunctions** (*both–and, either–or, neither–nor, not only–but also*) connect both complete sentences and elements within the sentence. Within the sentence *either–or* and *neither–nor* are used alike:

> I will $\begin{cases} \text{either} \\ \text{neither} \end{cases}$ meet you in the lobby $\begin{cases} \text{or} \\ \text{nor} \end{cases}$ come to your room.

As a connector of complete sentences, *neither–nor* requires the subject–auxiliary shift; *either–or* does not:

> Neither <u>will I</u> meet you in the lobby, nor <u>will I</u> come to your room.
>
> Either <u>I will</u> meet you in the lobby, or <u>I will</u> come to your room.

Not only–but also can be used both within and between sentences:

> <u>Not only</u> the coaches and players <u>but also</u> the fans had high hopes of defeating the Crimson Tide.
>
> <u>Not only</u> did the government's experts underestimate the mortgage crisis that 2008 would bring, <u>but</u> they <u>also</u> delayed in taking action to change its course.

This sentence would be equally grammatical with either *but* or *also*, rather than both.

Both–and does not connect complete sentences; it connects elements within the sentence only:

> Franco is a good sport, <u>both</u> on <u>and</u> off the playing field.
>
> <u>Both</u> Jeanne <u>and</u> Marie worked hard to get their manuscript finished on schedule.

Conjunctive Adverbs (Adverbial Conjunctions).   As their name suggests, the **conjunctive adverbs** join sentences to form coordinate structures as other conjunctions do, but they do so with an adverbial emphasis. The following list also includes some of the most common simple adverbs and adverbial prepositional phrases that function as sentence connectors:

Result:	*therefore, consequently, as a result, of course*
Concession:	*nevertheless, yet, at any rate, still, after all, of course*
Apposition:	*for example, for instance, that is, namely, in other words*
Addition:	*moreover, furthermore, also, in addition, likewise, further*
Time:	*meanwhile, in the meantime*
Contrast:	*however, instead, on the contrary, on the other hand, in contrast, rather*
Summary:	*thus, in conclusion, then*
Reinforcement:	*further, in particular, indeed, above all, in fact*

Conjunctive adverbs differ from other conjunctions in that, like many other adverbials, they tend to be movable within their clause; they need not introduce the clause:

> My tax accountant is not cheap; <u>however</u>, the amount of tax she saves me is far greater than her fee.
> My tax accountant is not cheap; the amount of tax she saves me, <u>however</u>, is far greater than her fee.

The punctuation of coordinate sentences with conjunctive adverbs is explained on page 218. Their rhetorical effects are discussed on page 329.

Subordinating Conjunctions.   The subordinators are conjunctions too, although their function is not to connect independent ideas as equals but rather to show a relationship between two ideas in which one of them is a *dependent* or *subordinate clause*. Like the conjunctive adverbs, the **subordinating conjunctions** are both single words and phrases:

Time:	*when, whenever, after, as, before, once, since, till, until, now that, while, as long as, as soon as*
Concession:	*though, although, even though, if, while*
Contingency:	*if, once*
Condition:	*if, in case, as long as, unless, provided that*
Reason:	*because, since, as long as*
Result:	*so that*
Comparison:	*as, just as, as if*
Contrast:	*while, whereas*

Most subordinate clauses come both before and after the main clause. This movability feature provides a test to differentiate between subordinators and coordinators. The coordinators—the conjunctive adverbs as well as the coordinating conjunctions—introduce only the second clause:

We decided to walk because we had missed the last bus.

Because we had missed the last bus, we decided to walk.

We decided to walk, for we had missed the last bus.

*For we had missed the last bus, we decided to walk.

We missed the bus, so we decided to walk.

*So we decided to walk, we missed the bus.

When set off by commas, subordinate clauses can also come between the subject and the predicate, where they will get added emphasis:

The City Council members, <u>before they adjourned their meeting</u>, voted to give a special award to the recycling center.

None of the players, <u>as they sat in the dugout</u>, heard the fans fighting in the stands just above them.

In addition to these simple and phrasal subordinators, we have a small group of correlative subordinators—two-part structures, one of which is part of the main clause: *as–so, the–the, no sooner–than.*

<u>As</u> General Motors goes, <u>so</u> goes the nation.

The more I go on fad diets, the more weight I seem to add.

He had no sooner arrived than he started to give orders.

Another two-part subordinator occurs in the clause of comparison:

There were more people at the political rally than we expected.

The governor gave a much longer speech than the program called for.

Adverbial subordinate clauses are discussed in Chapter 6. Subordinate clauses that are more clearly sentence modifiers and elliptical clauses are discussed in Chapter 9.

INTERROGATIVES

As their name implies, the interrogatives—*who, whose, whom, which, what, how, why, when, where*—introduce questions:

What are you doing here?

How did you get here?

When are you leaving?

The function of such questions, of course, is to elicit particular information.

The interrogatives also introduce clauses that fill NP slots in the sentence patterns. Such clauses are sometimes referred to as *indirect questions:*

Tell me why he came.

I wonder who came with him.

Whose car he drove is a mystery to me.

These clauses, which function as nominals, are discussed in Chapter 8. (We should note that the interrogatives are the same words that in other contexts are classified as relative pronouns or relative adverbs. For that reason the term *interrogative* more accurately labels a function than a word class.)

EXPLETIVES

Rather than providing a grammatical or structural meaning as the other structure-word classes do, the **expletives**—sometimes defined as "empty words"—generally act simply as operators that allow us to manipulate sentences in a variety of ways. In the diagrams of these sentences, the expletives are independent of the basic sentence.

There. The *there* transformation, as we saw in Chapter 5, enables us to delay the subject in certain kinds of sentences, thus putting it in the position of main stress, which generally falls in the predicate half of the sentence:

> An airplane is landing   There's an airplane landing
>   on the freeway.   →   on the freeway.

The expletive *there* plays no grammatical role in the sentence. To analyze the sentence, you have to discover its underlying form by eliminating the expletive and shifting the subject in front of the *be*.

The *there* transformation as a rhetorical tool is discussed in Chapter 15.

That. One of our most common expletives, *that,* introduces a nominal clause:

> I hope <u>that our exam is easy</u>.

Unlike the relative pronoun *that*, which introduces adjectival clauses, the expletive *that* plays no part in the clause.

"Expletive" is not the only label given to this use of the word *that*; it is sometimes called a "nominalizer" because its function is to turn a clause into a nominal, that is, a noun phrase substitute. And sometimes it is called a "subordinator." The label "expletive" is used by traditional grammarians to emphasize the "empty word" quality of *that*, in that it serves strictly as an operator; it plays no role in the clause itself. The use of *that* in nominal clauses is taken up in detail in Chapter 8.

Or. The expletive *or* introduces an explanatory appositive:

> The study of sentences, <u>or</u> syntax, helps us appreciate how much we know when we know language.

> The African wildebeest, <u>or</u> gnu, resembles an ox.

This *or* should not be confused with the conjunction *or*, which indicates an alternative (as in coffee <u>or</u> tea). The expletive introduces an equivalent in an appositive role. The diagram shows its expletive role:

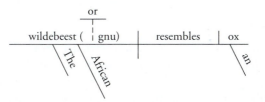

As. Another fairly common expletive introduces certain object complements in Patterns IX and X:

> We elected him <u>as</u> president.

The diagram shows the role of *as* outside of the grammatical structure of the sentence:

Leaving out the *as* does not change the meaning of this sentence; whether to choose it or not is usually a matter of emphasis or rhythm. With verbs like *refer to, think of,* and *know,* however, *as* is required with the object complement:

> I refer to Professor Buck <u>as</u> a woman of character.
>
> I think of her <u>as</u> a woman of many talents.
>
> I think of her <u>as</u> exceptionally clever.
>
> I know her <u>as</u> a friend.

If* and *Whether (or not). These two expletives serve as nominalizers, turning yes/no questions into nominal clauses:

> I wonder <u>if the test</u>
> <u>will be easy</u>.

> It doesn't matter <u>whether</u>
> <u>I study or not</u>.

(You'll recall that for the other kind of questions—the information, or *wh-* questions—interrogative words act as nominalizers: I wonder <u>what</u> <u>I should study</u>.)

PARTICLES

The particle, which combines with a verb to produce a phrasal verb (look *up,* find *out,* turn *in,* look *into*), can be thought of as an alternative function that prepositions and adverbs perform rather than a word class of its own. Both transitive and intransitive verbs combine with particles:

> We <u>turned in</u> at midnight. (intransitive)
>
> The police <u>looked into</u> the allegations. (transitive)

Phrasal verbs are discussed on pages 40–41 and 43–44.

Exercise 57

Label the class of each underlined word.

1. I found some rare stamps <u>and</u> postmarks <u>on</u> <u>an</u> old envelope <u>in</u> the attic.

2. <u>Four</u> friends of mine <u>from</u> the dorm waited in line <u>for</u> sixteen hours, <u>for</u> they were determined to get tickets <u>for</u> the World Series.

3. <u>As</u> the experts predicted, the Republicans chose <u>an</u> ultraconservative <u>as</u> their party's candidate <u>at</u> the convention.

4. We should <u>be</u> arriving <u>by</u> six, <u>but</u> don't wait for us.

5. Our group <u>of</u> tourists will take <u>off</u> at dawn <u>if</u> the weather permits.

6. We <u>are</u> now studying the structure <u>of</u> sentences, <u>or</u> syntax, in <u>our</u> English class.

7. We <u>will</u> warm up <u>with</u> a game of one-on-one <u>while</u> we wait for the rest of the players.

8. We had <u>too</u> many problems with our <u>two</u> new puppies, so we gave them both <u>to</u> the neighbors.

CHAPTER *13*
Key Terms

Adverbial conjunction

Article

Auxiliary

Conjunction

Conjunctive adverb

Coordinating conjunction

Correlative conjunction

Definite article

Demonstrative pronoun

Determiner

Expanded determiner

Explanatory appositive

Expletive

Indefinite article

Indefinite pronoun

Intensifier

Interrogative

Mass noun

Modal-like verb

Number

Particle

Phrasal preposition

Possessive noun

Possessive pronoun

Postdeterminer

Predeterminer

Preposition

Qualifier

Semi-auxiliary

Subject–verb agreement

Subordinating conjunction

QUESTIONS
?
for DISCUSSION

1. Prepositions and particles are among the most difficult words in the language for foreign speakers to master. Why do you suppose this is so? Look at the following sentences. How would you explain the selection of prepositions to a learner of English?

   Be sure to fill out the form carefully.

   Be sure to fill in the form carefully.

   I like to jog in the early morning.

   I like to jog on a sunny morning.

   Our house burned down last week.

   All of my books burned up.

   I'm working on my math.

   I'm really working at it.

2. In answering an interviewer's question, an economist recently said, "I do not foresee any improvement in the economy, absent any change in the elements that are driving it." What part of speech is *absent*?

3. In an article entitled "The Big Nine" (*Atlantic*, March 1988), Cullen Murphy reports on a 1923 study in which the lexicographer G. H. McKnight identified nine words in our language that account for one-quarter of all spoken words. (A list of forty-three accounts for one-half.) Here are the nine: *and, be, have, it, of, the, to, will,* and *you*. Identify their word classes.

   Murphy did his own research of written texts, ranging from an IRS document to the "Wizard of Id" comic strip, and came up with similar results. You might find it interesting to evaluate your own writing. Then write a paragraph in which you use none of the nine—just to see if you can do it. Describe the difference—perhaps in tone or in rhythm—if any.

4. The *New Yorker* reported an apology printed by a Sydney, Australia, newspaper for inadvertently changing a word in a reader's letter to the editor. The correspondent had written, "The number of speakers became unmanageable." The paper changed *the* to *a*. How can one little structure word make such a difference?

5. One difference between the form-class words and the structure words, in addition to the size of their separate vocabularies, is the size of the words themselves. We can cite a few nouns that have fewer than three letters (which seems to be the requirement for crossword puzzles!)—*ox, ax* (also spelled *axe*), *ex* (obviously an abbreviation), *ma*, and *pa*. And here are three verbs—*be, do,* and *go* (the first two of which also fill the auxiliary function). Maybe you can think of others. But certainly most two-letter words are members of the structure classes or pronouns. Interestingly, some of those little ones have homophones in the form classes. Which of the following have homophones that qualify for the crosswords?

> *in   an   or   so   to   we   no   I   do   be*

CLASSROOM APPLICATIONS

1. Sometimes the source of ambiguity in headlines and telegrams is the lack of structure words. Demonstrate the double meaning of the following ambiguous passages by adding structure words:

   PENTAGON REQUESTS CUT
   SHIP SAILS TODAY
   UNION DEMANDS CHANGE
   POLICE PATROLS STRIP

   Now come up with headlines of your own that have more than one meaning.

2. One of the assessment tools commonly used in the field of English as a Second Language (ESL) is the "Cloze" test, which consists of a prose passage with deletions at regular intervals. Language proficiency is then judged on the student's ability to fill in the blanks correctly. Here are two Cloze passages with every fifth word deleted. The first is from the opening paragraph of Shelby Foote's first volume of *The Civil War: A Narrative*. The second is the last paragraph in a *Time* article about weather on the occasion of the 1993 Mississippi flood. Fill in each blank with what you think has been deleted; then compare your answers with those of your classmates. Is there more agreement among you on the form-class words or on

the structure words? Which blanks do you think would be the most difficult for a nonnative speaker?

A. It was a Monday _____ Washington, January 21; Jefferson Davis _____ from his seat in _____ Senate. South Carolina had _____ the Union a month _____, followed by Mississippi, Florida, _____ Alabama, which seceded at _____ rate of one a _____ during the second week _____ the new year. Georgia _____ out eight days later;_____ and Texas were poised _____ go; few doubted that _____ would, along with others._____ more than a decade _____ had been intensive discussion _____ to the legality of _____, but now the argument _____ no longer academic.

B. What is new about _____ weather is that, for _____ first time, some of _____ factors that help shape _____ may be man-made. Experts _____ it may be decades _____ we are certain what _____ the buildup of greenhouse _____ or the depletion of _____ ozone layer has had _____ the global climate. Last _____ flooding and heat wave _____ as a warning that _____ we wait for the _____ to tell us what's _____ with the weather, it _____ be too late to _____ anything about it.

CHAPTER

14

Pronouns

CHAPTER PREVIEW

Pronouns are among our most common words. You will rarely encounter a passage of two or more sentences that doesn't contain several pronouns. In fact, the sentence you just finished reading contains three.

We looked briefly at pronouns in earlier chapters when we substituted them for noun phrases in order to demonstrate where the subject ended and the predicate began:

> The county commissioners (they) have passed a new ordinance.
>
> The mayor's husband (he) spoke against it.
>
> The mayor (she) was upset with him.

These substitutions—*they, he,* and *she*—are among the personal pronouns, the kind you probably recognize most readily. But there are many other classes of pronouns, and in this chapter we will look at them all, pointing out where a conscious understanding of the system can be helpful to you as a writer. By the end of this chapter you will be able to

- Recognize and correct errors in *pronoun-antecedent agreement.*
- Choose the standard *case* for pronouns.
- Use *reflexive* and *demonstrative* pronouns appropriately and effectively.
- Identify pronouns in these subclasses: *intensive, reciprocal, relative, interrogative,* and *indefinite.*

As their name suggests, **pronouns** are words that stand for nouns. Perhaps a more accurate label would be *pronomial,* because they actually stand for

289

any construction that functions as a nominal in the sentence. We refer to the noun or nominal that the pronoun stands for as its **antecedent**. Not all pronouns are alike. The label *pronoun* actually covers a wide variety of words, many of which function in quite different ways. A brief description of the main classes of pronouns follows.

PERSONAL PRONOUNS

The **personal pronouns** are the ones we usually think of when the word *pronoun* comes to mind. We generally label them on the basis of person and number:

PERSON	NUMBER		
	Singular	*Plural*	
1st	I	we	[person(s) speaking]
2nd	you	you	[person(s) spoken to]
3rd	he she it	they	[person(s) spoken about]

For example, we refer to *I* as the "first-person singular" pronoun and *they* as the "third-person plural." In addition, the third-person singular pronouns include the feature of **gender**: masculine *(he)*, feminine *(she)*, and neuter *(it)*.

The term **pronoun–antecedent agreement** describes our selection of the pronoun in reference to the noun or noun phrase (or nominal) it replaces: The personal pronoun "agrees with" its antecedent in both number and, for third-person singular, gender. Note that the second person *(you)* has neither gender nor number distinctions.

Case. The forms given in the preceding set are in the subjective (traditionally called "nominative") case; this is the form used when the pronoun serves as the subject or subject complement. The personal pronouns also inflect for the **possessive** case, as nouns do, and the **objective** case, an inflection that nouns do not have.[1]

[1.] In traditional grammar, the case labels often used are those of Latin: **nominative** (subjective); **genitive** (possessive); and **accusative** (objective). In addition to these three, Latin has separate cases for indirect objects (dative) and objects of prepositions (ablative). For most Latin nouns, these five categories mean at least four different case endings, along with several more for plural nouns.

Subjective:	I	we	you	he	she	it	they
Possessive:	my	our	your	his	her	its	their
	(mine)	(ours)	(yours)	(his)	(hers)		(theirs)
Objective:	me	us	you	him	her	it	them

The possessive forms of pronouns function as determiners. The objective case is used for pronouns in all the object slots: direct object, indirect object, and object complement. A pronoun as object of the preposition is also in the objective case, with one exception: The preposition *of* usually takes the possessive case, producing a structure called the "double possessive":

> Tim's friend = a friend <u>of Tim's</u>
> his friend = a friend <u>of his</u>
> my class = a class <u>of mine</u>

With common nouns we often use the *of* prepositional phrase in the place of the possessive noun:

> the car's engine = the engine <u>of the car</u>
> the day's end = the end <u>of the day</u>

Alternative forms of the possessive case, shown in parentheses in the previous chart, are used when the headword of the noun phrase is deleted:

> This is <u>my book</u>.   This is <u>mine</u>.
> This is <u>her book</u>.   This is <u>hers</u>.

Possessive nouns can also be used without headwords when the headword is understood by the reader or listener:

> This is <u>John's book</u>.   This is <u>John's</u>.
> <u>Mary's book</u> is missing.   <u>Mary's</u> is missing.

The third-person singular *it*, the most neutral of the personal pronouns, is sometimes used as an "anticipatory" subject, as we saw in the discussion of cleft sentences (pages 98–100) and nominals (page 184). In some cases it has clear pronoun status, as in this passage from Robert Frost's poem "Stopping by Woods on a Snowy Evening":

> My little horse must think <u>it</u> queer
> <u>To stop without a farmhouse near</u>.

In other cases the *it*, while acting as a grammatical subject, remains essentially an empty word:

> It is raining
> It's a nice day.

The plural pronoun *they* can also have neutral status:

> They say best men are moulded out of faults. [Shakespeare]

Usage Matters   **The Unwanted Apostrophe**

If, in an essay about your cat, you write,

> The cat caught it's tail in the door,

you will probably find a circle around *it's* when the teacher returns your paper. Here's the rule you violated:

PERSONAL PRONOUNS HAVE NO APOSTROPHES IN THE POSSESSIVE CASE.

If you're thinking that this rule appears to defy the possessive noun rule—well, you're right. But that rule—"add an apostrophe-plus-s to make singular nouns possessive"—applies to nouns only, not to personal pronouns. If you add the apostrophe to *its*, you've written either *it is* or *it has*. *Cat's* and other nouns with an apostrophe-plus-s, on the other hand, have three potential meanings: *the cat is, the cat has,* and possession—that is, belonging to the cat.

Adding the apostrophe-plus-s to the pronoun *it* for possessive case may indeed seem logical—but it's incorrect! In this case, logic is working against you!

(Note, however, we do use the apostrophe-plus-s for the possessive of indefinite pronouns: *someone's cat; everybody's* business, and so forth—as you'll see later in this chapter, on page 301.)

The Missing Pronoun. We should also note that our system of personal pronouns—or, to be more accurate, a gap in the system—is the source of a great deal of the sexism in our language. Missing from the system is a singular third-person pronoun that refers to either gender. Our plural pronoun (*they*) includes both male and female; but when we need a pronoun to refer to an unidentified person, such as "the writer" or "a student" or "the doctor," the long-standing tradition has been to use the masculine (*he/his/him*):

> The writer of this news story should have kept <u>his</u> personal
>   opinion out of it.

In this situation, we could avoid the sexism of *his* either by eliminating the determiner or substituting *the*. Perhaps someday the plural pronoun will be accepted for both singular and plural, a usage known as the "singular *they*," which has become quite common in speech:

> Someone broke into our car last night; *they* stole our tape deck and all our tapes.

(This issue is discussed further in the "Usage Matters" feature on pages 301–302.) The topic is covered in great detail in Haussamen's *Revising the Rules*, found in the reference list at the end of Chapter 1.

Exercise 58

Substitute personal pronouns for the underlined nouns and noun phrases in the following sentences.

1. <u>Luis and Maria</u> have bought a new house.
2. <u>Bev and I</u> will be going to the game with <u>Otis</u>.
3. <u>Betsy</u> bought <u>that beautiful new car of hers</u> in Charlotte.
4. Both of <u>her cars</u> are gas guzzlers.
5. There have always been uneasy feelings between <u>the neighbors and my husband</u>.
6. I want <u>Tony</u> to approve of <u>the project</u>.
7. The kids gave <u>their father and me</u> a bad time.
8. <u>My brother, who works for the Navy in California,</u> spends <u>his weekends</u> in Las Vegas.

Usage Matters   Case

The difference between *who* and *whom*, discussed in a previous "Usage Matters" (pages 140–141), is identical to the difference between *I* and *me* or between *she* and *her* or between *he* and *him* or *they* and *them*. We say

| I know him. | *and* | He knows me. |
| She helps them. | *and* | They help her. |

We also say

> The man <u>who loves me</u> is coming to visit,

where *who* is the subject in its own clause, the subject of the verb *love*, and

> The man <u>whom I love</u> is coming to visit,

where *whom* is the direct object of *love*.

The topic under discussion here is that of **case**. If you are a native speaker of English, nothing in the previous discussion comes as a surprise. Chances are you've never been tempted to say,

> *Him knows I.   *or*   *Them helps she.

However, you may have been tempted to say—you may even have heard yourself say—

> The stranger <u>who I helped this morning</u> was very grateful,

even though *who* functions as the direct object in the adjectival clause. For some reason, *who* doesn't sound as strange, or as ungrammatical, as

> *Amy knows I.   *or*   *They help she.

If you consider the position of *who* in its clause, you can probably figure out why that sentence about the stranger is so easy to say—and why it sounds o.k.

The point is that we do *say* it. The fact that we do is one of the differences between speech and writing. But in writing, you'll want to figure out the appropriate *case* for the object position:

> The stranger <u>whom I helped this morning</u>...

The direct object, of course, is not the only object in our sentences. The object of the preposition is probably even more common. And except for the preposition *of* (noted on page 291), prepositional phrases require the objective case when the object is a pronoun:

> I bought this <u>for him</u>.   Pam bought this <u>for me</u>.
>
> I gave it <u>to them</u>.   They came <u>with her</u>.

Again, you're probably not tempted to say "for he" or "to they" or "for I" or "with she." You automatically use the objective case of personal pronouns after prepositions. And native speakers are probably never tempted to say,

> *This secret is just <u>between we</u>.
>
> *This secret is just between <u>Joe and they</u>.

So why do you suppose it's so common to hear,

> *This secret is just <u>between Joe and I</u>.

> *and*

> *This secret is just <u>between you and I</u>?

Perhaps the people who use *I* instead of *me* in these sentences are the same people who, as children, were corrected by their parents or by a teacher when they said, "Joe and me are going to the park." The lesson stuck—and it got applied in places where it didn't belong.

REFLEXIVE PRONOUNS

Reflexive pronouns are those formed by adding *-self* or *-selves* to a form of the personal pronoun:

PERSON	SINGULAR	PLURAL
1st	myself	ourselves
2nd	yourself	yourselves
3rd	himself herself itself	themselves

The reflexive pronoun is used as the direct object, indirect object, and object of the preposition when its antecedent appears in the same clause, usually as the subject:

John cut <u>himself.</u>

I glanced at <u>myself</u> in the mirror.

I cooked dinner for Shelley and <u>myself.</u>

Joe cooked dinner for Gary and <u>himself.</u>

Investigating Language 14.1

For each of the italicized noun phrases in the following sentences, substitute either a personal pronoun or a reflexive pronoun. Assume that a name or noun phrase appearing more than once in a sentence refers to the same person or people in each instance:

1. Randall cut *Randall* while *Randall* was shaving.
2. The Kim sisters threw a party for *the Kim sisters.*
3. Although Juan ran a good race, two other runners finished ahead of *Juan.*
4. The wardrobe mistress gave *the wardrobe mistress* all the credit for the play's success.
5. The students said that *the students* understood the assignment.

Formulate a rule to explain the system you used to choose the class of pronoun. In what way do the following sentences depart from the system you described:

6. Joe cooked dinner for Gary and myself.
7. We decided that Gary and myself would do the dishes.

The rule you formulated for the first five sentences probably explains that the reflexive pronoun is used only when those identical noun phrases appear in the same clause, as in sentences 1, 2, and 4. In sentences 3 and 5, the repeated noun phrase appears in a second clause. However, in the last two examples, those requirements are absent: In 6 there is no antecedent for *myself* in the sentence; in 7, *Gary and myself* and its antecedent *we* are in separate clauses. Although sentences like the last two are fairly common in speech, the written standard calls for personal pronouns:

> Joe cooked dinner for Gary and me.
>
> We decided that Gary and I would do the dishes.

Both versions are unambiguous; both forms of the first-person pronoun, *me* and *myself*, can refer only to the speaker. However, with third-person pronouns different forms produce different meanings:

> Joe cooked dinner for Gary and <u>himself</u> (Joe).
>
> Joe cooked dinner for Gary and <u>him</u> (someone else).

Exercise 59

Fill the blanks with the appropriate reflexive pronouns.

1. Gabrielle gave _____ a black eye when she fell.
2. Li and Mei-Ling cooked _____ salmon for dinner.
3. The ceramic figurine sat by _____ on the shelf.
4. We sat by _____ in the front row.
5. Paulo cooked a delicious Mexican feast for Rosa and _____.
6. Wearing our new designer jeans, Sheila and I admired _____ in the mirror.

INTENSIVE PRONOUNS

Also known as the *emphatic reflexive pronouns*, the **intensive pronouns** have the same form as the reflexives. The intensive pronoun serves as an appositive to emphasize a noun, but it need not directly follow the noun:

> I <u>myself</u> prefer chocolate.
> I prefer chocolate <u>myself</u>.
> <u>Myself</u>, I prefer chocolate.

Because *myself* is in apposition to *I* in all three versions, the diagram will not distinguish among them:

I (myself)	prefer	chocolate

RECIPROCAL PRONOUNS

Each other and *one another* are known as the **reciprocal pronouns.** They serve either as determiners (in the possessive case) or as objects, referring to previously named nouns. *Each other* generally refers to two nouns; *one another* to three or more.

> Juan and Claudia help <u>each other</u>.
> They even do <u>each other's</u> chores.
> All the students in my study group help <u>one another</u> with their homework.

DEMONSTRATIVE PRONOUNS

In our discussion of determiners we noted that the selection of a determiner is based on certain inherent features, such as definite or indefinite, countable or noncountable. The **demonstrative pronouns**, one of the subclasses of determiners, include the features of "number" and "proximity":

PROXIMITY	NUMBER	
	Singular	*Plural*
Near	this	these
Distant	that	those

> <u>That</u> documentary we saw last night really made me think, but <u>this</u> one is simply stupid.
> <u>Those</u> trees on the ridge were almost destroyed by gypsy moths, but <u>these</u> seem perfectly healthy.

Like other determiner classes, the demonstrative pronoun can be a substitute for a nominal as well as a signal for one:

These old shoes and hats   will be perfect for the costumes.

These   will be perfect for the costumes.

To be effective as a nominal, the demonstrative pronoun must replace or stand for a clearly stated antecedent. In the following example, *that* does not refer to "solar energy"; it has no clear antecedent:

Our contractor is obviously skeptical about solar energy. That
doesn't surprise me.

Such sentences are not uncommon in speech, nor are they ungrammatical. But when a *this* or *that* has no specific antecedent, the writer can usually improve the sentence by providing a noun headword for the demonstrative pronoun—by turning the pronoun into a determiner:

Our contractor is obviously skeptical about solar energy. That
attitude (or His attitude) doesn't surprise me.

A combination of the two sentences would also be an improvement over the vague use of *that:*

Our contractor's skepticism about solar energy doesn't surprise me.

The vague reference of *this* and *that* has the same fuzzy quality as the broad-reference relative clause, which you read about in Chapter 9:

Our contractor is skeptical about solar energy, which doesn't
surprise me.

RELATIVE PRONOUNS

The **relative pronouns** are *who*, *which*, and *that;* they introduce clauses that modify the nouns that are the antecedents of these pronouns. *Who* inflects for both possessive and objective cases: *whose* (possessive) and *whom* (objective). The case of *who* is determined by the part it plays (its function) in its own clause:

The man who lives across the street sold me his car.

In this sentence *who* renames *man*, its antecedent, and plays the part of subject in the relative (adjectival) clause. In the next sentence the relative pronoun is in the possessive case form, *whose:*

The man whose car I bought was not very honest about the gas
mileage.

Here *whose*, the possessive relative pronoun, again stands for *man;* in its own clause it acts as the determiner for *car*, the role that possessives normally play.

Whose also acts as the possessive form of *which:*

> The wooded ridge across the valley, <u>whose trees were infested by gypsy moths</u>, turned brown in mid-June.

The relative pronoun *that* is generally subjective or objective, never possessive:

> I lost the backpack <u>that I bought yesterday</u>.

That renames *backpack* and acts as the object within its own clause. In object position, *that* can be omitted:

> I lost the backpack <u>I bought yesterday</u>.

When *that* is the subject of the clause, however, it cannot be omitted:

> The route <u>that will get us there fastest</u> is straight across the mountain.

The *wh-* relative pronouns also have an expanded form with the addition of *-ever*, known as **indefinite relative pronouns:** *whoever, whosever, whomever,* and *whatever*. The expanded relatives have indefinite referents rather than specific ones as the simple relatives do:

> I will give a bonus to <u>whoever works the hardest</u>.
> I will pay you <u>whatever you deserve</u>.
> I will call <u>whomever the doctor recommends</u>.

What is also considered an indefinite relative pronoun when it introduces adjectival clauses and means "that which":

> I will pay you <u>what you deserve</u>.

The relative (adjectival) clauses are also discussed in Chapter 7.

INTERROGATIVE PRONOUNS

The list of **interrogative pronouns** is similar to that of the relatives: *who* (*whose, whom*), *which,* and *what*. The interrogatives, as their name suggests, are among the question words that produce information questions (in contrast to yes/no questions):

> <u>What</u> do you want for lunch?
> <u>Whose</u> car is that?
> <u>Which</u> section of history did you get?

As we saw in Chapter 3, the interrogative word plays a part in the sentence. For example, in the first preceding sample sentence, *what* fills the direct object slot: "You do want *what* for lunch." In a sentence such as "What flavor do you prefer?" the interrogative *what* acts as a determiner for the noun *flavor*. In the other two examples listed, *whose* and *which* also act as determiners: *whose car, which section*. Because of this modifying function, *which*, *what*, and *whose* are sometimes classified as **interrogative adjectives**.

The interrogative pronouns also introduce nominal clauses and, like the relative pronouns, play a part in the clause. There is an indirect question involved in such clauses—either implied or stated, asked or answered:

> Tell me <u>what you want for lunch</u>.
>
> I know <u>who gave you that black eye</u>.

Nominal clauses are discussed in Chapter 8.

INDEFINITE PRONOUNS

The **indefinite pronouns** include a number of words listed earlier as determiners:

enough	many	all	either	more
few	much	both	neither	most
fewer	several	any	none	each

One is also commonly used as a pronoun (as are the other cardinal numbers—*two*, *three*, etc.) along with its negative, *none*. As a pronoun, *one* often replaces only the headword, rather than the entire noun phrase:

> *The blue <u>shoes</u> that I bought yesterday* will be perfect for the trip.
>
> *The blue <u>ones</u> that I bought yesterday* will be perfect for the trip.

The personal pronoun, on the other hand, would replace the entire noun phrase:

> <u>*They*</u> will be perfect for the trip.

The pronouns *every, any, no,* and *some* can be expanded with *-body, -thing,* and *-one*:

some	{ body, thing, one	every	{ body, thing, one
any	{ body, thing, one	no	{ body, thing, one (two words)

(Note that *every* and *no*, which function as determiners, do not function as pronouns except in the expanded forms shown here.)

These pronouns can take modifiers in the form of clauses and phrases:

> <u>Anyone</u> *who wants extra credit in psych class* can volunteer for tonight's experiment.

They can also be modified by verb phrases:

> <u>Everyone</u> *reporting late for practice* will take fifteen laps.

And by prepositional phrases:

> <u>Nothing</u> *on the front page* interests me anymore.

Unlike most nouns, the expanded indefinite pronouns can be modified by single adjectives in postheadword position:

> I don't care for <u>anything</u> *sweet*.
> I think that <u>something</u> *strange* is going on here.

And unlike other pronouns, when the expanded indefinite pronouns are used in the possessive case—as they are when functioning as determiners—they require an apostrophe + s, just as possessive nouns do:

> <u>Somebody's</u> books are in the back seat.
> The teacher ignored <u>everyone's</u> complaints about the exam schedule.

Usage Matters   Problem Pronouns

In the previous section, you saw the system for expanding indefinite pronouns to form common words like *somebody* and *anyone* and *everyone*. When we use these pronouns as sentence subjects, we treat them as singular in terms of the verb:

> Everyone in class <u>is</u> invited to the picnic.
> Everybody <u>plans</u> to be there.

Clearly, however, the referent of these pronouns is plural; that is, both *everyone* and *everybody* refer to more than one person. That's why, when we need a personal pronoun, we choose *they:*

> When everyone arrived, <u>they</u> organized a softball game.
> Everybody had a good time, didn't <u>they</u>?

In these examples, there's really no alternative to this use of the plural *they* even though the indefinite pronouns require a singular verb. However, in some cases *they* will sound awkward:

> Someone called last night, but <u>they</u> didn't leave a message.

Here the problem is a different one. Here *someone* is actually singular—but we have no singular pronoun that refers to a person whose sex is unknown. (On page 292 you read about this problem in the section called "The Missing Pronoun.") In the past, until a few decades ago, writers had no qualms about using the masculine pronoun in this situation; it was standard usage:

> Someone called last night, but <u>he</u> didn't leave a message.

However, this use of *he* is no longer standard. In Chapter 15 we look further at this issue in the section called "Using Gender Appropriately" (pages 336–339).

ELL Issues   The "Some/Any" Rule

Although the restrictions are not apparent in their forms, the choice of *some* and *any*, as well as their expanded versions with *body*, *thing*, and *one*, is usually determined by the presence or absence of *not* or another negative, such as *never, rarely, seldom*, and the like:

> Do you want <u>some</u> dessert?
>
> No, I do<u>n't</u> want <u>any</u>.
>
> I saw <u>someone</u> you know at the concert.
>
> I did<u>n't</u> see <u>anyone</u> I know.

The adverbs *somewhere* and *anywhere* carry the same restriction:

> My sister is <u>somewhere</u> in the mall.
>
> I'm <u>not</u> going <u>anywhere</u> until she shows up.

We should emphasize that while these examples follow the standard rule, it is not unusual to hear variations. In the first example, for instance, the response "No, I don't want some" would sound a bit odd—but would probably not be judged ungrammatical.

Exercise   60

Underline the pronouns in the following sentences. Identify the subclass to which each pronoun belongs.

1. When Roberto ordered a pizza with everything, I ordered one too.
2. Millie and Bev shopped at almost every store in the mall but couldn't find any shoes they liked.

3. Someone was standing in the shadows, but we couldn't see who it was.

4. All that I had for lunch was that overripe banana.

5. Booker and Marcus didn't eat much either, but they both ate more than I did.

6. I myself will go along with whatever you decide.

7. One hour of studying was enough for me.

8. Quarreling among themselves, the committee members completely disregarded one another's suggestions.

9. At the end of most months, I find myself without funds.

10. The employment office will find a job for whoever wants one.

CHAPTER *14*
Key Terms

Antecedent	Personal pronoun
Case	Plural
Demonstrative pronoun	Possessive case
Emphatic reflexive pronoun	Pronoun
Gender	Pronoun–antecedent agreement
Indefinite pronoun	Proximity
Indefinite relative pronoun	Reciprocal pronoun
Intensive pronoun	Reflexive pronoun
Interrogative adjective	Relative pronoun
Interrogative pronoun	Sexism
Number	Singular
Objective case	Subjective case
Person	

QUESTIONS
?
for DISCUSSION

1. The relative pronoun agrees with its antecedent in person and number but not necessarily in case. How do the following sentences illustrate that statement?

> I don't know the women who live next door.
>
> It was I whom you spoke with on the phone.

2. How do you explain the ambiguity of this sentence?

   > The white horse by the rail looked faster than the one in the paddock.

3. In Chapter 3, Discussion Question 8 (page 62), we looked at the following ambiguous sentence:

   > Rosa called her Aunt Betty.

   What is the source of the ambiguity? Would a sentence about Mario and Uncle Ben instead of Rosa and Aunt Betty be equally ambiguous? What's the difference?

4. What is the difference in the meaning of *one* in the following sentences?

   > <u>One</u> farmer told me there hadn't been rain in eight weeks.
   >
   > <u>One</u> can only hope that the weather changes soon.

5. The following sentences include clauses introduced by expanded, or indefinite, relative pronouns:

   > I will give a bonus to whoever works hardest.
   >
   > I will pay you whatever you deserve.
   >
   > I will call whomever the doctor recommends.

   Explain why a traditional diagram of such sentences would look like this:

   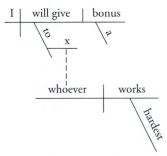

   How should we diagram the sentences with *whatever* and *whomever*?

6. How do you explain the use of *we* and *us* in the following sentences?

   > We graduates lined up to go into the gym.
   >
   > The speaker told us graduates that we were the hope of the future.

Is *we* used correctly in the following sentence?

    It wasn't a good idea for we dishwashers to go on strike.

7. Here's a statement with a single, straightforward meaning:

    I invited everyone in the class to my party.

The follow-up sentence is not quite as clear; in fact, it's ambiguous:

    Everyone didn't come.

Here's another ambiguous sentence:

    Everything doesn't cause cancer.

Paraphrase the two negative sentences in two ways to demonstrate their meanings. Then consider the meaning of *everyone* and *everything* and explain why their use with the negative should produce ambiguity.

CLASSROOM APPLICATIONS

1. In this chapter you have seen eight subclasses of pronouns. Although they are all words you commonly use, you may not have realized they are all pronouns. Write a passage with as few sentences as possible using at least one pronoun from each of the eight subclasses: personal, reflexive, intensive, reciprocal, demonstrative, relative, interrogative, and indefinite.

2. The following passage, from "The Winter of Man," an essay by Loren Eiseley, was published in 1972, a time when the masculine pronoun was accepted as a generic singular. Note too the use of *man* in reference to humans in general.

> Students of the earth's climate have observed that man, in spite of the disappearance of the great continental ice fields, still lives on the steep edge of winter or early spring. The pulsations of these great ice deserts, thousands of feet thick and capable of overflowing mountains and valleys, have characterized the nature of the world since man, in his thinking and speaking phase, arose. The ice which has left the marks of its passing upon the landscape of the Northern Hemisphere has also accounted, in its long, slow advances and retreats, for movements, migrations and extinctions throughout the plant and animal kingdoms. Though man is originally tropical in his origins, the ice has played a great role in his unwritten history. At times it has

constricted his movements, affecting the genetic selection that has created him. Again, ice has established conditions in which man has had to exert all his ingenuity in order to survive. By contrast, there have been other times when the ice has withdrawn farther than today and then, like a kind of sleepy dragon, has crept forth to harry man once more. For something like a million years this strange and alternating context has continued between man and the ice.

Revise the passage in gender-neutral language.

Grammar for Writers

For some of you, this book has been your introduction to the study of grammar. Terms like *noun* and *adjective* and *predicate* and *participle* were completely new to you or, at best, distant echoes from a long-ago classroom. Others of you brought a fairly substantial understanding of parts of speech and sentences from grammar classes that may have begun in the fifth grade and continued through the twelfth, very likely starting every year with parts of speech and ending with complex sentences. The majority of you are probably somewhere in between, with memories of a grammar unit for a year or two, perhaps in the seventh and eighth grades.

Those differing backgrounds reflect actual differences in the way in which grammar is taught throughout this country. Grammar is not a subject area that curriculum experts agree on; it is, in fact, an area fraught with controversy and misunderstanding. Part of that misunderstanding lies in the problem of definition.

In Chapter 1 we looked at three definitions of *grammar:*

1. The rules in our heads that enable each of us to produce language.

2. The subject matter of books like this one, with its description of sentences and the rules that produce them.

3. The do's and don't's of usage, known as "linguistic etiquette."

For many people, it is only this third definition—the social rules of usage, those traditional rules about correctness—that they remember from their grammar classes. Grammar brings to mind red marks on essays pinpointing comma splices and spelling errors; it recalls warnings about ending sentences with prepositions or beginning them with conjunctions. It's understandable for people to assume that the purpose of studying grammar is to avoid error. This definition and this purpose—and the methods of teaching that reflect such a definition and purpose—contribute to the misunderstanding.

If the purpose of studying grammar is to avoid error, then it should follow that learning the "rules of grammar" will make you a better writer because you will avoid errors in your compositions. There are two problems with this assumption: First, the purpose for studying grammar goes far beyond that of avoiding error; and, second, composition teachers realized long ago that error-free writing is not necessarily effective writing. To write effectively, you must be sensitive to your readers, to take into account what they already know, what they expect, what they need to know. You must think about how the words and the structures you choose will accomplish your purpose.

Unfortunately, methods of teaching grammar have been slow to change. The traditional view of language as a set of rules to be memorized ignores all of the insights of modern linguistics. Instead, teachers should help their students recognize and explore their own innate competence and then help them use that knowledge when they write.

Composition teachers know that students who understand the structure of their language are in a position to recognize their own weaknesses and strengths as writers, to revise and edit their own writing; further, they can offer helpful evaluations in peer-review sessions. Students who have explored their own language expertise, who have acquired a vocabulary for discussing language, hold a decided advantage over those who have not.

We firmly believe that understanding English grammar—the title and theme of this book—does make a difference for writers and teachers of writing: It does so by enhancing a writer's confidence, by giving the writer control, by illuminating all the choices that are available. That control and those choices are the subject matter of Chapter 15, "Rhetorical Grammar." And because punctuation is such an important skill for both writing competence and writing confidence, we have pulled together punctuation lessons from throughout the book into Chapter 16, "Purposeful Punctuation."

Rhetorical Grammar

CHAPTER PREVIEW

Although the term *rhetorical* and its noun form, *rhetoric*, have not been used up to now, you'll find a description of rhetoric in Chapter 1 under the topic "Language Variety":

> In our written language, too, what is appropriate or effective in one situation may be completely out of place in another. The language of email messages and texting are obviously different from the language you use in a job-application letter. Even the writing you do in school varies from one class or one assignment to another. The personal essay you write for your composition class has a level of informality that would be inappropriate for a business report or a history research paper. As with speech, the purpose and the audience make all the difference.

Rhetoric means that the topic, the purpose, and the audience will make a difference in the way you write, and your rhetorical situation will determine the grammatical choices you make, choices about sentence structure and vocabulary, even about punctuation.

In this chapter we will discuss the ways that the grammar knowledge you have gained in the preceding chapters can make a difference to you as a writer and, perhaps, as a teacher of writing. By the end of the chapter you will be able to

- Use the *known–new contract* to increase *cohesion*.
- Manipulate *rhythm* and *end focus* to control the way your sentences are read.
- Choose precise verbs and avoid *nominalizations*.

- Shift *adverbials* for emphasis and variety.
- Make effective use of *metadiscourse*.
- Improve *style* with variations in sentences and punctuation.
- Avoid *sexist* language.

SENTENCE PATTERNS

Basic Sentences. In Chapter 2 we recognized that such simple two-word sentences as "Mary laughed" and "Cats fight" rarely show up in actual prose. However, it's fairly common to see bare-bones sentence patterns just a bit longer than two words used both as topic sentences and as attention-getters. Here, for example, are two passages, both of which include a basic sentence that stands out and calls attention to itself. We have added the underlining.

The first, from Steven Pinker's *Language Instinct*, begins the discussion of his case for calling language an instinct:

> The trail begins with the study of how the particular lan-
> guages we find in the world today arose. Here, one would
> think, linguistics runs into the problem of any historical
> science: no one recorded the crucial events at the time they
> happened. Although historical linguists can trace modern
> complex languages back to earlier ones, this just pushes the
> problem back a step; we need to see how people create a
> complex language from scratch. <u>Amazingly, we can.</u> (p. 32)

The second is from Stephen E. Ambrose's *Undaunted Courage*, his book about the Lewis and Clark expedition:

> Fewer than one out of ten Americans, about half a million
> people, lived west of the Appalachian Mountains, but as the
> Whiskey Rebellion had shown, they were already disposed
> to think of themselves as the germ of an independent nation
> that would find its outlet to the world marketplace not across
> the mountains to the Atlantic Seaboard, but by the Ohio and
> Mississippi river system to the Gulf of Mexico. <u>The threat of
> secession was quite real.</u> The United States was only eighteen
> years old, had itself come into existence by an act of rebellion
> and secession, had changed its form of government just twelve
> years earlier, and thus was in a fluid political situation. (p. 52)

In both of these cases, the underlined sentence is functioning as the topic sentence. The first one is an elliptical sentence, with an understood verb, which we can recover from the previous sentence: *Amazingly, we can see that*. Perhaps this doesn't qualify as bare bones, but by truncating it, the author has made it an attention-getter.

Cohesion. An important concept for helping you to understand sentence patterns back in Chapter 3 was the recognition that sentences consist of a series of slots, or positions, some required and some optional, filled by structures of various forms. Your understanding of these sentence parts can be helpful in thinking about sentence **cohesion**, the ties that connect each sentence to what has gone before—the glue that gives a paragraph and an essay unity. Part of that glue is provided by information in the sentence that the reader knows or expects, information that has already been mentioned.

The following paragraph opens a *Parade* magazine article by Bob Reiss titled "Stopping Drugs at Sea" (January 31, 2010):

> Every day, <u>a high-stakes battle</u> affecting the security and well-being of millions of Americans is played out far off our shores. <u>The conflict</u> occurs across more than 6 million square miles of ocean—an area larger than the size of the contiguous United States—where smugglers transport cocaine and other illegal drugs from South America. <u>Their cargo</u> is ultimately intended for sale in our cities and towns—but not if the U.S. Coast Guard stops it first.

The first sentence introduces the topic with the noun phrase *a high-stakes battle.* The subject of the second sentence uses a synonym for the known information, *conflict;* and the new information in the predicate of the second sentence becomes the subject of the third, *their cargo.*

This known-to-new sequence is fairly typical for cohesive paragraphs, where the new information of one sentence becomes the known information of the next. In fact, the known–new sequence is so pervasive a feature of our prose that it is sometimes referred to as the **known–new contract**. The writer has an obligation, a contract of sorts, to fulfill expectations in the reader—to keep the reader on familiar ground. The reader has every right to expect each sentence to be connected in some way to what has gone before, to include a known element. This schema, where the new information in one sentence becomes the known information of the next, might be diagrammed in this way:

A—B, B—C, C—D

One of our most common known elements, certainly as strong as the repeated noun or noun phrase, is the pronoun. Consider how often the subject slot of the second sentence in a passage is filled by a pronoun, such as *she* or *he* or *it* or *they*. That pronoun is automatically tied to its antecedent, a previously mentioned nominal that it stands for. If there is no obvious antecedent, then the pronoun is not doing its cohesive job.

In the following passage, part of the opening paragraph of an essay by Annie Dillard, from her book *Teaching a Stone to Talk*, the first sentence introduces the topic, *a weasel*, in the subject slot—another basic sentence pattern. And, as you can see, the subjects of the next three sentences are the pronoun *he:*

> A weasel is wild. Who knows what **he** thinks? **He** sleeps in his underground den, his tail draped over his nose. Sometimes **he** lives in his den for two days without leaving. Outside, **he** stalks rabbits, mice, muskrats, and birds, killing more bodies than **he** can eat warm, and often dragging the carcasses home.

The pattern of known and new information in this passage, which is fairly common in descriptive writing, has a different schema from the earlier paragraph discussed. Here, where succeeding sentences repeat the subject, the schema would look like this:

$$A—B, A—C, A—D$$

Cohesion can also be enhanced by the information in an opening adverbial slot. For example, the opening of the fifth sentence in the weasel passage, *Outside*, provides a cohesive tie by contrasting with the "inside" designation *in his den* of sentence four. In narrative writing, adverbials of place or time often serve as the glue that connects sentences and paragraphs.

How can the known–new principle of cohesion help you as a writer? Are you supposed to stop after every sentence and estimate the cohesive power of your next subject? No, of course not. That's not the way writers work. But when you are revising—and by the way, revision goes on all the time, even during the first draft—you will want to keep in mind the issues of the known–new contract and reader expectation. You can learn to put yourself in your reader's shoes to see if you've kept your part of the bargain.

SENTENCE RHYTHM

One of the most distinctive features of any language—and one of the most automatic for the native speaker—is its sense of rhythm. Our language has a rhythm just as surely as music does—a regular beat. That sense of rhythm is tied up with the sentence patterns and with the known–new contract. If you read the opening sentence in this paragraph out loud, you'll hear yourself saying "one of the most" in almost a monotone; you probably don't hear a stressed syllable, a beat, until you get to *distinctive:*

one of the most disTINCtive

And you probably rush through those first four words so fast that you pronounce "of" without the *f*, making "one of" sound like the first two words in "won a prize."

The rhythm of sentences, what we call the **intonation** pattern, can be described as valleys and peaks, where the loudest syllables, those with stress, are represented by peaks:

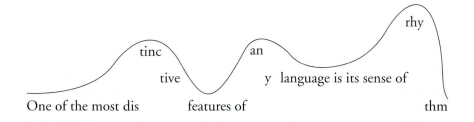

Not all the peaks are of the same height—we have different degrees of stress—but they do tend to come at fairly regular intervals. As listeners we pay attention to the peaks—that's where we'll hear the information that the speaker is focusing on. As speakers, we manipulate the peaks and valleys to coincide with our message, reserving the loudest stress, the highest peak, for the new information, which will be our main point of focus.

End Focus. The rhythm of a sentence is closely tied both to its two-part subject–predicate structure and to the known–new contract. The topic, or theme, stated in the subject will usually be a valley or low peak in the intonation contour, especially if it is known information. The prominent peak of stress, the focus on the new information, will come in the predicate; it will be close to the end of the sentence. Linguists describe this common rhythm pattern as **end focus**. It is a rhythm that experienced writers are sensitive to. Good writers, you can be sure, are tuned in to the rhythm of their own inner voice as they write; they understand how to manipulate sentences in order to control the way the reader reads them and to prevent misreading.

Read the following passage aloud and listen to the intonation pattern you give to the underlined sentence:

> Did you hear what happened? <u>Barbara wrecked her motorcycle yesterday</u>. She was on her way to work when the car in front of her stopped suddenly—and she didn't.

You probably read that second sentence with the stress on *motor*. In a different context, however, the rhythm could change if the purpose of the sentence has changed. In the following passage, the known information has changed. Again, read it aloud and listen to the intonation:

> Sue told me that Barbara had an accident this morning on her way to work. But I think she got her facts wrong. <u>Barbara wrecked her motorcycle yesterday</u>.

This time you probably put the main stress on *yesterday;* in this context it would make no sense to stress *motorcycle.* Try reading the passage that way, and you'll easily recognize the problem: All the information in the last sentence up to the word *yesterday* is already known. In this context it is old information: "Barbara wrecked her motorcycle" is a repetition, albeit more specific, of "Barbara had an accident." As a reader, you know intuitively that it's not time to apply stress until you get beyond that old information, until you get to *yesterday*, the new focus.

You'll note, however, that the principle of end focus is still operating, with the main stress on the last sentence element. But imagine how awkward the sentence would be if the adverb *yesterday* were shifted to the beginning of the sentence. It would certainly be grammatical from a structural point of view; as you know, adverbials are movable, especially adverbials of time. Even in opening position the reader might recognize *yesterday* as the new information and give it main stress. But the sentence would certainly have lost its natural rhythm. Read the passage aloud and you'll hear the problem:

> Sue told me that Barbara had an accident this morning on her way to work. But I think she got her facts wrong. Yesterday Barbara wrecked her motorcycle.

Although sentence variety is certainly commendable, you won't want to shift an adverbial to the opening slot just for the sake of variety—certainly not if that adverbial is the new information.

Investigating Language   15.1

Read the following passages, listening carefully to the intonation contour of each sentence. Indicate the words (or syllables) that get main stress. Compare your reading with that of your classmates. Identify the new information in each sentence. Does its position and emphasis fulfill the known–new contract?

1. Never invest in something you don't understand or in the dream of an artful salesperson. Be a buyer, not a sellee. Figure out what you want (be it life insurance, mutual funds or a vacuum cleaner) and then shop for a good buy. Don't let someone else tell you what you need—at least not if he happens to be selling it. [Andrew Tobias, *Parade*]

2. To simulate chance occurrences, a computer can't literally toss a coin or roll a die. Instead, it relies on special numerical recipes for

generating strings for shuffled digits that pass for random numbers. Such sequences of pseudorandom numbers play crucial roles not only in computer games but also in simulations of physical processes. [I. Peterson, *Science News*]

3. Frank evaluation of its [caffeine's] hazards is not easy. There is a vast literature on the effects of caffeine on the body, and for every study reaching one conclusion, seemingly there is another that contradicts it. Although most major health risks have been ruled out, research continues at a steady clip. [Corby Kummer, *Atlantic Monthly*]

FOCUSING TOOLS

Because end focus is such a common rhythm pattern, we can think of it as a part of the contract between writer and reader. The reader expects the main sentence focus to be in the predicate unless given a signal to the contrary. And we do have several such signals at our disposal.

Several of the sentence transformations we looked at in Chapter 5 allow the writer to shift the focus of the sentence, pointing the reader to a particular slot. The *it*-cleft transformation is one of the most versatile. Here are three variations of the sentence about Barbara, each of which guarantees that the reader will put the emphasis exactly where the writer intends for it to be:

1. It was Barbara who wrecked her motorcycle yesterday.
2. It was her motorcycle that Barbara wrecked yesterday.
3. It was yesterday that Barbara wrecked her motorcycle.

If sentence 3 had been included in that earlier passage about the accident, it would have been impossible for the reader to miss the new information; in the cleft transformation the emphasis is clearly on *yesterday*.

The *it*-cleft is not a structure you will want to overuse, but it certainly is useful—and almost foolproof—when it comes to controlling the rhythm of a sentence and directing the reader's focus.

Another cleft transformation, also described in Chapter 5, uses a *what* clause to direct the reader's attention. In the following sentence you will probably put the emphasis on *bothers:*

Mike's cynical attitude toward the customers really bothers me.

Here are two variations using the *what*-cleft:

What bothers me is Mike's cynical attitude toward the customers.
What bothers me about Mike is his cynical attitude toward the customers.

Although all three versions mean essentially the same thing, the choice in a particular context will be determined in part by what the reader already knows—and consequently expects. And in the case of both cleft variations, their use assumes background knowledge that the reader and writer share.

Another common sentence variation you saw in Chapter 5 is the *there* transformation, which allows the writer to focus on the subject by shifting it to the slot following *be*—either the predicating *be* or the auxiliary *be:*

> Several hundred people were crowding the courtroom.
> There were several hundred people crowding the courtroom.
>
> Another big crowd was in the hallway.
> There was another big crowd in the hallway.

The last paragraph in the previous Investigating Language exercise includes two *there* transformations in the second sentence:

> There is a vast literature on the effects of caffeine on the body, and for every study reaching one conclusion, seemingly there is another that contradicts it.

Here the author undoubtedly wants the reader to put main stress on *vast literature* and on *another*.

The anticipatory *it* can also change sentence rhythm, as we saw in the discussion of nominals (page 184):

> It takes stamina and perseverance to be a successful farmer.
>
> It's fun to play computer games.

Do writers consciously call up such focusing devices from their grammar tool kits as they write? Do they tell themselves, "Time to use my trusty *it*-cleft, or should I delay this subject with the *there* transformation?" No, they probably don't. They may not even know labels like "transformation" and "cleft." But as experienced writers and readers, they're tuned in to sentence rhythm as they compose—especially as they revise. And you can be sure that in reading their own prose, whether silently or aloud, they are paying attention to the way in which the reader will read the sentence.

CHOOSING VERBS

Most writing teachers would probably agree that choosing verbs is one of the writer's most important jobs. The verb, after all, occupies the central, pivotal slot of the sentence pattern. A well-chosen verb not only heightens the drama of a sentence and makes its meaning clear; it can send a message to the reader that the writer has crafted the sentence carefully, that the idea matters.

Sometimes the culprit that keeps a sentence from sending that message is the phrasal verb, the verb + particle combination we saw in Chapter 3, known as an idiom: *turn down, bring about, put up with, take up, do away with, get on with, give up.* There's nothing wrong with these common idioms—and they certainly are common, part of our everyday speech. But the single-word synonym may be more precise—and it's always tighter:

> The legislature turned down the governor's compromise proposal.
> The legislature rejected . . .

> The lawyer turned down the prosecutor's offer of a plea bargain.
> The lawyer refused . . .

> The police are looking into the rumors about corruption.
> The police are investigating . . .

> The police are looking into the evidence.
> The police are analyzing . . .

Certainly another difference between the phrasal verb and its one-word counterpart is the level of formality: *To investigate* and *to analyze* sound more formal than *to look into.* In informal contexts, the idiom may be the best choice—for example, in a personal essay or narrative, or for a general audience, such as you might address in a letter to the editor of a newspaper. But for research papers or technical reports—and certainly for résumés and letters to prospective employers—the single-word version might be more effective. So one step in your revision process is to look carefully at (to *scrutinize*) the verbs that you have chosen—and recognize that you have a choice.

You may also have introduced some flabbiness simply by selecting a common garden-variety verb. In Chapter 4, you saw a list of the ten most frequently used verbs in English: *be, have, do, say, make, go, take, come, see,* and *get.* In many cases these are the verbs that take part in idioms. And because they have so many nuances of meaning, you can often find a more precise one.

Exercise 61

Revise the following passages by finding more precise alternatives to the italicized verbs. In some cases you will have to make changes other than just the verb substitution.

1. The small band of rebels *fought off* the army patrol for several hours, then *gave up* just before dawn. News reports about the event did not *give any specific details about* how many troops were involved.

2. The majority leader *has* a great deal of influence in the White House. He or she can easily *find a way around* the established procedures and go directly to the president.

3. Several economists are saying that they *look forward to* an upturn in the stock market during the second half of the year. Others, however, maintain that interest rates must *stop their fluctuating* if the bull market is to prevail.

4. The night-shift workers took their complaints to the shop steward when the managers tried to *force* them into *giving up* their ten-cent wage differential.

5. The chairman of the Senate investigating committee *spoke against* the practice of accepting fees for outside speeches. He said that the new rules will *put a stop to* all such questionable fund raising. To some observers, such practices *are the same thing as* bribery. Several senators have promised to *come up with* a new compromise plan.

6. Dorm life changed drastically when colleges *did away with* their traditional "in loco parentis" role. In the old days, of course, there were always students who *paid no attention to* the rules. At some schools, where the administration would not *put up with* violations, students were routinely *kicked out*.

The Overuse of *Be*.   Another major culprit contributing to flabbiness is the overuse of *be* as the main verb. *Be* sentences commonly serve not only as topic sentences (as in the paragraph you're now reading), but also as supporting sentences throughout the paragraph. You might be surprised, in checking a paragraph or two of your own prose, at how often you've used a form of *be* as the link between the known and the new information. An abundance of such examples—say, more than two or three in a paragraph—may constitute a clear "revise" message.

Sometimes you can eliminate *be* simply by substituting a different verb. We used this technique in rewriting the second sentence of the previous section:

> Most writing teachers would probably agree that choosing verbs
>
> is one of the writer's most important jobs. The verb, after all, ~~is~~ ^{occupies}
>
> the central, pivotal slot of the sentence pattern.

You may have noticed *be* in the first sentence too, which we didn't change. We could have written, "choosing verbs *constitutes* one of the writer's most important jobs," but that sounds a bit forced; it interferes with the natural rhythm.

Another technique for eliminating the flabbiness that *be* often brings with it is [Oops! There it is again!] to make use of appositives and absolute phrases and other kinds of modifiers to combine sentences, to combine ideas. For example, in the following passage the second and third sentences can become appositives, nominals that rename another nominal, which you studied in Chapter 8.

Last year scientists announced the discovery of the smallest known primate. It is one of several species of Eosimias (dawn monkey). This extinct animal was no longer than a human thumb.

Revision: Last year scientists announced the discovery of the smallest known primate, one of several species of Eosimias (dawn monkey), an extinct animal no longer than a human thumb.

In combining the following sentences, we have turned the subject complement of the second one, where *be* is the main verb, into a sentence appositive, punctuated with a dash:

The play opened to rave reviews and standing-room-only crowds; it was a smashing success.

Revision: The play opened to rave reviews and standing-room-only crowds—a smashing success.

The sentence appositive acts as a summary statement that gives special focus to the idea of the main clause.

The Linking *Be* and Metaphor.   There is one use of the linking *be* that deserves more attention: its role—and its power—in **metaphor**. When *be* links a subject complement to its subject in an unexpected way—that is, when the two referents are not, in reality, the same—the statement is anything but weak.

A successful Broadway musical was based on a metaphor:

Life is a cabaret.

In several plays Shakespeare used the stage metaphor for life. This is Macbeth speaking:

Life's but a walking shadow, a poor player
That struts and frets his hour upon the stage.

and this one is from *As You Like It:*

All the world's a stage.

Charles Schulz, the creator of "Peanuts," used metaphor for two popular titles to express the philosophy of his characters:

> *Happiness Is a Warm Puppy*
> *Happiness Is a Thumb and a Blanket.*

These Pattern 3 sentences are anything but weak.

The Passive Voice. In Chapter 5 you learned how to transform a sentence in the active voice into the passive voice by adding *be* + *-en* to the verb and shifting the object to subject position; the active subject can become the object of a preposition:

> Active: *The committee discussed the report.*
> Passive: *The report was discussed by the committee.*

It's certainly possible that everything you've read in other books or heard from teachers about the passive voice has been negative—admonitions to avoid it because of wordiness or vagueness.

It's true, of course, that some passive sentences could be improved by being revised into the active (including, perhaps, the one you are now reading!)—*but not because they're passive.* The reason lies elsewhere: perhaps because they have the wrong focus. In that case, it's the focus that's the problem—not the mere fact of their being passive.

As with cleft sentences and the *there* transformation, the passive voice enables the writer to shift emphasis in the sentence, so that the reader will put the focus where it should be—on the new information. That passive shift can also provide transition between sentences. When the object of the action is the known information—when it is the topic under discussion—the passive transformation can shift that information to the subject slot, where we generally find the topic.

In this paragraph from *Time* about the destruction of the Brazilian rain forests, note that in the second sentence, which is passive, the known information of the subject provides transition:

> If Americans are truly interested in saving the rain forests, they should move beyond rhetoric and suggest *policies* that are practical—and acceptable—to the understandably wary Brazilians. *Such policies* cannot be presented as take-them-or-leave-them propositions. If the U.S. expects better performance from Brazil, Brazil has a right to make demands in return. [emphasis added]
>
> MICHAEL D. LEMONICK

In the first sentence, *policies* is new information in object position; in the second it is known and it has become the topic—and the subject.

THE ABSTRACT SUBJECT

One common cause of abstraction is **nominalization**, verbs that have been turned into nouns. We saw the process of nominalization in Chapters 11 and 12 in connection with derivational affixes, the word endings that change the class of the word. Remember that a verb is an action word. A verb *shows* the action; but a noun simply *names* the action:

> The governor's <u>opposition</u> to abortion has caused many pro-choice organizations to work against his reelection.

> There is a growing <u>recognition</u> that forests are more valuable when left standing.

> The school's attempts at <u>reduction</u> of student cheating have been unsuccessful.

Our language, of course, is filled with nominalized verbs—most of which are useful, legitimate ways of expressing ideas. In this paragraph, for example, you have seen *action* and *connection*, both of which began as verbs (*act, connect*) and are now ordinary, everyday nouns.

Who Is Doing What? Because nominalized verbs are so common and so easy to produce, they can become a trap for the unwary writer, introducing abstraction where concrete ideas belong. It's during the revision stage of writing that you'll want to be on the lookout. Ask yourself, Is the agent there and, if so, is it functioning as the subject? In other words, does the sentence explain *who is doing what?* If the answer is no, your sentence may be a prime candidate for revision.

Another source of abstraction and flabbiness is the sentence with a verb phrase or a clause as subject, rather than the usual noun phrase. You learned in Chapter 8 that these structures are grammatical, common substitutes for noun phrases. But because they are abstractions, they too may be pitfalls for the unwary writer. Again, the source of the problem may be that of the missing or misplaced agent:

> <u>The canceling of the after-school drama program by the school board</u> caused the community to raise strong objections.

> With the opening of China to certain aspects of capitalism, <u>what is happening</u> is that American companies are looking for ways of expanding their markets and their product lines to take advantage of the situation.

> <u>Analyzing the situation in the Far East</u> has shown that opportunities for investment are growing.

Although we need context to tell us the best way to revise these sentences, we can see and hear a problem. The sentences seem to be about actions—but they can't show the action in a strong and concrete way because the agents of those actions are not there in subject position. This kind of agentless sentence should send up a red flag—a signal that here's a possible candidate for revision.

Exercise 62

Here are some sentences that might sound familiar—that is, you may write like this yourself. Try to achieve a more direct style and tone as you revise the sentences. Be especially alert to nominalizations and passives. The first three items are the examples from the preceding discussion. Remember to ask yourself, "Who is doing what?"

1. The canceling of the after-school drama program by the school board caused the community to raise strong objections.

2. With the opening of China to certain aspects of capitalism, what is happening is that American companies are looking for ways of expanding their markets and their product lines to take advantage of the situation.

3. Analyzing the situation in the Far East has shown that opportunities for investment are growing.

4. In the biography of Lyndon Johnson by Robert Caro, an account of the Senate election of 1948 is described in great detail.

5. When Julie filled out an application for a work-study job, she was surprised to learn that a detailed financial statement would have to be submitted by her parents.

6. Getting his new pizza parlor to finally turn a profit has meant a lot of hard work and long hours for Tim.

7. The broadening of one's view of life and the establishment of worthy goals are both important aims of education.

8. The encouragement of the thinking process is also an important educational aim. Strategies should be developed by students for the understanding of problems and for their solutions.

THE SHIFTING ADVERBIALS

One of the writer's most versatile sentence elements is the adverbial, in terms of both form and position. As you recall from Chapter 6, the adverbs and prepositional phrases and noun phrases and verb phrases and clauses that add adverbial information can open the sentence or close it, or they can interrupt it somewhere in the middle. Sentence variety by itself is, of course, not a reason for opening or closing a sentence with an adverbial structure. Rather, you should understand the effects on cohesion and reader expectation that adverbials will have in different positions.

In Chapter 3 we labeled the adverbial function as "optional," but that label is somewhat misleading. Even though an adverbial is rarely needed from a grammatical point of view, the adverbial information is often the main idea—the new information of the sentence. For example, in the sentence,

> I got up <u>early</u> <u>to study for my Spanish test,</u>

the two adverbials are optional in terms of the sentence pattern: *I got up* is a grammatical Pattern VI sentence. But the person saying or writing that sentence probably does so to convey time or purpose. It's the information in one or both adverbials that actually provides the main focus of the sentence.

The decision about placement of adverbials, then, is connected to sentence focus and to the concept of known and new information. If the adverbial is the main focus, it probably belongs at or near the end of the sentence. We saw an example of this situation earlier in this chapter with the sentence "Barbara wrecked her motorcycle yesterday," where the adverb *yesterday* supplied the new information. In opening position, the adverbial will usually tie the sentence to what has gone before, either because it is the known information or because it is providing a cohesive element, such as time sequence, with an adverbial like *then* or *later that day* or *on the following afternoon.*

The opening adverbial in the sentence you just read provides that cohesive tie: *In opening position* contrasts with the discussion in the previous sentence about closing position. In a sense it is known information, even though opening position had not been discussed in the paragraph up to that point: Common sense tells us that a sentence has an opening as well as a closing position.

The versatility of adverbials lies not only in the variety of positions they can occupy; it lies also in the variety of their forms. They can be short and brisk, or they can be long and relaxed, changing the tone and pace of the sentence.

> I haven't been feeling well <u>lately.</u>
>
> I haven't been feeling well <u>since September.</u>
>
> I haven't been feeling well <u>since the beginning of the semester.</u>
>
> I haven't been feeling well <u>since September, when the semester started.</u>

The Adverbial Clause. In Chapters 6 and 9 we emphasized the movable nature of adverbial and subordinate clauses. They are both movable and versatile: Our long list of subordinators enables us to connect ideas for a wide variety of reasons. Certainly subordinate clauses are common structures in our language: In speech we use them often and automatically. In writing, of course, they are not automatic, nor are they always used as effectively as they could be. Two problems that show up fairly often are related to the meaning of the sentence: (1) The wrong idea gets subordinated; and (2) the meaning of the subordinator is imprecise.

Here, for example, are two related ideas that a writer might want to combine into a single sentence:

> We worked hard for the candidates.
> We suspected they didn't stand a chance.

Here are some possibilities for connecting them:

> <u>While</u> we worked hard for the candidates, we suspected they didn't stand a chance.
>
> <u>Although</u> we worked hard for the candidates, we suspected they didn't stand a chance.
>
> We worked hard for the candidates, <u>even though</u> we suspected they didn't stand a chance.

We need context, of course, to know precisely what the connection between the two ideas should be, but given no other information, the last version expresses what would appear to be the logical relationship.

Perhaps an even more common problem than the imprecise subordinator is the compound sentence with no subordination—the sentence with two independent clauses, two equal focuses, that would be more accurate and effective with a single focus. The most common culprit is the compound sentence connected by *but:*

> The prime rate went down two percentage points during the last quarter, but government economists are still worried about high inflation and low productivity.

Because *but* is a coordinating conjunction, just as *and* is, the sentence has two ideas that, by reason of the structure, can be considered only as equals. But are they? Probably not.

Here's another compound sentence with *but*, a paragraph opener in an article about sleep. The paragraph preceding this one gives examples of accidents on the job connected with work schedules:

> The biological clock is flexible enough to adjust to slight changes in a person's work schedule, *but* in many industries rotations in shift

work are so drastic that they play havoc with body rhythms, leaving employees unable to sleep at home and impairing their productivity at work. [emphasis added]

ERIK ECKHOLM, *New York Times Magazine*

Here the two clauses are clearly not equal: The main idea is the second clause. The idea in the first clause, although it has not previously appeared in the article, is presented as understood, as information the reader is assumed to know—the known information. The new information is in the second clause. Making the first clause subordinate will help the reader focus on the new idea:

> *Although* the biological clock is flexible enough to adjust to slight changes in a person's work schedule, in many industries rotations in shift work are so drastic that they play havoc with body rhythms, leaving employees unable to sleep at home and impairing their productivity at work.

Remember that a compound sentence has two points of focus that, in terms of structure, are equal. The compound sentence is effective only when that structure accurately reflects the relationship of the two ideas. If a single point of focus would be more accurate, then a subordinating conjunction should introduce one of the two ideas.

Exercise 63

Combine each of the following groups of sentences into a single sentence by using subordination. In some cases you will want to reword the sentence. Remember that the subordinator you select will signal the relationship between the two ideas. You can probably come up with more than one possibility for each.

1. The famous Gateway Arch is in St. Louis.
   Kansas City claims the title "Gateway to the West."

2. Our spring semester doesn't end until the second week of June.
   Many students have a hard time finding summer jobs.

3. Thomas Jefferson acquired the Ozark Mountains for the United States in 1803.
   That was the year of the Louisiana Purchase.
   We bought the Louisiana Territory from Napoleon.

4. Many attorneys are unacquainted with oil and gas laws.
   They are unable to offer advice concerning oil and gas leases to their clients.

5. The neighbors added a pit bull to their pet population, which now numbers three unfriendly four-legged creatures.
   We have decided to fence in our backyard.

6. The human circulatory system is a marvel of efficiency.
   It is still subject to a wide variety of degenerative diseases.

7. Carbohydrates—starches—are the body's prime source of energy.
   Fad diets that severely restrict the intake of starches are nearly always ineffective.
   Such diets can also be dangerous.

8. Auto companies offered enticing cash rebates to buyers of new cars last January.
   Car sales increased dramatically.

The Adverbs of Emphasis.   As you know, the adverbials are versatile structures. They provide their information of time, place, manner, and the like in a variety of shapes; and they give the writer special flexibility because they can fill so many different slots—at the beginning, the middle, and the end of sentences. But there's another group of adverbials, mainly single-word adverbs, whose purpose is to emphasize a particular structure and thus control the pace and rhythm of the sentence.

Read the following sentences and note where you apply the main stress:

I hardly slept last night.

I slept hardly at all last night.

My roommate never has trouble sleeping.

Some people are always looking for trouble.

Joe tells me that he rarely stays awake past midnight.

You probably put the emphasis on *hardly, all, never, always,* and *rarely.*

Given these examples, you can think of other words that you use for emphasis: other negatives, such as *seldom, barely, scarcely;* other time and frequency words, such as *afterwards, finally, sometimes;* and others expressing duration, such as *already, no longer, still.*

It's possible, of course, to write sentences in which these words would not have main stress, where the principle of end focus, for example, would still be in effect. But certainly these are words that you, as a writer, need to recognize; they often wield the power in a sentence, controlling its intonation contour and making a difference in the message.

The Common *Only.*   One of our most versatile—but also most frequently misused—adverbials of emphasis is the common *only.* Like other emphasizers, *only* can change the focus of the sentence by directing the reader's attention to a particular word:

> I'm taking <u>only twelve</u> credits this semester.
>
> The car <u>only looks</u> old; it's really quite new.
>
> Joe isn't <u>only handsome</u>; he's rich too.
>
> Paul cleans house <u>only on Saturdays</u>.

When you read these sentences, you'll find yourself putting nearly equal emphasis on both *only* and the word that follows it.

But there's also a common problem with *only:* It's frequently misplaced—and most of the time we don't even notice!

> I'm only taking twelve credits this semester.
>
> Paul only cleans house on Saturdays.
>
> We're only going to be gone for two or three days.
>
> Jane refuses to watch the Super Bowl; she only likes baseball.

A well-placed *only* can strengthen the sentence focus. It sends a message to the reader that the writer has crafted the sentence carefully.

METADISCOURSE

In our discussion of sentence modifiers in Chapter 9, we contrasted the use of *clearly* in two sentences:

> Mark did not explain the situation clearly.
>
> Clearly, Mark did not explain the situation.

In the first, *clearly* is an adverbial modifying *explain;* in the second it adds emphasis, indicating the writer's commitment to the truth of the statement. This kind of attitude message is called **metadiscourse**, or discourse about discourse. Here are some further sample sentences from Chapter 9 that include sentence modifiers as attitude markers:

> <u>Frankly</u>, I didn't expect sailing to be so much work.
>
> <u>To our amazement</u>, the driver of the Corvette walked away from the accident.
>
> <u>To my regret</u>, I have never seen the Grand Canyon.

These words and phrases add a feeling of informality that may not be appropriate in a formal paper; and, in fact, examples like these are probably more common in speech than in writing. But, certainly, attitude statements like these (and like the "certainly" in this sentence) make a difference in the writer's voice, the sense of connection to the reader.

Here are some examples from the text itself. The first one is from the introduction to Part V (page 308):

> Unfortunately, methods of teaching grammar have been slow to change.

And this one is from the section in this chapter called "Choosing Verbs" (page 316):

> The verb, after all, occupies the central, pivotal slot of the sentence pattern.

Neither *unfortunately* nor *after all* contributes to the truth of its sentence; neither alters the fact of the statement in any way, so we certainly can't call them adverbials. Then why add those extra words? In both cases they are sending a message to you, the reader, from us, the authors of your grammar book. And don't assume that they are "extra" words: They're important.

In the first example, the word *unfortunately* tells you what we think about the grammar-teaching situation; it tells you what side we're on, in case you didn't know.

The signal in the second example, *after all*, is even more important. Without it, if we had written, simply,

> The verb occupies the central, pivotal slot of the sentence pattern,

you might have become indignant, at least momentarily, to think that we think that after fourteen chapters of studying sentences you still haven't figured out that verbs occupy an important place! The phrase *after all* is there to tell you that we are well aware that you do indeed already know the importance of verbs.

Here's another example from the text. This one opens the section in Chapter 2 on the noun phrase (page 18):

> The term *noun phrase* may be new to you, although you're probably familiar with the word *phrase*. . . .

Think of what the words *may* and *probably* are doing in that sentence: Their purpose is called **hedging**. We don't know for sure that the term *noun phrase* is new to you, but we suspect it is; we do think you're familiar with the more common term *phrase*. In both cases, however, we're hedging our bets; *may* and *probably* allow us to do that. Writers have a fairly large repertoire of hedging words: *fairly* is one of them, along with *could, might, perhaps, at times, sometimes, almost, usually*, and many other such words and phrases that qualify our statements, that add a note of probability to what otherwise might come across as certainty, when certainty may not be appropriate or possible.

Another important purpose of metadiscourse is cohesion. Cohesive signals act as guideposts that clarify the purpose or direction of a passage and connect it to what has gone before. For example, when a sentence begins, as this one does, with the phrase "for example," you know the sentence will discuss an example of the concept just mentioned. The phrase may not be necessary—many examples go unmarked because they are expected—but sometimes that specific signal is very important.

Other connectors you're familiar with, such as *first, in the first place, second, next,* and *finally,* clearly add to the ease of reading, the flow of the text. Those that signal contrasting pairs of ideas—*on the one hand/on the other hand*—are also especially helpful to keep the reader on course. These are among the connectors called *conjunctive adverbs* that you studied in Chapter 10 on coordination and in the "Conjunction" section of Chapter 12, "The Structure Classes."

STYLE

Everything we write, we write "with style," in one sense of the word—when the word refers simply to an individual's way of writing. You have your own style of writing, just as you have your own style of walking and whistling and wearing your hair. We also use the word *style* to characterize the overall impression of a piece of writing, such as the plain style, the pompous style, the official style. When you follow advice about being brief and using simple words, the outcome will be a plain style; words that are too fancy will probably result in a pompous style.

The word *style* is also used in connection with variations in sentence structure, with the structural and punctuation choices that you as a writer can use to your advantage. For example, in the second sentence of the previous paragraph, three verb phrases in a series are connected with two *and*s and no commas:

> walking and whistling and wearing your hair

It could have been written with two commas and only one *and*:

> walking, whistling, and wearing your hair

Or only commas:

> walking, whistling, wearing your hair

Such stylistic variations have traditionally occupied an important place in the study of rhetoric. In fact, the Greeks had names for every deviation from ordinary word order and usage, and Greek orators practiced using them. Some of the more common ones you're familiar with, such as "figures of speech" as simile, metaphor, and personification. But many of them, you probably don't even notice—such as the shift, in both this sentence and the previous one, of the direct object to opening position. In this section we will examine the rhetorical effects that these and other variations in sentence structure and punctuation can have.

Word Order Variation. Variation from the standard subject–verb–object word order is fairly common in poetry; it can be effective in prose as well, partly because it is uncommon. In the following sentence, Charles Dickens made sure that the reader would hear the contrast between *has* and *has not:*

> Talent, Mr. Micawber has; money, Mr. Micawber has not.

Another fairly common rearrangement occurs when a clause as direct object opens the sentence, as you saw in the previous paragraph.

> Which of these calls seemed more mysterious, it is not possible
>   to say.
>
> JAMES AGEE

Robert Frost used this variation, too, in the first line of his famous poem "Stopping by Woods on a Snowy Evening":

> Whose woods these are, I think I know.

Notice that all these variations put special emphasis on the verb, the slot that would normally be in a valley when the sentence has a direct object.
  With certain adverbs in opening position, the subject and the auxiliary can be reversed:

> Never before had I seen such an eerie glow in the night sky.
> Rarely do I hear such words of praise.

You'll notice that the opening adverbial is a peak of stress.
  The following sentence, written by Winston Churchill, illustrates another kind of shift in word order. Here the very last noun phrase in the sentence is the grammatical subject:

> Against Lee and his great Lieutenant [Stonewall Jackson], united for a year of intense action in a comradeship which recalls that of Marlborough and Eugene, were now to be marshaled *the overwhelming forces of the Union.* [emphasis added]

When you read this sentence aloud, you can hear your voice building to a peak of stress on *overwhelming forces,* just as Churchill planned. In fact, it's hard to read the sentence without sounding Churchillian.

Ellipsis. Another fairly common stylistic variation is the use of ellipsis, where part of the sentence is simply left out, or "understood," usually for the purpose of avoiding repetition. In the following description of Stonewall Jackson, Churchill used ellipsis in both sentences. In the first, he left out the linking verb in all but the first clause. The tightness of the sentence actually reflects the description of Jackson's character:

> His character was stern, his manner [was] reserved and usually forbidding, his temper [was] Calvinistic, his mode of life [was] strict, frugal, austere.

> Black-bearded, pale-faced, with thin, compressed lips, aquiline nose, and dark, piercing eyes, he slouched in his weather-stained uniform a professor-warrior; yet [he was] greatly beloved by the few who knew him best, and [he was] gifted with that strange power of commanding measureless devotion from the thousands whom he ruled with an iron hand.

Notice also in the last sentence that in the clause after the semicolon both the subjects and the verbs are understood.

The Coordinate Series. Many of the structural variations that writers use for special effects occur in connection with coordinate structures—pairs and series of sentences and sentence parts. One effective way of changing the emphasis in coordinate structures entails a small deviation from the usual way of using conjunctions, as you saw in the example about "walking, whistling, and wearing your hair." In a series of three or more structures, we generally use commas between the parts of the series, and we use a conjunction before the final member. Here's another example:

> At the class reunion, we laughed, reminisced, and sang the old songs.

Here are two variations. Read them aloud and listen to the differences.

> At the class reunion we laughed and reminisced and sang the old songs.

> At the class reunion we laughed, reminisced, sang the old songs.

The differences are subtle, but meaningful. The first variation puts emphasis on each verb with a fairly equal beat: / and / and /. It also puts a lilt in your voice. The second variation, the one without conjunctions, has an open-ended quality, as though the list were incomplete. The writer seems to be saying, "I could go on and on; I could tell you much more."

The following sentence, from Churchill's description of Stonewall Jackson, includes that second technique. The phrases themselves have no conjunctions, as a regular series would, nor does the final series of adjectives:

> His character was stern, his manner reserved and usually forbidding,
> his temper Calvinistic, his mode of life strict, frugal, austere.

The omission of the conjunction contributes to the strictness and frugality of style that echo the words themselves. With conjunctions, the sentence would lose that echo:

> His mode of life was strict and frugal and austere.

The Introductory Appositive Series. In the following passages, the sentence opens with a series of noun phrases that act as appositives to the subject. In the first example, Churchill describes Queen Victoria:

> High devotion to her royal task, domestic virtues, evident sincerity
> of nature, a piercing and sometime disconcerting truthfulness—all
> these qualities of the Queen's had long impressed themselves upon
> the mind of her subjects.

The following description is from a *Time* article on the Vikings, written by Michael D. Lemonick and Andrea Dorfman:

> Ravagers, despoilers, pagans, heathens—such epithets pretty
> well summed up the Vikings for those who lived in the British Isles
> during medieval times.

Often the noun phrase series is in apposition to a pronoun as subject, as in this example from William Golding:

> Political and religious systems, social customs, loyalties and tradi-
> tions, they all came tumbling down like so many rotten apples
> off a tree.

Notice, too, in these examples that the series does not include a conjunction before the last member.

The Deliberate Sentence Fragment. The sentence fragments that composition teachers flag with a marginal "frag" are the unintentional kind, usually the result of punctuation errors, the most common being the subordinate clause punctuated as a full sentence. But not all fragments are errors. Experienced writers know how to use them effectively—noun phrases or verb phrases that invariably call attention to themselves. The first two examples are from novels of John le Carré:

> They remembered the tinkling of falling glass all right, and the timid brushing noise of the young foliage hitting the road. <u>And the mewing of people too frightened to scream.</u>
>
> *The Little Drummer Girl*

> Our Candidate begins speaking. <u>A deliberate, unimpressive opening</u>.
>
> *A Perfect Spy*

Barack Obama opens Chapter 5 of his memoir, *Dreams from My Father,* with three sentence fragments in two sentences. The second sentence has two fragments, an absolute phrase and a noun phrase:

> Three o'clock in the morning. The moon-washed streets empty, the growl of a car picking up speed down a distant road.

In the following paragraph, which opens "Geraldo No Last Name" by Sandra Cisneros, we are hearing fragmented thoughts—ideal candidates for sentence fragments.

> She met him at a dance. Pretty too, and young. Said he worked in a restaurant, but she can't remember which one. Geraldo. That's all. Green pants and Saturday shirt. Geraldo. That's what he told her. And how was she to know she'd be the last one to see him alive. An accident, don't you know. Hit and run.

Repetition.   Repetition has come up before in these pages—in both a positive and a negative sense. On the positive side, repetition gives our sentences cohesion: The known–new contract calls for the repetition, if not of words, then of ideas. It is part of the glue that holds sentences together. But we also have a negative label for repetition when it has no purpose, when it gets in the reader's way: Then we call it redundancy. If you've heard warnings about redundancy, if you've seen "red" in the margins of your essays, you might hesitate to use repetition deliberately. But don't hesitate. It's easy to distinguish redundancy from good repetition, from repetition as a stylistic tool.

The Greek rhetoricians had labels for every conceivable kind of good repetition—from the repetition of sounds and syllables to that of words and phrases in various locations in the sentence. We'll confine our discussion to repetition in coordinate structures that will make the reader sit up and take notice.

Consider the Gettysburg Address. Which of Lincoln's words, other than "Fourscore and seven years ago," do you remember? Probably "government of the people, by the people, and for the people." It's hard to imagine those words without the repetition: "Of, by, and for the people" just wouldn't have the same effect. And think about President Kennedy's stirring words, with his repetition of *any:*

> [W]e shall pay any price, bear any burden, meet any hardship, support any friend, oppose any foe to assure the survival and the success of liberty.

Notice, too, that the conjunction has been omitted before the last member of the series. He seems to be saying, "I could go on and on with my list."

You don't have to be a president to use that kind of repetition, nor do you have to reserve it for formal occasions. Whenever you use a coordinate structure, there's an opportunity for you to add to its impact with repetition, simply by including words that wouldn't have to be included. The following sentence, from an essay in *Time* by Charles Krauthammer, could have been more concise, but it would have lost its drama:

> There is not a single Western standard, there are two: what we demand of Western countries at peace and what we demand of Western countries at war.

And here is the second paragraph of the *Time* article about the Vikings by Michael D. Lemonick and Andrea Dorfman, with four repetitions of *they were.* The first paragraph began with that opening appositive series we saw earlier:

> But that view is wildly skewed. The Vikings were indeed raiders, but they were also traders whose economic network stretched from today's Iraq all the way to the Canadian Arctic. They were democrats who founded the world's oldest surviving parliament while Britain was still mired in feudalism. They were master metalworkers, fashioning exquisite jewelry from silver, gold and bronze. Above all, they were intrepid explorers whose restless hearts brought them to North America some 500 years before Columbus.

In the following one-sentence paragraph from *Undaunted Courage,* Stephen E. Ambrose describes the birthplace of Meriwether Lewis with repeated *where* clauses:

> Lewis was born in a place where the West invited exploration but the East could provide education and knowledge, where the

hunting was magnificent but plantation society provided refinement and enlightenment, where he could learn wilderness skills while sharpening his wits about such matters as surveying, politics, natural history, and geography.

Notice, too, the parallelism of the *where* clauses, each including a contrasting pair of descriptors.

ANTITHESIS

In his book on classical rhetoric, Edward P. J. Corbett defines **antithesis** as "the juxtaposition of contrasting ideas, often in parallel."[1] Among his examples are the words of Neil Armstrong as he stepped on the moon in 1969:

> That's one small step for a man, one giant leap for mankind.

Benjamin Franklin included this example in a letter he wrote in 1783:

> There never was a good war, or a bad peace.

As you see, the contrasting ideas in these sentences come from opposites: *small/giant; good/bad.* In his book *The Discoverers*, Daniel Boorstein provides antithesis with the simple *not from—but from* in discussing the origin of clocks:

> The first steps toward the mechanical measurement of time, the beginnings of the modern clock in Europe, came not from farmers or shepherds, not from merchants or craftsmen, but from religious persons anxious to perform promptly and regularly their duties to God.

In his book *Making Our Democracy Work*, Associate Justice of the Supreme Court Stephen Breyer quotes former Justice Robert H. Jackson's juxtaposition of *final* and *infallible:*

> [W]e are not final because we are infallible; rather, we are infallible only insofar as our word is final.

Note the opposite word meanings in the following passage from a *New York Times* book review by Martha Bayles:

> Precise detail adds texture, but profuse detail adds tedium. . . .

---

1. *Classical Rhetoric for the Modern Student*, 2nd ed. (New York: Oxford University Press, 1971), p. 464.

And here the contrast is a pair of adverbials:

> The surprise isn't how often we make bad choices; the surprise is
> how seldom they defeat us.

We should also note in all of these examples, in both this and the previous
section on repetition, the importance of **parallel structure**.

The use of the stylistic devices we have taken up in this chapter will
invariably call attention to themselves. For that reason, you will reserve
these structures for important ideas, for those times when you want your
reader to sit up and take notice. Like the gourmet cook who knows that
too many spices can overwhelm a dish, you won't want to overwhelm
your reader. But you will want to recognize that, like the spice that turns
a bland sauce into fine cuisine, these stylistic tools can make the difference
between ordinary and powerful prose.

USING GENDER APPROPRIATELY

As you learned in Chapter 14, the system of personal pronouns has a gap.
And it is that missing pronoun—the lack of a gender-neutral pronoun in
the third-person singular slot—that is responsible for a great deal of the
sexism in our language. You'd think that *he* and *she* and *it* would be up to
the task of covering all the contingencies, but they're not. When we need
a pronoun to refer to an unidentified person, such as "the writer" or "a
student" or just "someone," our long-standing tradition has been to use
the masculine:

> The writer of this news story should have kept <u>his</u> personal opinion
> out of it.
>
> Someone left <u>his</u> book on the table.

But that usage is no longer automatically accepted. Times and attitudes
change, and we have come to recognize the power of language in shaping
those attitudes. So an important step in reshaping society's view of women
has been to eliminate the automatic use of *he* and *his* and *him* when the
sex of someone referred to could just as easily be female.

In a paragraph we looked at earlier in this chapter in connection with
sentence rhythm, the writer has made an effort to avoid sexism with the
generic *salesperson*, a title that has all but replaced the masculine *salesman*.
But notice the pronoun in the last sentence:

> Never invest in something you don't understand or in the
> dream of an artful salesperson. Be a buyer, not a sellee. Figure out
> what you want (be it life insurance, mutual funds or a vacuum

cleaner) and then shop for a good buy. Don't let someone else tell you what you need—at least not if <u>he</u> happens to be selling it.

Andrew Tobias

In speech we commonly use *they* for both singular and plural:

> Don't let someone else tell you what you need—at least not if <u>they</u> happen to be selling it.

Eventually, perhaps, the **singular *they,*** as it is called, will become the accepted form in both speech and writing; after all, in the second person (*you/your/you*), we make no distinction between singular and plural, so it's not unreasonable to do the same in the third person. But such changes come slowly. What should we do in the meantime?

One common, but not necessarily effective, way to solve the problem of the pronoun gap is with *he or she:*

> . . . at least not if <u>he or she</u> happens to be selling it.

An occasional *he or she* will work in most situations like this one, but more than one in a paragraph will change the rhythm of the prose, slow the reader down, and call attention to itself when such attention is simply uncalled for.

Often the plural is an easy and obvious solution. For example, in the following passages from books about language, the change to plural does not affect the overall meaning or intent:

> Of all the developments in the history of ~~man~~ [the human race], surely the most remarkable was language, for with it ~~he was~~ [our ancestors were] able to pass on ~~his~~ [their] cultural heritage to succeeding generations who then did not have to rediscover how to make a fire, where to hunt, or how to build another wheel.

Charles B. Martin and Curt M. Rulon

> It has been said that whenever ~~a person~~ [people] ~~speaks~~ [speak], ~~he is~~ [they are] either mimicking or analogizing.

Charles Hockett

We should emphasize that these two passages were written several decades ago, when the masculine pronoun was the norm. Chances are, they would not have been written in this way today. All of us who are involved with words, who are sensitive to the power of language, have gone through a consciousness-raising in the matter of sexist language.

Here, then, are some of the ways in which you can make up for the pronoun gap when you write and/or revise your own sentences:

1. USE THE PLURAL:

   Every writer should be aware of the power of language when <u>he</u> chooses <u>his</u> pronouns.

   Revision: Writers should be aware of the power of language when <u>they</u> choose <u>their</u> pronouns.

2. USE *HE OR SHE* IF YOU CAN USE IT ONLY ONCE:

   Revision: Every writer should be aware of the power of language when <u>he or she</u> chooses pronouns.

3. TURN THE CLAUSE INTO A VERB PHRASE, THUS ELIMINATING THE PROBLEM SUBJECT:

   Revision: Every writer should be aware of the power of language when <u>choosing pronouns</u>.

This third method of revision is often a good possibility because the offending pronoun nearly always shows up in the second clause of a passage, often as part of the same sentence. In our example, we have turned the complete subordinate clause into an elliptical clause—that is, a clause with something missing. In this case what's missing is the subject. (The elliptical clause, which has some hidden pitfalls, is discussed in Chapter 9.)

4. AVOID *HIS* AS A DETERMINER, EITHER BY SUBSTITUTING ANOTHER ONE OR, IN SOME CASES, DELETING THE DETERMINER:

   The writer of the news story should have kept <u>his</u> opinion out of it.

   Revision: The writer of the news story should have kept (<u>all</u>) opinion out of it.

5. REWRITE THE ADVERBIAL CLAUSE AS A RELATIVE (WHO) CLAUSE:

   When <u>a person</u> buys a house, <u>he</u> should shop carefully for the lowest interest rate.

   Revision: <u>A person who</u> buys a house should shop carefully for the lowest interest rate.

The relative clause with its neutral *who* eliminates the necessity of a personal pronoun to rename *a person*.

6. CHANGE THE POINT OF VIEW:

Revision 2nd person: As a writer <u>you</u> should be aware of the power of language when you choose (your) pronouns.

Revision 1st person: As writers, <u>we</u> should be aware of the power of language when we choose (our) pronouns.

This emphasis on the variety of ways available for making our thoughts known applies to topics on grammar and style throughout all the chapters. As you read in the opening of Part V, "Grammar for Writers," we firmly believe that understanding those choices, understanding English grammar, does make a difference for writers and teachers of writing.

CHAPTER 15
Key Terms

Absolute phrase	Metadiscourse
Abstract subject	Metaphor
Adverbial clause	Nominalization
Adverbs of emphasis	Parallel structure
Antithesis	Passive voice
Appositive	Repetition
Cleft transformation	Rhetorical grammar
Cohesion	Rhythm
Coordinate series	Sentence fragment
Ellipsis	Sentence rhythm
End focus	Sexist language
Gender	Shifting adverbial
Hedging	Singular *they*
Intonation	Style
Introductory appositive series	Word-order variation
Known–new contract	

CHAPTER
16

Purposeful Punctuation

CHAPTER PREVIEW

As you know, the purpose of punctuation is to indicate the grammatical structures in a written text. It makes the writer's meaning clear to the reader by marking boundaries, signaling levels of importance, and indicating linkages. Our summary here is organized according to these purposes.

Throughout the previous chapters we have explained punctuation in the context of the sentence patterns and their expansions. The first highlighted punctuation rule you saw—or, more accurately, nonpunctuation rule—came in Chapter 3 after the description of the basic patterns:

Do not put single commas between the required slots.

In describing the various expansions of the required and optional slots, we have discussed the standard punctuation conventions, fully recognizing that many of those conventions are simply general guidelines. We strongly believe, however, that students—indeed, all of us who write— should know the standard punctuation conventions thoroughly and follow them as closely as possible, always with the reader in mind.

Our purpose in this chapter is not to answer all of your punctuation questions. A handbook will explain single quotes and footnotes and ellipses points and question marks within quotations and such. Rather, our purpose throughout the chapters—and summarized here—is to help you understand how punctuation contributes to meaning and to give you confidence as you express your meaning in prose.

MAKING CONNECTIONS

Compounding Sentences (see pages 216–219)

1. Use a comma between the independent clauses of a compound sentence when they are joined by a coordinating conjunction (*and, but, or, nor, for, yet*):

> *There is a difference between the music of Bach and Mozart, and it is a difference worth discovering.*

> *The trial lasted for almost three months, yet it took the jury only three hours to render a verdict.*

The comma may be omitted if the clauses are very short and closely connected:

> *Meg played the piano and Thom sang.*

To use the comma without the conjunction produces a nonconventional connection called the **comma splice**. Writers do use comma splices on certain occasions, especially when combining two or three short sentences for special attention:

> *They graduated on Friday, they got married on Sunday, they moved to Alaska on Monday.*

2. Use a semicolon between independent clauses not joined by a coordinating conjunction:

> *There is a difference between the music of Bach and Mozart; it is a difference worth discovering.*

The semicolon sends a message to the reader: Notice the tight connection.

3. Use a semicolon between the clauses of a compound sentence when a conjunctive adverb (such as *nonetheless, however, therefore*) or an adverbial phrase (such as *in that case, as a result, on the other hand*) introduces the second clause (see page 218):

> *The issues were difficult to sort out; however, the judges had to make a decision.*

> *The contract negotiations lasted for two years; as a result, many workers quit their jobs and found other ones.*

The movability of the conjunctive adverb, set off by commas, enables the writer to change the focus in the second clause: The word just preceding it gets the main stress.

4. Use a semicolon between clauses joined by a coordinating conjunction if one or both of the clauses includes commas:

> *During the Italian Renaissance the inside of the pomegranate, which is divided into compartments containing colorful seeds, was the basis*

for a popular fabric design; and in the Middle East this beautiful fruit figured prominently in the decorative arts.

The reader knows immediately on reaching the semicolon that another complete sentence is coming; that immediacy would be missing with only a comma as the signal.

5. Use a colon between the clauses of a compound sentence when the second clause explains or amplifies the first clause (see page 219):

After reading the letter, he did something that surprised me: He laughed and tore it up.

My uncle was not wasteful: he was uncommonly thrifty.

You have the choice of using either a capital or a lowercase letter on the second clause. Notice how the first clause sets up an expectation in the reader. The colon says, "Here comes the information that you're expecting" or "Here's what I promised." In the second example, the *not* in the first clause sets the reader up for a contrast in the second.

Compounding Structures Within Sentences (see pages 209–212)

For compound pairs of words, phrases, and clauses that occur within the sentence, do NOT use a comma with the conjunction:

High ceilings and cathedral windows are two features that I look for in a house. (compound subject)

The skiers cleaned their boots and sprayed them with a water repellent. (compound predicate)

The new citizens promised that they would obey the laws of the country and that they would uphold the principles of the Constitution. (compound direct object)

Exceptions:

You may use a comma with compound elements when the conjunction is *but:*

I love mangos and peaches, but not apricots.

You may also use a comma to give special emphasis to the second element in a compound:

The judge listened to our side of the story, and then ruled against us.

A dash would give the second element even more emphasis:

The judge listened to our side of the story—and then ruled against us.

Connecting More Than Two Parts: The Series (see pages 211–212)

1. Use commas to separate three or more items in a series or list:

Tacos, cheeseburgers, and low-carb salads are the most popular foods served in the cafeteria.

The subway carries children going to school, adults going to work, and tourists going to the next historic site on their itinerary.

Note that the serial comma, the comma before the conjunction in a series, is left out by some writers and in some publications:

Tacos, cheeseburgers and low-carb salads are the most popular foods served in the cafeteria.

You can read about the importance of the serial comma on page 211.

2. Use semicolons to separate items in a series or list when one or more of the items already includes a comma:

The estate included lands and buildings; a portfolio of stocks, IRAs, and government bonds; and an extensive collection of art works.

SEPARATING PRENOUN MODIFIERS
(see pages 132–134)

1. Use a comma to separate two or more coordinate modifiers that describe the same noun. Coordinate modifiers, which describe the noun independently, require commas if they could be joined with *and*. Another way to test the need for the comma is to reverse their order. If this is possible, the comma is necessary. These adjectives are opinions, subjective qualities:

The film was censored for its raucous, vulgar language.

A friendly, sensitive, intelligent counselor helped us with the complicated paperwork.

Note that no comma comes between the final modifier and the noun.

2. Do NOT use a comma between cumulative modifiers. Cumulative modifiers, which describe the combination of the next modifier plus the noun it modifies, cannot be joined with *and;* and their order cannot be changed.

We gave her a crystal perfume bottle.

A set of large shiny new brass pots hangs over the stove.

In contrast to the coordinate modifiers, the cumulative modifiers will generally follow a set order: size, shape, condition or age, color, origin, or material:

large shiny new brass pots

Any coordinate adjectives will precede the cumulative modifiers in the string:

beautiful large shiny new brass pots

3. Use a hyphen to join the elements of compound modifiers when the first modifier applies to the second modifier, not to the headword:

> *Everybody needs a home-cooked meal now and then.*
>
> *They attended a four-hour seminar on long-range planning.*

Also use hyphens in a complete phrase that fills the modifier slot:

> *The results from this study are based on out-of-date statistics.*

But do not use hyphens in compound modifiers containing an *-ly* adverb:

> *The senator presented his proposal in clearly defined terms.*

IDENTIFYING ESSENTIAL AND NONESSENTIAL STRUCTURES (see pages 151–154)

1. Use commas to set off phrases or clauses that merely comment on the nouns they modify, rather than defining or restricting their meaning. In other words, a nonessential phrase or clause could be omitted without changing the meaning of the sentence.

Adjective clause:

> *A popular concept in today's corporate world is time management, which has four distinct phases.*

Participial phrase:

> *The line judge, blocked by the player's movement, could not tell whether the ball was in or out.*

Appositive:

> *Richard Wagner, the composer of* Tristan and Isolde, *was a leading exponent of German romanticism.*

2. Do NOT set off phrases or clauses that are needed to identify the nouns they modify. Omitting an essential phrase or clause would alter the meaning of the sentence.

> *Time management is a concept that has become popular in today's corporate world.*
>
> *A line judge who is blocked by the player's movement cannot tell whether the ball is in or out.*
>
> *The composer Richard Wagner was a leading exponent of German romanticism.*

3. Use commas to set off transitional phrases and parenthetical comments that interrupt the flow of the sentence (see page 123):

> *Honesty, in my opinion, should always be tempered with kindness.*
>
> *Being totally honest is, after all, sometimes an excuse for being cruel.*

4. Use commas to set off nouns of direct address (see page 193):

> *The fact is, my friends, we have no choice in this matter.*
>
> *Mr. Ortiz, can you send us a copy of the accident report?*

5. Use a comma to set off the reporting tag (e.g., *she said, he replied, Darwin observed*) from a direct quotation:

> *Eleanor Roosevelt said, "No one can make you feel inferior without your consent."*
>
> *"No one can make you feel inferior," Eleanor Roosevelt said, "without your consent."*
>
> *"No one can make you feel inferior without your consent," Eleanor Roosevelt observed.*

Note that the comma between the verb (*said*) and the quotation constitutes an exception to the highlighted rule mentioned in the chapter preview (see page 340).

SIGNALING SENTENCE OPENERS

Put a comma after the following introductory structures:

A long prepositional phrase:

> *After a heavy downpour with lightning and high winds, the yard was littered with branches.*

A single-word sentence modifier:

> *Surprisingly, the roof was still intact.*

Adverbial clause or verb phrase:

> *Just to be thorough, my roommate checked the basement.*
>
> *As he feared, he found an inch and a half of water down there.*

Absolute phrase:

> *The electricity having gone out, our sump pump had quit working.*

Participial phrase:

> *Sighing heavily, we got out the wet-vac and went to work.*

SIGNALING EMPHASIS

1. Use a colon to introduce a list of appositives renaming a noun:

> *The study of grammar includes three areas: phonology, morphology, and syntax.*
>
> *For this class students need the following equipment: a laptop computer, a spiral notebook, a pen, colored pencils, and a calculator.*

Note that a complete sentence precedes the colon. Do not use a colon when the list of items fills a complement slot:

> *The equipment needed for this class includes a laptop computer, a spiral notebook, a pen, colored pencils, and a calculator.*

2. Use dashes to highlight explanatory or amplifying structures, such as appositives, modifiers, and parts of compounds:

> *Foods high in protein—meats, fish, eggs, and cheese—should be part of everyone's daily diet.*
>
> *This provision will prevent corporations—large and small—from buying influence with campaign contributions.*
>
> *The stores were filled with holiday shoppers—even more so than last year.*
>
> *The soloist had a lean face, a long nose—and cold blue eyes.*

Note that no punctuation precedes or follows a dash.

3. Use parentheses to downplay explanatory or amplifying material:

> *Foods high in protein (meats, fish, eggs, and cheese) should be part of everyone's daily diet.*
>
> *The stores were filled with holiday shoppers (even more so than last year).*

USING APOSTROPHES FOR CONTRACTION AND POSSESSIVE CASE (see pages 240–244)

1. Use an apostrophe to show where a letter or letters are missing in a contraction:

> *doesn't* = does not
>
> *won't* = will not
>
> *class of '75* = class of 1975

2. Use an apostrophe plus *s* to form the possessive of a singular noun or an irregular plural noun:

> *the soldier's uniform* = the uniform of the soldier
>
> *a year's lease* = a lease for one year
>
> *the boss's daughter* = the daughter of the boss
>
> *my children's clothes* = the clothes of my children

Note: Exceptions include certain words with more than one sibilant (*s* or *z*) sound in the last syllable (Jesus', Moses') and proper nouns ending in an *–eez* sound: Aristophanes' plays, Ramses' tomb.

3. Use an apostrophe alone to form the possessive of a regular plural noun:

> *the soldiers' uniforms* = the uniforms of more than one soldier
>
> *the Mendozas' house* = the house of the Mendozas

4. Use an apostrophe plus *s* to form the possessive of indefinite pronouns:

> *someone's bright idea*
>
> *nobody's business*

5. Do NOT add an apostrophe to the possessive forms of personal pronouns: *ours, yours, his, hers, its, theirs.*

Exercise 64

The following passages are punctuated according to our conventional rules. However, the proliferation of commas tends to detract from their readability. Revise the punctuation with the reader in mind:

1. During the second two-year stretch of a president's term in office, he may find himself on the defensive, even with his own party, and, when, as frequently happens, his party loses a number of Senate and House seats in the midterm election, that second stretch can become even more defensive.

2. In recent years, the public attitude toward smoking, except perhaps in the tobacco-growing states, has changed so fast, with smoke-free zones everywhere, including restaurants, office buildings, and shopping malls, it could almost be called a revolution, and even outdoor stadiums, such as Oriole Park at Camden Yards and Jacobs Field in Cleveland, have established a no-smoking policy.

Exercise 65

Experiment with commas, colons, and dashes as you revise and/or combine the following sentences.

1. The cost of repairs to the nation's public transportation facilities is an expenditure that cannot be delayed much longer if the system is to survive. Roads, bridges, and railroads are all in need of repair.

2. To many people, the mushroom is a lowly fungus. It has little food value. To other people, it is a gourmet's delight.

3. The Chinese banned the import of certain American goods, such as cotton, synthetic fibers, and soybeans. The restriction has had an adverse effect on the U.S. economy, especially on the farmers.

4. According to fashion experts, the crew cut will be back in style before long. That particular haircut was more or less the hallmark of the 1950s.

5. My favorite activities are skiing, playing golf, and bowling; unfortunately, they cost more than my budget can stand.

6. Alexander Graham Bell is remembered as the inventor of the telephone. Most people probably don't know that Bell succeeded his father-in-law as president of the National Geographic Society.

7. Many scientists believe that sightings of "cryptids" are mistakes. Cryptids include Big Foot, the Loch Ness monster, and Yeti, known as the Abominable Snowman. Mistaken sightings can be attributed to unfamiliarity with known animals, rather than to delusions.

8. Eugene Schiffelin was a New Yorker. In 1890 he decided to introduce all the birds mentioned in Shakespeare's works into America. The only mention of the starling in Shakespeare is a single instance in *Henry IV*. Schiffelin loosed 60 starlings in Central Park. Today millions of starlings live here. They are voracious and aggressive and smart. They have blanketed the United States. In many places they blacken the sky.

Glossary of Grammatical Terms

(For further explanation of the terms listed here, check the Index for page references.)

Absolute adjective. An adjective with a meaning that is generally not capable of being intensified or compared, such as *unique* or *perfect* or *square*. Careful writers avoid such usages as "very perfect" or "more unique."

Absolute phrase. A noun phrase related to the sentence as a whole that includes a postnoun modifier (often a participial phrase). One kind of absolute explains a cause or condition ("*The weather being warm*, we decided to have a picnic"); the other adds a detail or a point of focus to the idea in the main clause ("He spoke quietly to the class, *his voice trembling*").

Accusative case. The Latin term denoting the case of nouns and pronouns functioning as direct objects and as objects of certain prepositions.

Active voice. A feature of transitive verb sentences in which the subject is generally the agent and the direct object is the goal or objective of the action. Voice refers to the relationship of the subject to the verb. See also *Passive voice*.

Adjectival. Any structure, no matter what its form, that functions as a modifier of a noun—that is, that functions as an adjective normally functions. See Chapter 7.

Adjectival clause. See *Relative clause*.

Adjective. One of the four form classes, whose members act as modifiers of nouns; most adjectives can be inflected for comparative and superlative degree (*big, bigger, biggest*); they can be qualified or intensified (*rather big, very big*); they have characteristic derivational endings such as *-ous* (*famous*), *-ish* (*childish*), *-ful* (*graceful*), and *-ary* (*complementary*).

Adjective phrase. A modified adjective, such as an adjective with a qualifier (*very happy, extremely happy*), a comparative or superlative word (*more generous, most generous*), or with a complement (*happy to see you, happy that you could come*).

Adverb. One of the four form classes, whose members act as modifiers of verbs, contributing information of time, place, reason, manner, and the like. Like adjectives, certain adverbs can be qualified (*very quickly, rather fast*); some can be inflected for comparative and superlative degree (*more quickly, fastest*); they have characteristic derivational endings such as *-ly* (*quickly*), *-wise* (*lengthwise*), and *-ward* (*backward*).

Adverbial. Any structure, no matter what its form, that functions as a modifier of a verb—that is, that functions as an adverb normally functions. See Chapter 6.

Adverbial objective. The traditional label given to the noun phrase that functions adverbially: "Joe went *home*"; "It was cold *last night*."

Adverb phrase. A modified adverb, such as an adverb with a qualifier (*very quickly, rather quickly*) or with *more* or *most* (*more quickly, most anxiously*).

Affix. A morpheme, or meaningful unit, that is added to the beginning (prefix) or end (suffix) of a word to change its meaning or its grammatical role or its form class: (prefix) *un*likely; (suffix) unlike*ly*.

Agent. The initiator of the action in the sentence, the "doer" of the action. Usually the agent is the subject in an active sentence: "*John* groomed the dog"; "*The committee* elected Pam." In a passive sentence the agent may be the object of the preposition *by:* "Pam was elected by *the committee*."

Agreement. (1) Subject–verb. A third-person singular subject in the present tense takes the *-s* form of the verb: "*The dog barks* all night"; "*He bothers* the neighbors." A plural subject takes the base form: "*The dogs bark*"; "*They bother* the neighbors." (2) Pronoun–antecedent. The number of the pronoun (whether singular or plural) agrees with the number of its antecedent: "*The boys* did *their* chores"; "*Each girl* did *her* best."

Allomorph. A variation of a morpheme, usually determined by its environment. For example, the three allomorphs of the regular plural morpheme are determined by the final sound of the nouns to which they are added: /s/ *cats;* /z/ *dogs;* and /əz/ *churches.*

Ambiguous. The condition in which a structure has more than one possible meaning. The source may be lexical ("She is *blue*") or structural ("*Visiting relatives* can be boring") or both ("The detective looked *hard*").

Antecedent. The noun or nominal that a pronoun stands for.

Anticipatory *it*. The use of the pronoun *it* in subject position in order to delay the actual subject: "It was Mary who had the accident in Phoenix." See also *Cleft sentence.*

Antithesis. The juxtaposition of contrasting ideas: "I come to bury Caesar, not to praise him."

Appositive. A structure, often a noun phrase, that renames another structure: "My neighbor, *a butcher at Weis Market*, recently lost his job." Clauses ("It is nice *that you could come*") and verb phrases ("My favorite hobby, *collecting stamps*, is getting expensive") can also function as appositives.

Article. One of the determiner classes, including the indefinite *a*, or *an*, which signals only countable nouns, and the definite *the*, which can signal all classes of nouns.

Aspect. The perfect (*have* + *en*) and progressive (*be* + *ing*) auxiliaries, which denote such features of verbs as completion, duration, and repetition—time elements not related to past, present, or future.

Attributive adjective. The adjective in prenoun position: "my *new* coat"; "the *big* attraction." See also *Predicative adjective*.

Auxiliary. One of the structure-class words, a marker of verbs. Auxiliaries include forms of *have* and *be*, as well as the modals, such as *will*, *shall*, and *must*, and the "stand-in auxiliary" *do*.

Base form of the verb. The uninflected form of the verb. In all verbs except *be*, the base form is the present tense: *go*, *help*. The base form also serves as the infinitive, usually preceded by *to*.

Base morpheme. The morpheme that gives a word its primary lexical meaning: *help*ing, re*flect*.

Be patterns. The sentence patterns in which a form of *be* is the main verb: Patterns I, II, and III.

Bound morpheme. A morpheme that cannot stand alone as a word. Most affixes are bound (help*ing*; *re*act); some base morphemes are also bound (con*cise*; *leg*al).

Case. A feature of nouns and certain pronouns that denotes their relationship to other words in a sentence. Pronouns have three case distinctions: subjective (e.g., *I*, *they*, *who*); possessive (e.g., *my*, *their*, *whose*); and objective (e.g., *me*, *them*, *whom*). Nouns have only one case inflection, the possessive (*John's*, the *cat's*). The case of nouns other than the possessive is sometimes referred to as common case.

Catenative verb. A transitive verb that can take another verb as its object: "I *like* to jog"; "We *enjoy* jogging."

Clause. A structure with a subject and a predicate. The sentence patterns are clause patterns. Clauses are either independent or dependent.

Cleft sentence. A sentence variation that provides a way of shifting the stress or focus of the sentence: "A careless bicyclist caused the accident" → "It was a careless bicyclist who caused the accident"; "What caused the accident was a careless bicyclist."

Cohesion. The grammatical, lexical, and semantic connections between sentences. Cohesive ties are furnished by pronouns that have antecedents in previous sentences, by adverbial connections, by known information, and by knowledge shared by the reader.

Collective noun. A noun that refers to a collection of individuals: *group, team, family*. Collective nouns can be replaced by both singular and plural pronouns, depending on the meaning.

Command. See *Imperative sentence.*

Common case. See *Case.*

Common noun. A noun with general, rather than unique, reference (in contrast to proper nouns). Common nouns may be countable (*house, book*) or noncountable (*water, oil*); they may be concrete (*house, water*) or abstract (*justice, indifference*).

Comparative degree. See *Degree.*

Complement. A structure that "completes" the sentence. The term includes those slots in the predicate that complete the verb: direct object, indirect object, subject complement, and object complement. Certain adjectives also have complements—clauses and phrases that pattern with them: "I was *certain that he would come;* I was *afraid to go.*"

Complementary infinitive. An infinitive that functions as the main verb. "I'm going *to move* next week"; "I have *to find* a new apartment." There is a modal-like quality in "going to" and "have to."

Complex sentence. A sentence that includes at least one dependent clause.

Compound-complex sentence. A sentence that includes at least two independent clauses and one dependent clause.

Compound sentence. A sentence with two or more independent clauses.

Compound word. A word that is a combination of two or more free morphemes acting as a unit. Some compound words are closed (*highlight*), some are hyphenated (*high-handed*), and some are open, written as separate words (*high school*).

Conditional mood. The attitude of probability designated by the modal auxiliaries *could, may, might, would,* and *should.*

Conjunction. One of the structure classes, which includes connectors that coordinate structures of many forms (e.g., *and, or*), subordinate sentences (e.g., *if, because, when*), and coordinate sentences with an adverbial emphasis (e.g., *however, therefore*).

Conjunctive adverb. A conjunction that connects two sentences with an adverbial emphasis, such as *however, therefore, moreover,* and *nevertheless.*

Coordinating conjunction. A conjunction that connects two or more sentences or structures within a sentence as equals: *and, but, or, nor, for,* and *yet.*

Coordination. A way of expanding sentences in which two or more structures of the same form function as a unit. All the sentence slots and modifiers in the slots, as well as the sentence itself, can be coordinated. See Chapter 10.

Correlative conjunction. A two-part conjunction that expresses a relationship between the coordinated structures: *either–or, neither–nor, both–and, not only–but also.*

Countable noun. A noun whose referent can be identified as a separate entity; the countable noun can be signaled by the indefinite article, *a,* and numbers: *a house; an experience; two eggs; three problems.*

Declarative sentence. A sentence in the form of a statement (in contrast to a command, a question, or an exclamation).

Deep structure. A term from transformational generative grammar that refers to the underlying semantic and syntactic relationships of the sentence, in contrast to surface structure, which is the sentence as it is actually written or spoken.

Definite article. The determiner *the,* which generally marks a specific or previously mentioned noun: *"the* man on *the* corner."

Degree. The variations in adjectives that indicate the simple quality of a noun, or positive degree ("Bill is a *big* boy"); its comparison to another, the comparative degree ("Bill is *bigger* than Tim"); or to two or more, the superlative degree ("Bill is the *biggest* person in the whole class"). Certain adverbs also have degree variations, usually designated by *more* and *most.*

Demonstrative pronoun. The pronouns *this* (plural *these*) and *that* (plural *those*), which function as nominal substitutes and as determiners. They include the feature of proximity: near (*this, these*); distant (*that, those*).

Dependent clause. A clause that functions as an adverbial, adjectival, nominal, or sentence modifier (in contrast to an independent, or main, clause).

Derivational affix. A morpheme that is added to a form-class word, either to change its class (*friend* → *friendly; act* → *action*) or to change its meaning (*legal* → *illegal; boy* → *boyhood*).

Determiner. One of the structure-class words, a marker of nouns. Determiners include articles (*a, the*); possessive nouns and pronouns (e.g., *Chuck's, his, my*); demonstrative pronouns (*this, that*); quantifiers (e.g., *many, several*); indefinite pronouns (e.g., *each, every*); and numbers.

Dialect. The shared linguistic features of a group of people, often one from a particular region or of a particular ethnic or social background.

Direct address. See *Vocative.*

Direct object. A nominal slot in the predicate of the transitive sentence patterns. The direct object names the objective or goal or the receiver of the verb's action: "We ate *the peanuts*"; "The boy hit *the ball*"; "I enjoy *playing chess.*"

***Do* support.** The addition of the stand-in auxiliary *do* to a verb string that has no other auxiliary. The question, the negative, and the emphatic transformations all require an auxiliary. *Do* also substitutes for a repeated verb phrase in compound sentences: "Bryan liked the movie, and I *did* too."

Dynamic. Words that exhibit features related to qualities capable of change. Dynamic verbs can combine with the progressive aspect, *be + -ing*: "I *am leaving* now"; dynamic adjectives can follow the progressive form of *be:* "He is being *silly*." See also *Stative*.

Edited American English. The variety of English usage that is widely accepted as the norm for the public writing of school essays, newspapers, magazines, and books. It is sometimes referred to as EAE.

Elliptical clause. A clause in which a part has been left out but is "understood": "Chester is older *than I (am old)*"; "Bev can jog farther *than Otis (can jog)*"; "*When (you are) planning your essay*, be sure to consider the audience."

Emphatic sentence. A statement in which the main stress has been shifted to the auxiliary: "I AM trying." When there is no auxiliary, the stand-in auxiliary *do* is added to carry the stress: "I DO want to go."

End focus. The common rhythm pattern in which the prominent peak of stress falls on or near the final sentence slot.

Exclamatory sentence. A sentence that expresses excitement or emotion. It may include a shift in the word order of a basic sentence that focuses on a complement: "What a beautiful day we're having!" It is characterized by heightened pitch and stress and is usually punctuated with an exclamation point.

Expanded determiner. The determiner, together with pre- and postdeterminers that qualify and quantify and in other ways alter its meaning.

Expletive. A word that enables the writer or speaker to shift the stress in a sentence or to embed one sentence in another: "A fly is in my soup → *There* is a fly in my soup"; "I know *that* he loves me." The expletive is sometimes called an "empty word" because it plays a structural rather than a lexical role.

Finite verb. The first element in the verb string; the auxiliary or main verb that carries the tense, either present or past: "Connie *was* being silly"; "I *eat* too much junk food."

Flat adverb. A class of adverb that is the same in form as its corresponding adjective: *fast, high, early, late, hard, long,* etc.

Form. The inherent features, the shapes, of words and phrases and clauses, as distinguished from their function in the sentence—characterized in words by prefixes and suffixes, in phrases by headwords and their objects or complements or modifiers, and in clauses by subjects and predicates.

Form classes. The large, open classes of words that provide the lexical content of the language: nouns, verbs, adjectives, and adverbs. Each has characteristic derivational and inflectional morphemes that distinguish its forms. See Chapter 12.

Free modifier. A nonrestrictive, nondefining modifier that is set off by commas and can usually occupy a position at the beginning, at the end, or in the middle of the sentence: "He spoke quietly to the class, *his voice trembling*"; "*Looking pale and nervous,* she stood at the podium"; "New England in the autumn, *because of the brilliant maples and birches,* has become a tourist destination."

Free morpheme. A single morpheme that is also a complete word (in contrast to a bound morpheme, which is not).

Function. The role that a particular structure plays, or the slot that it fills, in a sentence (or in any larger structure). In "The book on the table is mine," "table" functions as the *object of a preposition* in the prepositional phrase "on the table"; the prepositional phrase functions as an *adjectival,* modifying "book." The entire noun phrase "the book on the table" functions as the *subject* in its sentence.

Functional shift. The conversion of one word class to another, simply by changing its function: "He *bottled* the wine" (noun to verb); "She *lowered* the curtain" (adjective to verb); "We took a *swim*" (verb to noun).

Future time. Unlike the present and past, future time is not designated by a distinctive verb form. We have other ways of doing so: with the modal auxiliaries *shall* and *will* ("*I'll* see you tonight"); with the auxiliary *be* + *going to* ("*I'm going to* buy the cheese this afternoon"); and with adverbials of time ("We're having mac and cheese *tonight*").

Gender. A feature of personal pronouns and certain nouns that distinguishes masculine (*he*), feminine (*she*), and neuter (*it*). Nouns with gender distinctions include *waiter, waitress, actor, actress, girl, boy, man, woman, ewe, ram.*

Genitive case. The Latin term for possessive case.

Gerund. An *-ing* verb functioning as a nominal: "I enjoy *jogging*"; "*Running* is good exercise."

Gerund phrase. A gerund together with all of its complements and modifiers.

Grammatical. Usage that conforms to the rules that native speakers follow or that native speakers would find acceptable in a given situation. See also *Ungrammatical.*

Headword. The word that fills the noun slot in the noun phrase: "the little *boy* across the *street*." The verb is the headword of the verb phrase; the preposition is the headword of the prepositional phrase.

Hedging. A metadiscourse signal that helps readers interpret the writer's degree of certainty: *perhaps, possibly, might, seems,* etc.

Helping verb. See *Auxiliary.*

Heteronyms. Words that are spelled the same but differ in both meaning and pronunciation: *bass/bass*; *wound/wound*; *Polish/polish.*

Homonyms. Words and morphemes that have the same sound and the same spelling but have different meanings: *saw/saw*; farm*er*/bright*er.*

Homophones. Words that have the same sound, but with both different meanings and different spellings: *sale/sail; to/too/two.*

Idiom. A combination of words, a set phrase, whose meaning cannot be predicted from the meaning of the individual words.

Imperative sentence. The sentence in the form of a command. The imperative sentence includes the base form of the verb and usually an understood subject (*you*): "*Eat* your spinach"; "*Finish* your report as soon as possible"; "You *go* on without me."

Indefinite article. The determiner *a*, or *an*, which marks an unspecified count noun. See also *Definite article.*

Indefinite pronoun. A large category that includes quantifiers (e.g., *enough, several, many, much*), universals (*all, both, every, each*), and partitives (*any, either, neither, no, some*). Many of the indefinite pronouns can function as determiners.

Indefinite relative pronoun. The relative pronouns with *-ever* added, which have indefinite referents; they introduce adjectival clauses: "I will give a bonus to *whoever* works the hardest" (i.e., to the person who works the hardest).

Independent clause. The main clause of the sentence; a compound sentence has more than one independent clause.

Indicative mood. The expression of an idea as fact (as opposed to probability). Verb phrases without modal auxiliaries and those with *will* and *shall* are considered the indicative mood: "We *will* go soon"; "We *are going* tomorrow." "When *are* you *going?*" See also *Subjunctive mood* and *Conditional mood.*

Indirect object. The nominal slot following the verb in a Pattern VIII sentence. In a sentence with a verb like *give*, the indirect object is the recipient; the direct object is the thing given: "We gave *our friends* a ride home." The indirect object can be shifted to the slot following the direct object with the preposition *to* or *for:* "Joe gave a message to Kim"; "Sam bought a ticket for his dad."

Infinitive. The base form of the verb (present tense), usually expressed with *to*, which is called the "sign of the infinitive." The infinitive can function adverbially ("I stayed up all night *to study* for the exam"); adjectivally ("That is no way *to study*"); or nominally ("*To stay up* all night is foolish"). The only verb with an infinitive form separate from the present tense is *be.*

Infinitive phrase. The infinitive together with all of its complements and modifiers.

Inflection. See *Inflectional suffix.*

Inflectional suffix. Morphemes that are added to the form classes (nouns, verbs, adjectives, and adverbs) to change their grammatical role in some way. Nouns have two inflectional suffixes (*-s* plural and *-'s* possessive); verbs have four (*-s*, *-ing*, *-ed*, and *-en*); adjectives and some adverbs have two (*-er* and *-est*).

Intensifier. See *Qualifier.*

Intensive pronoun. A pronoun that serves as an appositive to emphasize a noun or pronoun. It is formed by adding *-self* or *-selves* to a personal pronoun: "I *myself* prefer chocolate."

Interjection. A word considered independent of the main sentence, often punctuated with an exclamation point: "*Ouch!* My shoe pinches"; "*Oh!* Is that what you meant?"

Interrogative. One of the structure classes. Sometimes referred to as "*wh*-words," the interrogatives—*where, when, who, what,* and *how*—introduce questions and nominal clauses, filling the roles of nouns, adjectives, and adverbs in their clauses: "*Where* is she going?" "I wonder *who* is going with her."

Interrogative sentence. A sentence that is a question in form: "Are you leaving now?" "When are you leaving?"

Intonation. The rhythmic pattern of a spoken sentence, affected by its stress and pitch and pauses.

Intransitive verb. The verbs of Pattern VI sentences, most of which require no complement to be complete.

Irregular verb. Any verb in which the *-ed* and *-en* forms are not that of the regular verb; in other words, a verb in which the past-tense and past-participle forms are not simply the addition of *-d*, *-ed*, or *-t* to the base form.

It-cleft. See *Cleft sentence.*

Known–new contract. A common feature of prose in which the known information opens the sentence and the new information occupies the point of main focus at or near the end of the sentence.

Linking verb. The verbs of Patterns IV and V, which require a subject complement to be complete.

Main verb. The verb that fills the last slot in the verb-expansion formula. See also *Predicating verb.*

Manner adverb. An adverb that answers the question of "how" or "in what manner" about the verb. Most manner adverbs are derived from adjectives with the addition of *-ly: quickly, merrily, candidly.*

Mass noun. See *Noncountable noun.*

Metadiscourse. Any words that are included in a message beyond the subject of the message itself: such connectors as *for example, finally, in the first place*; attitude markers, such as emphatic words (*clearly, certainly*); hedges (*possibly, perhaps*); and other comments of the author directed to the reader.

Metaphor. A figure of speech in which an attribute is applied to something or someone that is literally untrue but that expresses a sense of connection. When we call Superman *a man of steel*, we are using the term "steel" metaphorically, to attribute the qualities of steel to Superman. Many common expressions are based on metaphor: *the eye of the hurricane, a carpet of grass, a movie that bombed.*

Modal auxiliary. The auxiliary that occupies the opening slot in the verb-expansion rule and may affect what is known as the mood of the verb, conveying probability, possibility, obligation, and the like.

Mood. A quality of the verb denoting fact (indicative), a condition contrary to fact (subjunctive), and probability or possibility (conditional).

Morpheme. A sound or combination of sounds with meaning.

Morphology. The study of morphemes. See Chapter 11.

Nominal. Any structure that functions as a noun phrase normally functions. See Chapter 8.

Nominal clause. A clause that fills a noun phrase (NP) slot.

Nominalization. The process of producing a noun by adding derivational affixes to another word class, commonly a verb: *legalize-legalization; regulate-regulation; friendly-friendliness.*

Nominative case. The Latin term for subjective case.

Noncountable noun. Nouns referring to what might be called an undifferentiated mass—such as *wood, water, sugar, glass*—or an abstraction—*justice, love, indifference.* Whether or not you can use the indefinite article, *a*, is probably the best test of countability: If you can, the noun is countable.

Nonfinite verb phrase. A verb phrase that functions other than as a predicate. Verbs and verb phrases acting as adjectivals, adverbials, and nominals within the sentence are nonfinite.

Nonrestrictive modifier. A modifier in the noun phrase that comments about the noun rather than defines it. Nonrestrictive modifiers following the noun are set off by commas.

Noun. One of the four form classes, whose members fill the headword slot in the noun phrase. Most nouns can be inflected for plural and possessive (*boy, boys, boy's, boys'*). Nouns have characteristic derivational endings, such as *-tion* (*action, compensation*), *-ment* (*contentment*), and

-ness (*happiness*). Nouns can also function as adjectivals and adverbials (The *neighbor* children went *home*).

Noun clause. See *Nominal clause*.

Noun phrase (NP). The noun headword with all of its attendant pre- and postnoun modifiers.

Number. A feature of nouns and pronouns, referring to singular and plural.

Object complement. The slot following the direct object, filled by an adjectival (Pattern IX) or a nominal (Pattern X). The object complement has two functions: (1) It completes the idea of the verb; and (2) it modifies (if an adjective) or renames (if a nominal) the direct object: "I found the play *exciting*"; "We consider Pete *a good friend.*"

Object of preposition. The nominal slot—usually filled by a noun phrase — that follows the preposition to form a prepositional phrase.

Objective case. The role in a sentence of a noun phrase or pronoun when it functions as an object—direct object, indirect object, object complement, or object of the preposition. Although nouns do not have a special form for objective case, many of the pronouns do; personal pronouns and the relative pronoun *who* have separate forms when they function as objects. See Chapter 14.

Optional slot. The adverbial information that can be added to all the sentence patterns; such information is not required for grammaticality.

Parallel structure. A coordinate structure in which all the coordinate parts are of the same grammatical form.

Participial phrase. A participle together with all of its complements and modifiers.

Participle. The *-ing* and *-en* verb (or verb phrase) functioning as an adjectival or adverbial. See also *Present participle* and *Past participle*.

Particle. A word that combines with a verb to form a phrasal verb: look *up*, look *into*, put *up with*.

Passive voice. A feature of transitive sentences in which the direct object (the objective or goal) is shifted to the subject position and *be* +*-en* is added to the verb. The term *passive* refers to the relationship between the subject and verb: "Ed ate the pizza" → "The pizza *was eaten* by Ed."

Past participle. The *-en* form of the verb.

Past tense. The *-ed* form of the verb, usually denoting a specific past action.

Person. A feature of personal pronouns that distinguishes the speaker or writer (first person), the person or thing spoken to (second person), and the person or thing spoken of (third person).

Personal pronoun. The pronoun that refers to a specific person or thing. In the subjective case the personal pronouns are *I, you, he, she, we, you, they,* and *it.* The personal pronouns have variant forms for objective and possessive case.

Phoneme. The smallest unit of sound that makes a difference in meaning.

Phonology. The study of phonemes.

Phrasal preposition. A preposition consisting of two or more words, a simple preposition preceded by a word from another category, such as an adverb or adjective: *according to, aside from, because of, prior to.*

Phrasal verb. A verb–particle combination that produces a meaning that cannot be predicted from the meaning of the parts: *look up, put up with, make up.*

Phrase. A word or group of words that functions as a unit within the sentence.

Plural. A feature of nouns and pronouns denoting more than one, usually signaled in nouns by the inflectional ending *-s* (or *-es*).

Positive degree. See *Degree.*

Possessive case. The inflected form of nouns (*John's, the dog's*) and pronouns (*my, his, your, her, their,* etc.) usually indicating ownership.

Predicate. One of the two principal parts of the sentence, the comment made about the subject. The predicate includes the verb, together with its complements and modifiers.

Predicate adjective. The adjective that functions as a subject complement.

Predicate nominative. The noun or nominal that functions as a subject complement.

Predicating verb. The function of the verb slot in the sentence patterns, consisting of the main verb together with its auxiliaries. The verb-expansion rule in Chapter 4 accounts for the auxiliary–verb combinations of the predicating verb.

Predicative adjective. The adjective that occupies a complement slot in the sentence as subject complement or object complement.

Prefix. An affix added to the beginning of the word to change its meaning (*un*likely, *il*legal, *pre*scribe, *re*new) or its class (*en*able, *be*little).

Preposition. A structure-class word found in pre-position to—that is, preceding—a nominal. Prepositions can be classed according to their form as simple (*above, at, in, of,* etc.) or phrasal (*according to, instead of,* etc.).

Prepositional phrase. The combination of a preposition and a nominal, which is known as the object of the preposition.

Prescriptive grammar. An approach to teaching grammar, the purpose of which is to prescribe "proper" usage, rather than to describe how the language is actually used. It is sometimes referred to as "linguistic etiquette."

Present participle. The *-ing* form of the verb.

Present tense. The base form and the *-s* form of the verb: *help, helps.* The present tense denotes a present point in time ("I *understand* your position"), a habitual action ("I *jog* five miles a day"), or the "timeless" present ("Shakespeare *helps* us understand ourselves").

Pronoun. A word that substitutes for a noun—or, more accurately, for a nominal—in the sentence.

Pronoun–antecedent agreement. See *Agreement.*

Proper noun. A noun with individual reference to a person, a historical event, or other name. Proper nouns are capitalized.

Qualifier. A structure-class word that qualifies or intensifies an adjective or adverb: "We worked *rather* slowly"; "The work was *very* difficult."

Reciprocal pronoun. The pronouns *each other* and *one another,* which refer to previously named nouns.

Referent. The thing (or person, event, concept, action, etc.)—in other words, the reality—that a word stands for.

Reflexive pronoun. A pronoun formed by adding *-self* or *-selves* to a form of the personal pronoun, used as an object in the sentence to refer to a previously named noun or pronoun: "I gave *myself* a haircut."

Regionalism. A characteristic feature of the pronunciation or structure of the language spoken in a particular region of the country.

Regular verb. A verb in which the *-ed* form (the past tense) and the *-en* form (the past participle) are formed by adding *-ed* (or, in some cases, *-d* or *-t*) to the base. These two forms of a regular verb are always identical. "I *walked* home"; "I have *walked* home every day this week."

Relative adverb. The adverbs *where, when,* and *why,* which introduce adjectival clauses.

Relative clause. A clause introduced by a relative pronoun (*who, which, that*) or a relative adverb (*when, where, why*) that generally modifies a noun. The broad-reference *which* clause functions as a sentence modifier.

Relative pronoun. The pronouns *who* (*whom, whose*), *which,* and *that* in their role as introducers of a relative clause.

Restrictive modifier. A modifier in the noun phrase whose function is to restrict the meaning of the noun. A modifier is restrictive when it is needed to identify the referent of the headword. The restrictive modifier is not set off by commas.

Retained object. The direct object of a Pattern VIII sentence that is retained in its original position when the sentence is transformed into the passive voice: "The judges awarded Mary the prize" → "Mary was awarded *the prize.*"

Sentence. A word or group of words based on one or more subject–predicate, or clause, patterns. The written sentence begins with a capital letter and ends with terminal punctuation—a period, question mark, or an exclamation point.

Sentence modifier. A word or phrase or clause that modifies the sentence as a whole. See Chapter 9.

Sentence patterns. The simple skeletal sentences, made up of two or three or four required elements, that underlie our sentences, even the most complex among them. Ten such patterns will account for almost all the possible sentences of English. See Chapter 3.

Serial comma. The comma that is used before the conjunction in a series: "On our fishing trip to Alaska, we caught salmon, halibut, and the elusive Arctic grayling." Some publications, as a matter of policy, omit the serial comma.

Simple preposition. A one-word preposition. See also *Phrasal preposition.*

Singular. A feature of nouns and pronouns denoting one referent.

Singular *they.* The use of the plural pronoun *they* (*their, them*) in reference to a singular antecedent whose sex is unknown. It is especially common in reference to the indefinite pronouns, such as *someone, everyone, everybody,* which take singular verbs, even when they refer to more than one person: "Everyone is expected to do *their* best"; "Someone called but *they* didn't leave a message." This use of the plural pronoun is an alternative to *his or her/he or she.* Although common in speech, it is not generally accepted in formal writing.

Standard English. See *Edited American English.*

Stand-in auxiliary. The auxiliary *do* (*does, did*), which we add to sentences when we transform them into questions, negatives, and emphatic statements when there is no auxiliary in the original.

Stative. Words that exhibit features relating to an unchanging state, in contrast to those that change. Stative verbs do not pattern with the progressive aspect: *"I am *resembling* my mother." Stative adjectives generally do not follow the progressive form of *be:* *"He is *being* tall." See also *Dynamic.*

Structuralism. An approach to analyzing grammar, associated with mid-twentieth-century linguists, in which the purpose is to describe how the language is actually used in its various dialects, not to prescribe a "correct" version.

Structure classes. The small, closed classes of words that explain the grammatical or structural relationships of the form classes. See Chapter 13.

Subject. The opening slot in the sentence patterns, filled by a noun phrase or other nominal, that functions as the topic of the sentence.

Subject complement. The nominal or adjectival in Pattern II, III, IV, and V sentences following the verb, which renames or modifies the subject. The passive version of a Pattern IX or X sentence will also have a subject complement, the nominal or adjectival that in the active voice functions as the object complement.

Subjective case. The role in the sentence of a noun phrase or a pronoun when it functions as the subject of the sentence. Personal pronouns have distinctive forms for subjective case: *I, he, she, they,* etc.

Subject–verb agreement. See *Agreement.*

Subjunctive mood. An expression of the verb in which the base form, rather than the inflected form, is used (1) in certain *that* clauses conveying strong suggestions or resolutions or commands ("We suggest that Mary *go* with us"; "I move that the meeting *be* adjourned"; "I demand that you *let* us in"), and (2) in the expression of wishes or conditions contrary to fact ("If I *were* you, I'd be careful"; "I wish it *were* summer"). The subjunctive of the verb *be* is expressed by *were* or *be*, even for subjects that normally take *is* or *was*.

Subordinate clause. A dependent clause introduced by a subordinating conjunction, such as *if, since, because,* and *although.*

Subordinating conjunction. See *Subordinator.*

Subordinator. A subordinating conjunction that turns a complete sentence into a subordinate clause and expresses the connection between the subordinate clause and the main clause.

Substantive. A structure that functions as a noun; a nominal.

Suffix. An affix added to the end of a form-class word to change its class (act → act*ion*; laugh → laugh*able*) with derivational suffixes or to change its grammatical function (boy → boy*s;* walk → walk*ing*) with inflectional suffixes. See also *Derivational affix* and *Inflectional suffix.*

Superlative degree. See *Degree.*

Surface structure. A term used by transformational grammarians to designate the sentences of the language as they are spoken and written. See also *Deep structure.*

Syntax. The structure of sentences; the relationship of the parts of the sentence.

Tense. A grammatical feature of verbs and auxiliaries relating to time. Three verb forms indicate tense: the base form and the *-s* form (present) and the *-ed* form (past). Note that "tense" in relation to the modal auxiliaries refers only to form, not to time.

Tensed verb. A verb string that includes T(tense). In contrast, gerunds, infinitives, and participles have no tense marker.

***There* transformation.** A variation of a basic sentence in which the expletive *there* is added at the beginning and the subject is shifted to a position following *be:* "A fly is in my soup" → "There is a fly in my soup."

Third-person singular. The personal pronouns *he, she,* and *it.* The term is also used in reference to the *-s* form of the verb.

Transformational grammar (also called transformational generative, or T-G). A theory of grammar that attempts to account for the ability of native speakers to generate and process the sentences of their language.

Transitive verb. The verbs of Patterns VII through X, which require at least one complement, the direct object, to be complete. With only a few exceptions, transitive verbs are those that can be transformed into the passive voice.

Ungrammatical. Usage that does not conform to the rules that native speakers follow. Usage that varies from one dialect or speech community to another is not necessarily ungrammatical. "I ain't coming" is an unacceptable usage to many, although it follows the "rules." However, it is not part of the prestige, or standard, dialect and would be inappropriate in most formal and business situations. See also *Grammatical* and *Edited American English.*

Verb. One of the four form classes, traditionally thought of as the action word in the sentence. A better way to recognize the verb, however, is by its form, its *-s* and *-ing* endings. Verbs also have an *-ed* and an *-en* form, although in the case of some irregular verbs these forms are not readily apparent. And every verb, without exception, can be marked by auxiliaries. Many verbs also have characteristic derivational forms, such as *-ify (typify), -ize (criticize),* and *-ate (activate).*

Verb phrase (VP). A verb together with its complements and modifiers; the predicate of the sentence is a verb phrase. See also *Gerund phrase, Infinitive phrase,* and *Participial phrase.*

Verb-expansion rule. The formula that describes our system for expanding the verb with auxiliaries to express variations in meaning. See Chapter 4.

Vocative. The noun or noun phrase of direct address, considered a sentence modifier: *"Mike,* is that you?"

***What*-cleft.** See *Cleft sentence.*

***Wh*-question.** A question that is introduced by an interrogative, such as *who, which, when, where, why,* or *how,* that asks for information of content, in contrast to a yes/no question.

Yes/no interrogative. The words *if* and *whether* (*or not*) that introduce nominal clauses that ask or suggest a *yes/no* question: "I wonder *if Kim is coming*"; "I wonder *whether or not she's coming.*"

Yes/no question. A question that calls for a *yes* or *no* response. It is characterized by the opening auxiliary, in contrast to the interrogative that opens the *wh*-question: "*Are* you being served?" "*Did* the Orioles win?"

Appendix:
Sentence Diagramming

Our use of sentence diagramming to teach grammar reflects the purpose described by Alonzo Reed and Brainerd Kellogg, who created this system of illustrating sentences well over a century ago: "to picture the complete analysis of the sentence, with principal and subordinate parts in their proper relation" (p. vi).[1]

We would extend that statement of purpose to emphasize the role of a visual method for helping students recognize and differentiate the sentence patterns as well. We believe that the sentence patterns, introduced in Chapter 3, provide a practical framework for organizing the details of clauses, along with their modification and subordination and coordination.

Reed and Kellogg acknowledge the criticism that diagramming alters the order of sentence parts. They maintain, however—and we agree—that this alternation "is a merit, for it teaches the pupil to look through the literary order and discover the logical order" (p. vii). We also agree that engaging in "the logical analysis of the sentence . . . is to learn to think" (p. v).

We would add that, in conjunction with diagramming, the sentence patterns provide an organized set of tools for thinking. The ten diagrams on page 55 make clear the basic structure of the patterns, as well as their similarities and differences. For example, there is only one pattern, the intransitive Pattern VI, in which the predicate requires no structure beyond the verb; the diagrams also clarify that only transitive patterns include the vertical line that identifies a direct object; and the slanted lines in Patterns II and III explain why *be* qualifies as a linking verb.

When you recognize that it's the verb that determines the sentence pattern, you can then understand—and visualize—that the same features apply when the verb form is no longer that of predicating verb. For example, when an

---

[1] Alonzo Reed and Brainerd Kellogg, *Higher Lessons in English* (New York: Maynard, Merrill & Co., 1902). Between 1877 and 1913, twenty-five editions were published.

active Pattern VII verb functions as an adverbial (infinitive) or adjectival (participle) or nominal (gerund), it will be followed by a direct object. It's important to recognize that the various requirements of the sentence patterns (direct object, indirect object, subject complement, etc.) apply to the verbs in all their functions, not just when they are the predicating verbs.

Throughout the text we have included diagrams to illustrate the various sentence expansions. You will find them listed in the Index under the name of the structure. We are including in this Appendix a few diagrams for structures not covered in the book. However, we do not assume that every sentence is amenable to diagramming. And we would also note that many teachers using the text consider diagrams optional for their students; the sentence patterns and their formulas can easily be understood without them.

VARIATIONS FROM REED & KELLOGG

1. One major change from the R&K system occurs in Patterns IX and X, the two transitive patterns that include object complements. The R&K diagram locates the object complement between the verb and the direct object:

They explain that the line separating the verb from the object complement slants toward the OC to show that the complement belongs to the object. In our version, too, the OC line slants toward the object, but our diagram also maintains the linear order of the sentence:

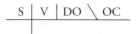

This version also illustrates that the connection between the direct object and its complement is similar to the connection between the subject and the subject complement in linking verbs.

2. Another difference, fairly minor, concerns the line that connects a subordinate clause with the main clause. We show it as a dotted line; the R&K system uses a line that is half solid and half dotted when the word expresses both an adverbial and a connective purpose, such as *when, where, after*, and so forth; we make no distinction based on meaning.

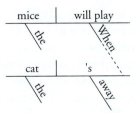

EXCEPTIONS TO R&K DIAGRAMS

Not all structures are amenable to diagramming. One example is the noun phrase in which the headword has an expanded determiner, as discussed on pages 269–270:

> *All of the **cookies*** are gone.

In this sentence, *cookies* is the headword, preceded by an expanded determiner. However, the traditional diagram would show *All* as the headword:

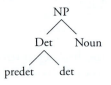

In this case, a tree diagram would make the relationship clear:

ADDITIONAL DIAGRAMS

In the diagram of the **noun phrase**, no matter where in the sentence it appears and no matter how many modifiers it includes, the headword is on a horizontal line with the determiner, adjective(s), and modifying noun(s) slanting down from it:[2]

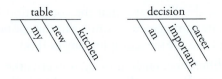

[2.] The relationship of prenoun modifiers is not always represented accurately by the diagram. For example, the first diagram does not indicate that *new* modifies *kitchen table*, not just *table*; in the second example, the adjective *important* modifies *career decision*, not just *decision*.

When the modifiers themselves have modifiers, either qualifiers or other nouns, the diagram will make that clear:

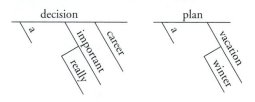

When the determiner is a possessive noun, it may have a determiner of its own: my daughter's car, the car's electrical system:

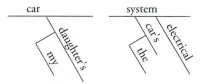

As the diagrams illustrate, the whole phrases "my daughter" and "the car" have been made possessive. You can show that *my daughter's* and *the car's* constitute a single modifier of the headword by substituting a possessive pronoun: *her* car, *its* electrical system.

In Chapter 5 we saw the ***what*-cleft**, a way of changing sentence focus; the result is a nominal clause, like those you saw in Chapter 8:

A branch in the road caused ⟶ What caused the accident was
the accident. a branch in the road.

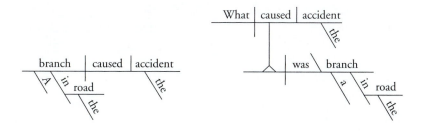

Elliptical **clauses of comparison** were discussed in the chapter on sentence modifiers (pages 197–199):

I'm a year older than my sister.

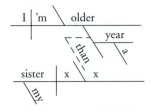

My roommate studies harder than I do.

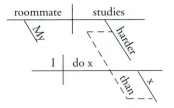

Some elliptical sentences we saw were ambiguous:

The Packers beat the Patriots worse than the Panthers.

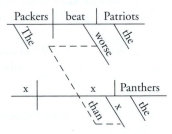

Answers to the Exercises

CHAPTER 2

Exercise 1, page 19

1. The students   their long trip
    d   H   d   H

2. our new neighbors   the hall   our best friends
    d   H   d   H   d   H

3. Mickey's roommate   the library   the weekends
    d   H   d   H   d   H

4. A huge crowd   the streets   the big parade
    d   H   d   H   d   H

5. This new lasagna recipe   an enormous crowd
    d   H   d   H

6. Jessica   her new boyfriend   some cookies
    H   d   H   d   H

Exercise 2, page 21

1. They   2. He   3. She
4. They   5. They   6. It

Exercise 3, page 25

1. adj, adv   2. adv, adv   3. adj, adv
4. adj   5. adv, adv   6. adv, adv, adv

CHAPTER 3

Exercise 4, page 34

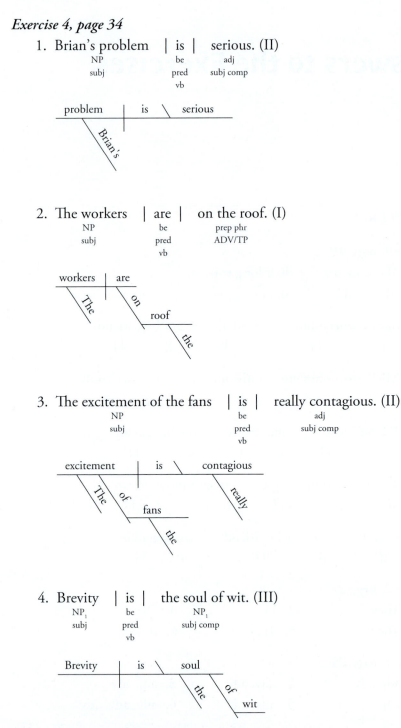

1. Brian's problem | is | serious. (II)
   NP   be   adj
   subj   pred   subj comp
                      vb

2. The workers | are | on the roof. (I)
   NP   be   prep phr
   subj   pred ADV/TP
                   vb

3. The excitement of the fans | is | really contagious. (II)
   NP   be   adj
   subj   pred subj comp
                                 vb

4. Brevity | is | the soul of wit. (III)
   NP₁   be   NP₁
   subj   pred subj comp
              vb

5. The final exam | was | at four o'clock. (I)

     NP   be   prep phr

     subj   pred vb   ADV/TP

6. The kids | are | very silly. (II)

     NP   be   adj

     subj   pred vb   subj comp

7. The basketball team | is | on a roll. (II)

         NP   be   prep phr

         subj   pred   subj comp

                 vb

8. A foolish consistency | is | the hobgoblin of little minds. (III)

        NP_1 be NP_1

        subj   pred   subj comp

                   vb

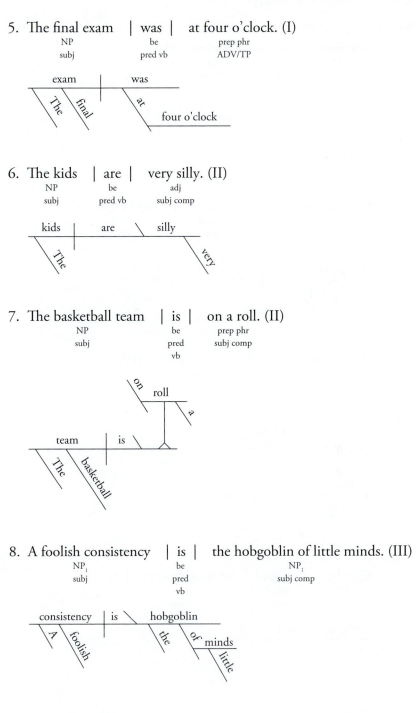

Exercise 5, page 36

1. The baby | looks | healthy. (IV)
   NP   lnk vb   adj
   subj   pred vb   subj comp

2. Our new neighbors | became | our best friends. (V)
   NP$_1$ lnk vb   NP$_1$
   subj   pred vb   subj comp

3. The piano | sounds | out of tune. (IV)
   NP   lnk vb   prep phr
   subj   pred vb   subj comp

4. October | turned | extremely cold. (IV)
   NP   lnk vb   adj
   subj   pred vb   subj comp

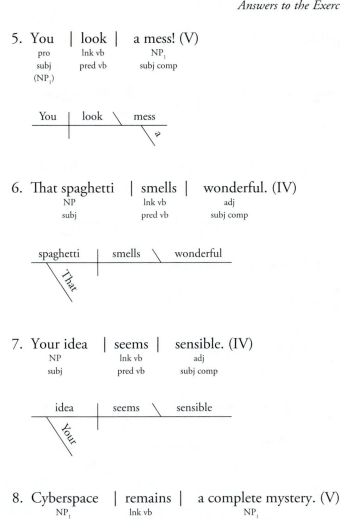

5. You | look | a mess! (V)
   pro   lnk vb   NP₁
   subj   pred vb   subj comp
   (NP₁)

You | look \ mess
              ə

6. That spaghetti | smells | wonderful. (IV)
       NP   lnk vb   adj
      subj   pred vb   subj comp

spaghetti | smells \ wonderful
   That

7. Your idea | seems | sensible. (IV)
      NP   lnk vb   adj
     subj   pred vb subj comp

idea | seems \ sensible
  Your

8. Cyberspace | remains | a complete mystery. (V)
      NP₁   lnk vb   NP₁
     subj   pred vb   subj comp

Cyberspace | remains \ mystery
                        ə complete

Exercise 6, page 39

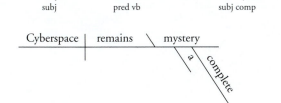

1. The rug in the dining room is dirty.   (II)
              adj

2. We rarely dine in the dining room.   (VI)
              adv

3. The break between classes seems very short on sunny days.   (IV)
        adj   adv

4. At the diner on Water Street, we chatted aimlessly until midnight.   (VI)
              adj   adv
   adv

5. Daylilies grow wild in our backyard.   (VI—or, perhaps, IV)
                      adv

6. In 1638 a young philanthropist of Puritan background became the
   adv   adj
   founder of the oldest university in the U.S.   (V)
                              adj
                      adj

7. The name of that young man was John Harvard.   (III)
            adj

8. My cousin from Iowa City works for a family with seven children.   (VI)
            adj   adj
                      adv

Exercise 7, page 41

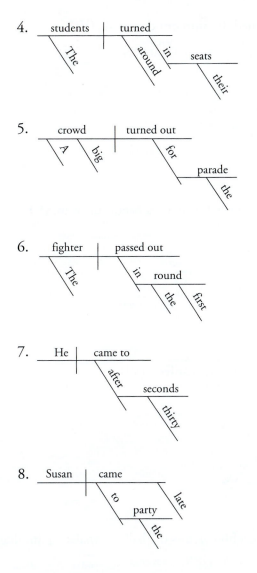

4. students | turned
   The / around in seats their

5. crowd | turned out
   A big / for parade the

6. fighter | passed out
   The / in round the first

7. He | came to
   after seconds thirty

8. Susan | came
   to party the late

Exercise 8, page 44

1. The boys | prepared | a terrific spaghetti dinner. (VII)
   NP₁   tr vb   NP₂
   subj   pred vb   dir obj

   boys | prepared | dinner
   The /   a terrific spaghetti

2. An old jalopy | turned | into our driveway. (VI)

     NP   int vb   prep phr
     subj   pred vb   opt ADV

3. The ugly duckling | turned into | a beautiful swan. (V)

     NP₁   lnk vb   NP₁
     subj   pred vb   subj comp

4. The fog | comes | on little cat feet. (VI)

     NP   int vb   prep phr
     subj   pred vb   opt ADV

5. On Sundays | the neighbor across the hall | walks | his dog |

    prep phr   NP₁   tr vb   NP₂
    opt ADV   subj   pred vb   dir obj

at 6:00 A.M. (VII)

    prep phr
    opt ADV

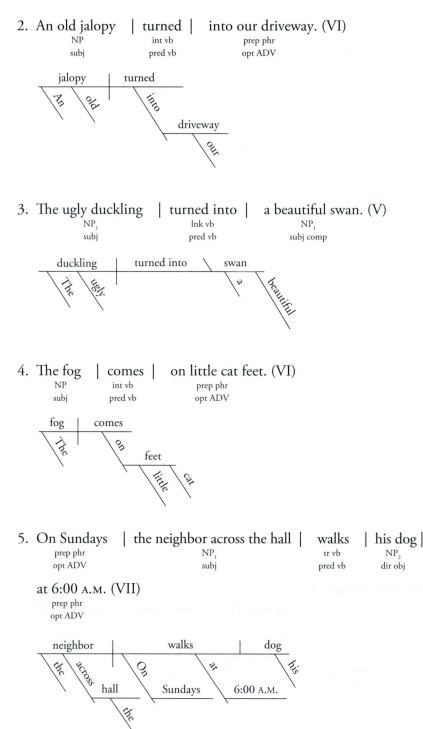

6. Betsy | often | jogs | with her dog. (VI)
    NP   adv   int vb   prep phr
    subj   opt ADV   pred vb   opt ADV

7. After two months | the teachers | called off | their strike. (VII)
    prep phr   NP₁   tr vb   NP₂
    opt ADV   subj   pred vb   dir obj

8. The whole gang | reminisced | at our class reunion |
    NP   int vb   prep phr
    subj   pred vb   opt ADV

about the good old days. (VI)
    prep phr
    opt ADV

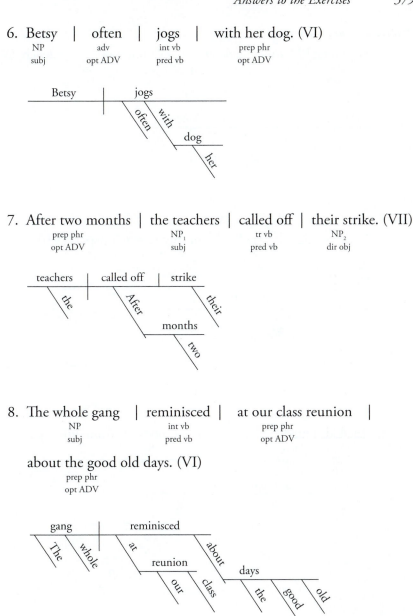

Exercise 9, page 46

1. For lunch | Manny | made | himself | a humongous sandwich. (VIII)

    prep phr   NP₁   tr vb   pro   NP₃

    opt ADV   subj   pred vb   ind obj   dir obj

                             (NP₂)

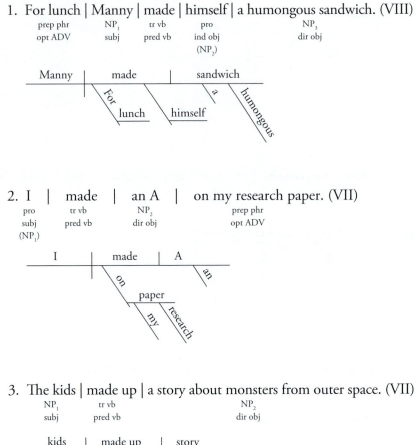

2. I | made | an A | on my research paper. (VII)

  pro   tr vb   NP₂   prep phr

  subj   pred vb   dir obj   opt ADV

  (NP₁)

3. The kids | made up | a story about monsters from outer space. (VII)

    NP₁   tr vb   NP₂

    subj   pred vb   dir obj

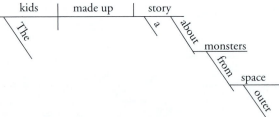

4. The teacher | wrote | a lot of comments | in the margins. (VII)

    NP₁   tr vb   NP₂   prep phr

    subj   pred vb   dir obj   opt ADV

5. My advisor | wrote | a letter of recommendation | for me. (VIII)

NP₁	tr vb	NP₂	prep phr
subj	pred vb	dir obj	ind obj
			NP₃

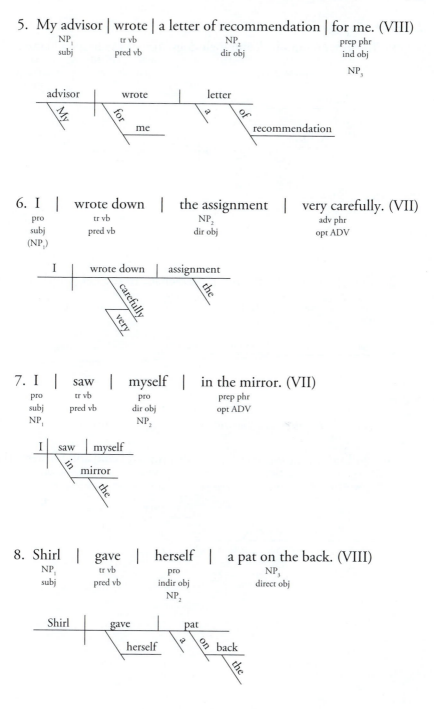

6. I | wrote down | the assignment | very carefully. (VII)

pro	tr vb	NP₂	adv phr
subj	pred vb	dir obj	opt ADV
(NP₁)			

7. I | saw | myself | in the mirror. (VII)

pro	tr vb	pro	prep phr
subj	pred vb	dir obj	opt ADV
NP₁		NP₂	

8. Shirl | gave | herself | a pat on the back. (VIII)

NP₁	tr vb	pro	NP₃
subj	pred vb	indir obj	direct obj
		NP₂	

Exercise 10, page 50

1. The kids on our block and their dogs | drive | my mother | crazy. (IX)

    NP₁   tr vb   NP₂   adj
    compound subj   pred vb   dir obj   obj comp

```
            kids
    The          on
                      block
                           our
                                          and      drive | mother  \ crazy
                                                                  my
            dogs
                 their
```

2. She | calls | them | a menace to the neighborhood. (X)

    pro   tr vb   pro   NP₂
    subj   pred vb dir obj   obj comp
    (NP₁)   (NP₂)

```
    She | calls | them  \ menace
                        a    to
                                neighborhood
                                          the
```

3. On Friday | the weather | suddenly | turned | cold and blustery. (IV)

    prep phr   NP   adv   lnk vb   compound adj
    opt ADV   subj   opt ADV   pred vb   subj comp

4. The teacher | was | unhappy | with our test scores. (II)

NP₁ — subj

be — pred vb

Adj — subj comp

prep phr — opt ADV

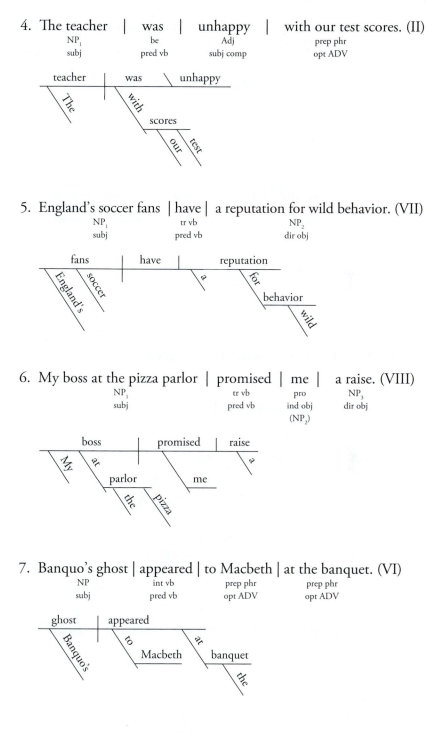

5. England's soccer fans | have | a reputation for wild behavior. (VII)

NP₁ — subj

tr vb — pred vb

NP₂ — dir obj

6. My boss at the pizza parlor | promised | me | a raise. (VIII)

NP₁ — subj

tr vb — pred vb

pro — ind obj (NP₂)

NP₃ — dir obj

7. Banquo's ghost | appeared | to Macbeth | at the banquet. (VI)

NP — subj

int vb — pred vb

prep phr — opt ADV

prep phr — opt ADV

8. The new arrivals at the animal shelter | appeared | und. (IV)

NP   lnk vb   adj

subj   pred vb   sub comp

9. Both Alaska and Hawaii | attained | statehood | in 1959. (VII)

NP₁   tr vb   NP₂   prep phr

subj   pred vb   dir obj   opt ADV

10. According to the latest census, | Wyoming | is |

prep phr   NP₁   be

opt ADV   subj   pred vb

our least populous state. (III)

NP₁

subj comp

11. Some people | consider | Minnesota's winters | excessively long. (IX)

NP₁   tr vb   NP₂   adj phr

subj   pred vb   dir obj   obj comp

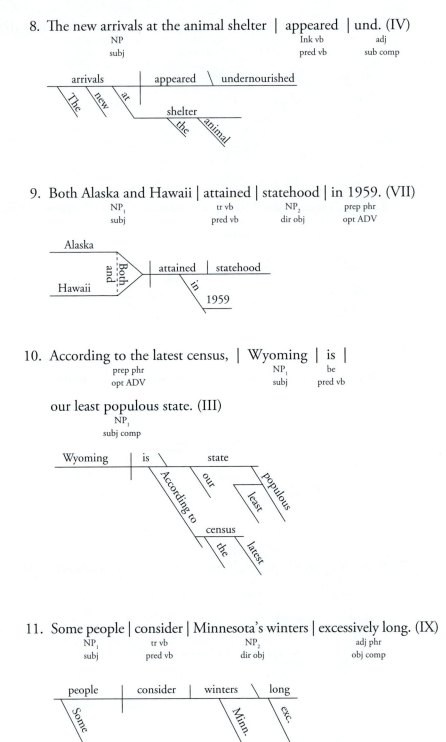

12. Emily | selected | peach and lavender |
    NP₁   tr vb   compound NP₂
    subj   pred vb   dir obj

as the color scheme for her wedding. (X)
                        NP₂
                     obj comp

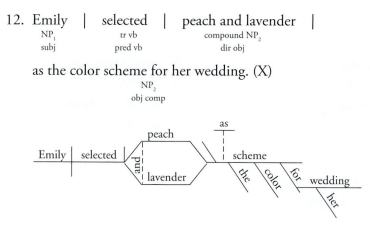

(Note: *for her wedding* could also be considered adverbial.)

CHAPTER 4

Exercise 11, page 65

1. have	has	had	having	had
2. do	does	did	doing	done
3. say	says	said	saying	said
4. make	makes	made	making	made
5. go	goes	went	going	gone
6. take	takes	took	taking	taken
7. come	comes	came	coming	come
8. see	sees	saw	seeing	seen
9. get	gets	got	getting	got, gotten
10. move	moves	moved	moving	moved
11. prove	proves	proved	proving	proved, proven
12. put	puts	put	putting	put
13. think	thinks	thought	thinking	thought
14. beat	beats	beat	beating	beat, beaten
15. meet	meets	met	meeting	met

Exercise 12, page 71

A.

1. has worked
2. will be playing
3. was being
4. is having

5. should have had
6. had had
7. could have been
8. may have been trying

B.

1. past + be + -ing + study
2. pres + have + -en + find
3. past + lose
4. pres + have + -en + be + -ing + skip
5. past + can + be
6. pres + seem
7. pres + will + be + -ing + have
8. past + shall + have + -en + study

CHAPTER 5

Exercise 13, page 89

1. The Emancipation Proclamation was signed by President Lincoln in 1862.
2. Several sensational news stories have been published by the campus paper this semester.
3. A run-off election will be held in two weeks.
4. The suspect is being kept in solitary confinement.
5. I am pleased by your positive attitude.
6. Bill was being teased about his new mustache by his fraternity brothers.
7. Your computer files should be backed up on a regular basis.
8. Power lines have been knocked down by heavy thunderstorms in three counties.

Exercise 14, page 92

1. *Avatar* was given rave reviews by many critics.
2. The third graders are being given too much homework.
3. Three finalists have been chosen for the science award.
4. The staircase walls have been turned into an art museum by these colorful murals.
5. Roger Federer is often referred to as the greatest tennis player of all time.
6. Some of our most intricate fugues were composed by Bach.

Exercise 15, page 93

1. The cheerleading squad led the football team onto the field. (VII)
2. A committee chooses the cheerleaders in the spring. (VII)
3. The managing editor had warned the new reporters about late submissions. (VII)
4. The judges have chosen three finalists for the science award. (VII)
5. Someone manufactured dental floss for the first time in 1882. (VII)
6. People in financial circles are talking about the possibility of recession. (VII)
7. The critics called the play a smashing success. (X)
8. Someone has rendered the poison harmless. (IX)

Exercise 16, page 98

1. expletive (VII)
2. adverb (I)
3. expletive (I)
4. expletive (I)
5. adverb (I)
6. adverb (VI)
7. expletive (I)
8. adverb (VI)

CHAPTER 6

Exercise 17, page 113

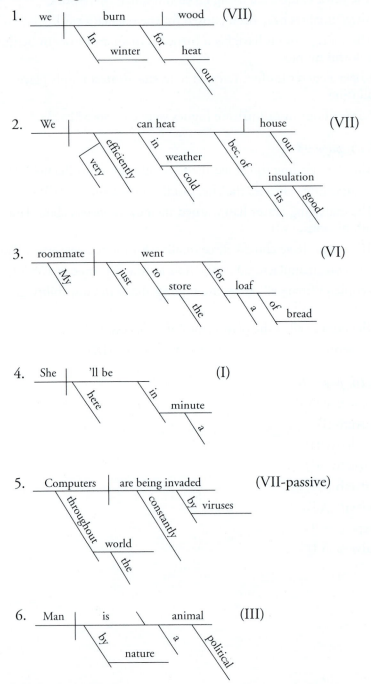

Exercise 18, page 114

1. I'm going to wax the car parked in the garage.

   I'm going into the garage to wax the car.

2. We watched the game from the porch.

   We watched the game being played on the porch.

3. Fred tripped his teammate who was holding the bat.

   Fred stuck the bat out and tripped his teammate.

4. Susan washed the stones she found in the riverbed.

   Susan went to the river to wash the stones she found.

Exercise 19, page 116

1. Pete is working <u>nights</u> <u>this week</u>. (VI)

                   N   NP

2. I was awake <u>the whole night</u>. (II)

                NP

3. I'll see you <u>soon</u>. (VII)

              adv

4. <u>This morning</u> Pam threw away the leftover spaghetti. (VII)

      NP

5. George will do dishes <u>next time</u>. (VII)

                     NP

6. I love weekends. (VII)

7. Bill works <u>weekends</u>. (VI)

             N

8. <u>At the first sign of winter</u> the birds flew <u>south</u>. (VI)

        prep phr   adv

Exercise 20, page 120

1. Our cat <u>often</u> jumps <u>up</u> <u>on the roof</u> <u>to reach the attic window</u>.
   (main clause: VI; infinitive: VII)

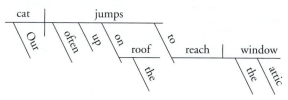

2. <u>Sometimes</u> she <u>even</u> climbs the ladder <u>to get there</u>. (main clause: VII; infinitive: VI)

3. <u>Last night</u> my computer blinked <u>ominously</u> <u>during an electrical storm</u>. (VI)

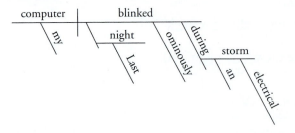

4. I <u>immediately</u> turned it off. (VII)

5. We went <u>to the mall</u> <u>last Saturday</u> <u>to check out the big sales</u>. (main clause: VI; infinitive: VII)

6. <u>Afterwards</u> we stayed <u>home</u> <u>to watch the playoff game with Uncle Dick</u>. (main clause: VI; infinitive: VII)

Exercise 21, page 123

4.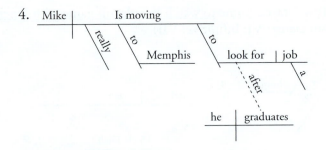

(Note: The adverbial clause could also be interpreted as a modifier of the main verb.)

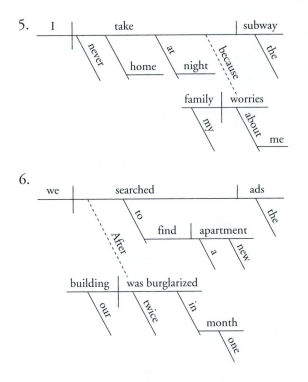

5.

6.

CHAPTER 7

Exercise 22, page 134

A. 1. <u>Some</u> movie <u>reviewers</u>
    (D)   (n)   (H)

  2. <u>a</u> riveting, ambitious <u>example</u>
    (D) (part)   (adj)   (H)

3. The film's central premise
 (D) (D) (adj) (H)

4. a worldwide social revolution
 (D) (adj) (adj) (H)

5. two middle-class college boys
 (D) (adj) (n) (n) (H)

6. a brilliant sequence
 (D) (adj) (H)

7. his Facebook co-founders
 (D) (n)   (H)

8. a wild party
 (D) (adj) (H)

9. the exclusive college clubs
 (D) (adj)   (n) (H)

10. a derisive contrast
 (D) (adj) (H)

11. their computers
 (D)   (H)

12. the beautiful young things
 (D) (adj) (adj) (H)

13. a future entrepreneur and billionaire
 (D) (adj)   (H)   (H)

14. the born-to-rule kids
 (D) (part ph) (H)

B. 1. The department's personnel committee
    (D)   (n)   (H)

  the main office this morning
  (D) (adj) (H) (D) (H)

 2. Our whole family the new Sunday brunch menu the cafeteria
  (D) (adj) (H) (D) (adj) (n) (n) (H) (D) (H)

 3. Serena's daughter an expensive-looking copper-colored bracelet
  (D) (H) (D) (adj) (part) (n) (part) (H)

  the subway station
  (D) (n) (H)

 4. The bicycle-safety commission the new regulations
  (D) (n) (n) (H) (D) (adj) (H)

  their regular meeting this noon
  (D) (adj) (H) (D) (H)

 5. Her lovely, gracious manner the start
  (D) (adj) (adj) (H) (D) (H)

6. Any mother   the job   several air-traffic controllers
   (D) (H)   (D) (H)   (D)   (n)   (n)   (H)

7. The rising interest rates   a serious concern
   (D) (part)   (n)   (H)   (D) (adj)   (H)

   every cost-conscious citizen
   (D)   (n)   (adj)   (H)

Exercise 23, page 137

1. with a cast on his left foot

2. of the museum (*near the visitors' information booth* could modify either *museum* or *meet*)

3. after the game (*at Bob's house* could modify either *party* or *game*)

4. of computer viruses

5. from within

6. for my science course, from Stanford

7. (*of any size* could modify either *loans* or *businesses*)

8. with the weakest qualifications, about the selection process

Exercise 24, page 143

1. who traveled overland . . . mid-1800s; modifies *pioneers; who =* subj; VI

2. that the pioneers traveled; modifies *routes; that =* dir obj; VII

3. which appeared . . . days; modifies *Chimney Rock; which =* subj; VI

4. who braved . . . foot; modifies *families; who =* subj; VII

5. that those . . . wagon wheels . . . prairie; modifies *ruts; that =* dir obj; VII

6. which . . . journey: modifies *Cont. Divide; which =* subj; III

7. which led to. . . GSL: modifies *Mormon Trail; which =* subj; VI
   where the followers . . . home; modifies *GSL; where =* ADV; VII

8. who had been promised . . . Oregon; modifies *farmers . . . families*:
   who = subj; VIII (pass)

9. when two golden spikes . . . railway; modifies *1869; when =* ADV; VII (pass)

10. which became obsolete . . . telegraph; modifies *Pony Ex; which =* subj (IV)

Exercise 25, page 146

Here are some possibilities; you will think of others.

1. Bill owns <u>that expensive sports car standing in the driveway</u>. (Note that the indefinite *an* becomes definite with *that*.)

2. I am babysitting for <u>the baby sleeping upstairs in the crib</u>.

3. Some of <u>the fans lining up at the ticket office</u> will probably be disappointed.

4. <u>The students searching the Internet</u> want to find material for their research projects.

5. The defense could not stop <u>the fullback charging through the line</u>.

6. <u>The teachers walking the picket line</u> have been on strike for eight days.

Exercise 26, page 149

1. The award <u>given every year to the outstanding volunteer</u> has
                           (VIII passive)
been announced.

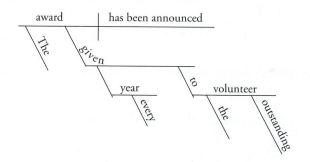

2. <u>Being a philosopher</u>, she can propose a problem for every solution.
        (III)

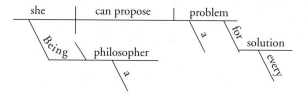

3. He has all the gall of a shoplifter <u>returning an item for a refund</u>.
(VII)

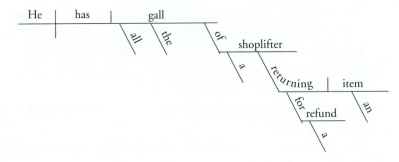

4. The hostess gave the <u>departing</u> guests some leftover food for
(VI)

their pets.

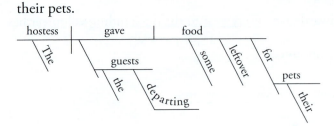

(The prepostional phrase could also be interpreted as adverbial.)

5. <u>Finding the price reasonable</u>, they rented the apartment on the spot.
(IX)

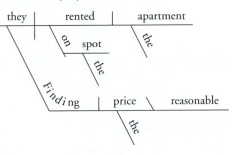

6. Congress shall make no law <u>abridging the freedom of speech or</u>
(VII)

of the press.

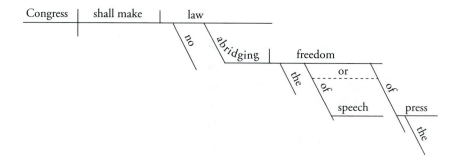

7. Some agencies will not fund research <u>involving genetic manipulation</u>.
(VII)

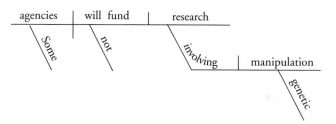

8. The teachers' union has finally approved the last two <u>disputed</u>
(VII passive)

sections of the contract <u>offered by the school district</u>.
(VII passive)

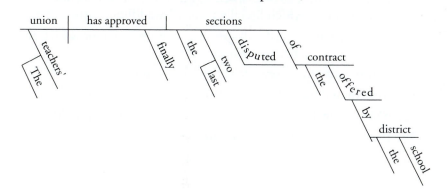

Exercise 27, page 151

Here are some possibilities; you will probably think of others.

1. Because the house needed considerable repair, my parents were able to buy it for little money.
2. Having misunderstood the assignment, I got a low grade on my paper.
3. The archeologists could not decipher the inscription, which was covered with the grime of centuries.
4. The bus left without the woman who was still searching for change in her purse.
5. The patient spent four hours on the operating table while doctors performed a double bypass on her (or his) severely blocked arteries.
6. Once considered only an average player, Chris has greatly improved his game in the last three months.
7. The dean of men surprised several members of the football team as they were breaking in through the window of the girls' dormitory.
8. Seen from miles away, the mountain might be mistaken for a cloud.

Exercise 28, page 154

1. Johannes Gutenberg, who had . . . goldsmith, developed . . . ; that changed the world of printing—*restrictive*, no comma
2. using movable metal type—*restrictive*, no commas
3. Movable type, often regarded . . . millennium, changed . . . ; [that] people read books—*restrictive*, no comma
4. a communal event, where one person . . . people.
5. printed before 1501—*restrictive*, no commas; is called an incunabulum, which literally means "swaddling clothes."
6. that transfers . . . printed—*restrictive*, no comma; on which it is printed—*restrictive*, no comma
7. that bypass . . . plates—*restrictive*, no comma
8. Text messaging, which is called . . . Asia, has become . . .
9. SMS is hugely popular in India, where companies provide . . .
10. that made . . . papers—*restrictive*, no comma

Exercise 29, page 158

1. in which players . . . target (relative clause)
2. which originated . . . Netherlands (relative clause); of bowling and shuffleboard (prep phrase); of billiards and chess (prep phrase)
3. that is 42 . . . wide (relative clause); of four players to a side (prep phrase); to a side (prep phrase)
4. that is . . . away (relative clause)
5. called Blue Hone (participial phrase); which is . . . resiliency (relative clause)
6. of the wrist (prep phrase); imparting . . . named (participial phrase); for which . . . named (relative clause)
7. on a team (prep phrase); to knock . . . bounds (infinitive phrase)
8. of curling equipment (prep phrase); used by players . . . stone (participial phrase); of a teammate's stone (prep phrase)
9. whose stones . . . target (relative clause); of the target (prep phrase); that is closer (relative clause)
10. where there are . . . circuit (relative clause); who play . . . circuit (relative clause)

CHAPTER 8

Exercise 30, page 166

1. <u>simple ballads sung to guitar music</u>
2. <u>son of the legendary songwriter Woody Guthrie</u>
3. <u>An offbeat film about illegal trash dumping</u>
4. <u>the search for personal freedom</u>
5. <u>a contemporary folk singer and songwriter; *Soul Journey* and *Time (The Revelator)*</u>
6. *Casey*

Exercise 31, page 170

A.
1. Flying a supersonic jet—VII, subject; main clause: III
2. playing practical jokes on his players—VII, direct object; main clause: VII
3. telling a few jokes—VII, object of preposition; main clause: VI
4. staying awake in my eight o'clock class—IV, subject complement; main clause: III
5. Leaving the scene of the accident—VII, subject; main clause: III
6. seeing the suspect near the entrance of the bank—VII, direct object; main clause: VII

7. going to college—VI, object of preposition; main clause: VI
8. Thinking a problem through—VII, subject; main clause: VII

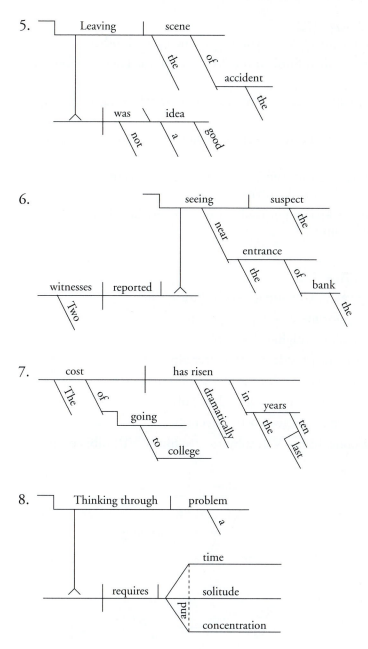

Exercise 32, page 172
Here are some possibilities; you may come up with others.

1. After we had finished the decorations, the ballroom looked beautiful.
2. You will reduce your revising time by following a few helpful pointers.
3. In making a career decision, you will find your counselor a big help.
4. By signing this waiver, the tenant gives up any right to make claims against the owner.
5. Our backpacks got really heavy after we hiked up that steep mountain trail.

Exercise 33, page 175

1. to give . . . Christmas—VIII, direct obj
2. to beg for mercy—VI, subj comp
3. To walk . . . night—VI, subj
4. to become president—V, direct obj
5. to never take . . . lunch—VII, appositive
6. to distract . . . nest—VII, direct obj
7. to shock . . . views—VII, direct obj
8. To know him—VII, subj; to love him—VII, subj comp

1.

2.

3.

4.

5.

6.

7.

8.

Exercise 34, page 177

1. <u>for you to tell the truth</u>, infinitive (subj comp)
2. <u>remaining silent</u>, gerund (obj of prep)
3. <u>to ignore . . . order</u>, infinitive (appositive)
4. <u>Raising . . . profile</u>, gerund (subj)
5. <u>to write . . . assignment</u>, infinitive (direct obj)
6. <u>your proofreading . . . me</u>, gerund (direct obj)
7. <u>to watch . . . morning</u>, infinitive (direct obj)
8. <u>The baby's crying</u>, gerund (subj)

1.

7.

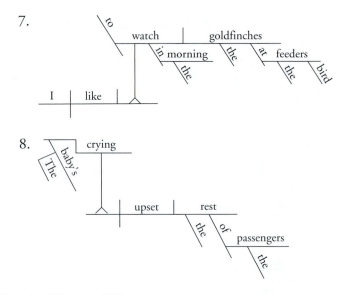

8.

Exercise 35, page 179

Here are some possibilities; you will undoubtedly think of others.

1. You should know <u>that this flight has been cancelled</u>. (dir obj)
2. <u>That the airlines overbook their flights</u> makes everyone angry. (subj)
3. My parents realize <u>that I can't call them every day</u>. (dir obj)
4. <u>That my flight will be late</u> has not occurred to them. (subj)
5. The truth is <u>that they never asked me about my travel plans</u>. (subj comp)
6. The fact <u>that I might keep them waiting</u> disturbs me. (appositive)

Exercise 36, page 181

1. Main clause: VII; nominal *where* clause (dir obj): VII
2. Main clause: VII; adverbial *when* clause: VII
3. Main clause: IV; adverbial *when* clause: VI
4. Main clause: III; nominal *when* clause (subj): VI
5. Main clause: VI; adverbial *where* clause: VI
6. Main clause: VIII; adverbial *when* clause: VII; nominal *where* clause (dir obj): VII
7. Main clause: VII; adverbial *when* clause: VII; nominal *where* clause (dir obj): VI
8. Main clause: VII; nominal *where* clause (dir obj): VII (passive)
9. Main clause: VII; adverbial *when* clause: III
10. Main clause: VII; nominal *where* clause (dir obj): I; adverbial *when* clause: VI

Exercise 37, page 182

1. <u>how awesome a redwood tree could be</u> (dir obj)
2. <u>that it was too short</u> (subj comp)
3. <u>What Carlos said about his cousin</u> (subj)
4. <u>why people fear intimacy</u> (obj of prep)
5. <u>that they could have a dog</u> (dir obj)
6. <u>Who invented calculus</u> (subj)
7. <u>which twin was Elaine</u> (dir obj)
8. <u>if we could come for the weekend</u> (dir obj)
9. <u>he would explain his explanation</u> (dir obj)
10. <u>that they should replay the point</u> (appositive)

1.

2.

3.

4.

5.

6.

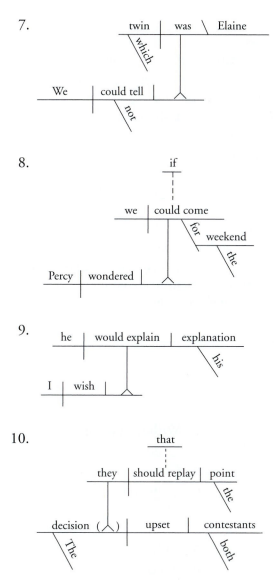

7.

8.

9.

10.

Exercise 38, page 183

1. (In 1874), (in London), (today)—adv
   [for . . . game], [of . . . game], [that was . . . today] [of . . . today]—adj
   <u>what we play today</u>—nom cl, o. p.
2. <u>how graphite . . . tennis</u>—nom cl, d. o.; [of tennis]—adj.
3. <u>Multiplying . . . serve</u>—gerund ph, subj; [of . . . serve],
   [that many . . . enjoy]—adj.

4. [Introduced in 1970], [of tennis]—adj.; (in 1970),
   (by . . . attractive)—adv.;
   <u>making the matches . . . attractive</u>—gerund ph, o. p.

5. (In . . . final), (in . . . won)—adv.; [which . . .won]—adj.;
   <u>to convert . . . won</u>—infinitive ph, d.o.

6. (Unless . . . injured), (because . . . losing)—adv.;
   <u>to beat her</u>—infinitive ph, delayed subj.

7. <u>to win . . . retires</u>—infinitive ph, subj comp;
   (before . . . retires)—adv.

8. (Two years) (after . . . baby)—adv.; <u>getting . . . baby</u>—gerund
   ph, o. p.

9. (Instead . . . shot) (when . . .lob)—adv.; <u>using . . . shot</u>—gerund
   ph, o. p.; <u>to hit . . . lob</u>—infinitive ph, d.o.

10. (Although . . . chemistry) (in . . . results)—adv.; [who . . tennis],
    [in . . . tennis]—adj.; <u>that . . . chemistry</u>—nom cl, d. o., <u>that
    common . . . results</u>—nom cl, appositive

CHAPTER 9

Exercise 39, page 195

1. <u>Amazingly</u>
2. (none)
3. <u>Well</u>
4. (none)
5. <u>Strangely</u>
6. (none)
7. <u>Without a doubt</u>
8. <u>no doubt</u>
9. (none)
10. <u>my friend</u>

Exercise 40, page 197

1. (no commas)
2. us, although
3. over, we
4. coffee, since (optional)
5. rent, even
6. (no commas)
7. apartment, even (optional)
8. heat, get

Exercise 41, page 199

A. 1. When you are late for work, the subway is better than the bus.

2. If bread is kept too long in hot weather, mold will grow on it.

3. While we were driving to the game on Saturday, an accident tied
   up traffic for over an hour.

B. 1. I picked up a midwestern accent while *I was* living in Omaha.
    2. My accent is not as noticeable as Carlo's *accent is* [noticeable].
    3. Holmes hit Ali harder than Norton *hit Ali* (or *Holmes hit Norton*).
    4. If *it is* necessary, strain the juice before adding the sugar.
    5. While *I was* waiting . . .
    6. If *your paper is* handed in late . . .
    7. Love goes toward love, as schoolboys *go* from their books. But love *goes* from love, *as schoolboys go* toward school with heavy looks.
    8. The weather in Little Rock is not as humid *as it is in* New Orleans.

Exercise 42, page 202

1. <u>her tail . . . metronome</u> (part)
2. <u>their arms . . . shoulders</u> (part)
3. <u>The rain having . . . hour</u> (part)
4. <u>her book . . . floor</u> (adj phr); <u>her eyes . . . flames</u> (adj phrase)
5. <u>the streets . . . light</u> (NP); <u>the planet . . . edges</u> (part); <u>the sky . . . infinity</u> (NP)
6. <u>his bunched shirt . . . blades</u> (prep ph); <u>his toes . . . floor</u> (part); <u>the aunt's arms . . . shoulders</u> (prep. phrase)

Exercise 43, page 204

1. Cleaning the basement this morning wasn't very much fun.
2. It surprised me that Otis didn't want to stay for the second half of the game.
3. The president criticized the Congress rather severely in his press conference; some observers considered his criticism quite inappropriate.
4. Contrary to the prediction of the weather service, the first snowstorm of the season in Denver was both early and severe.
5. Our having company for dinner three times this week probably means hot dogs for the rest of the month.

CHAPTER 10

Exercise 44, page 212

1. (no commas)
2. now, I

3. tires, shock absorbers, and brake linings

4. 1970s, a 1959 Chevy, required

5. (no commas)

6. Corvette, the car

Exercise 45, page 216

There's more than one possibility in each case.

1. I can't decide which activity I prefer: swimming . . . or jogging . . .

2. I almost never watch television. Either there is nothing on that appeals to me or the picture . . .

3. I don't enjoy flying, and I don't feel like taking the train.

4. Either the superintendent or the members of the school board make the final decision.

5. Either the recipe was printed wrong, or I misread it.

6. I was unhappy with what he said and how he said it.

7. The coach announced an extra hour of drill on Saturday and no practice on Sunday.

8. My history class, as well as both English classes, requires . . .

9. For my birthday dinner, Aunt Rosa has promised to fix her famous lasagna and to bake my favorite cake.

10. For the picnic we brought lemonade and baskets of chicken.

CHAPTER 11

Exercise 46, page 229

nov | a   aud | it | or

re | nov | at | ion   aud | ience

in | nov | ate   in | aud | ible

nov | ice   aud | it | or | ium

nov | el | ist   aud | io

  nov = new   aud = hear

dur | able   con | ceive

en | dure   cap | able

dur | ation   sus | cept | ible

dur | ing   cap | ture

en | dur | ance   inter | cept

  dur = hard   cap (cept) = take

Exercise 47, page 230
Check your answers with the dictionary and/or your instructor.

Exercise 48, page 236

1. pre cis ion (bound + bound + bound; affix, base, affix)
     d   d

   (Note: d = derivational; i = inflectional)

2. candid ate (free + bound; base, affix)
         d

3. de tour ed (bound + free + bound; affix, base, affix)
    d   i

4. ex cess ive ly (bound + bound + bound + bound; affix, base, affix, affix)
    d   d d

5. un a ware (bound + bound + free; affix, affix, base)
    d d

6. money (free; base)

7. side walk s (free + free + bound; base, base, affix)
           i

8. pro mot ion (bound + bound + bound; affix, base, affix)
     d   d

9. il leg al (bound + bound + bound; affix, base, affix)
    d   d

10. weal th y (free + bound + bound; base, affix, affix)
        d d

11. tele vis ion (bound + bound + bound; affix, base, affix)
       d   d

12. re vis es (bound + bound + bound; affix, base, affix)
      d   i

CHAPTER 12

Exercise 49, page 241

1. pleasure
2. regulation, regulator
3. stealth
4. seizure
5. derivation, derivative
6. retirement, retiree
7. formula, formation
8. revival

Exercise 50, page 242

1. teacher's, teachers'
2. horse's, horses'
3. sister's husband's, sisters' husbands'
4. son's, sons'

Exercise 51, page 244

1. Price's
2. Hedges'
3. James's
4. Massachusetts'
5. Linus's
6. neighbor's
7. neighbors'
8. Miss Piggy's
9. women's
10. Confucius'

Exercise 52, page 255

friendly	friendlier	friendliest
helpful	more helpful	most helpful
wise	wiser	wisest
awful	more awful	most awful
rich	richer	richest
mellow	mellower	mellowest
expensive	more expensive	most expensive
valid	more valid	most valid
pure	purer	purest
able	abler (more able)	ablest (most able)

Exercise 53, page 260

1. grief | grieve | grievous | grievously
2. variation | vary | variable | variably
   variance | | various | variously
   variety
3. ability | enable | able | ably
4. defense | defend | defensive | defensively

5. economy	economize	economical economic	economically
6. pleasure	please	pleasant	pleasantly
7. type	typify	typical	typically
8. prohibition	prohibit	prohibitive	prohibitively
9. critic criticism	criticize	critical	critically
10. validation validity	validate	valid	validly
11. appreciation	appreciate	appreciative	appreciatively
12. beauty	beautify	beautiful	beautifully
13. acceptance	accept	acceptable	acceptably
14. purity	purify	pure	purely
15. continuation continuity	continue	continuous continual	continuously continually

(Note: You may think of other possibilities.)

CHAPTER 13

Exercise 54, page 268

1. my, enough, her
2. John's, the
3. Every, this, a
4. more, the week's
5. less, last
6. either, no

Exercise 55, page 271

1. <u>have been</u> (having)
2. <u>should have</u> (eaten)
3. <u>can't</u> (look)
4. <u>will be</u> (helping)
5. <u>has to</u> (leave)
6. <u>are</u> (frustrating)
7. <u>can</u> (be)
8. <u>should</u> (continue)

Exercise 56, page 277

1. in, since
2. because of
3. in spite of
4. Prior to, in

5. According to, of, in
6. with (on = particle)
7. Except for, in, of, out of
8. Between, until

Exercise 57, page 285

1. <u>and</u>—coordinating conjunction; <u>on</u>—preposition; <u>an</u>—determiner; <u>in</u>—preposition
2. <u>Four</u>—determiner; <u>from</u>—preposition; <u>for</u>—preposition; <u>for</u>—coordinating conjunction; <u>for</u>—preposition
3. <u>As</u>—subordinating conjunction; <u>an</u>—determiner; <u>as</u>—expletive; <u>at</u>—preposition
4. <u>be</u>—auxiliary; <u>by</u>—preposition; <u>but</u>—coordinating conjunction
5. <u>of</u>—preposition; <u>off</u>—particle (part of verb); <u>if</u>—subordinating conjunction
6. <u>are</u>—auxiliary; <u>of</u>—preposition; <u>or</u>—expletive; <u>our</u>—determiner
7. <u>will</u>—auxiliary; <u>with</u>—preposition; <u>while</u>—subordinating conjunction
8. <u>too</u>—qualifier; <u>two</u>—determiner; <u>to</u>—preposition

---

CHAPTER 14

Exercise 58, page 293

1. They
2. We, him
3. She, it

4. them
5. them *or*
   them and him

6. him, it
7. us
8. He, them

Exercise 59, page 296

1. herself
2. themselves

3. itself
4. ourselves

5. himself
6. ourselves

Exercise 60, page 302

1. <u>everything</u>—indefinite; <u>I</u>—personal; <u>one</u>—indefinite
2. <u>every</u>—indefinite; <u>any</u>—indefinite; <u>they</u>—personal
3. <u>Someone</u>—indefinite; <u>we</u>—personal; <u>who</u>—interrogative; <u>it</u>—personal
4. <u>All</u>—indefinite; <u>that</u>—relative; <u>I</u>—personal; <u>that</u>—demonstrative
5. <u>much</u>—indefinite; <u>they</u>—personal; <u>both</u>—indefinite; <u>more</u>—indefinite; <u>I</u>—personal
6. <u>I</u>—personal; <u>myself</u>—intensive; <u>whatever</u>—indefinite relative; <u>you</u>—personal
7. <u>enough</u>—indefinite; <u>me</u>—personal
8. <u>themselves</u>—reflexive; <u>one another's</u>—reciprocal
9. <u>most</u>—indefinite; <u>I</u>—personal; <u>myself</u>—reflexive
10. <u>whoever</u>—indefinite relative; <u>one</u>—indefinite

---

CHAPTER 15

There is no one correct answer for any of the exercise items in this chapter. The answers given here are simply suggestions.

Exercise 61, page 317

1. The small band of rebels *resisted* the army patrol for several hours, then *surrendered* just before dawn. News reports . . . did not *specify* . . .
2. The majority leader *wields* a great deal of influence in the White House. He or she can easily *circumvent* . . .
3. Several economists are saying that they *anticipate* an upturn . . . Others, however, maintain that interest rates must *stabilize* if . . .
4. The night-shift workers . . . tried to *compel* them to *relinquish* . . .
5. The chairman . . . *denounced* the practice . . . He said that the new rules will *eliminate* . . . To some observers, such practices *signify* [or *constitute*] bribery. Several senators have promised to *formulate* . . .
6. Dorm life changed drastically when colleges *abrogated* [or *abolished*] . . . In the old days . . . students who *defied* [or *disregarded, disobeyed*] the rules. At some schools . . . would not *tolerate* . . . routinely *expelled*.

Exercise 62, page 322

1. The community objected strongly when the school board cancelled the after-school drama program.
2. Now that China has opened its doors to certain aspects of capitalism, American companies are looking for ways to expand their markets and their product lines.
3. Analysts of the situation in the Far East agree that opportunities for investment there are growing.
4. In his biography of Lyndon Johnson, Robert Caro describes the 1948 Senate election in great detail.
5. When Julie applied for a work-study job, she was surprised to learn that her parents would have to submit a detailed financial statement.
6. Tim worked long and hard before his new pizza parlor finally turned a profit.
7. Two important aims of education are to broaden one's view of life and to establish worthy goals.
8. Another important aim of education is to help students learn to think: to develop strategies for understanding and solving problems.

Exercise 63, page 325

1. Even though the famous Gateway Arch is in St. Louis, it is Kansas City that claims the title "Gateway to the West."
2. Many students have a hard time finding summer jobs because our spring semester doesn't end until the second week of June.
3. Thomas Jefferson acquired the Ozark Mountains for the United States when he negotiated the Louisiana Purchase with Napoleon in 1803.
4. Many attorneys are unable to offer advice to their clients concerning oil and gas leases because they are unacquainted with the relevant laws.
5. When the neighbors added a pit bull to their pet population, which now numbers three unfriendly four-legged creatures, we decided to fence in our backyard.
6. Even though the human circulatory system is a marvel of efficiency, it is still subject to a wide variety of degenerative diseases.
7. Because carbohydrates are the body's prime source of energy, fad diets that severely restrict them are not only ineffective, they are often dangerous.
8. When the auto companies offered cash rebates last January, sales of new cars increased dramatically.

CHAPTER 16

Exercise 64, page 347

1. During the second two-year stretch of a president's term in office, he may find himself on the defensive, even with his own party; when—as frequently happens—his party loses a number of Senate and House seats in the midterm election, that second stretch can become even more defensive.

2. In recent years, the public attitude toward smoking (except perhaps in the tobacco-growing states) has changed so fast, with smoke-free zones everywhere, including restaurants, office buildings, and shopping malls, it could almost be called a revolution; even outdoor stadiums, such as Oriole Park at Camden Yards and Jacobs Field in Cleveland, have established a no-smoking policy.

Exercise 65, page 347

1. The cost of repairs to the nation's public transportation facilities—roads, bridges, and railroads—is an expenditure that cannot be delayed much longer if the system is to survive.

2. To many people, the mushroom is a lowly fungus with little food value; to others, it is a gourmet's delight.

3. A Chinese restriction on importing certain American goods, such as cotton, synthetic fibers, and soybeans, has had an adverse effect on the U.S. economy—especially on the farmers.

4. According to fashion experts, the crew cut—the haircut that was more or less the hallmark of the 1950s—will be back in style before long.

5. Unfortunately, my favorite activities—skiing, playing golf, and bowling—cost more than my budget can stand.

6. Most people probably don't know that Alexander Graham Bell, the inventor of the telephone, succeeded his father-in-law as president of the National Geographic Society.

7. Many scientists believe that sightings of "cryptids"—including Big Foot, the Loch Ness monster, and Yeti, the Abominable Snowman—are simply mistakes, attributable to unfamiliarity with known animals, rather than to delusions.

8. Eugene Schiffelin, a New Yorker, decided to introduce all the birds mentioned in Shakespeare's works into America. In 1890—because of a single mention in *Henry IV*—he loosed 60 starlings into Central Park. Today millions of aggressive and smart and voracious starlings have blanketed the United States; in many places they blacken the sky.

Index

superlative degree of, 22, 253–55
volitional vs. nonvolitional, 83
Adjective test frame, 252, 261
ADV/TP. *See* Adverbial of time or place
Adverb-forming suffixes, 257–59
Adverbial, 19, 25, 37–38, 108–27
   adverb, 109–12
   clause, 121–23, 323–24. *See also*
      Subordinate clause.
   conjunction. *See* Conjunctive adverb.
   defined, 25, 121, 350
   diagramming of, 38, 58, 112, 122–23
   of emphasis, 326–27
   to express future, 72
   as function, 105
   infinitive, 117–19
   introductory, 191–92
   movability of, 37–38, 109–12, 127,
      322–23
   nouns and noun phrases, 114–16
   objectives, 115
   as optional slot, 37–38
   participles, 121, 151
   in Pattern I, 32–33
   in Pattern VI, 38
   placement of, 373
   prepositional phrase, 24–25, 37–38,
      112–14
   punctuation of, 123–24
   required, 32, 51
   in sentence pattern formula, 31, 32,
      37–38
   shifting, in writing, 322–27
   of time or place, 31–33, 259
   verb phrases, 117–19
   versatility of, 322–23
Adverbial objective, 115
   defined, 350
Adverb phrase, 38
   defined, 350
Adverbs, 22–24, 109–12, 257–60
   as adjectivals, 158
   as adverbials, 109–12
   of concession, 259
   defined, 350
   degree of, 22, 110, 254, 259
   derivational suffixes of, 23,
      257–59, 260
   diagramming of, 32, 38, 58, 110

   of direction, 259
   of duration, 259
   of emphasis, 326–27
   flat, 259
   of frequency, 110, 111–12, 259
   hyphens with, 133
   inflectional suffixes of, 22, 231, 259
   interrogative, 52
   introductory, 190–91
   locative. *See* Adverbs, of place.
   of manner, 23, 110–11, 133, 190, 254,
      257–58, 262
     defined, 357
     degree of, 22, 110, 254
     and hyphens, 133
     as qualifiers, 273–74
     as sentence modifiers, 190
   movability of, 23–24, 110, 127
   negative, 111–12
   of place, 23, 31, 32, 97, 110–11, 259
     compared with expletive *there,* 97, 98
   qualifiers with, 22, 38, 58, 110, 273
   relative, 142
   as sentence modifiers, 190–91
   of sequence, 259
   there, 96–97, 110–11
   of time, 23, 31, 32, 110–11, 259
Affixes, 229–34
   creating words with, 257
   defined, 350
African American Vernacular English.
     See AAVE
Agent, 87–88, 92, 321–22
   defined, 350
Agreement
   defined, 350
   pronoun-antecedent, 290, 303–304
   subject-verb, 97, 130, 213–15,
      223, 270
     with collective nouns, 130, 246
     with compound subjects, 213–15
     exception to rule, 97
     with indefinite pronouns, 247
     with quantified phrases, 270
     in *there* transformation, 97
Ain't, 8–10
Allomorphs, 233–34
   defined, 350
Always, 111